Yale Studies in English, 184

Colley Cibber as Lord Foppington

Colley Cibber: Three Sentimental Comedies

LOVE'S LAST SHIFT: OR,
THE FOOL IN FASHION

THE CARELESS HUSBAND

THE LADY'S LAST STAKE: OR,
THE WIFE'S RESENTMENT

Edited with an Introduction and Notes by

Maureen Sullivan

NEW HAVEN AND LONDON, YALE UNIVERSITY PRESS, 1973

Library of Congress catalog card number: 73-77168
International standard book number: 0-300-01532-1

Designed by Sally Sullivan and set in IBM Baskerville type.
Printed in the United States of America by The Murray Printing Co., Inc., Forge Village, Massachusetts.

Published in Great Britain, Europe, and Africa by Yale University Press, Ltd., London.
Distributed in Latin America by Kaiman & Polon, Inc., New York City; in Australasia and Southeast Asia by John Wiley & Sons Australasia Pty. Ltd., Sydney; in India by UBS Publishers' Distributors Pvt., Ltd., Delhi; in Japan by John Weatherhill, Inc., Tokyo.

Contents

Illustrations

Preface

Colley Cibber won his immortality as the hero of *The Dunciad,* in which the clouds of dullness, inflated not a little by storms of personal animosity, obscured his long career in the theater. Cibber was a gifted comic actor, an influential manager of the Theatre Royal in Drury Lane, and a successful playwright. He has also left ample evidence that as a poet, and as a man, he was a fit subject for the satire of Pope's circle. His *Apology,* for all its historical interest, is animated by unconcealed vanity; his performances as laureate were abysmal; his conduct as a businessman was often scandalous. Because these were aspects of his life that captivated an age of satire, and because Cibber complacently bolstered his own reputation for folly, we can only too easily overlook his real achievement as a playwright, though his plays constitute the largest and certainly the best part of his work.

Many of his contemporaries praised his plays. Even Pope himself deplored the public's neglect of *The Careless Husband.*[1] In 1764 David Erskine Baker wrote, "The Audience has, through a Course of upwards of sixty Years, received great Pleasure from many of his Plays, which have constantly formed Part of the Entertainment of every Season, and many of them repeatedly performed with that Approbation they undoubtedly merit."[2] Twenty years later, Thomas Davies, in his reminiscences of the theater, praised Cibber lavishly as the writer who "first taught the stage to talk decently and morally."[3] Though the notion of Cibber as the father of sentimental comedy has persisted into the twentieth century,[4] more recent criticism rejects the notion of a "first" sentimental dramatist. We can, however, safely say that in his best comedies Cibber gave us, clearly outlined for the first time, the plot, characters, language, and attitudes of sentimental comedy.

Between 1696 and 1745 Cibber wrote twenty-five pieces for the stage—twelve comedies, six tragedies, two ballad operas, two masques, a farce, an interlude, and a "comical tragedy."[5] In addition, he had, as manager of the Theatre Royal in Drury Lane, a hand in many other productions. Some of these are only attributions and complicate the task of compiling a definitive list of his works.[6] Even with those plays generally believed to be his own, an editor finds difficulties. Only a very few of Cibber's plays can be considered truly original. His enemies openly called him a plagiarist; Pope wrote of "Fletcher's half-eat scenes," of "crucify'd Molière," and of "hapless Shakespear" filling out the "pleasing memory of all he stole."[7] These accusations seem well founded when we examine the extent of Cibber's literary debts. Eight of the twelve comedies and four of the six tragedies are adaptations, combinations, or completions of other men's plays.[8] It must be remembered, of course, that in that era no great store was set upon creation *ex nihilo;* in reworking older plays, Cibber was doing what many playwrights before him had done. Then too, as manager of Drury Lane, he had an obligation to produce workable, popular stage entertainment. He enjoyed more than moderate success, and many of his plays, with their borrowed plots, were performed over and over again.

Of Cibber's four original comedies, one was an admitted failure.[9] To the other three, *Love's Last Shift: Or, The Fool in Fashion, The Careless Husband,* and *The Lady's Last Stake: Or, The Wife's Resentment,* he owes his reputation as an able comedian and his place in the history of comedy. Yet little has been done to preserve them during the last two hundred years. Though three collections of Cibber's plays appeared during his life and two shortly after his death, and though several of the plays were frequently reprinted in the eighteenth and nineteenth centuries, no collection or selection of his plays has appeared since 1777.[10]

This edition offers critical texts of the three plays. They are important to a study of English comedy, and they offer evidence of the actual merit of a man known to us only through the caricatures his enemies have left. Cibber's best comedies shed on his reputation a light which dispels, at least for a moment, the utter darkness to which *The Dunciad* would abandon him.

The large quarto edition of 1721, *Plays Written by Mr. Cibber. In Two Volumes,* provides the copy-text for all three plays in this edition. The right of the 1721 edition to be regarded as the final authentic version of the texts is substantial. First and most important, we know from his *Apology* that Cibber took some pains with the preparation of this edition, choosing only what he must have considered his best work. He wrote of his second play, *Woman's Wit; or The Lady in Fashion:* "I confess, so bad was my second, that I do not chuse to tell you the Name of it; and that it might be peaceably forgotten, I have not given it a Place in the two Volumes of those I publish'd in Quarto in the Year 1721."[11] Secondly, Cibber made the first and only clearly authorial alterations in this edition of *Love's Last Shift* and *The Lady's Last Stake.*[12] In *The Careless Husband,* the significant authorial revisions were made in the Third Edition of 1712, which might indeed have been considered as possible copy-text in this case. However, the 1721 large quarto edition introduces a few further apparently authorial revisions and thus seems to be, like the texts of *Love's Last Shift* and *The Lady's Last Stake,* Cibber's final version of the text.

The nature of the revisions Cibber made in all three plays suggests that, in this elegant subscription edition, he was preparing his "literary works," polishing phrase and idiom, cleaning up coarse dialogue, and even, in *Love's Last Shift,* cutting out a scene of irrelevant horseplay. In addition, the deletion of many stage directions relevant to stage performance only and the insertion of more precise marking of asides indicate that Cibber was transforming acting texts into reading texts. This, then, is the edition which ought to serve as copy-text for a modern critical edition of *Love's Last Shift, The Careless Husband,* and *The Lady's Last Stake.*

For this edition, collations have been made of multiple copies of the copy-text and at least one copy each of all London editions printed during Cibber's lifetime. All substantive variants have been recorded in the textual notes, which, together with a comparative analysis of the texts and a description of the textual procedure, are included in Appendix III below.

I wish to thank, first of all, Professor Maynard Mack, who advised me while I was preparing the dissertation which was the beginning of this edition. I owe special thanks also to the reference staffs of the Beinecke Rare Book Library at Yale, the Rare Book Collection and Furness Memorial Library at the University of Pennsylvania, the Folger Shakespeare Library, the British Museum, the Library of Congress, and the Library Company of Philadelphia.

I have depended for primary materials chiefly on the collections in the Yale University Library and the Folger Shakespeare Library, and for certain supplementary materials on the rare book collections in the libraries of Harvard, Princeton, Duke, Rochester, and Northwestern universities, the University of Chicago, the University of Amsterdam, and the British Museum. To I. G. Philip, Keeper of Printed Books at the Bodleian Library, to T. C. Skeat, Keeper of Manuscripts at the British Museum, to John Irwin, Keeper of the Indian Department of the Victoria and Albert Museum, and to W. A. Taylor, City Librarian of Birmingham, I am grateful for help in solving special textual and editorial problems. I owe thanks to Yvonne Noble, who helped me in my search for the music to the plays, to Wayne H. Phelps, who offered invaluable advice and assistance at every stage in the preparation of the manuscript, to my copy editor Dr. Lila Freedman, and to Stephen Lappert and Dana Cecelia Joseph, who, most heroically, read the proof. To Sister Vincentia Burns, O.P., my friend and teacher, I give thanks for sustaining encouragement. To my family, and especially to the memory of my father, I dedicate this book.

The editor's task is a humbling one. It requires such vigilant attention to the problems and errors of the past that the special peripheral vision which ought to keep watch on one's own accuracy and consistency is often obscured. For errors which may have intruded into this edition under such conditions, I beg my readers' indulgence.

M.S.

Wethersfield, Connecticut

Introduction

The Plays

Love's Last Shift, Cibber's first play, was produced at the Theatre Royal in Drury Lane in January, 1695/6.[1] The play, acted by Christopher Rich's company, was a great success; Davies reports that "the joy of unexpected reconcilement, from Loveless's remorse and penitence, spread such an uncommon rapture of pleasure in the audience, that never were spectators more happy in easing their minds by uncommon and repeated plaudits."[2] Cibber himself could not resist preserving a compliment from the Lord Chamberlain, whom he remembers as having said, *"That it was the best First Play that any Author in his Memory had produc'd; and that for a young Fellow to shew himself such an Actor and such a Writer in one Day, was something extraordinary."*[3]

Cibber had joined the Drury Lane company in 1690 and, after an inauspicious start, fell by chance into two roles that launched his career as a comic actor. In 1693 he replaced the actor Edward Kynaston, who was ill, in the role of Lord Touchwood in Congreve's *The Double Dealer.*[4] Two years later he acted the part of Alderman Fondlewife in *The Old Batchelor,* taking part with other members of his company in mimicking the actors who had made the play famous, but who had deserted Drury Lane under the leadership of the actor Thomas Betterton and had opened a rival theater in Lincoln's Inn Fields.[5] Cibber's success as Fondlewife produced no further favors for him as an actor at that time. He therefore took matters into his own hands in Cibberian fashion: "My early Success in the *Old Batchelor* . . . having open'd no farther way to my Advancement, was enough, perhaps, to have made a young Fellow of more Modesty despair; but being of a Temper not easily disheartend'd,

I resolv'd to leave nothing unattempted that might shew me in some new Rank of Distinction. Having then no other Resource, I was at last reduc'd to write a Character for myself."[6] In this way Sir Novelty Fashion was born.

Besides Cibber himself in the role of the egregious fop he was to make his trademark, the cast included some of the best actors and actresses of the Drury Lane company. Mrs. Jane Rogers, whom Cibber remembers for her prudery—"Her Fondness for Virtue on the Stage she began to think might perswade the World that it had made an Impression on her private Life"[7]—played Amanda. John Verbruggen, "that rough Diamond,"[8] played Loveless. His talents had suited him for the title role in Southerne's tragedy *Oroonoko;* he was also to play the part of Mirabell in *The Way of the World.* His variety no doubt contributed to his success as Cibber's hero, a role that demanded something of both tragic and comic skills. In addition, his personal habits must have added authenticity to his portrayal of Loveless; he is reputed to have been so far from sober at the première of Vanbrugh's *The Relapse* on November 12, 1696, that he was "on the verge of assaulting Mrs. Rogers [Amanda] in actuality instead of doing so only vicariously."[9] The clowning of Will Penkethman must have brought Snap to life vividly, especially as that able comedian was in the habit of joking with the audience directly, much as Snap does from beneath the table in Act IV of *Love's Last Shift.*[10] Cibber's wife Katherine played Hillaria, and Mrs. Susannah Verbruggen, the former Mrs. Mountfort, was Narcissa.

Love's Last Shift was a success from the start, so much so that it inspired Vanbrugh's sequel, *The Relapse,* in the very next season. It continued a success through the century, being acted, according to *The London Stage,* more than two hundred times during Cibber's lifetime. He could justly claim, in 1740, that it was, along with *The Relapse,* "in a continued and equal Possession of the Stage for more than forty Years."[11]

The Careless Husband opened at Drury Lane on December 7, 1704, and had a brilliant first season with ten performances during December alone. Like *Love's Last Shift,* it was performed in London more than two hundred times during Cibber's life. Unlike the earlier play, it appeared in America; it was given in New York on December 3, 1753.[12] Horace Walpole called it as perfect as a Molière comedy, and David Erskine Baker said it contained "the most elegant Dialogue, and the most perfect knowledge of the Manners of Persons in real high Life extant in any dramatic Piece that has yet appear'd in any Language whatever."[13]

The Careless Husband provided another occasion for Cibber to play Sir Novelty Fashion, upon whom Vanbrugh had conferred the title of Lord Foppington. But the acknowledged star of the play was the celebrated Anne Oldfield. She had joined the Drury Lane company in 1699 and had impressed Cibber with little more than her "Person" until she made a success of her portrayal of Leonora in John Crowne's *Sir Courtly Nice* at Bath in 1703. This encouraged him to take up *The Careless Husband,* the first two acts of which he had written the summer before, but had cast aside "in despair of having Justice done to the Character of Lady *Betty Modish.*"[14] In a burst of generosity unusual for him in such cases, Cibber credits Mrs. Oldfield with much of the success of his play: "Whatever favourable Reception this Comedy has met with from the Publick, it would be unjust in me not to place a large Share of it to the Account of Mrs. *Oldfield;* not only from the uncommon Excellence of her Action, but Even from her personal manner of Conversing. There are many Sentiments in the Character of Lady *Betty Modish* that I may almost say were originally her own, or only dress'd with a little more care than when they negligently fell from her lively Humour."[15]

The Lady's Last Stake did not share the fortunes of *Love's Last Shift* or *The Careless Husband.* The first recorded performance was at the Queen's Theatre, Haymarket, on December 13, 1707, during the time when Cibber had broken with Christopher Rich, the patentee and manager of Drury Lane, and had gone to work with Owen Swiney at the Haymarket. The dispute between the Drury Lane actors and Rich arose chiefly because of Rich's increasing use of operas and other spectacular entertainments to attract audiences, to the detriment of dramatic performances, and quite literally at the expense of the actors in the company. Cibber and many other members of the company, unable to tolerate Rich's practices any longer, left him for Swiney.[16] *The Lady's Last Stake,* an obvious attempt to repeat the success of *The Careless Husband,* was probably the last hope of Cibber and Swiney to save the Haymarket theater, but the competition from Rich's operas proved too strong.[17] The play survived only to its third day that December, but its Epilogue—a comic depiction of the theatrical troubles—was spoken several more times during the same month. The failure of *The Lady's Last Stake* may have been partly owing to the warfare of the theaters, rather than to any great flaws in the play itself. Cibber himself thought that the poor acoustics of the Haymarket—better suited to and eventually reserved for opera—were to blame. The play, he found, had a much better reception when it was acted at Drury Lane.[18] *The London Stage* records thirty-five performances in Cibber's lifetime, not a bad score when plays were dying by the hundreds every season.

The play had a remarkably good cast. Anne Oldfield played Mrs. Conquest, a role well-suited to her vivacity; Mrs. Rogers, playing Lady Gentle, had the opportunity to repeat the qualities she had portrayed earlier in Amanda; and Mrs. Elizabeth Barry, whom Cibber praised extravagantly for her dignity, majesty, tenderness, and power to excite pity, played Lady Wronglove.[19] Robert Wilks, Cibber's fellow actor and later one of the actor-managers of Drury Lane, played Lord Wronglove. Wilks, the chief actor at Drury Lane at the time of the theatrical dispute, was famous for his acting of both tragic and comic roles. He often performed with Anne Oldfield, and Cibber notes that "their frequently playing against one another in our best Comedies, very happily supported that Humour and Vivacity which is so peculiar to our *English Stage.*"[20] Of course, in *The Lady's Last Stake* Wilks did not get to play opposite Mrs. Oldfield; that pleasure fell to Cibber himself, who played Lord George Brilliant, a curious role for him. Undoubtedly he was able to do justice to Brilliant's moments of foppish affectation, but one wonders if the audience, so accustomed to Sir Novelty Fashion and Lord Foppington, could support Cibber's portrayal of Brilliant's appeal as the romantic hero and good-natured man.

All three plays dramatize, though with subtle variations and differing degrees of skill, the triumph of true and virtuous love over the worldly, conventional "love-attitudes" presented in Restoration comedy of manners. In each play Cibber's main plot develops the theme sentimentally—that is, earnestly and emotionally—while the subplot repeats and expands it in the witty terms of the comedy of manners. Cibber's sentimental aims did not prevent his using the attitudes of the comedy of manners, which was, after all, a proven success and the tradition in which he had his training. His witty subplots, however, are so closely interwoven with their main plots that they too become sentimentalized, concluding in the celebration of virtuous love, whether in their own action, or by merging into the main plot.

In *Love's Last Shift,* the main plot is that of the faithful Amanda's recapture of her wandering husband Loveless, a conventional rake, by means of a bed-trick which leads him to believe her a mistress.[21] Amanda—"she who is to be loved"—represents true love, faithful, unchanging, and understood as part of a higher ordination: she sees Loveless as "the Man I'm bound by Heaven to Love" (III.i.75-76). Loveless, like the traditional hero of the comedy of manners, equates love with adventure and pleasure and abandons her merely because she is a wife. When her disguise proves to him that she can give him great pleasure, he is converted, admitting:

> *'Twas heedless Fancy first, that made me stray,*
> *But Reason now breaks forth, and lights me on my Way.*
> [V.ii.229-30]

His final words confirm what Amanda has known all along:

> The greatest Happiness we can hope on Earth,
> *And sure the nearest to the Joys above,*
> *Is the chaste Rapture of a virtuous Love.*
> [V.iv.49-52]

The subplot repeats all this on a different level and in a lighter tone. It involves the carrying out of a ruse which will enable the Worthy brothers to marry the women of their choice despite parental objections. Young Worthy, a good-hearted rake not unlike Loveless in some of his poses, contrives the deception that makes the "right" marriages possible, but first he must exorcise some of the conventional attitudes that stand in the way. He must subdue his brother's jealousy of Hillaria, correct Hillaria's weakness for fashionable flirtation, school his own Narcissa out of a preference for a talked-about courtship over marriage, and prove to old Sir

William that fortune is not the foundation for marriage. His success in each of these quests is but a reflection of his triumph as the engineer of the intrigue that brings Loveless to the bed of his unknown Amanda, to the renunciation of his raking ways, and finally to marital joy.

Thus the two plots in *Love's Last Shift* are united by their parallel themes and by the interaction of the characters. Young Worthy's acrobatics keep him swinging from one plot to the other; the ladies seek each other out for advice, thus linking Amanda's love-sufferings with the coquettish complaints of Hillaria and Narcissa. The ultimate evidence of unity of theme and action comes at the end of the play in the wedding celebration. The two plots merge; the newly married couples become novices, learning from the "remarried" Amanda and Loveless the dangers and the rewards of marriage. In one of the last scenes of the play, one in which the serious attitudes of sentimental love transform the game-playing of the witty lovers, Loveless instructs Narcissa: "Love's a tender Plant which can't live out of a warm Bed: You must take care, with undissembled Kindness, to keep him from the Northern Blast of Jealousy" (V.iii.43-46).

A further support to the thematic unity of *Love's Last Shift* is the sentimental dedication to a belief in native goodness of heart, which underlies the notion of conversion, covers a multitude of sins, and ultimately gives its possessor success. We must presume that Loveless has a good heart, for his conversion is regarded as an awakening. He himself sees all that has gone before as but "Shadows of substantial Bliss" (V.ii.193). Young Worthy's membership in the same "raking Brotherhood" is absolved by his promotion of the plot to bring Loveless to account. Even Sir William Wisewoud learns to value goodness of heart, and reveals something of it himself when he forgives Young Worthy for tricking him not only of his daughter, but of his five thousand pounds.

The only unreclaimed figure in the play is Sir Novelty Fashion, whose newfangledness makes him a representative of the old conventionalism. When he comes to join in a celebration of marital joy, his own cause for happiness is not marriage, but having finally escaped his mistress. He is a "Weed" that continues to grow "as rank as ever" (V.iii.63,64), with no understanding of what has been happening all around him. He continues to believe that "'tis mechanical to marry the Woman you love: Men of Quality shou'd always marry those they never saw" (III.i.102-04). His role, besides providing the only real laughing comedy in the play, serves a unifying function as well. All the other characters in the play, in one way or another, reflect his acceptance of fashion as the measure of all actions. In every case this code of behavior is the obstacle which must be overcome if the characters are to avoid being fools.

For all its careful integration of plots and unity of theme, *Love's Last Shift* seems somehow to offend probability, perhaps even tempt the spectator to laugh at the wrong time, for the wrong motives. The reason for this is undoubtedly the great difference in tone between main plot and subplot. The main plot combines the doctrinal assumptions and stark characterization of a morality play—vice against virtue—with the improbable intrigue of romance. The combination balances uneasily with the smooth, easy wit and the perfectly plausible trick—a mere substitution of names on the marriage papers—of the subplot. This has led, naturally enough, to accusations of hypocrisy, of putting a "superficial veneer over manners not far removed from those of the court of Charles," and of encouraging still the "evil, gallant heroes."[22] Cibber's statement in the Epilogue that his hero is "lew'd for above four Acts" seems to be supported by the ecstatic suggestiveness of the seduction in Act IV. To be sure, Loveless does not repent until Act V, but it is to his repentance that the four acts of "lewdness" lead. Young Worthy prepares the means of conversion in the first act, and Amanda discusses its possibilities in the second. Besides this, the theme of virtuous love is made apparent in Amanda's first speeches. It is worth remembering too that this, Cibber's first play, was transitional and experimental, imposing the attitudes of sentimental morality on the materials of Restoration comedy, playing up to the new spirit, but unwilling to relinquish the successes of the past.

In *The Careless Husband,* Cibber's most famous play, the apparent moral ambivalence and the unevenness of tone found in *Love's Last Shift* have disappeared and are replaced by a more balanced and polished treatment of similar actions and themes. Again the wandering husband is converted, but this time gracefully; Sir Charles and Lady Easy continue the roles of Loveless and Amanda, but their conflict and its resolution are more subtle than those in the earlier play. Lady Easy is as confident of her goodness—

in this case it reveals itself in her patience—as Amanda is, but she understands its practical worth as well: "to reproach him with my Wrongs, is taking on my self the Means of a Redress, bidding Defiance to his Falshood, and naturally but provokes him to undo me" (I.i.4-7). When she finds Sir Charles asleep with her maid, she resists the impulse to wake and rebuke him, and merely covers his bared head with her scarf, an action which is both sentimental—a melodramatic manifestation of her patience—and shrewd—an accurate evaluation of her husband's temper. Sir Charles, too, though indifferent to his wife, recognizes her goodness from the start, and admits the psychological effectiveness of her imperturbability: "Well! one way or other this Woman will certainly bring about her Business with me at last; for tho' she can't make me happy in her own Person, she lets me be so intolerably easie with the Women that can, that she has at least brought me into a fair way of being as weary of them too" (I.i.268-72).

Here, as in *Love's Last Shift,* Cibber develops a pair of closely related actions bound together by the interaction of their characters and the repetition of theme. Sir Charles directs Morelove's eventual triumph over Lady Betty, and Lady Easy is Lady Betty's adviser. The play involves only seven characters grouped in two love-triangles: one made up of Sir Charles, Lady Easy, and Lady Graveairs and the maid Edging, who play two aspects of the same role; and one made up of Lord Morelove, Lady Betty, and the flirtatious Lord Foppington, who is Sir Novelty Fashion in later years and higher rank. In the sentimental plot, Lady Easy, like Amanda, wins her errant husband back to virtuous love, but she does so on a different level; where Amanda proved to Loveless that marital love gives pleasure surpassing that of an illicit amour, Lady Easy brings Sir Charles to the realization that, with her grace and patience, she is personally worthy of his love and respect. The schematic arrangement of characters in *The Careless Husband* highlights her good qualities for Sir Charles, as well as for the audience; his love affairs—the fashionable, serious alliance with Lady Graveairs and the pantry flirtation with Edging—bring down upon him insults and accusations, harangues and huffs. In contrast to these women, Lady Easy comes to represent to him a precious jewel that he has worn close to him, so close that he has not been curious to "look upon its Lustre" (V.vi.78).

The intrigue of the subplot is set against all this and, despite its resemblance to the comedy of manners, repeats the central theme on another level. Lady Betty, a fuller embodiment of the qualities Cibber presented in Narcissa and Hillaria in *Love's Last Shift,* is "careless," refusing to behave seriously and reveling, like Sir Charles, in a modish desire to dominate in love. Sir Charles must root out that affectation in her by abusing her so violently that she is forced to seek refuge in Morelove's chivalry, the very quality she had declared to be unfashionable and dreary.

If Lady Betty is a reflection of Sir Charles, Lord Morelove is a parody of Lady Easy. He is serious about love and marriage, confronting Sir Charles and Lord Foppington with the declaration: "If I were married, I would as soon part from my Estate, as my Wife" (II.ii.138-39). But unlike Lady Easy, Morelove is too agitated by his love for Lady Betty to affect the ease and carelessness Sir Charles tells him is necessary to win her out of her affected aversion. In this action, a third party serves as a grotesque caricature of both patience and frivolity. Lord Foppington is the supremely careless lover; as Sir Charles says to Morelove: "he's able to give you Advice; for tho' he's in Love with the same Woman, yet to him she has not Charms enough to give a Minute's Pain" (I.i.385-87). The consummately easy man is no real lover, as Lady Betty discovers, but rather, as Sir Charles will see in his own case, a fool.

Though it deals with similar materials and themes, *The Careless Husband* is a better play than *Love's Last Shift,* owing, no doubt, to its subtle balance of elements. In the first place, its sentimental plot—the conversion of Sir Charles Easy—and its witty plot—the conversion of Lady Betty—are given nearly equal weight and develop as parallel interests, bound together by a limited cast of characters who are integral to both actions. This balance is further supported by a brilliant trick in one, and a brilliant heroine in the other. Perhaps more important is the internal economy of the two plots. *Love's Last Shift* develops around a purely romantic disguise-trick; *The Careless Husband,* while not eschewing the romantic element altogether, relies on psychological probability. When Lady Easy lays her scarf over her husband's head, and when he awakens, finds it, and repents, the audience accepts the situation because the trick is not merely an extravagant gesture, but the plausible outgrowth of what husband and wife have already shown themselves to be. Lady Easy is not a mere type of patience; rather, she has a specific goal in mind to which she recognizes patience as the most efficacious means.

Her psychological plausibility further manifests itself in the cleverness with which she manipulates her conversation with Sir Charles in Act I. He wants to find out if she suspects him of philandering; she knows this and will not satisfy him by responding like a jealous wife. Her answers to his questions are so complacent that he, unwitting, is forced to reveal the extent of his amours—as suppositions: "Suppose now my Lady *Graveairs* and I were great—" and "the Duce take me, if I would not as soon have an Affair with thy own Woman" (I.i.213, 228-29). Her replies to his leading questions seem innocent only to him, however, for when, in response to his last remark, she says, "Indeed, my Dear, I should as soon suspect you with one as t'other" (I.i.230-31), we realize that she is in control. When she places the scarf on his head, she claims it is an act of love and mercy; it is, in fact, a confrontation, silent, tactful, and effective. And Sir Charles, in whose disposition the willingness to be confronted and converted has been evident from the beginning, realizes ruefully that she has known all along, and that he has been a hypocrite and a fool.

The affairs of Lady Betty and Lord Morelove proceed according to the rules of witty comedy. The conventional nature of this action is typified in Lord Foppington's false wit, especially in his extended pursuit of the hunting metaphor in Act III, and in his arrangement of a tennis-match of barbed comments in Act IV. Yet even in this subplot, Cibber adds touches of a psychological truth, not usually found in the comedy of manners, to distinguish it from the ordinary. One of these is the added twist in Sir Charles's plan for Morelove—the abuse of Lady Betty—after he finds he cannot induce Morelove to remain indifferent. Another is the good humor of all the participants when their affectations have been exposed: Lady Betty admits that Sir Charles's deception was "the only thing that cou'd have prevail'd upon my Temper" (V.vii.249-50); Lord Foppington reflects, upon being abandoned: "[I] do not positively remember, that the *Non-Chalence* of my Temper ever had so bright an Occasion to shew it self before" (V.ii.193-95). All are allowed to change their ways with the same grace that Sir Charles changed his. In fact, Sir Charles brings Lady Betty and Lord Morelove together with words that reinforce the similarities of action and tone in the two plots: "Well, Madam, now the worst that the World can say of your past Conduct is, that my Lord had Constancy, and you have try'd it" (V.vii.254-56).

The success of *The Careless Husband* inspired Cibber to use some of its elements again. In the Prologue to *The Lady's Last Stake, or The Wife's Resentment* he claims his intention is to try a variation of the plot of the earlier play, if only to satisfy the many who found Lady Easy's patience intolerable:

He gives you now a Wife, he's sure's in Fashion,
Whose Wrongs use modern Means for Reparation.
No Fool, that will her Life in Sufferings waste,
But furious, proud, and insolently chaste;
Who more in Honour jealous, than in Love,
Resolves Resentment shall her Wrongs remove.
[Prologue, 21-26]

So he creates Lady Wronglove, a resentful wife who will not tolerate her husband's affairs, and Lord Wronglove, an irascible husband who is goaded by her resentment to flaunt them. It is apparent from the start that the misconduct of each is prompted by the sins of the other, and it is impossible to assign the first offense to either. While we may suspect that Lady Wronglove's girlhood espousal of a kind of courtly "daunger" was the first obstacle to conjugal love, we cannot hold her entirely responsible. Lord Wronglove is a conventional rake, but one more like Sir Charles Easy than like Loveless, with something of Sir Charles's redeeming ability to laugh at himself and his amours. Yet there is a nastiness in him that was not in Cibber's earlier heroes. While he claims a libertine right to his pleasures, the greatest pleasure his adventures afford is the baiting of his wife.

If it is difficult to discern the first offender, it is equally difficult to recognize the first stirrings of native goodness in either. There would seem to be no solution, and indeed there is none of the sort that saved Loveless. But a new figure materializes to effect the necessary awakening and reconciliation. In Act IV both husband and wife entrust their misery to Sir Friendly Moral, who, by talking about it, encourages them to recognize and reject some of their rigidities. In the final act, Sir Friendly manages to reduce Lady Wronglove to tears, introduces her husband at that moment, and unites their "softened" hearts.

The subplot revolves around Lord George Brilliant, a would-be rake whom Wronglove accuses of denying his true feelings for Mrs. Conquest only because her fortune is too small, and of contriving a passion for the virtuous Lady Gentle as a diversion. Mrs. Conquest, patient and witty, is confident that Brilliant loves her, and needs only to be made aware of the fact by some awakening incident. When Brilliant carries out his plan to compromise Lady Gentle by winning at cards, Mrs. Conquest, disguised as her own brother, intervenes and challenges him. In the episode that follows, she arranges to be "wounded." The trick works. Still in disguise, she absolves Brilliant of any guilt in her "death," he is moved by her generosity to admit his love for the "sister," she reveals herself, and they are to be married on the spot.

The interrelationship of the two plots in *The Lady's Last Stake,* like those of *Love's Last Shift* and *The Careless Husband,* depends upon the friendship of the characters. In this play, however, the bond between plots is looser; there is no one like Young Worthy or Sir Charles Easy who is integral to both plots. As a result, the two plots tend to separate and even to compete with each other. The play ends with the awakening of Lord George, at which the presence of the Wrongloves seems quite accidental. As for the parallel action, it too is less obviously parallel than in the earlier plays, where both plots move toward marriage or "remarriage." In *The Lady's Last Stake* some degree of thematic unity grows out of the fact that all the characters come to an awakening and give up their wrong notions of love and honor: the Wrongloves learn selflessness in love; Lord George, the follies of raking; and Lady Gentle, the vulnerability of a virtuous wife. But this is a rather subtle and tenuous unity and does not prevent the sense that there are too many actions in the play.

Perhaps the real reason for the weakness of *The Lady's Last Stake* lies in Cibber's attempt to capitalize on the success of *The*

Careless Husband by showing us the wife's other possible course of action. The tale of a wife whose patience finally wins the esteem of a philandering, but fundamentally good-natured and sensitive husband is, in its simple, fabulous outlines, genuinely sentimental. That of a wife who rises to the bait, growing more and more frenzied and increasingly degraded, is too real and resists a sentimental conclusion. The difficulty is compounded by the fact that Cibber seems to have had a good ear for the dialogue of irreparable quarrels between husband and wife. The best scenes in the play are those where Lord and Lady Wronglove are farthest from reconciliation. An outstanding example of this is the quarrel in Act IV (i.82-116) where, in a mounting rage, each picks out of the other's accusations some particular detail—the choice of irrelevancies is excruciatingly personal and real—on which to base his own next outburst.

In *Love's Last Shift* the errant hero is a figure in a moral fable, the outcome of which is apparent from the very beginning; Sir Charles and Lady Easy exhibit a plausibility which vivifies, but does not destroy their moral typicality. Lord and Lady Wronglove are not moral types at all, but are, rather, strikingly singular individuals. The torments they visit upon one another are not, like the sins Loveless commits against Amanda, generalized violations of the marriage vows, but carefully sharpened barbs which they, through long familiarity, use to probe each other's weaknesses. The conflict is not a sentimental one, and thus the sentimental resolution is more awkward here than in the other plays. Whether this points to an inherent weakness in sentimental comedy, or to Cibber's inability to sustain a necessary typicality would be difficult to determine. It may, in fact, be Cibber's way of reminding those who found Lady Easy's patience intolerable that they had missed the point of the play. There was no alternative.

The Lord George-Lady Gentle plot offers a fairly clear-cut moral example, but Lord George's adventures with Mrs. Conquest seem to exhibit the same ambiguity of attitude that troubles the main plot, perhaps because Lord George is not a real rake and Mrs. Conquest is a witty female *eiron* rather than the embodiment of the emotions of virtue. The play, unlike *Love's Last Shift* and *The*

Careless Husband, ends not with a song to celebrate the triumph of virtuous love, but with the high spirits that Lord George and Mrs. Conquest have sustained throughout:

> *Lord Geo.* I fancy . . . I begin to make a very ridiculous Figure here, and have given my self the Air of more Looseness than I have been able to come up to.
> *Mrs. Con.* I'm afraid that's giving your self the Air of more Virtue than you'll be able to come up to—. [V.v.170-74]

The Contexts

> *Ramble.* Ay, marry, that Play [*Love's Last Shift*] was the Philosopher's Stone; I think it did wonders.
> *Sullen.* It did so, and very deservedly; there being few Comedies that came up to't for purity of Plot, Manners and Moral.
>
> *A Comparison Between the Two Stages,* p. 25

To praise Cibber as the standard-bearer of a new kind of comedy which reformed the old is misleading. Besides imputing to him a greatness he did not have, it implies that a different and superior kind of comedy at a given moment supplanted the comedy of manners. There are, however, elements of perverse truth in the encomiums of Davies and of the author of the *Comparison;* what Cibber offered in *Love's Last Shift, The Careless Husband,* and *The Lady's Last Stake,* though they bore many resemblances to earlier comedy, was startlingly unlike the best plays of his predecessors.

The striking quality of Cibber's three comedies—and of sentimental comedies generally—is the dramatization in everyday dress of moral commonplaces, the confident assumptions that good always triumphs over evil, that man has only to see or feel the right to do it, that whatever the past has been, conversion is permanent, and that man is happy in being good. The dramatization of these assumptions produces the other distinguishing feature of Cibber's plays, a language that is essentially the language of religious ecstasy and conversion. Made up of stock phrases and colored by high emotion, the speeches of Cibber's reclaimed heroes and heroines express what amounts to a kind of Renaissance *admiratio* for the goodness which has rescued them. Loveless, for example, tells Amanda:

> . . . while in my Arms I thus can circle thee, I grasp more Treasure, than in a Day the posting Sun can travel o'er. Oh! why have I so long been blind to the Perfections of thy Mind and Person? Not knowing thee a Wife, I found thee charming beyond the Wishes of luxurious Love. Is it then a Name, a Word shall rob thee of thy Worth? Can Fancy be a surer Guide to Happiness than Reason? Oh! I have wander'd like a benighted Wretch, and lost my self in Life's unpleasing Journey. [V.ii. 220-28]

A number of studies have been made to identify the constituent characteristics of sentimental comedy, and its chroniclers agree on the basic elements: a moral problem that provides the plot, fundamentally good characters who grapple with the problem and solve it in accordance with Christian ethics, and sympathetic emotions that accompany triumph.[23] Joseph Wood Krutch's characterization of sentimental drama locates its quintessential spirit in audience response—in sharing the joys and sorrows of the characters, in admiring virtue, in believing that it will triumph, and in rejoicing personally when it does.[24] From another point of view, sentimentalism is a technique: for John Harrington Smith it is the "exemplary method"; according to Arthur Sherbo, the sentimental dramatist indulges in "repetition and prolongation" of the intricacies of the moral dilemma or of the virtues and the sufferings of the characters.[25] Related to this is the "emphasis and direction" by which the dramatist reiterates certain ideas and plays on certain emotions so that the climax is natural and expected.[26]

All the critics of sentimental comedy find fault with its thundering improbability, especially in the unlikely conversions of the wicked. In doing so, however, they urge the objections of a Restoration wit or a twentieth-century theater-goer and overlook the nature of sentimental comedy. Cibber himself hinted at this special nature in the Prologue to *Love's Last Shift:* "Neglected Virtue is at least shewn fair." This he quickly says is "enough o'Conscience," no doubt wishing to placate those in his audience—still very much attuned to the comedy of manners—who preferred racy intrigue. The Prologue to *The Careless Husband,* a decade later, gives clearer expression to the sentimental spirit:

> *Wretches so far shut out from Sense of Shame*
> Newgate *or* Bedlam *only shòu'd reclaim;*
> *For Satyr ne'er was meant to make wild Monsters tame.*
> *No, Sirs—*
> *We rather think the Persons fit for Plays,*
> *Are they whose Birth and Education says*
> *They've ev'ry Help that shou'd improve Mankind,*
> *Yet still live Slaves to a vile tainted Mind.*
>
> [Prologue, 15-22]

The inference is that plays should instruct directly, that characters should inspire emulation or give warning. The Prologue to *The Lady's Last Stake* refers to the depiction of the lady gamester's plight as "*the friendly Muses tender'st way*" to deliver the warning.

It is in Richard Steele that we find the ultimate expression of what Cibber hinted at in prologues and epilogues. To show "neglected" virtue merely fair is no longer sufficient. In the Preface to *The Conscious Lovers* Steele redefines the nature of comedy. To those who found his hero's virtue and the tearful reunion of father with long-lost daughter "no Subjects of Comedy" he says that he "cannot be of their Mind; for any thing that has its Foundation in Happiness and Success, must be allow'd to be the Object of Comedy, and sure it must be an Improvement of it, to introduce a Joy too exquisite for Laughter, that can have no Spring but in Delight .... To be apt to give way to the Impressions of Humanity is the Excellence of a right Disposition, and the natural Working of a well-turn'd Spirit."[27]

Sentimental comedy is radically opposed to the comedy of manners. Its supporters saw it as a triumph over the "immorality" of the earlier comedy, and its critics, like Goldsmith, considered it a betrayal of true "laughing" comedy.[28] The comedy of manners expresses aristocratic laughter at the complications of life. The salon and the park circumscribe its universe; the graces expected in those precincts become commandments; the polished gentleman, man of the world, is hero. His life is a game devoted to keeping order in that world, to overcoming obstacles that threaten his mastery. He is most frequently balked in the fulfillment of his own sexual desires and must somehow reconcile the inconsistency between what society expects and what he wants.[29] The risks he runs in trying to slight neither are, even for him, exceedingly laughable.

The desire to win motivates him, but the game itself contributes enticing pleasure to the final conquest; thus intrigue becomes the substance, the stuff from which plots are made. Critics have almost universally acknowledged the intellectual quality of the comedy of manners; it inheres in the spirit of game.[30] There is immense pleasure in the mind's arrangements and in the triumph of victory, and still no shackles upon the player at all. Neither is the spectator committed.

The hero of the comedy of manners has always charmed or outraged the critics. His view of life as a game to be won by the clever has given him a role and a language, both highly specialized. He is an *eiron,* a manipulator of his own and others' desires according to a code of behavior established by his society. He is descended from the Vice of the morality play, what Bernard Spivack calls the "homiletic showman, intriguer extraordinary, and master of dramatic ceremonies."[31] In Etherege's *The Man of Mode,* for example, Dorimant loves not only the game, but the awareness of play: "next to the coming to a good understanding with a new Mistress, I love a quarrel with an old one."[32] His pleasure in dominion is so great that he not only plays one mistress off against another, but participates in the scene himself, first insulting Loveit into a rage, then declining to stay where his love is not wanted, and finally—because Loveit will not be cast aside—accusing her of a flirtation with the fool Sir Fopling Flutter.[33] He delights in masquerading as the prig Courtage to win the approval of Harriet's mother and to elicit her avowal that "a dozen such good men" as himself would be "enough to attone for that wicked *Dorimant.*"[34] Though he gives up his "liberty" to Harriet at the end of the play, agreeing to live in the country, he does not reject his mistresses. He encourages Loveit with the revelation that Harriet is to be a wife, not a competing mistress, and seems surprised when Bellinda says she hopes they will never meet again.

The nature of the dominion Dorimant retains at the conclusion of *The Man of Mode* may be ambiguous; Horner's survival as master in Wycherley's *The Country Wife* is unqualified. He is the "intriguer extraordinary"; capitalizing on the expectations of his society, he has prepared a scheme that eliminates all unnecessary preliminaries and provides him the promise of endless pleasure. But even pleasure seems secondary to satisfaction with a successful process. Horner's defense of his deceit seems chiefly to be that it saves him time:

> ask but all the young Fellows of the Town, if they do not lose more time, like Huntsmen, in starting the game, than in running it down; one knows not where to find 'em, who will, or will not; Women of Quality are so civil, you can hardly distinguish love from good breeding, and a Man is often mistaken; but now I can be sure, she that shews an aversion to me loves the sport. . . . Now may I have, by the reputation of an Eunuch, the Priviledges of One; and be seen in a Ladies Chamber in a morning as early as her Husband; kiss Virgins before their Parents, or Lovers; and may be, in short, the *Pas par tout* of the Town.[35]

Congreve's Mirabell is a manipulator, too, but an *eiron* of a different sort. Like Dorimant and Horner, he has participated in the world and uses its follies to his own advantage, but unlike them, he manipulates the code of behavior in order to transcend it. By enumerating and denying the fashionable conventions, both he and Millamant prepare ideal grounds for a lasting bond. His provisos require that she give up all coquettish forms which lead to usurping "the mens prerogative." Hers ask that they avoid the standards of the town: "let us be very strange and well-bred: let us be as strange as if we had been married a great while; and as well bred as if we were not marri'd at all."[36] The difference in *The Way of the World* is a crucial one. Here the stake of the game is marriage, and the victory understood to be a permanent one.

The aesthetic view of life accounts for the carefully planned repartee that constitutes the verbal wit of Restoration comedy. Wit is more than mere verbal agility, an added grace in a courtly world; it is the manifestation of the ideals of the time.[37] Wit comprehends fancy and judgment; it is the mastery of images, and what Dryden called propriety, the "clothing of those thoughts with such expressions as are naturally proper to them."[38] Verbal wit is the natural expression of the rake-hero. The game that he plays with his life and others' is a metaphor for the sexual encounter. Most fittingly, it is acted out in the drawing room by means of witty conversation which is a carefully woven fabric of images and figures. The metaphorical vision may express itself simply, in the descriptive terms the characters apply to themselves or to things outside. Thus, when Horner proclaims, at the end of his long description of the women who are revealed to him by his pretended impotence, that he has become the "*Pas par tout*" of the town, he is indulging in no purely ornamental label; this is how he sees himself. Earlier in the same speech he spoke of "Huntsmen," "game," and "running it down," because this is precisely what he has arranged.

The witty dialogue is another means by which the metaphor is expressed. Hero and heroine, by the very fact of their formal repartee, are engaging in a game, matching metaphors. In *The Country Wife,* for example, Lady Fidget, Mrs. Dainty, and Mrs. Squeamish join Horner in pursuit of the following simile:

> *Dain.* The filthy Toads chuse Mistresses now, as they do Stuffs, for having been fancy'd and worn by others.
> *Squeam.* For being common and cheap.
> *Lady.* Whilst Women of Quality, like the richest Stuffs lye untumbled, and unask'd for.
> *Hor.* Ay, neat, and cheap, and new, often they think best.
> *Dain.* No, Sir, the Beasts will be known by a Mistriss longer than by a suit.[39]

The give-and-take of Congreve's brilliant dialogue is the epitome of wit. At the same time, it embodies a consciousness that it is wit and somehow not real, as the following conversation of Mirabell, Millamant, and Witwoud shows:

> *Mrs. Mil.* One no more owes one's Beauty to a Lover, than one's Wit to an Eccho. They can but reflect what we look and say; vain and empty Things if we are silent or unseen, and want a being.
> *Mir.* Yet to those two vain empty Things you owe the two greatest Pleasures of your Life.
> *Mrs. Mil.* How so?

Mir. To your Lover you owe the pleasure of hearing your selves prais'd; and to an Eccho the pleasure of hearing your selves talk.
Wit. But I know a Lady that loves talking so incessantly, she won't give an Eccho fair play; she has that everlasting Rotation of Tongue, that an Eccho must wait till she dies, before it can catch her last Words.
Mrs. Mil. O Fiction.[40]

With Congreve something of the real world often breaks through. Millamant's impatient "O Fiction" stops the playing on words which otherwise might have gone on forever. Consciousness that words are part of the game brings the "proviso" scene as well to a conclusion. Mirabell offers a set of conditions to which Millamant coquettishly objects throughout, yet at the very end he says, without being contradicted, "Then wee're agreed."[41]

Those characters who are not true wits usually sin against language as well as against the code of the fashionable world. Witwoud, the false wit in *The Way of the World,* is incapable of holding the delicate balance of verbal wit. He cannot refrain from the excessive example that pushes wit over the edge into word-play that must be acknowledged, then and there, as "fiction." The extreme of the false wit is perhaps Sparkish in *The Country Wife;* he desires the reputation of a wit, which he thinks he can gain by being spoken of wittily as a fool and a cuckold. Accordingly, scorning to be "jealous, like a Country Bumpkin," he sends Alithea, his bride-to-be, off into a corner with Harcourt, who loves her. When Alithea protests that Harcourt has insulted him, Sparkish feels he has at last arrived in the world of wit: "but if he does rail at me, 'tis but in jest I warrant; what we wits do for one another, and never take any notice of it."[42]

The hero of the comedy of manners uses wit to accomplish his design, but he is obviously capable, as his successes testify, of distinguishing between it and reality. The fool or false wit lacks the detachment necessary to make such a distinction. It is, in fact, by mistaking appearance for reality that he becomes a fool. Naive characters like Mrs. Pinchwife disregard wit altogether and fasten on the real significance of action. Mrs. Pinchwife does not understand the language of the town, but she knows what Horner is about; she does not, however, realize that he is playing a game. Thus, her responses are literal, both verbally and psychologically. Instructed by her husband to write a letter discouraging Horner, she adds on her own:

> —for I'm sure if you and I were in the Countrey at Cards together,—*so*—I cou'd not help treading on your Toe under the Table—*so*—or rubbing knees with you, and staring in your face, 'till you saw me—*very well*—and then looking down, and blushing for an hour together—*so*—[43]

By writing what she feels, she sets herself apart from the world of manners, which demands the detachment that is wit in both living and speaking.

For this reason, figures like Mrs. Pinchwife appear seldom in the comedy of manners. The only other outstanding example, also Wycherley's, is Manly, in *The Plain Dealer.* He is excluded from the society of wits by his spleen, not by naiveté, but the effect in the play is similar. Mrs. Pinchwife cannot help calling a spade a spade, Manly will not avoid it: he "wou'd give fauning Slaves the Lye, whilst they embrace or commend [him]."[44] These "realists" are too thoroughly "engaged" in themselves and their own circumstances to participate in the game of wit.[45] But, like the fools who are also wrapped up in themselves, Margery Pinchwife and Captain Manly are important in the comedy of manners for two reasons: their failures enhance the successes of the true wits; at the same time, their inability to play, whether through folly, innocence, or intransigence, identifies wit—and the comedy of manners—as a game.

In contrast to the aesthetic view, sentimental comedy is pragmatic. Cibber's Sir Friendly Moral urges the new ethos: "Come! come! lets not contend for Victory, but Truth" (*The Lady's Last Stake,* III.i.536). To understand how the change from one attitude to the other came about we must look to Restoration London. The comedy of manners was written for an aristocratic audience by aristocrats, and though some of its attitudes were aped by every sort of playwright, including Cibber, it spoke to an elite; it reflected the life and ideas of the court of Charles II.

The vivacity of its action and the brilliance of its dialogue gave it a fame, however, that has tended to obscure its limited reach. For example, during the first twenty years of the Restoration there were only two major companies of actors in London: Killigrew's King's Men and Davenant's Duke's Men. By 1682, difficulties, chiefly financial, forced the union of the two companies, and until the actor Thomas Betterton broke away from the Theatre Royal in Drury Lane to open his own theater in Lincoln's Inn Fields in 1695, there was only one official company acting in London.[46] Even this division seems to have represented the will of the actors, rather than the demands of the spectators, for, as a contemporary pamphlet reports, the town was unable "to furnish out two good Audiences every Day."[47]

The audiences of Restoration comedy were, then, a relatively small group. The great numbers of merchants and businessmen bred in the Puritan tradition still shared, up to a point, the creed that had produced Stephen Gosson and William Prynne and had closed the London theaters in 1642. The paradigm of the citizen's life was Christian's progress to the heavenly city, and a question still to be asked was "*What shall I do to be saved?*"[48] Earnestness about salvation precluded joking on the subject of human weaknesses and difficulties, especially those of the flesh, which the Christian knew ought to be mortified. A sober respect for the social institutions necessary to his progress in the world—especially marriage and inheritance—made the jibing of the comic wits unacceptable. Added to this, resentment at the ridiculous depiction of his class on the stage set the average Puritan in opposition to the essential character of the comedy of manners—its detachment.[49]

In the writings of Sir Richard Blackmore, at the end of the century, we find an example of the arguments of the middle class against the comedy of manners. They are important, not only because they represent the middle-class view, but also because they reveal it in a man who was clearly no mere shopkeeper. In Blackmore, the City Knight and physician-turned-poet, there burned a middle-class fervor which was directed against wit and the "Wits" as the corrupters of both taste and morality.[50] He made war on Dryden, Congreve, Wycherley, and, we presume, all authors of comedy of manners. These men belonged to a world from which every social and intellectual barrier excluded him. He, in turn, rejected their plots, characters, and language as "a general *Confederacy* to ruin the End of their own Art."[51] In accepting as the primary end of poetry the instruction of the mind and regulation of manners, he was in agreement with his enemies, but his acknowledgment that poetry ought to delight is grudging. It was, he thought, to this "inferiour End" that the wits devoted themselves solely, "for no higher Purpose than to please the Imagination of vain and wanton People."[52] The power to delight was, for him, the power to move the emotions, and thus a means of facilitating instruction: "A Poet should imploy all his Judgment and Wit, exhaust all the Riches of his Fancy, and abound in Beautiful and Noble Expression, to divert and entertain others; but then it must be with this Prospect, that he may hereby engage their Attention, insinuate more easily into their Minds, and more effectually convey to them wise Instructions."[53] For Blackmore, the comedy of manners betrayed the spectator by misusing both of the powers of wit—inventiveness and felicity of expression—in scandalous characterization and scurrilous language. In his opposition to a purely intellectual wit, and his insensitivity to satiric purpose in the comedy of manners, Blackmore illustrates one of the several attitudes that helped prepare the way for sentimental comedy.

The doctrine of benevolence preached by latitudinarian clergymen of the Established Church contributed another attitude, especially in its rejection of the Hobbesian view of man as a beast of prey.[54] Though anti-Puritan in spirit, Latitudinarianism shared the Puritan earnestness about life and encouraged virtuous living as a preparation for eternity. Archbishop Tillotson, for example, preached that plays fostered infidelity and vice. They could, however, be "innocently diverting" and "instructing and useful" if they would but take into account that "the two great ends for which this faculty of Speech is given us, are to glorifie God our Maker, and to edifie Man our Neighbour."[55] The ideal man, according to Isaac Barrow, is not the man of the world, but one who is "like *David, fulfilling all God's will, and having respect to all God's commandments.*"[56] Such a man will see all things *sub specie aeternitatis,* not as a satirist or laughing philosopher.

One of the most significant contributions of latitudinarian doctrine and Puritan belief to sentimental attitudes is the conviction that virtuous living is, apart from being necessary to salvation, pleasant and profitable to practice. Tillotson, in *The present and future Advantage of an Holy and Virtuous Life,* a sermon with a practical middle-class orientation, enumerates virtue's present advantages: it brings peace of mind, a good name, blessings upon one's posterity, and it promotes our "outward temporal Interest."[57]

That this idealization of the good man was not restricted to the pulpit is shown in Richard Steele's *The Christian Hero.* This little book, first published in 1701 while Steele was serving in the Guards, bears the subtitle *An Argument Proving that no Principles But Those of Religion Are Sufficient to Make a Great Man.* It adds to the ideas of uprightness and justice the notion of benevolence. Steele writes confidently of man's natural inclination to good, of Christianity's supreme efficacy in directing him, and in feeling as the right spur to all action. "The Eternal God," he writes, ". . . presses us by Natural Society to a close Union with each other." By this union "we lament with the Unfortunate, and rejoice with the Glad; for it is not possible for an human Heart to be averse to any thing that is Human."[58] By Steele's time the scope of these ideas was far-reaching. Virtue, the support of the Puritan wayfarer, had almost imperceptibly enlarged into virtue, the support of society, "*that* which is the Prop and Ornament of human Affairs; which upholds Communitys, maintains Union, Friendship, and Correspondence amongst Men."[59]

It was natural that a desire for moral reform would spring from this temper. The London of the seventies and eighties seemed to those inspired by either Puritan or latitudinarian zeal to be a city of fornication, blasphemy, drunkenness, gaming, cursing and swearing, violations of the Sabbath, and scurrilous stage plays. The movement to reform the manners of England did not really take shape, however, until the accession of William and Mary. Both King and Queen, from the very beginning of their reign, were vitally concerned with reform. In a letter to the Bishop of London, dated February 13, 1689, William wrote: "We most earnestly Desire, and shall Endeavour a General Reformation of the Lives and Manners of all Our Subjects, as being that which must Establish Our Throne, and Secure to Our People their Religion, Happiness and Peace, all which seem to be in great Danger at this time, by reason of that overflowing of Vice, which is too Notorious in this as well as other Neighbouring Nations."[60] In July 1691 Queen Mary wrote a letter to the justices of the peace in Middlesex, urging them to enforce "*those Laws which have been made, and are still in Force against the Prophanation of the* Lord's-Day, Drunkenness, Prophane Swearing and Cursing, *and all other* Lewd, Enormous, *and* Disorderly Practices."[61] Mary's letter stirred the London Court of Aldermen as well as the justices of Middlesex, and ultimately, from groups already formed or forming, the Societies for the Reformation of Manners were established. Begun in the vague desire to promote reform, the societies soon, and logically enough, instituted a system of informing on offenders and issued blank warrants for their members' convenience.

An account of the growth of the societies in the nineties records that after the accession of William and Mary, a handful of zealous men undertook to carry out their monarchs' wishes. These were joined by others until the societies included a wide range of members, from those prominent in law and Parliament, who brought the offenders to punishment, down to common informers.[62] During the last decade of the century and the early years of the eighteenth century, the societies throve, if the hundreds of sermons delivered before them are any evidence. But they had an inherent weakness in the means by which they acquired their information. In a contemporary pamphlet entitled *A Comparison Between the Two Stages,* Sullen, Ramble, and Critick discuss what could happen when informers were suspected everywhere:

> *Sull.* But did you hear the News?
> *Ramb.* What News?
> *Sull.* The Trial between the *Play-Houses* and *Informers,* for *Prophane, Immoral, Lewd, Scandalous,* and I don't know how many sad things utter'd and spoken on the stage.
> *Cri.* Who were the Persons that spoke 'em, and what were the words?
> *Sull. Batterton* [*sic*], *Brace-girdle, Ben. Johnson,* and others; but the words may not be repeated: Are you so cunning? For ought I know, *Critick,* you're a Spy; they are sly Rogues, they

> say, and lurk in all Companies for matter of Accusation, that a Man is not safe, tho' he be with the Minister of the Parish.[63]

The author of *The Laureat,* another anonymous pamphlet, recalls similar happenings and indicates that royal authority, where it once encouraged the seeking out of vice, was finally forced to counsel restraint; he writes that Queen Anne at one point refused to prosecute accused performers because she was "well satisfied" that those who informed against them "liv'd upon their Oaths, and that what they did, proceeded not from Conscience, but from Interest."[64]

The high point of the movement to reform manners, Jeremy Collier's *A Short View of the Immorality, and Profaneness of the English Stage,* caused no surprise when it appeared in 1698. It was neither the first nor the last of the diatribes directed at the stage as a great source of the immorality of the times, but it was certainly the most famous and, because of this, probably the most effective. Not even Congreve was able to propose a sufficiently withering response. Collier, a non-juring Anglican clergyman, tried to conduct his argument along critical lines, though the shrillness of his preacher's rhetoric often distracts the reader from his literary ideas. He begins with flat statement: "The Business of *Plays* is to recommend Virtue, and discountenance Vice; To shew the Uncertainty of Humane Greatness, the suddain Turns of Fate, and the Unhappy Conclusions of Violence and Injustice: 'Tis to expose the Singularities of Pride and Fancy, to make Folly and Falsehood contemptible, and to bring every Thing that is Ill Under Infamy, and Neglect."[65] This leads him to reject the rake as hero, because he will inspire emulation.[66] He condemns fidelity to sordid reality: "Must we relate whatever is done, and is every Thing fit for Representation?" He recommends that the playwright make a "golden world," a world which, curiously enough, he feels is closer to the real London of his day: "Must Life be huddled over, Nature left imperfect, and the Humour of the Town not shown?"[67] He deplores the lack of decorum in the characterization especially of women and clergymen; these stage types are not only unseemly, but untrue.[68] He thinks English plays more pagan than those of the ancients because they treat deity lightly. He finds idolatry in the lines: "'Tis Heaven to have thee, and without thee Hell."[69] He discovers blasphemy in "I am thinking that tho' Marriage makes Man and Wife one Flesh, it leaves them two Fools." "This Jest," writes Collier, "is made upon a Text in *Genesis,* and afterwards applyed by our Saviour to the Case of Divorse."[70]

With his microscopic eye and literal mind, Collier became a joke to the wits. Such myopia seemed to support the caricatures of the bourgeois moralist that had already appeared on the stage. Congreve's Alderman Fondlewife, in *The Old Batchelor,* illustrates the heavy-handed, dull-witted Puritan when he offers counsel to his lovely young wife: "Wife have you throughly consider'd how detestable, how hainous, and how Crying a Sin, the Sin of Adultery is? have you weigh'd it I say? For it is a very weighty Sin; and although it may lie heavy upon thee, yet thy Husband must also bear his part: for thy iniquity will fall upon his Head."[71]

The middle-class moralist may have seemed, to the comedians he threatened, a hypocrite and a gull, a fanatic and a freak. Yet he made his point. Moderated in tone and polished by wit, his voice and ideas became increasingly the voice and ideas of the town. They reached their most urbane form in *The Spectator,* where Addison wrote with a purpose clearly instructive. He was to balance wit and morality in such a way that he would "refresh [his readers'] Memories from Day to Day, till [he had] recovered them out of that desperate State of Vice and Folly into which the Age is fallen."[72] *The Spectator* marks the successful completion of the citizen's struggle for social acceptance; the arrival of Sir Andrew Freeport, noble, generous, frugal, and diligent, in the polite world of the Spectator Club indicates that the citizen and his values have achieved recognition.[73]

Earlier indications show that bourgeois hostility to the stage was also changing. Samuel Pepys, a snobbish member of the urbane upper-middle class and an avid playgoer, records the presence of increasing numbers of citizens in the audience: "The house was full of citizens, and so the less pleasant"; and on another occasion: "Not so well pleased with the company at the house to-day, which was full of citizens, there hardly being a gentleman or woman in the house."[74] Evidence of the growing importance of bourgeois opinion turns up in his account of attendance at *Tu Quoque,* which he found silly and wearying, but which, he allowed, "will please the citizens."[75] That Pepys should consider pleasing the citizens a legitimate concern tells something about the effect of the middle class upon the stage. Growing in size and influence during the Restoration, the middle class was, by reason of its celebration of the virtues of earnestness and diligence, fundamentally opposed to the cynical temper of the comedy of manners. Yet the citizen, as always, sought respectability, social acceptance, and entertainment; he could not stay away from the playhouse. So he brought with him his tastes and demanded that they be met. After the Revolution of 1688 he found he had a "middle-class" King and Queen who immediately joined the battle on his side. He had, too, the indispensible support of preachers who reached every level in a plea for holy living. By the end of the seventeenth century his class was economically the most powerful, even if not the ruling class. The triumph of his attitudes made the perpetuation of true comedy of manners impossible. Some of the appearances remained in plot, in characters, and in dialogue, presumably as signs of gentility. But the direction was totally different; the hero of the new comedy was at heart the Christian hero.

Sentimental comedy derives its special qualities from this background; in the most general terms, it is an attempt to accommodate the middle-class ethic to the stage. For its plot it takes the solution of a moral problem, and since lust and adultery were so central in the Puritan scheme of sin, the solution usually asserts the triumph of chastity, the nobility of marital fidelity. The audience expected an explicit moral lesson, and this, in turn, required stylized characterization and edifying speech. A more courtly theater, years earlier, had presented these qualities in a different form in the tragedy, tragicomedy, and heroic drama of the early years of the Restoration. In these forms we find nobility of character and high sentiment flourishing in moral struggle.

The special contribution of Restoration tragedy was pathos, that of tragicomedy, the contrived happy ending usually brought about through a change of heart on the part of the blocking character. But it is in the heroic drama that we can see most clearly the roots of the literary tradition out of which sentimental comedy grew.[76] From the years just preceding the Restoration and for at least twenty years after, the heroic plays of Davenant, Howard, Orrery, and Dryden brought to the stage what Dryden defined, in part, as "examples of moral virtue."[77] Here moral virtue was usually represented in great men whose loves conflicted with their loyalties as princes or warriors. The plots of these plays were complex and episodic, each episode intensifying the hero's conflict. The idealization which manifested itself in the prince-hero from exotic lands or remote times, and in the singleness of focus on his trial, extended to language as well. It too was idealized, licensed, like all of the heroic drama, by the contemporary understanding of the laws of the heroic poem, which permitted, even instructed, the dramatist to draw "all things as far above the ordinary proportion of the stage, as that is beyond the common words and actions of human life."[78]

To link Cibber's early comedies with Restoration heroic drama is not to suggest that Cibber thought he was writing a bourgeois adaptation of heroics, though in a way this is what he turned out. On a very basic level both sentimentalism and the heroic vision are wish-fulfillment: sentimental comedy asserts the possibility of the Christian ethic; heroic drama supports belief in a heroic way of life, what one critic has called a response to "the absence of what is most passionately desired, yet not believed any longer to exist."[79] The apparent aims of Cibber's comedies and the kinds of characters and language they required were much like those of the heroic drama. There is even a tactical similarity between the two. Davenant's *The Siege of Rhodes* (1656) appeared while the theaters were still officially closed by those whom Dryden called "good people, who could more easily dispossess their lawful sovereign than endure a wanton jest."[80] Davenant was "forced to turn his thoughts another way, and to introduce the examples of moral virtue writ in verse, and performed in recitative music."[81] *Love's Last Shift* appeared at a similar critical point in the history of the theater, and while Cibber's Epilogue seems to indicate a cavalier treatment of the moral problem in the play and thus to prevent us from seeing in it a wholehearted acquiescence in the moralists' demands, it cannot be denied that the play made some response to the censures then abounding.

The main objective of both types of drama was acknowledged to be homiletic. Dryden's heroes are to provide " guides and patterns of . . . imitation. . . . The feigned hero inflames the true; and the dead virtue animates the living."[82] Cibber, in praising Addison's *Cato* for the patriotism it stirs, asks, about plays of the heroic sort: "have they not vastly the Advantage of any other Human Helps to Eloquence? What equal Method can be found to lead or stimulate the Mind to a quicker Sense of Truth and Virtue, or warm a People into the Love and Practice of such Principles as might be at once a Defence and Honour to their Country?"[83] Inherent in these views is an emotionalism common to both heroic and sentimental drama. Heroic drama inflames and animates, sentimental drama quickens and warms. Steele's belief that comedy should produce a "joy too exquisite for laughter" is but the next step in emotional response.

Heroic drama aimed at producing admiration for the quality of greatness in princes and warriors. The heroes of sentimental comedy are not princes; in their world, as in that which Milton speaks of in the opening lines of Book IX of *Paradise Lost,* the quest for virtue is itself a heroic struggle and affirms the heroism of the aspiring Christian and the saint. Yet the prince-warrior and the sentimental hero have certain qualities in common. Eugene M. Waith describes the former as the Herculean hero, "a warrior of great stature who is guilty of striking departures from the morality of the society in which he lives."[84] In Dryden's Almanzor, Aurengzebe, and Morat we are aware of the interaction of greatness and powerful pride or passion. The sentimental hero does not, on any level, share the stature of the heroic figure. Yet the divinity that makes the Herculean hero what he is may find a sentimental analogue in the humanity of heroes like Loveless and Sir Charles Easy, a humanity which provides susceptibility to the weaknesses of the world and the flesh on the one hand, and the strength of good nature and reasonableness on the other.

The tendency of sentimental comedy to idealize women is another attitude that Cibber may have inherited from heroic drama. The "good" women of Dryden's plays, for example, are loving, long-suffering, and, above all, queenly and honorable. Furthermore, they urge upon errant heroes a sense of honor equal to their own. Not only does Almahide repeatedly profess her duty to wed King Boabdelin, her father's choice, despite her steadily increasing attraction to Almanzor, but she asks him to equal her fidelity.[85]

When Amanda, in *Love's Last Shift,* refers to Loveless as "the Man I'm bound by Heaven to Love" we can hear an echo, not, perhaps, of the same code of honor which binds Almahide, but of feminine perseverance in maintaining an important order. Indamora foreshadows Amanda in the confidence she has in her own virtue: "Honour, like mine, serenely is severe," she protests.[86] Her claim that "All greatness is in virtue understood; / 'Tis only necessary to be good"[87] recalls both Amanda's stock-in-trade and that of all reclaimed sinners in sentimental comedy, an open acceptance of the supreme value of goodness.

Exaltation of the hero above the common order and insistence on elevated language—with rhyme as the most suitable vehicle—are two of the most important and controversial features of heroic drama. Dryden thought "that serious plays ought not to imitate conversation too nearly,"[88] and that heroic plays were entitled to even further magnification above ordinary life. Thus, to idealized characters he would give an equally idealized speech. When, toward the end of *The Conquest of Granada,* Part I, Almanzor frees the captive Almahide, they engage in the following exchange:

> *Almahide.* Almanzor can from every subject raise
> New matter for our wonder and his praise.
> You bound and freed me; but the difference is,
> That showed your valor; but your virtue this.
> *Almanzor.* Madam, you praise a funeral victory,
> At whose sad pomp the conqueror must die.
> *Almahide.* Conquest attends Almanzor everywhere;
> I am too small a foe for him to fear. . .
> *Almanzor.* Madam I cannot on bare praises live;
> Those, who abound in praises, seldom give.[89]

Here language is raised above the ordinary partly by the rhymed verse, partly by the formality of its arrangement, and these combine to produce a strange effect. The rhyme and the formal figurative language create the impression of originality; at the same time, closer examination shows that in the figures lurk some all too familiar commonplaces. There is nothing new in the idea of the pyrrhic victory, nor in the adage, "Those, who abound in praises, seldom give." These are highly organized commonplaces, princely in their phrasing, but not altogether unlike the commonplaces of sentimental comedy.

In the heroic drama, commonplaces function as identifications of self, necessary to the depicting of "examples" of virtue. These identifications, especially in emotional moments, grow into extended explanations of the speaker and his motives. When Almanzor first sees Almahide he says to himself:

I'm pleased and pained, since first her eyes I saw,
As I were stung with some tarantula.
Arms, and the dusty field, I less admire,
And soften strangely in some new desire;
Honour burns in me not so fiercely bright,
But pale as fires when mastered by the light:
Even while I speak and look, I change yet more,
And now am nothing that I was before.
I'm numbed, and fixed, and scarce my eyeballs move:
I fear it is the lethargy of love!
'Tis he; I feel him now in every part:
Like a new lord he vaunts about my heart;
Surveys, in state, each corner of my breast,
While poor fierce I, that was, am dispossessed.
I'm bound; but I will rouse my rage again;
And, though no hope of liberty remain,
I'll fright my keeper when I shake my chain.[90]

As an example of self-conscious rhetoric in drama this is excellent. It evaluates an inner state with immediacy and detailed accuracy; it expresses emotion and simultaneously calculates the consequences present and future; and finally it registers the hero's resolution about the way to behave despite his inner turmoil. It is vividly, distressingly imagistic, with its tarantula metamorphosing, by the end of the passage, into a usurping lord.[91] The moral purpose of sentimental comedy requires similar rhetoric. Loveless's admission of his "deep Lethargy of Vice," his enslavement to "loose Desires," his acute awareness of waking "with Joy, to find [his] Rapture real," and his open acknowledgment that he has been subdued are in some degree derivations from this earlier heroic sentiment.

The extended analysis of self and of others is, in the heroic drama, what Kathleen Lynch has called the language of Platonic convention. The convention provides a love that is ordained by fate, pure and selfless, almost transcending passion. It imposes on the lovers a ritual that begins with their learning to analyze their own emotions and to express the analysis verbally and formally in a "catechism" of love.[92] The final step in this part of the convention is the "similitude debate," in which the principals argue favorite themes. The nature and duties of love and friendship, the merits of constancy, the effects of jealousy—these are argued formally in speeches embellished with rhetorical figures and often having what Miss Lynch calls "significant consequences."[93] In other words, the elaborate language is capable of effecting a change in the hearer. In this respect, such language is especially appropriate to the homiletic nature of both heroic drama and sentimental comedy.

Cibber did not go to heroic drama for the material—plot, characters, setting—of his plays. He chose instead the comedy of manners, already a proved success and, at least in setting, more familiar to a bourgeois audience. In *Love's Last Shift,* in *The Careless Husband,* and in *The Lady's Last Stake* there is plenty of coquetry, gallantry, and dialogue at least "like" wit. Each of the chief male figures—Loveless, Young Worthy, Sir Charles Easy, Lord Wronglove, and Lord George—plays, or tries to play, the *eiron.* The old spirit is invoked, but the insistent moral direction transforms the plays. If the characters and spectators accept from the start the eventual restoration of a moral order, and if the would-be *eiron* is the man most in need of reclaiming and turns out to have a tender heart after all, then ironic outlook and witty dialogue are only aspects of the fallen world to be purged away.

The driving moral purpose behind the plot produces the two great weaknesses of sentimental comedy, improbable incidents and unnatural language. In *Love's Last Shift* the difficulty is Loveless's conversion. The fact that Loveless, whose creed is founded on the appeal of new pleasures and their rapid evaporation, should find himself permanently changed by an instance of those transitory joys is astounding. If he is what he claims to be, the night with Amanda proves nothing; the portrait of the rake is too well drawn in the first place to admit of such a sudden reversal. Similarly, Amanda's early self-righteousness makes it awkward to conceive of her as a seductress. If this is not enough, a string of improbabilities builds up to the conversion. Loveless believes in Amanda's death; Sly, unquestioned, "mistakes" Loveless for another; Amanda succeeds with her disguise; finally, because of her inheritance she can relieve all Loveless's debts. It is no wonder that Vanbrugh, in *The Relapse,* has Loveless fall again, gives Amanda severe temptations against her virtue, and, in short, questions the complacent assumptions of *Love's Last Shift.* The reunion of the Wrongloves poses a similar problem. It is, of course, not impossible that two people as thoroughly miserable as they are should clutch at the words of a reasonable man; it may be even more likely than Amanda's test. The improbability lies in the assumption that a piece of good advice and a moment's manipulation of emotion can provide the basis for permanent reconciliation. Just as the raking Loveless is so well drawn that we question the stability of his new virtue, so the proud, quarrelsome Wrongloves are so vividly executed that their eleventh-hour humility and tenderness are unconvincing. *The Careless Husband* exhibits the same complacency as the other two plays, even though action here is more closely related to character. Lady Easy's scarf trick is like Amanda's test in its improbability; the sudden conversion of Sir Charles—though he may be said to have been better prepared psychologically—puts him in a class with Loveless and Lord Wronglove.

In all three plays the language of the emotional moments also grates. Consider Amanda's "All the Comfort of my Life is, that I can tell my Conscience, I have been true to Virtue," or Loveless's "Have I not used thee like a Villain? For almost ten long Years depriv'd thee of my Love, and ruin'd all thy Fortune! But I will labour, dig, beg, or starve to give new Proofs of my unfeign'd Affection." The same effect is created by Sir Charles's "Receive me then intire at last, and take what yet no Woman ever truly had, my conquer'd Heart," by Lord Wronglove's plea to his wife, "Yet nearer, closer to my Heart. . . . Thus blending our dissolving Souls in dumb inutterable Softness," and by Lady Wronglove's description of her heart that "fears, yet wishes, that burns and blushes." All these speeches, like those in the heroic drama, derive their improbability and exaggeration not from the revelation of hidden depths of the heart, but from the enunciation, in excruciating detail, of the most banal stock responses.

What has to be remembered is that these plays are no more closely related to ordinary human reality than heroic plays, or even the comedies of wit. They are exempla in illustration of a point of view. Their characters are not real people with real mental processes, but types of human strength and weakness necessary to the exemplum. They speak their unlikely speeches not to reveal a psychological reaction to their distress, but to insist upon their identities, to say over and over again, "I am the virtuous woman," or "I am the repentant sinner." This is, I think, the only thing we can make of Amanda's avowal that her fidelity to virtue is "All the Comfort" of her life, or of Loveless's admission of his villainy.

Sentimental comedy encourages the wayward and affirms what the righteous are presumed to know intuitively, by presenting an ideal world ultimately triumphant. In earlier English drama, as Ernest Bernbaum writes: "Whenever the human aspiration toward goodness was to be gratified by the presentation of ideally virtuous persons, these were placed in a background remote from the usual course of human experience. In other words, the perfect place for perfect characters was romantic drama. . . . Such virtuous characters as the eighteenth-century drama of sensibility was to place in the environment of ordinary life, were, previous to its rise, placed in romantic comedy, pastoral drama, and heroic tragedy,—types which did not profess to hold a true mirror up to nature."[94] A closer look at Cibber's comedies, always treated by the critics as exercises in illogical behavior and excessive emotion, will reveal that they are, in fact, a species of romance. In setting and costume, they purvey the familiar matter of every day, but the theme of virtue's triumph is presented in terms of the story of the beautiful princess who rescues the handsome prince from the wicked spell which has turned him into a beast. This is the plot of *Love's Last Shift* and, with some variations, of *The Careless Husband* and *The Lady's Last Stake.* Each of the plays concludes ideally; the conversion of Loveless and of Sir Charles Easy, and the reconciliation of the Wrongloves are what "should be" according to the beliefs and desires of the audience. It is as romance that sentimental comedy participates in the equally romantic idealizations of heroic drama, where the hero always triumphs.

Wish-fulfillment is the stuff of romantic comedy, what Northrop Frye calls the "drama of the green world, its plot being assimilated to the ritual theme of the triumph of life and love over the waste land."[95] Like pure romance, comedy is a sequence of conflict, death-struggle, and rebirth. Romantic comedy appropriates many of the fairy-land embellishments of romance; the archetypal death-struggle and rebirth become almost literal, the hero or heroine seeming to die and then reviving in happy resolution, as in Shakespeare's comedies and romances. Though the comic world of Colley Cibber is far removed from the problem situations and enchanted lands of Shakespeare, there are things happening in *Love's Last Shift, The Careless Husband,* and *The Lady's Last Stake* that can be explained only in terms of a romantic removal into a "second world."[96] Amanda, for example, is believed dead by Loveless and "dies" to herself in assuming the disguise of a mistress. Like Shakespeare's Hero and Hermione, she wins her struggle with the enemy through her "death," and emerges triumphant, reborn into a new life. By the same means she brings about the redemption of Loveless. The dim "sweet Lodgings" of the mistress, which Loveless enters through the garden after first picking the lock on the garden door, become a kind of enchanted spot, contrived by Amanda as a magic world which will lead to the true one. Like Shakespeare's Helena, she assumes a disguise to win her point and casts it off at the beginning of a new life. The romantic implications come to a climax when Amanda proves her identity by revealing Loveless's name tattooed on her arm: "These speaking Characters, which in their cheerful Bloom [their] early Passions mutually recorded" (V.ii. 169-71). Loveless, of course, plays Claudio to her Hero, Bertram to her Helena, and Leontes to her Hermione. He too undergoes a symbolic death and rebirth, developed, in his case, in biblical terms. He puts off the old man when he changes his soiled linen for the clothing Amanda has laid out for him (IV.iii.9-11); when he confronts Amanda for the repentance scene, he appears in "new Cloaths" (V.ii.11s.d.). His life repeats the parable of the prodigal son, his fatted calf being the rich inheritance Amanda offers him, despite his having wasted her first fortune.

In *The Lady's Last Stake,* Lord George Brilliant and Mrs. Conquest also play recognizable romantic roles. Brilliant is better understood by being seen in the light of Shakespeare's Orlando; his carefully cultivated rakish passion for Lady Gentle is his form of love-sickness. He does not hang verses on trees, but his explosion into Wronglove's apartment after drinking tea with Lady Gentle shows him in the grip of a similar madness: "Tea! Thou soft, thou sober, sage, and venerable Liquid, thou innocent Pretence for bringing the Wicked of both Sexes together in a Morning; thou Female Tongue-running, Smile-smoothing, Heart-opening, Wink-tipping Cordial, to whose glorious Insipidity I owe the happiest Moment of my Life, let me fall prostrate thus, and s-p, s-p, s-p, thus adore thee. [*Kneels and sips the Tea*" (I.i.280-85). Mrs. Conquest plays Rosalind to school him out of that false passion into a recognition of his love for her. To do so, she assumes man's dress, becomes her own brother, challenges Brilliant, and leads him out into the park where she is "mortally" wounded. Brilliant repents, she reveals herself, and both put off the old life.

The wrangling Wrongloves fit into the schemes of romance less easily, for the psychological motivation in each case seems bitterly real. Their conversion, however, restates a romance formula with a rebirth like that of Loveless. They emerge from the moment of their harshest conflict like two people who have been long wandering under a spell from which only Sir Friendly Moral, the pedestrian Prospero, can release them. His reasonable words and skillful manipulation provide the magic power for breaking their spell. In *The Careless Husband,* Lady Easy's scarf, placed gently on the head of Sir Charles as he lies asleep beside the maid, equally shows the properties of a charm and awakens him in all senses of the word. When he comes to admit his guilt, he finds his wife at work altering the scarf; their new relationship has begun.

The drawing-room will never make as convincing a setting for romance as the Forest of Arden or Bohemia-by-the-Sea. Shakespeare's comedies and romances are convincing because they preserve romantic detail—fantastic kingdoms, enchanted forests, and magical powers. We accept their existence and thus anything that could happen in such a world. Sentimental comedy, on the other hand, never claims a magic world, only a world of faith. The belief in a triumphant moral order, the vision of life as a constant struggle to maintain it, the conviction that virtue protects the good man and that emotion moves the sinner—these become an effectual doctrinal mythology and supply whatever probability is wanting in the plots of the plays. In one way at least, sentimental comedy is more romantic than Shakespearean romantic comedy. The bare bones of the myth are more evident. We always have the moral fable clearly in mind, and if we are at any point tempted to forget it, one of the characters will remind us amply, in the most explicit terms.

Later sentimental comedies continued to treat life as romance; in fact, they became in many ways more conventionally romantic, bringing into play the suggestion of exotic adventures and the return of long-lost heirs and heiresses. Steele's *The Conscious Lovers* (1722)—regarded as the archetype of sentimental comedy by many—develops what was to become a favorite theme. Indiana, a poor orphan who, as a child, was captured by pirates while voyaging to join her father in the Indies, turns out to be an acceptable wife for Bevil, thus resolving his conflict between love and filial duty. While this theme persisted on the stage for half a century—it was still at work as late as Cumberland's *The West Indian* (1770)—sentimental romance, with its tendency to infinite reiteration, ultimately led away from dramatic comedy and emerged in the early novel, especially in the novels of Richardson. In both *Pamela* and *Clarissa,* Richardson develops long courtships, with abundant expansion of the conflict that precedes resolution.[97] He tries, through the epistolary form, to make the novel a study of the psychology of the courtship struggle, but preoccupation with a moral calls forth from every incident the stock response, just as it does in sentimental comedy. When Pamela suspects her master of trying to weaken her by kindness, to "melt" her, she says:

> I fear not, Sir, the Grace of God supporting me, that any Acts of Kindness would make me forget what I owe to my Virtue; but, Sir, I may, I find, be made more miserable by such Acts, than by Terror; because my Nature is too frank and open to make me wish to be ungrateful; and if I should be taught a Lesson I never yet learnt, with what Regret should I descend to the Grave, to

> think, that I could not hate my Undoer? And, that, at the last great Day, I must stand up as an Accuser of the poor unhappy Soul, that I could wish it in my Power to save![98]

Like Amanda's speeches in *Love's Last Shift,* Pamela's serve the twofold purpose of reiterating the moral and identifying the speaker. Both heroines are equally well answered by Cibber's Loveless: "How have I labour'd for my own undoing; while, in despite of all my Follies, kind Heav'n resolv'd my Happiness!" (V.ii.214-15).

LOVE's Laſt Shift:

OR,

The FOOL *in* FASHION.

A

COMEDY:

As it is Acted

At the THEATRE ROYAL

in *DRURY-LANE*,

By His MAJESTY's Servants.

Written by *C. CIBBER.*

----- *Fuit hæc Sapientia quondam,*
Concubitu prohibere vago, dare jure maritis.

Hor. de Art. Poet.

LONDON:

Printed in the Year M.DCC.XXI.

TO

RICHARD NORTON

OF

SOUTHWICK, Esq;

SIR,

Tho I can't, without Ingratitude, conceal the exceeding Favours which the Town have shewn this Piece; yet they must give me leave to own, that even my Vanity lay hush'd, quite stifled in my Fears, 'till I had securely fix'd its good Fortune, by publishing your Approbation of it: An Advantage, which, as it will confirm my Friends in their favourable Opinion, so it must, in some measure, qualify the Severity of the Malicious. After this Declaration, let the World imagine, how difficult it is for me, not to launch into your Character: But since your Candour and Depth of Judgment, are my chief Protection, I am loth to discompose you, by an ungrateful Repetition of those Virtues, which only please you in the Practice: The World as little wants the Knowledge of 'em, as you desire the Recital.

'Tis your Happiness, SIR, that your Fortune has fix'd you above the need of Praise, or Friends, yet both are equally unavoidable: For even to your Solitude, Praise will follow you, and grows fonder of you for your Coldness; she loves you for your Choice of Pleasures, those noble Pleasures of a sweet Retirement, from which nothing but the Consideration of your Country's Weal can draw you.

But as no Man can properly be made a Patron, whose Virtues have not in some sort qualified him for such a Care: So, SIR, it is sufficient for me, that your Life and Conversation are the best Heralds of your Power, and my Safety.

Here, SIR, I must beg Leave to clear myself from what the ill Wishes of some wou'd have the World believe, that what I now offer you, is Spurious, and not the Product of my own Labour. And tho' I am pleas'd that this Report seems to allow it some Beauties, yet I am sorry it has made a Discovery of some Persons, who think me worth their Malice. This DEDICATION were little better than an Affront, unless I cou'd with all Sincerity assure you, SIR, that the Fable is entirely my own; nor is there a Line or Thought throughout the whole, for which I am wittingly oblig'd either to the Dead, or Living: For I cou'd no more be pleas'd with a stoln Reputation, than with a Mistress, who yielded only upon the Intercession of my Friend. It satisfies me, SIR, that you believe it mine; and I hope, what others say to the contrary, is rather owing to an unreasonable Disgust, than their real Opinion. I am not ignorant of those Oversights I have committed, nor have the dissecting Criticks much discourag'd me: For 'tis their Diversion to find Fault; and to have none, is to them an unpardonable Disappointment; no Man can expect to go free, while they don't spare one another. But as I write not in Defiance of their Censure; so after having diverted you, SIR, I shall not trouble them with a *Preface.* Had it not succeeded, I should have had Modesty enough to impute it to my own want of Merit: For certainly the Town can take no Pleasure in decrying any Man's Labours, when 'tis their Interest to encourage 'em. Every Guest is the best Judge of his own Palate; and a Poet ought no more to impose good Sense upon the Galleries, than dull Farce upon the undisputed Judges. I first consider'd who my Guests were, before I prepared my Entertainment: And therefore I shall only add this, as a general Answer to all Objections, that it has every way exceeded mine, and hitherto has not wrong'd the *House*'s Expectation: That Mr. *Southern*'s good Nature (whose own Works best recommend his Judgment) engaged his Reputation for the Success; which its Reception, and your Approbation, SIR, has since redeem'd, to the intire Satisfaction of,

SIR,
Your most Devoted,
Humble Servant,
Colley Cibber.

PROLOGUE,
By a FRIEND.

Spoken by Mr. *VERBRUGGEN.*

Wit bears so thin a Crop, this duller Age,
We're forc'd to glean it from the barren Stage:
E'en Players, fledg'd by nobler Pens, take wing
Themselves, and their own rude Composures sing.
Nor need our young one dread a Shipwreck here;
Who trades without a Stock, has nought to fear.
In ev'ry Smile of yours, a Prize he draws;
And if you damn him, he's but where he was.
Yet where's the Reason for the critick Crew,
With killing Blasts, like Winter, to pursue
The tender Plant, that ripens but for you?
Nature, in all her Works, requires Time;
Kindness, and Years, 'tis makes the Virgin climb,
And shoot, and hasten to the expected Prime;
And then, if untaught Fancy fail to please,
Y'instruct the willing Pupil by Degrees;
By gentle Lessons you your Joys improve,
And mould her awkward Passion into Love.
Ev'n Folly has its Growth: Few Fools are made;
You drudge and sweat for't, as it were a Trade.
'Tis half the Labour of your trifling Age,
To fashion you fit Subjects for the Stage.
Well! If our Author fail to draw you like;
In the first Draught, you're not t'expect Vandike.
What tho' no Master-stroke in this appears,
Yet some may Features find resembling theirs.

Nor do the bad alone his Colours share;
Neglected Virtue is at least shewn fair,
And that's enough o'Conscience for a Play'r.
But if you'd have him take a bolder Flight,
And draw your Pictures by a truer Light,
You must your selves, by Follies yet unknown,
Inspire his Pencil, and divert the Town.
Nor judge, by this, his Genius at a stand;
For Time, that makes new Fools, may mend his Hand.

Dramatis Personae.

MEN.

Sir *William Wisewoud.* A rich old Gentleman, that fansies himself a great Master of his Passion, which he only is in trivial Matters.	Mr. *Johnson.*
Loveless. Of a debaucht Life, grew weary of his Wife in six Months; left her, and the Town, for Debts he did not care to pay; and having spent the last part of his Estate beyond Sea, returns to *England* in a very mean Condition.	Mr. *Verbruggen.*
Sir *Novelty Fashion.* A Coxcomb that loves to be the first in all Foppery.	Mr. *Cibber.*
Elder Worthy. A sober Gentleman of a fair Estate in Love with *Hillaria.*	Mr. *Williams.*
Young Worthy. His Brother, of a looser Temper, Lover to *Narcissa.*	Mr. *Horden.*
Snap. Servant to *Loveless.*	Mr. *Penkethman.*
Sly. Servant to *Young Worthy.*	Mr. *Bullock.*
A Lawyer.	Mr. *Mills.*

WOMEN.

Amanda. A Woman of strict Virtue, married to *Loveless* very young, and forsaken by him.	Mrs. *Rogers.*
Narcissa. Daughter to Sir *William Wisewoud,* a Fortune.	Mrs. *Verbruggen.*
Hillaria. His Niece.	Mrs. *Cibber.*

Flareit. A kept Mistress of Sir *Novelty*'s.	Mrs. *Kent.*
Woman to *Amanda.*	Mrs. *Lucas.*
Maid to *Flareit.*	

Servants, &*c.*

The SCENE *London.*

Love's Last Shift:

OR,

The FOOL in FASHION.

ACT I. SCENE I.

SCENE *the Park.*

Enter Loveless, *and* Snap (*his Servant.*)

Lov. Sirrah! leave your Preaching:—Your Counsel, like an ill Clock, either stands still, or goes too slow:—You ne'er thought my Extravagancies amiss, while you had your share of 'em, and now I want Money to make my self drunk, you advise me to live sober, you Dog.—They that will hunt Pleasure as I ha' done, Rascal, must never give over in a fair Chase.

Snap. Nay, I knew you wou'd never rest, till you had tir'd your Dogs.—Ah, Sir! what a fine Pack of Guineas have you had! and yet you wou'd make 'em run 'till they were quite spent.—Wou'd I were fairly turn'd out of your Service.—Here we have been three Days in Town, and I can safely swear I have liv'd upon picking a hollow Tooth ever since.

Lov. Why don't you eat then, Sirrah?

Snap. E'en because I don't know where, Sir.

Lov. Then stay 'till I eat, Hang-Dog! Ungrateful Rogue! to murmur at a little fasting with me, when thou hast been an equal Partner of my good Fortune.

Snap. Fortune!—It makes me weep, to think what you have brought your self and me to! How well might you ha' liv'd, Sir, had you been a sober Man.—Let me see!—I ha' been in your Service just ten Years:—In the first you marry'd, and grew weary of your Wife: In the second you whor'd, drank, gam'd, run in Debt, mortgaged your Estate, and was forc'd to leave the Kingdom: In the third, fourth, fifth, sixth, and seventh you made the Tour of *Europe,* with the State and Equipage of a *French* Court-Favourite, while your poor Wife at Home broke her Heart for the loss of you: In the eighth and ninth you grew poor, and little the wiser: and now in the tenth you are resolv'd I shall starve with you.

Lov. Despicable Rogue! can'st thou not bear the Frowns of a common Strumpet, Fortune?

Snap. –S'bud, I never think of the Pearl Necklace you gave that damn'd *Venetian* Strumpet, but I wish her hang'd in't!

Lov. Why, Sirrah! I knew I cou'd not have her without it, and I had a Night's Enjoyment of her was worth a Pope's Revenue for't.

Snap. Ah! you had better ha' laid out your Money here in *London;* I'll undertake you might have had the whole Town over and over for half the Price. –Beside, Sir, what a delicate Creature was your Wife! She was the only celebrated Beauty in Town; I'll undertake there were more Fops and Fools run mad for her:–S'bud she was more plagu'd with 'em, and more talked of than a good Actress with a Maiden-head! Why the Devil cou'd not she content you?

Lov. No, Sirrah! the World to me is a Garden stockt with all sorts of Fruit, where the greatest Pleasure we can take, is in the Variety of Taste: But a Wife is an Eternal Apple-tree; after a pull or two, you are sure to set your Teeth on Edge.

Snap. And yet I warrant you grudg'd another Man a Bit of her, tho' you valu'd her no more than you wou'd a half-eaten Pippin, that had lain a Week a sunning in a Parlour Window.–But see, Sir, who's this?–for methinks I long to meet with an old Acquaintance!

Lov. Ha! egad, he looks like one, and may be necessary, as the case stands with me.–

Snap. Pray Heaven he do but invite us to Dinner!

Enter Young Worthy.

Lov. Dear *Worthy!* let me embrace thee; the sight of an old Friend warms me, beyond that of a new Mistress.

Y. Wor. S'death, what Bully's this! Sir, your Pardon, I don't know you!

Lov. Faith, *Will,* I am a little out of Repairs at present: But I am all that's left of honest *Ned Loveless.*

Y. Wor. Loveless! I am amaz'd! What means this Metamorphosis!–

vantage you can draw from them. Prithee, how wilt thou live, now all your Money is gone?

Lov. Live! How dost thou live? thou are but a younger Brother, I take it.

Y. Wor. Oh, very well, Sir; (tho' faith my Father left me but 3000 *l.*) one of which I gave for a Place at Court, that I still enjoy; the other two are gone after Pleasure, as thou say'st. But beside this, I am supply'd by the continual Bounty of an indulgent Brother: Now, I am loth to load his good Nature too much, and therefore have e'en thought fit, like the rest of my raking Brotherhood, to purge out my wild Humours with Matrimony: By the way, I have taken care to see the Dose well sweetned with a swinging Portion.

Lov. Ah! *Will,* you'll find, marrying to cure Lewdness, is like surfeiting to cure Hunger: For all the Consequence is, you loath what you surfeit on, and are only chaste to her you marry.—But prithee, Friend, what is thy Wife that must be?

Y. Wor. Why, faith, since I believe the Matter is too far gone for any Man to postpone me, (at least, I am sure, thou wilt not do me an Injury, to do thy self no Good) I'll tell thee:—You must know, my Mistress is the Daughter of that very Knight to whom you mortgaged your Estate, Sir *William Wisewoud.*

Lov. Why, she's an Heiress, and has 1000 *l.* a Year in her own Hands, if she be of Age: But I suppose the old Man knows nothing of your Intentions. Therefore, prithee, how have you had Opportunities of promoting your Love?

Y. Wor. Why thus:—You must know, Sir *William* (being very well acquainted with the Largeness of my Brother's Estate) designs his Daughter for him; and to encourage his Passion, offers him, out of his own Pocket, the additional Blessing of 5000 *l.* This Offer, my Brother knowing my Inclinations, seems to embrace; but at the same time is really in Love with his Niece, who lives with him in the same House: And therefore, to hide my Design from the old Gentleman, I pretend Visits to his Daughter, as an Intercessor for my Brother only; and thus he has given me daily Opportunities of advancing my own Interest;—nay, and I have so contriv'd it, that I design to have the 5000 *l.* too.

Lov. How is that possible, since I see no hopes of the old Man's Consent for you?

Y. Wor. Have a Day's Patience, and you'll see the Effects on't: In a word, 'tis so sure, that nothing but Delays can hinder my Success; therefore I am very earnest with my Mistress, that To-morrow may be the Day: But a Pox on't, I have two Women to prevail with; for my Brother quarrels every other Day with his Mistress; and while I am reconciling him, I lose Ground in my own Amour.

Lov. Why, has not your Mistress told you her Mind yet?

Y. Wor. She will, I suppose, as soon as she knows it herself; for within this Week she has chang'd it as often as her Linen, and keeps it as secret to; for she wou'd no more own her Love before my Face, than she would shift herself before my Face.

Lov. Pshaw! she shews it the more, by striving to conceal it.

Y. Wor. Nay, she does give me some Proofs indeed; for she will suffer no Body but herself to speak ill of me, is always uneasy 'till I am sent for, never pleas'd when I am with her, and still jealous when I leave her.

Lov. Well! Success to thee, *Will;* I will send the Fiddles, to release you from your first Night's Labour.

Y. Wor. But, hark you! Have a Care of disobliging the Bride, though.—Ha! yonder goes my Brother! I am afraid his walking so early, proceeds from some Disturbance in his Love: I must after him, and set him right.—Dear *Ned,* you'll excuse me: Shall I see you at the *Blue Posts* between Five and Six this Afternoon?

Lov. With all my Heart:—But, d'ye hear!—Can'st not thou lend me the Fellow to that same *Guinea you gave my Man? I'll give you my Bond, if you mistrust me.

Y. Wor. Oh, Sir! Your Necessity is Obligation enough:—There 'tis, and all I have, faith; when I see you at Night, you may command me farther.—Adieu: At Six at farthest. [*Exit* Young Worthy.

Lov. Without fail. —So! Now, Rascal, you are an hungry, are you! Thou deserv'st never to eat again. —Rogue! grumble before Fortune had quite forsaken us!

Snap. Ah! dear Sir, the Thoughts of eating again, have so transported me, I am resolv'd to live and die with you.

Lov. Look ye, Sirrah, here's that will provide us of a Dinner, and a Brace of Whores into the Bargain; at least as Guineas and Whores go now.

Snap. Ah! good Sir! no Whores before Dinner, I beseech you.

Lov. Well, for once I'll take your Advice; for, to say the Truth, a

Man is as unfit to follow Love with an empty Stomach, as Business with an empty Head: Therefore I think a Bit and a Bottle won't be amiss first.

The Gods of Wine and Love were ever Friends;
For by the help of Wine, Love gains his Ends. [Exeunt.

Enter Elder Worthy *with a Letter.*

El. Wor. How hard is it to find that Happiness which our short-sighted Passions hope from Woman! 'tis not their cold Disdain or Cruelty should make a faithful Lover curse his Stars, that is but reasonable; 'tis the Shadow in our Pleasure's Picture! Without it, Love could ne'er be heightned! No, 'tis their Pride and vain Desire of many Lovers, that robs our Hope of its imagined Rapture: The Blind are only happy! For if we look through Reason's never-erring Perspective, we then survey their Souls, and view the Rubbish we were chaff'ring for: And such I find *Hillaria*'s Mind is made of. This Letter is an Order for the knocking off my Fetters, and I'll send it her immediately.

Enter to him Young Worthy.

Y. Wor. 'Morrow, Brother, [*Seeing the Letter.*] What! is your Fit return'd again? What Beau's Box now has *Hillaria* taken Snuff from? What Fool has led her from the Box to her Coach? What Fop has she suffer'd to read a Play or Novel to her? Or whose Money has she indiscreetly won at *Basset?*—Come, come, let's see the ghastly Wound she has made in your Quiet, that I may know how much Claret to prescribe you.

El. Wor. I have my Wound and Cure from the same Person, I'll assure you; the one from *Hillaria*'s Wit and Beauty, and the other from her Pride and Vanity.

Y. Wor. That's what I could ne'er yet find her guilty of: Are you angry at her loving you?

El. Wor. I am angry at my self, for believing she ever did.

Y. Wor. Have her Actions spoke the contrary? Come, you know she loves.

El. Wor. Indeed she gave a great Proof on't last Night here in the *Park,* by fastning on a Fool, and caressing him before my Face, when she might have so easily avoided him.

Y. Wor. What! and I warrant, interrupted you in the middle of your Sermon; for I don't question but you were preaching to her. But, prithee, who was the Fool she fasten'd upon?

El. Wor. One that Heaven intended for a Man; but the whole Business of his Life is, to make the World believe he is of another Species. A Thing that affects mightily to ridicule himself, only to give others a kind of Necessity of praising him. I can't say he's a Slave to any new Fashion, for he pretends to be Master of it, and is ever reviving some old, or advancing some new piece of Foppery; and tho' it don't take, is still as well pleased, because it then obliges the Town to take the more Notice of him: He's so fond of a publick Reputation, that he is more extravagant in his Attempts to gain it, than the Fool that fir'd *Diana*'s Temple to immortalize his Name.

Y. Wor. You have said enough to tell me his Name is Sir *Novelty Fashion.*

El. Wor. The same: But that which most concerns me, he has the Impudence to address to *Hillaria,* and she Vanity enough not to discard him.

Y. Wor. Is this all? Why, thou art as hard to please in a Wife, as thy Mistress in a new Gown: How many Women have you took in hand, and yet can't please your self at last?

El. Wor. I had need to have the best Goods, when I offer so great a Price as Marriage for them: *Hillaria* has some good Qualities, but not enough to make a Wife of.

Y. Wor. She has Beauty!

El. Wor. Granted.

Y. Wor. And Money.

El. Wor. Too much: Enough to supply her Vanity.

Y. Wor. She has Sense.

El. Wor. Not enough to believe I am no Fool.

Y. Wor. She has Wit.

El. Wor. Not enough to deceive me.

Y. Wor. Why then you are happy, if she can't deceive you.

El. Wor. Yet she has Folly enough to endeavour it: I'll see her no more, and this shall tell her so.

Y. Wor. Which in an Hour's time you'll repent, as much as ever—

El. Wor. As ever I should marrying her.

Y. Wor. You'll have a damn'd meaking Look, when you are forc'd to ask her Pardon for your ungenerous Suspicion, and lay the Fault upon excess of Love.

El. Wor. I am not so much in Love as you imagine.

Y. Wor. Indeed, Sir, you are in Love, and that Letter tells her so.

El. Wor. Read it, you'll find the contrary.

Y. Wor. Prithee, I know what's in't better than thou do'st: You say, 'tis to take your Leave of her; but I say, 'tis in hopes of a kind, excusive Answer: But, faith, you mistake her and your self too; she is too high-spirited, not to take you at your Word; and you are too much in Love, not to ask her Pardon.

El. Wor. Well, then, I'll not be too rash, but will shew my Resentment, in forbearing my Visits.

Y. Wor. Your Visits! Come, I shall soon try what a Man of Resolution you are; —for yonder she comes: Now, let's see if you have Power to move.

El. Wor. I'll soon convince you of that—Farewel. [*Exit.*

Y. Wor. Ha! Gone! I don't like that! I am sorry to find him so resolute: But I hope *Hillaria* has taken too fast hold of his Heart, to let this Fit shake him off: I must to her, and make up this Breach; for while his Amour stands still, I have no hopes of advancing my own. [*Exit.*

Enter Hillaria, Narcissa, *and* Amanda *in Mourning.*

Hil. Well, dear *Amanda,* thou art the most constant Wife I ever heard of, not to shake off the Memory of an ill Husband, after eight or ten years absence; nay, to mourn, for ought you know, for the living too, and such an Husband, that, tho' he were alive, would never thank you for it: Why d'ye persist in such a hopeless Grief?

Am. Because 'tis hopeless! For if he be alive, he is dead to me: His dead Affections, not Virtue's self can e'er retrieve: Wou'd I were with him, tho' in his Grave!

Hil. In my mind you are much better where you are! The Grave! Young Widows use to have warmer Wishes. But, methinks, the Death of a rich old Uncle should be a Cordial to your Sorrows.

Am. That adds to 'em; for he was the only Relation I had left, and was as tender of me as the nearest! He was a Father to me.

Hil. He was better than some Fathers to you; for he dy'd just when you had occasion for his Estate.

Nar. I have an old Father, and the Duce take me, I think he only lives to hinder me of my Occasions; but, Lord bless me, Madam, how can you be unhappy with 2000 *l.* a year in your own Possession?

Hil. For my part, the greatest Reason I think you have to grieve, is, that you are not sure your Husband's dead; for were that confirm'd, then indeed there were hopes that one Poison might drive out another; you might marry agen.

Am. All the Comfort of my Life is, that I can tell my Conscience, I have been true to Virtue.

Hil. And to an extravagant Husband, that cares not a farthing for you. But, come, let's leave this unseasonable Talk, and pray give me a little of your Advice. What shall I do with this Mr. *Worthy?* Wou'd you advise me to make a Husband of him?

Am. I am but an ill Judge of Men; the only one I thought my self secure of, most cruelly deceiv'd me.

Hil. A losing Gamester is fittest to give Warning: What d'ye think of him?

Am. Better than of any Man I know: I read nothing in him but what is some part of a good Man's Character.

Hil. He's jealous.

Am. He's a Lover.

Hil. He taxes me with a Fool!

Am. He wou'd preserve your Reputation; and a Fool's Love ends only in the ruin of it.

Hil. Methinks he's not handsome.

Am. He's a Man, Madam.

Hil. Why then e'en let him make a Woman of me.

Nar. Pray, Madam, what d'ye think of his Brother? [*Smiling.*

Am. I wou'd not think of him.

Nar. O dear, why, pray?

Am. He puts me in mind of a Man too like him; one that had Beauty, Wit, and Falshood!—

Nar. You have hit some part of his Character, I must confess, Madam; but as to his Truth, I'm sure he loves only me.

Am. I don't doubt but he tells you so, nay, and swears it too.

Nar. O Lord! Madam, I hope I may, without Vanity, believe him.

Am. But you will hardly, without Magick, secure him.

Nar. I shall use no Spells or Charms, but this poor Face, Madam.

Am. And your Fortune, Madam.

Nar. (Senseless Malice!) [*Aside.*] I know he'd marry me without a Groat.

Am. Then he's not the Man I take him for.

Nar. Why, pray—what do you take him for?

Am. A wild young Fellow, that loves every thing he sees.

Nar. He never lov'd you yet. [*Peevishly.*

Am. I hope, Madam, he never saw any thing in me to encourage him.

Nar. In my Conscience you are in the right on't, Madam; I dare swear he never did, nor e'er wou'd, tho' he gaz'd 'till Doom's-day.

Am. I hope, Madam, your Charms will prevent his putting himself to the trial, and I wish he may never—

Nar. Nay, dear Madam, no more railing at him, unless you wou'd have me believe you love him.

Hil. Indeed, Ladies, you are both in the wrong: You, Cousin, in being angry at what you desir'd, her Opinion of your Lover; and you, Madam, for speaking Truth against the Man she resolves to love.

Nar. Love him! Prithee, Cousin, no more of that old Stuff.

Hil. Stuff! Why, don't you own you are to marry him this Week? —Here he comes; I suppose you'll tell him another thing in his Ear.

Enter Young Worthy.

Hil. Mr. *Worthy,* your Servant! you look with the Face of Business: What's the News, pray?

Y. Wor. Faith, Madam, I have News for you all, and private News too; but that of the greatest Consequence, is with this Lady. Your Pardon, Ladies; I'll whisper with you all, one after another.

Nar. Come, Cousin, will you walk? the Gentleman has Business; we shall interrupt him.

Hil. Why really, Cousin, I don't say positively you love Mr. *Worthy,* but, I vow, this looks very like Jealousy.

Nar. Pish! Lord! *Hillaria,* you are in a very odd Humour to Day. But to let you see I have no such weak thoughts about me, I'll wait as unconcern'd as your self: (I'll rattle him.) [*Aside.*

Am. Not unpleasing, say you? Pray, Sir, unfold your self, for I have long despair'd of welcome News.

Y. Wor. Then, in a word, Madam, your Husband, Mr. *Loveless,* is in Town, and has been these three Days; I parted with him an Hour ago.

Am. In Town! you amaze me! for Heav'n's sake go on.

Y. Wor. Faith, Madam, considering *Italy,* and those Parts have furnish'd him with nothing but an Improvement of that Lewdness he carry'd over, I can't properly give you Joy of his Arrival: Besides, he is so very poor, that you wou'd take him for an Inhabitant of that Country. And when I confirm'd your being dead, he only shook his Head, and call'd you good-natur'd Fool, or to that effect; nay, tho' I told him his Unkindness broke your Heart.

Am. Barbarous Man! not shed a Tear upon my Grave? But why did you tell him I was dead?

Y. Wor. Because, Madam, I thought you had no mind to have your House plunder'd; and for another Reason, which if you dare listen to me, perhaps you'll not dislike: In a word, 'tis such a Stratagem, that will either make him asham'd of his Folly, or in love with your Virtue.

Am. Can there be a Hope, when ev'n my Death cou'd not move him to a relenting Sigh? Yet, pray instruct me, Sir.

Y. Wor. You know, Madam, 'twas not above four or five Months after you were marry'd, but (as most young Husbands do) he grew weary of you: Now, I am confident, 'twas more an Affectation of being fashionably Vicious, than any reasonable Dislike he cou'd either find in your Mind or Person: Therefore, cou'd you, by some Artifice, pass upon him as a new Mistress, I am apt to believe you wou'd find none of the wonted Coldness in his Love, but a younger Heat, and fierce Desire.

Am. Suppose this done: What wou'd be the Consequence?

Y. Wor. Oh, your having then a just Occasion to reproach him with his broken Vows, and to let him see the Weakness of his deluded Fancy, which ev'n in a Wife, while unknown, cou'd find those real Charms, which his blind, ungrateful Lewdness wou'd ne'er allow her to be Mistress of. After this, I'd have you seem freely to resign him to those fancy'd Raptures, which he deny'd were in a virtuous Woman: Who knows but this, with a little submissive Eloquence, may strike him with so great a sense of Shame, as may reform his Thoughts, and fix him yours?

Am. You have reviv'd me, Sir: But how can I assure my self he'll like me as a Mistress?

Y. Wor. From your being a new one.—Leave the Management of all to me; I have a Trick shall draw him to your Bed; and when he's there, faith, e'en let him cuckold himself; I'll engage he likes you as a Mistress, tho' he cou'd not as a Wife: At least, she'll have the Pleasure of knowing the difference between a Husband and a Lover, without the Scandal of the former. [*Aside.*

Am. You have oblig'd me, Sir; if I succeed, the Glory shall be yours.

Y. Wor. I'll wait on you at your Lodging, and consult how I may be farther serviceable to you: But you must put this in speedy execution, lest he shou'd hear of you, and prevent your Design; in the mean time, 'tis a Secret to all the World, but your self and me.

Am. I'll study to be grateful, Sir.

Y. Wor. Now for you, Madam. [*To* Hillaria.

Nar. So! I am to be last serv'd: Very well! [*Aside.*

Y. Wor. My Brother, Madam, confesses he scatter'd some rough Words last Night; and I take the liberty to tell you, you gave him some Provocation.

Hil. That may be; but I'm resolv'd to be Mistress of my Actions before Marriage, and no Man shall usurp a Power over me, 'till I give it him.

Y. Wor. At least, Madam, consider what he said, as the Effects of an impatient Passion, and give him leave, this Afternoon, to set all right agen.

Hil. Well, if I don't find my self out of order after Dinner, perhaps I may step into the Garden: But I won't promise you, neither.

Y. Wor. I dare believe you without it. —Now, Madam, I am your humble Servant. [*To* Narcissa.

Nar. And every Body's humble Servant. [*Walks off.*

Y. Wor. Why, Madam, I am come to tell you.—

Nar. What Success you had with that Lady, I suppose:—I don't mind Intrigues, Sir.

Y. Wor. I like this Jealousy, however, tho' I scarce know how to appease it. 'Tis Business of Moment, Madam, and may be done in a Moment.

Nar. Yours is done with me, Sir; but my Business is not so soon done as you imagine.

Y. Wor. In a word, I have very near reconcil'd my Brother and your Cousin, and I don't doubt but To-morrow will be the Day;

if I were but as well assur'd of your Consent for my Happiness too!

Nar. First tell me your Discourse with that Lady; and afterwards, if you can, look me in the Face.—Oh, are you studying, Sir?

Y. Wor. S'Death! I must not trust her with it; she'll tell it the whole Town for a Secret.—Pox! ne'er a Lye!

Nar. You said it was of the greatest Consequence too!

Y. Wor. A good Hint, faith. [*Aside.*] Why, Madam, since you will needs force it from me, 'twas to desire her to advance my Interest with you: But all my Intreaties cou'd not prevail; for she told me, I was unworthy of you: Was not this of Consequence, Madam?

Nar. Nay, now I must believe you, Mr. *Worthy,* and I ask your Pardon; for she was just railing against you for a Husband, before you came.

Y. Wor. Oh! Madam, a favour'd Lover, like a good Poem, for the Malice of some few, makes the generous Temper more admire it.

Nar. Nay, what she said, I must confess, had much the same effect, as the Coffee-Criticks ridiculing Prince *Arthur;* for I found a pleasing Disappointment in my reading you; and 'till I see your Beauties equal'd, I sha'n't dislike you for a few Faults.

Y. Wor. Then, since you have blest me with your good Opinion, let me beg of you, before these Ladies, to compleat my Happiness To-morrow. Let this be the last Night of your lying alone.

Nar. What d'ye mean?

Y. Wor. To marry you to-morrow, Madam.

Nar. Marry me! Who put that in your Head?

Y. Wor. Some small Encouragement which my Hopes have form'd Madam.

Nar. Hopes! Oh, Insolence! D'ye think I can be mov'd to love a Man, to kiss, and toy with him, and so forth!

Y. Wor. I'gad, I find nothing but down-right Impudence will do with her. [*Aside.*] No Madam, 'tis the Man must kiss, and toy with you, and so forth! Come, my dear Angel, pronounce the joyful Word, and draw the Scene of my eternal Happiness. Ah! methinks I'm there already, eager and impatient of approaching Bliss! Just laid within the bridal Bed; our Friends retir'd; the Curtains close drawn around us; no Light but *Caelia's* Eyes; no Noise but her soft trembling Words, and broken Sighs, that plead in vain for Mercy. And now a trickling Tear steals down her glowing Cheek, which tells the happy Lover at length she yields; yet vows she'd rather die. But still submits to the unexperienc'd Joy. [*Embracing her.*

Hil. What Raptures, Mr. *Worthy?*

Y. Wor. Only the force of Love in Imagination, Madam.

Nar. O Lord! dear Cousin! and Madam! let's be gone, I vow he grows rude! Oh, for Heav'n's sake! I sha'n't shake off my Fright these ten Days: O Lord! I will not stay—Be gone! for I declare I loath the Sight of you. [*Exit.*

Y. Wor. I hope you'll stand my Friend, Madam.

Hil. I'll get her into the Garden after Dinner. [*Exeunt.*

Y. Wor. I find there's nothing to be done with my Lady before Company; 'tis a strange affected Piece!—But there's no fault in her 1000 *l.* a Year, and that's the Loadstone that attracts my Heart.—The Wise and Grave may tell us of strange Chimera's call'd Virtues in a Woman, and that they alone are the best Dowry; but, faith, we younger Brothers are of another Mind.

Women are chang'd from what they were of old:
Therefore let Lovers still this Maxim hold,
She's only Worth, that Brings her Weight in Gold.

[*Exit.*

ACT II. SCENE I.

The SCENE *a Garden belonging to Sir* William Wisewoud*'s House.*

Enter Narcissa, Hillaria, *and Sir* Novelty Fashion.

Hil. Oh! for Heav'n's sake! no more of this Gallantry, Sir *Novelty:* For I know you say the same to every Woman you see.

Sir. Nov. Every one that sees you, Madam, must say the same. Your Beauty, like the Rack, forces every Beholder to confess his Crime—of daring to adore you.

Nar. Oh! I ha'n't Patience to hear all this! If he be blind, I'll open his Eyes.—I vow, Sir *Novelty,* you Men of Amour are strange Creatures: You think no Woman worth your while, unless you walk over a Rival's ruin to her Heart: I know nothing has encouraged your Passion to my Cousin more, than her Engagement to Mr. *Worthy.*

Hil. Poor Creature, now is she angry she ha'n't the Address of a Fop I nauseate! [*Aside.*

Sir Nov. Oh! Madam, as to that, I hope the Lady will easily distinguish the Sincerity of her Adorers. Tho' I must allow, Mr. *Worthy* is infinitely the handsomer Person!

Nar. O! fye, Sir *Novelty,* make not such a preposterous Comparison!

Sir Nov. Oh! Ged! Madam, there is no Comparison!

Nar. Pardon me, Sir! he's an unpolisht Animal!

Sir Nov. Why does your Ladyship really think me tolerable?

Hil. So! she has snapt his Heart already. [*Aside.*

Sir Nov. Pray, Madam, how do I look to day?—What, cursedly? I'll warrant; with a more hellish Complexion than a stale Actress in a Morning.—I don't know, Madam:—'Tis true—the Town does talk of me, indeed; —but the Dev'l take me, in my mind, I am a very ugly Fellow!

Nar. Now you are too severe, Sir *Novelty!*

Sir Nov. Not I, burn me:—For Heav'n's sake deal freely with me, Madam; and if you can, tell me—one tolerable thing about me?

Hil. 'Twou'd pose me, I'm sure. [*Aside.*

Nar. Oh! Sir *Novelty,* this is unanswerable; 'tis hard to know the brightest part of a Diamond.

Sir Nov. You'll make me blush, stop my Vitals, Madam.—I'gad I always said she was a Woman of Sense. Strike me dumb, I am in Love with her.—I'll try her farther. [*Aside.*]—But, Madam, is it possible I may vie with Mr. *Worthy?*—Not that he is any Rival of mine, Madam; for I can assure you, my Inclinations lie where, perhaps, your Ladyship little thinks.

Hil. So! now I am rid of him.

Sir Nov. But pray tell me, Madam; for I really love a severe Critick: I am sure you must believe he has a more happy Genius in Dress: For my part, I am but a Sloven.

Nar. He a Genius! unsufferable! Why, he dresses worse than a Captain of the Militia: But you, Sir *Novelty,* are a true Original, the very Pink of Fashion; I'll warrant you there's not a Milliner in Town but has got an Estate by you.

Sir Nov. I must confess, Madam, I am for doing good to my Country: For you see this Suit, Madam.—I suppose you are not ignorant what a hard time the Ribbon-Weavers have had since the late Mourning: Now my design is to set the poor Rogues up again, by recommending this sort of Trimming: The Fancy is pretty well for second Mourning.—By the way, Madam, I had fifteen hundred Guineas laid in my Hand, as a Gratuity, to encourage it: But, i'gad, I refus'd 'em, being too well acquainted with the Consequence of taking a Bribe in a national Concern!

Hil. A very charitable Fashion, indeed, Sir *Novelty!* But how if it should not take?

Nar. Ridiculous! Take! I warrant you, in a Week the whole Town will have it; tho' perhaps Mr. *Worthy* will be one of the last of 'em: He's a mere *Valet de Chambre* to all Fashion; and never is in any, till his Betters have left them off.

Sir Nov. Nay, Ged, now I must laugh; for the Dev'l take me, if I did not meet him, not above a Fortnight ago, in a Coat with Buttons no bigger than Nutmegs.

Hil. There, I must confess, you out-do him, Sir *Novelty.*

Sir Nov. Oh, dear Madam, why mine are not above three Inches diameter.

Hil. But, methinks, Sir *Novelty,* your Sleeve is a little too extravagant.

Sir. Nov. Nay, Madam, there you wrong me; mine does but just reach my Knuckles, but my Lord *Overdo*'s covers his Diamond Ring.

Hil. Nay, I confess, the Fashion may be very useful to you Gentlemen that make Campaigns; for shou'd you unfortunately lose an Arm, or so, that Sleeve might be very convenient to hide the defect on't.

Sir Nov. Ha! I think your Ladyship's in the right on't, Madam. [*Hiding his Hand in his Sleeve.*

Nar. Oh! such an Air! so becoming a Negligence! Upon my Soul, Sir *Novelty,* you'll be the Envy of the *Beau Monde!*

Hil. Mr. *Worthy!* A good Fancy were thrown away upon him! But you, Sir, are an Ornament to your Cloaths.

Sir Nov. Then your Ladyship really thinks they are—*Bien Entendue!*

Hil. A Merveil, Monsieur!

Sir Nov. She has almost as much Wit as her Cousin.—I must confess, Madam, this Coat has had a universal Approbation: For this Morning I had all the eminent Taylors about Town at my Levee, earnestly petitioning for the first Measure of it: Now, Madam, if you thought 'twou'd oblige Mr. *Worthy,* I wou'd let his Taylor have it before any of 'em.

Nar. See here he comes, and the Duce take me, I think 'twou'd be a great piece of good Nature; for I declare he looks as rough as a *Dutch* Corporal:—Prithee, Sir *Novelty,* let's laugh at him!

Sir Nov. O Ged! No, Madam, that were too cruel: Why you know he can't help it:—Let's take no notice of him.

Hil. Wretched Coxcomb. [*Aside.*

Enter Elder Worthy.

El. Wor. I find my Resolution is but vain, my Feet have brought me hither against my Will: But sure I can command my Tongue, which I'll bite off e'er it shall seek a Reconciliation. Still so familiar there! But 'tis no matter, I'll try if I can wear Indifference, and seem as careless in my Love, as she is of her Honour, which she can never truly know the worth of, while she persists to let a Fool thus play with it.—Ladies, your humble Servant.

Hil. Now can't I forbear fretting his Spleen a little. [*Aside.*] Oh! Mr. *Worthy,* we are admiring Sir *Novelty,* and his new Suit: Did you ever see so sweet a Fancy? He is as full of Variety as a good Play.

El. Wor. He's a very pleasant Comedy indeed, Madam, and drest with a great deal of good, Satyr, and no doubt may oblige both the Stage and the Town, especially the Ladies.

Hil. So! There's for me.— [*Aside.*

Sir Nov. O Ged! Nay, prithee, *Tom,* you know my Humour.—Ladies! Stop my Vitals! I don't believe there are five hundred in Town that ever took any notice of me.

El. Wor. Oh, Sir, there are some that take so much notice of you, that the Town takes notice of them for't.

Hil. It works rarely. [*Aside.*

Sir Nov. How, of them, *Tom,* upon my Account? O Ged, I wou'd not be the ruin of any Lady's Reputation, for the World. Stop my Vitals! I'm very sorry for't: Prithee, name but one that has a favourable Thought of me; and to convince you that I have no Design upon her, I'll instantly visit her in an unpowder'd Periwig.

El. Wor. Nay, she, I mean, is a Woman of Sense too.

Sir Nov. Phoo! Prithee, Pox, don't banter me! 'Tis impossible! What can she see in me?

El. Wor. Oh, a thousand taking Qualities! This Lady will inform you.—Come, I'll introduce you. [*Pulls him.*

Sir Nov. O Ged, no! Prithee!—Hark you in your Ear!—I am off of her! Demme, if I be'nt! I am, stop my Vitals!

El. Wor. Wretched Rogue! [*Aside.*] Pshaw! no matter; I'll reconcile you. Come, Madam.

Hil. Sir!

El. Wor. This Gentleman humbly begs to kiss your Hand.

Hil. He needs not your Recommendation, Sir.

El. Wor. True! a Fool recommends himself to your Sex, and that's the reason Men of common Sense live unmarry'd.

Hil. A Fool without Jealousy, is better than a Wit with ill Nature.

El. Wor. A friendly Office, seeing your Fault is ill Nature.

Hil. Believing more than we have, is pitiful.—You know I hate this Wretch, loath and scorn him.

El. Wor. Fools have a secret Art of pleasing Women: If he did not delight you, you wou'd not hazard your Reputation by encouraging his Love.

Hil. Dares he wrong my Reputation?

El. Wor. He need not; the World will do it for him, while you keep him Company.

Hil. I dare answer it to the World.

El. Wor. Then why not to me?

Hil. To satisfy you, were a Fondness I never shou'd forgive my self.

El. Wor. To persist in it, is what I'll ne'er forgive.

Hil. Insolence! Is it come to this? Never see me more.

El. Wor. I have lost the sight of you already; there hangs a cloud of Folly between you and the Woman I once thought you.

[*As* Hillaria *is going off, enter* Young Worthy.

Y. Wor. *What to our selves in Passion we propose;*
The Passion ceasing, do's the Purpose lose.

Madam, therefore, pray let me engage you to stay a little 'till your Resentment is over, that you may see whether you have reason to be angry, or no.

Sir Nov. [*to* Narcissa.] Pray, Madam, who is that Gentleman?

Nar. Mr. *Worthy*'s Brother, Sir, a Gentleman of no mean Parts, I can assure you.

Sir Nov. I don't doubt it, Madam:—He has a very good Periwig.

Hil. To be jealous of me with a Fool, is an Affront to my Understanding.

Y. Wor. Tamely to resign your Reputation to the merciless Vanity of a Fool, were no Proof of his Love.

Hil. 'Tis questioning my Conduct.

Y. Wor. Why, you let him kiss your Hand last Night before his Face.

Hil. The Fool diverted me, and I gave him my Hand, as I would lend my Money, Fan, or Handkerchief to a Legerdemain, that I might see him play all his Tricks over.

Y. Wor. O Madam! no Juggler is so deceitful as a Fop; for while you look his Folly in the Face, he steals away your Reputation with more ease than the other picks your Pocket.

Hil. Some Fools indeed are dangerous.

Y. Wor. I grant you, your Design is only to laugh at him: But that's more than he finds out: Therefore you must expect he will tell the World another Story; and 'tis ten to one but the Consequence makes you repent of your Curiosity.

Hil. You speak like an Oracle: I tremble at the Thoughts on't.

Y. Wor. Here's one shall reconcile your Fears:—Brother, I have done your Business: *Hillaria* is convinced of her Indiscretion, and has a Pardon ready, for your asking it.

El. Wor. She's the Criminal; I have no occasion for it.

Y. Wor. See, she comes toward you; give her a civil Word at least.

Hil. Mr. *Worthy,* I'll not be behind-hand in the Acknowledgment I owe you: I freely confess my Folly, and forgive your harsh Construction of it: Nay, I'll not condemn your want of good Nature, in not endeavouring, (as your Brother has done) by mild Arguments to convince me of my Error.

El. Wor. Now you vanquish me! I blush to be out-done in generous Love! I am your Slave, dispose of me as you please.

Hil. No more; from this Hour be you the Master of my Actions, and my Heart.

El. Wor. This Goodness gives you the Power, and I obey with Pleasure.

Y. Wor. So! I find I ha'n't preacht to no purpose! Well, Madam, if you find him guilty of Love, e'en let To-morrow be his Execution-Day; make a Husband of him, and there's the Extent of Love's Law.

El. Wor. Brother, I am indebted to you.

Y. Wor. Well, I'll give you a Discharge, if you'll but leave me half an hour in private with that Lady.

Hil. How will you get rid of Sir *Novelty?*

Y. Wor. I'll warrant you; leave him to me.

Hil. Come, Mr. *Worthy,* as we walk, I'll inform you how I intend to sacrifice that Wretch to your Laughter.

El. Wor. Not, Madam, that I want Revenge on so contemptible a Creature: But I think, you owe this Justice to your self, to let him see (if possible) you never took him for any other than what he really is.

Y. Wor. Well! Pox of your Politicks: Prithee consult of 'em within.

Hil. We'll obey you, Sir.—

[*Exeunt* Elder Worthy *and* Hillaria.

Y. Wor. Pray, Madam, give me leave to beg a Word in private with you. Sir, if you please. [*To Sir* Novelty, *who is taking Snuff.*

Sir Nov. Ay, Sir, with all my Heart.

Y. Wor. Sir.—

Sir Nov. Nay, 'tis right, I'll assure you. [*Offering his Box.*

Y. Wor. Ay, Sir;—but now the Lady wou'd be alone.

Sir Nov. Sir!

Y. Wor. The Lady wou'd be alone, Sir.

Sir Nov. I don't hear her say any such thing.

Y. Wor. Then I tell you so, and I wou'd advise you to believe me.

Sir Nov. I shall not take your Advice, Sir: But if you really think the Lady wou'd be alone, why—you had best leave her.

Y. Wor. In short, Sir, your Company is very unseasonable at present.

Sir Nov. I can tell you, Sir, if you have no more Wit than Manners, the Lady will be but scurvily entertain'd.

Nar. Oh, fie, Gentlemen, no quarreling before a Woman, I beseech you. Pray let me know the Business?

Sir Nov. My Business is Love, Madam.

Nar. And yours, Sir!

Y. Wor. What, I hope, you are no Stranger too, Madam? As for that Spark, you need take no Care of him; for if he stays much longer, I will do his Business my self.

Nar. Well, I vow, Love's a pleasant thing, when the Men come to cutting of Throats once. O Gad! I'd fain have them fight a little.—Methinks, *Narcissa* wou'd sound so great in an expiring Lover's Mouth.—Well, I am resolv'd Sir *Novelty* shall not go yet; for I will have the pleasure of hearing my self prais'd a little, tho' I don't marry this Month for't.—Come, Gentlemen, since you both say Love's your Business, e'en plead for your selves; and he that speaks the greater Passion, shall have the fairest Return.

Y. Wor. Oh, the Dev'l! now is she wrapt with the hopes of a little Flattery! There's no Remedy but Patience. S'Death! what a Piece have I to work upon?

Nar. Come, Gentlemen, one at a time. Sir *Novelty,* what have you to say to me?

Sir Nov. In the first place, Madam, I was the first Person in *England* that was complimented with the Name of *Beau,* which is a Title I prefer before Right Honourable: For that may be inherited: But this I extorted from the whole Nation, by my surprising Mien, and unexampled Gallantry.

Nar. So, Sir!

Sir Nov. Then another thing, Madam; It has been observed, that I have been eminently successful in those Fashions I have recommended to the Town; and I don't question but this very Suit will raise as many Ribbond-Weavers, as ever the clipping or melting Trade did Goldsmiths.

Nar. Pish! What does the Fool mean? he says nothing of me yet.

Sir Nov. In short, Madam, the Cravat-string, the Garter, the Sword-knot, the Centurine, the Bardash, the Steinkirk, the large Button, the long Sleeve, the Plume, and full Peruque, were all created, cry'd down, or revived by me: In a word, Madam, there has never been any thing particularly taking or agreeable for these ten Years past, but your humble Servant was the Author of it.

Y. Wor. Where the Devil will this end?

Nar. This is all extravagant, Sir *Novelty:* But what have you to say to me, Sir?

Sir Nov. I'll come to you presently, Madam, I have just done: Then you must know, my Coach and Equipage are as well known as my self; and since the Conveniency of two Play-houses, I have a better Opportunity of shewing them: For between every Act—Whisk—I am gone from one to th' other:—Oh! what Pleasure 'tis, at a good Play, to go out before half an Act's done!

Nar. Why at a good Play?

Sir Nov. O! Madam, it looks Particular, and gives the whole Audience an Opportunity of turning upon me at once: Then do they conclude I have some extraordinary Business, or a fine Woman to go to at least: And then again, it shews my Contempt of what the dull Town think their chiefest Diversion: But if I do stay a Play out, I always sit with my Back to the Stage.

Nar. Why so, Sir?

Sir Nov. Then every Body will imagine I have been tir'd with it before; or that I am jealous Who talks to Who in the King's Box. And thus, Madam, do I take more Pains to preserve a publick Reputation, than ever any Lady took, after the Small-Pox, to recover her Complexion.

Nar. Well, but to the Point: What have you to say to me, Sir *Novelty?*

Y. Wor. Now does she expect some Compliment shall out-flatter her Glass.

Sir Nov. To you, Madam?—Why, I have been saying all this to you.

Nar. To what End, Sir?

Sir Nov. Why, all this I have done for your sake.

Nar. What Kindness is it to me?

Sir Nov. Why, Madam, don't you think it more Glory to be belov'd by one eminently particular Person, whom all the Town knows and talks of; than to be ador'd by five hundred dull Souls that have lived incognito?

Nar. That, I must confess, is a prevailing Argument; but still you ha'n't told me, why you love me.

Y. Wor. That's a Task he has left for me, Madam.

Sir Nov. 'Tis a Province I never undertake, I must confess; I think 'tis sufficient, if I tell a Lady, why she shou'd love me.

Nar. Hang him! he's too conceited; he's so in love with himself, he won't allow a Woman the bare Comfort of a cold Compliment.— Well, Mr. *Worthy.*

Y. Wor. Why, Madam, I have observed several particular Qualities in your Ladyship, that I have perfectly ador'd you for; as, the majestick Toss of your Head;—your obliging-bow-Court'sy;—your satyrical Smile;—your blushing Laugh;—your demure Look;—the careless Tie of your Hood;—the genteel Flirt of your Fan;—the design'd Accident in your letting fall, and your agreeable Manner of receiving it from him that takes it up. *What he speaks, she imitates in dumb Shew.*

[*They both offer to take up her Fan; and in striving,* Young Worthy *pushes Sir* Novelty *on his Back.*

Sir Nov. [*adjusting himself.*] I hope your Ladyship will excuse my Disorder, Madam.—How now!

Enter a Footman to Sir Novelty.

Foot. Oh, Sir! Mrs. *Flareit*—

Sir Nov. Ha! speak lower: What of her?

Foot. By some unlucky Accident has discover'd your being here, and raves like a mad Woman: She's at your Lodging, Sir, and had broke you above forty Pounds worth of *China* before I came away; she talk'd of following you hither; and if you don't make haste, I'm afraid will be here, before you can get through the House, Sir.

Sir Nov. This Woman is certainly the Devil; her Jealousy is implacable; I must get rid of her, tho' I give her more for a separate Maintenance, than her Conscience demanded for a Settlement before Enjoyment.—See the Coach ready; and if you meet her, be sure you stop her with some pretended Business, 'till I'm got away from hence.—Madam, I ask your Ladyship ten thousand Pardons: There's a Person of Quality expects me at my Lodging, upon extraordinary Business.

Nar. What, will you leave us, Sir *Novelty?*

Sir Nov. As unwillingly as the Soul the Body: But this is an irresistable Occasion!—Madam, your most devoted Slave.—Sir, your most humble Servant.—Madam, I kiss your Hand.—O Ged, no farther, dear Sir, upon my Soul I won't stir if you do.—

[Young Worthy *sees him to the Door.*

[*Exit Sir* Novelty.

Y. Wor. Nay then, Sir, your humble Servant: So! this was a lucky Deliverance.

Nar. I over-heard the Business.—You see, Mr. *Worthy,* a Man must be a Slave to a Mistress sometimes, as well as a Wife; yet all can't persuade your Sex to a favourable Opinion of poor Marriage.

Y. Wor. I long, Madam, for an Opportunity to convince you of your Error; and therefore give me leave to hope To-morrow you will free me from the pain of farther Expectation, and make an Husband of me.—Come, I'll spare your Blushes, and believe I have already nam'd the Day.

Nar. Had not we better consider a little?

Y. Wor. No, let's avoid Consideration, 'tis an Enemy both to Love and Courage: They that consider much, live to be old Batchelors, and young Fighters. No! no! we shall have time enough to consider after Marriage.—But why are you so serious, Madam?

Nar. Not but I do consent To-morrow shall be the Day, Mr. *Worthy;* but I'm afraid you have not lov'd me long enough to make our Marriage be the Town-talk: For 'tis the Fashion now to be the Town-talk; and you know, one had as good be out of the World, as out of the Fashion.

Y. Wor. I don't know, Madam, what you call Town-talk; but it has been in the News-Letters above a Fortnight ago, that we were already married. Beside, the last Song I made of you, has been sung at the Musick-Meeting; and you may imagine, Madam, I took no little Care to let the Ladies and the Beaux know who 'twas made on.

Nar. Well, and what said the Ladies?

Y. Wor. What was most observable, Madam, was, that while it was singing, my Lady *Manlove* went out in a great Passion.

Nar. Poor jealous Animal! On my Conscience, that charitable Creature has such a Fund of kind Compliance for all young Fellows, whose Love lies dead upon their Hands, that she has been as great a Hindrance to us virtuous Women, as ever the Bank of *England* was to the City Goldsmiths.

Y. Wor. The Reason of that, is, Madam, because you virtuous Ladies pay no Interest: I must confess the Principal, our Health, is a little securer with you.

Nar. Well; and is not that Advantage worth entring into Bonds for? not but I vow, we virtuous Devils do love to insult a little; and to say Truth, it looks too credulous and easy in a Woman, to encourage a Man before he has sigh'd himself to a Skeleton.

Y. Wor. But Heaven be thank't, we are pretty even with you in the End; for the longer you hold us off before Marriage, the sooner we fall off after it.

Nar. What, then you take Marriage to be a kind of Jesuit's Powder, that infallibly cures the Fever of Love?

Y. Wor. 'Tis, indeed, a Jesuit's Powder, for the Priests first invented it; and only abstain'd from it, because they knew it had a bitter Taste; then gilded it over with a pretended Blessing, and so palm'd it upon the unthinking Laity.

Nar. Prithee don't screw your Wit beyond the compass of good Manners.—D'ye think I shall be tun'd to Matrimony by your railing against it? If you have so little Stomach to it, I'll e'en make you fast a Week longer.

Y. Wor. Ay, but let me tell you, Madam, 'tis no Policy to keep a Lover at a thin Diet, in hopes to raise his Appetite on the Wedding-Night; for then

We come like starving Beggars to a Feast,
Where, unconfin'd, we Feed with eager Haste,
Till each repeated Morsel palls the Taste.
Marriage gives Prodigals a boundless Treasure,
Who squander that, which might be lasting Pleasure;
And Women think they ne'er have Over-measure.

ACT III. SCENE I.

The SCENE *Sir* William Wisewoud*'s House*

Enter Amanda *and* Hillaria, *meeting.*

Am. My Dear, I have News for you.

Hil. I guess at it, and fain wou'd be satisfied of the Particulars: Your Husband is returned, and I hear knows nothing of your being alive: Young *Worthy* has told me of your Design upon him.

Am. 'Tis that I wanted your Advice in: What think you of it?

Hil. O! I admire it: Next to forgetting your Husband, 'tis the best Counsel was ever given you; for under the Disguise of a Mistress, you may now take a fair Advantage of indulging your Love; and the little Experience you have had of it already, has been just enough not to let you be afraid of a Man.

Am. Will you never leave your mad Humour?

Hil. Not till my Youth leaves me: Why should Women affect Ignorance among themselves? When we converse with Men, indeed, Modesty and good Breeding oblige us not to understand, what, sometimes, we can't help thinking of.

Am. Nay, I don't think the worse of you for what you say: For 'tis observ'd, that a bragging Lover, and an overshy Lady, are the farthest from what they would seem; the one is as seldom known to receive a Favour, as the other to resist an Opportunity.

Hil. Most Women have a wrong Sense of Modesty, as some Men of Courage; if you don't fight with all you meet, or run from all you see, you are presently thought a Coward, or an ill Woman.

Am. You say true; and 'tis as hard a matter, now-a-days, for a Woman to know how to converse with Men, as for a Man to know when to draw his Sword: For many times both Sexes are apt to over-act their Parts: To me the Rules of Virtue have been ever sacred; and I am loth to break 'em by an unadvised Undertaking: Therefore, dear *Hillaria*, help me, for I am at a loss.—Can I justify, think you, my intended Design upon my Husband?

Hil. As how, prithee?

Am. Why, if I court and conquer him, as a Mistress, am not I accessary to his violating the Bonds of Marriage? For tho' I'm his Wife, yet while he loves me not as such, I encourage an unlawful Passion; and tho' the Act be safe, yet his Intent is criminal: How can I answer this?

Hil. Very easily; for if he don't intrigue with you, he will with some Body else in the mean time, and I think you have as much Right to his Remains as any one.

Am. Ay! but I am assured, the Love he will pretend to me is vicious: And 'tis uncertain that I shall prevent his doing worse elsewhere.

Hil. 'Tis true, a certain Ill ought not to be done for an uncertain Good. But then again, of two Evils, chuse the least; and sure 'tis less criminal to let him love you as a Mistress, than to let him hate you as a Wife. If you succeed, I suppose you will easily forgive your Guilt in the Undertaking.

Am. To say truth, I find no Argument yet strong enough to conquer my Inclination to it. But is there no Danger, think you, of his knowing me?

Hil. Not the least, in my Opinion: In the first place, he confidently believes you are Dead: Then he has not seen you these eight or ten Years: Besides, you were not above sixteen when he left you: This, with the Alteration the Small-Pox have made in you, (tho' not for the worse) I think, are sufficient Disguises to secure you from his Knowledge.

Am. Nay, and to this I may add, the considerable Amendment of my Fortune; for when he left me, I had only my bare Jointure for a Subsistence: Beside my strange manner of receiving him.—

Hil. That's what I wou'd fain be acquainted with.

Am. I expect farther Instructions from Mr. *Worthy* every Moment; then you shall know all, my Dear.

Hil. Nay, he will do you no small Service: For a Thief is the best Thief-catcher.

Enter a Servant to Amanda.

Serv. Madam, your Servant is below, who says Young Mr.

Worthy's Man waits at your Lodgings with earnest Business from his Master.

Am. 'Tis well.—Come, my Dear, I must have your Assistance too.

Hil. With all my Heart, I love to be at the bottom of a Secret: For they say the Confident of any Amour, has sometimes more Pleasure in the Observation, than the Parties concern'd in the Enjoyment: But, methinks, you don't look with a good Heart upon the Business.

Am. I can't help a little Concern in a Business of such Moment: For tho' my Reason tells me my Design must prosper; yet my Fears say 'twere Happiness too great.—Oh! to reclaim the Man I'm bound by Heaven to Love, to expose the Folly of a roving Mind, in pleasing him with what he seem'd to loath, were such a sweet Revenge for slighted Love, so vast a Triumph of rewarded Constancy, as might persuade the looser part of Womankind ev'n to forsake themselves, and fall in Love with Virtue.

Re-enter the Servant to Hillaria.

Serv. Sir *Novelty Fashion* is below in his Coach, Madam, and enquires for your Ladyship, or Madam *Narcissa.*

Hil. You know my Cousin is gone out with my Lady *Tattletongue:* I hope you did not tell him I was within!

Serv. No, Madam, I did not know if your Ladyship wou'd be spoke with, and therefore came to see.

Hil. Then tell him I went with her.

Serv. I shall, Madam. [*Exit Servant.*

Hil. You must know, my Dear, I have sent to that Fury, Mrs. *Flareit,* whom this Sir *Novelty* keeps, and have stung her to some purpose with an account of his Passion for my Cousin: I ow'd him a Quarrel, for that he made between Mr. *Worthy* and me, and I hope her Jealousy will severely revenge it; therefore I sent my Cousin out of the way, because, unknown to her, her Name is at the bottom of my Design.—Here he comes: Prithee, my Dear, let's go down the Back-stairs, and take Coach from the Garden.—

[*Exeunt* Amanda *and* Hillaria.

Re-enter the Servant, conducting Sir Novelty.

Sir Nov. Both the Ladies abroad, say you? Is Sir *William* within?

Serv. Yes, Sir; if you please to walk in, I'll acquaint him that you expect him here.

Sir Nov. Do so, prithee;—and in the mean time let me consider what I have to say to him.—Hold! In the first place, his Daughter is in Love with me! Wou'd I marry her? Noh! Demm it, 'tis mechanical to marry the Woman you love: Men of Quality shou'd always marry those they never saw.—But I hear *Young Worthy* marries her To-morrow! which if I prevent not, will spoil my Design upon her. Let me see!—I have it!—I'll persuade the old Fellow, that I wou'd marry her my self! upon which he immediately rejects *Young Worthy,* and gives me free access to her! Good! What follows upon that? Opportunity, Importunity, Resistance, Force, Entreaty, Persisting!—Doubting, Swearing, Lying,—Blushes, Yielding, Victory, Pleasure!—Indifference:—O! here he comes *in ordine ad—*

Enter Sir William Wisewoud.

Sir Wil. Sir *Novelty,* your Servant: Have you any Commands for me, Sir?

Sir Nov. I have some Proposals to make, Sir, concerning your Happiness and my own, which perhaps will surprize you. In a word, Sir, I am upon the very brink of Matrimony.

Sir Wil. 'Tis the best thing you can pursue, Sir, considering you have a good Estate.

Sir Nov. But whom do you think I intend to marry?

Sir Wil. I can't imagine. Dear Sir, be brief, lest your Delay transport me into a Crime I wou'd avoid, which is Impatience. Sir, pray go on.

Sir Nov. In fine, Sir, 'tis to your very Daughter, the fair *Narcissa.*

Sir Wil. Humh! Pray, Sir, how long have you had this in your Head?

Sir Nov. Above these two Hours, Sir.

Sir Wil. Very good! then you ha'n't slept upon't?

Sir Nov. No! nor sha'n't sleep, for thinking on't. Did not I tell you I wou'd surprize you?

Sir Wil. O! you have indeed, Sir: I am amaz'd! I am amaz'd!

Sir Nov. Well, Sir, and what think you of my Proposal?

Sir Wil. Why truly, Sir, I like it not: But if I did, 'tis now too late; my Daughter is dispos'd of to a Gentleman that she and I like very well; at present, Sir, I have a little Business: If this be all, your humble Servant, I am in haste.

Sir Nov. Demme! what an insensible Blockhead's this? Hold, Sir: D'ye hear?—Is this all the Acknowledgment you make, for the Honour I design'd you?

Sir Wil. Why truly, Sir, 'tis an Honour that I am not ambitious of: In plain terms, I do not like you for a Son-in-Law.

Sir Nov. Now you speak to the Purpose, Sir: But prithee, what are thy Exceptions to me?

Sir Wil. Why, in the first place, Sir, you have too great a Passion for your own Person, to have any for your Wife's: In the next place, you take such an extravagant Care in the cloathing your Body, that your Understanding goes naked for't: Had I a Son so dress'd, I shou'd take the liberty to call him an egregious Fop.

Sir Nov. I'gad, thou art a comical old Gentleman, and I'll tell thee a Secret: Understand then, Sir, from me, that all young Fellows hate the Name of Fop, as Women do the Name of Whore: But, i'gad, they both love the Pleasure of being so: Nay, faith, and 'tis as hard a matter for some Men to be Fops, as you call 'em, as 'tis for some Women to be Whores.

Sir Wil. That's pleasant, i'faith. Can't any Man be a Fop, or any Woman be a Whore, that has a mind to't?

Sir Nov. No, faith, Sir; for let me tell you, 'tis not the Coldness of my Lady *Freelove*'s Inclination, but her Age and Wrinkles that won't let her cuckold her Husband. And again, 'tis not Sir *John Wou'dlook*'s Aversion to Dress; but his want of a fertile Genius, that won't let him look like a Gentleman: Therefore, in Vindication of all well-dress'd Gentlemen, I intend to write a Play, where my chiefest Character shall be a *downright English Booby,* that affects to be a Beau, without either Genius or foreign Education, and to call it, in Imitation of another famous Comedy, *He Wou'd if he Cou'd:* And now, I think, you are answer'd, Sir. Have you any Exceptions to my Birth, or Family, pray Sir?

Sir Wil. Yes, Sir, I have; you seem to be the Offspring of more than one Man's Labour; for certainly no less than a Dancing, Singing, and Fencing-Master, with a Taylor, Milliner, Perfumer, Peruque-Maker, and a *French Valet de Chambre,* cou'd be at the begetting of y

Sir Nov. All these have been at the finishing of me since I was made.

Sir Wil. That is, Heaven made you a Man, and they have made a Monster of you: And so farewel to ye! [*Is going.*

Sir Nov. Hark ye, Sir; am I to expect no farther Satisfaction in the Proposals I made you?

Sir Wil. Sir,—nothing makes a Man lose himself like Passion: Now I presume you are young, and consequently rash upon a Disappointment; therefore, to prevent any Difference that may arise by repeating my refusal of your Suit, I do not think it convenient to hold any farther Discourse with you.

Sir Nov. Nay, faith, thou shalt stay to hear a little more of my Mind first.

Sir Wil. Since you press me, Sir, I will rather bear with, than resist you.

Sir Nov. I doubt, old Gentleman, you have such a Torrent of Philosophy running thro' your *Pericranium,* that it has wash'd your Brains away.

Sir Wil. Pray, Sir, why do you think so?

Sir Nov. Because you chuse a beggarly, unaccountable sort of Younger-brotherish Rake-hell for your Son-in-Law, before a Man of Quality, Estate, good Parts and Breeding, Demme.

Sir Wil. Truly, Sir, I know neither of the Persons to whom these Characters belong; if you please to write their Names under 'em, perhaps I may tell you, if they be like or no.

Sir Nov. Why then, in short, I wou'd have been your Son-in-Law; and you, it seems, prefer *Young Worthy* before me. Now are your Eyes open?

Sir Wil. Had I been blind, Sir, you might have been my Son-in-Law; and if you were not blind, you wou'd not think that I design my Daughter for *Young Worthy.*—His Brother, I think, may deserve her.

Sir Nov. Then you are not jealous of *Young Worthy?* Humh!

Sir Wil. No, really, Sir, nor of you neither.

Sir Nov. Give me thy Hand: Thou art very happy, stop my Vitals! for thou do'st not see that thou art blind: Not jealous of *Young Worthy?* Ha! ha! How now!

Enter Sir Novelty*'s Servant, with a Porter.*

Serv. Sir, here's a Porter with a Letter for your Honour.

Port. I was order'd to give it into your own Hand, Sir, and expect an Answer.

Sir Nov. [reads.] *Excuse, my dear Sir* Novelty, *the forc'd Indifference I have shewn you, and let me recompence your past Sufferings with an Hour's Conversation, after the Play, at* Rosamond*'s* Pond, *where you will find an hearty Welcome to the Arms of your Narcissa!*– Unexpected Happiness! The Arms of your *Narcissa!* I'gad and when I am there, I'll make my self welcome. Faith, I did not think she was so far gone neither! But I don't question, there are five hundred more in her Condition.–I have a good mind not to go, faith! Yet, hang it, I will; tho', only to be reveng'd of this old Fellow! Nay, I'll have the Pleasure of making it publick too: For I will give her the Musick, and draw all the Town to be Witness of my Triumph! Where is the Lady?– [*To the Porter.*

Port. In a Hackney-Coach at the corner of the Street.

Sir Nov. Enough; tell her I will certainly be there.– [*Exit Porter.*] Well, old Gentleman! then you are resolv'd I shall be no Kin to you? Your Daughter is disposed of: Humh!

Sir Wil. You have your Answer, Sir; you shall be no Kin to me.

Sir Nov. Farewel, old Philosophy: And d'ye hear, I wou'd advise you to study nothing but the Art of Patience: You may have an unexpected Occasion for it. Hark you! wou'd not it nettle you damnably, to hear my Son call you Grandfather?

Sir Wil. Sir,–notwithstanding this Provocation, I am calm; but were I like other Men, a Slave to Passion, I shou'd not forbear calling you Impertinent! How I swell with rising Vexation!–Leave me, leave me; go, Sir, go, get you out of my House. [*Angrily.*

Sir Nov. Oh! have a care of Passion, dear *Diogenes:* Ha! ha! ha! ha

Sir Wil. So! [*Sighing.*] At last I have conquer'd it: Pray, Sir, oblige me with your Absence, [*taking off his Hat.*] I protest I am tired with you; pray leave my House. [*Submissively.*

Sir Nov. Demn your House, your Family, your Ancestors, your Generation, and your eternal Posterity. [*Exit.*

Sir Wil. Ah!–A fair Ridance; how I bless my self, that it was not in this Fool's Power to provoke me beyond that Serenity of Temper which a wise Man ought to be Master of: How near are Men to Brute when their unruly Passions break the Bounds of Reason? And of all Passions, Anger is the most violent; which often puts me in mind of that admirable Saying,

He that strives not to stem his Anger's Tide,
Does a mad Horse without a Bridle ride.

SCENE II.

The SCENE *changes to* St. James's-Park.

Enter Young Worthy *and* Loveless, *as from the Tavern;–* Snap *following.*

Y. Wor. What a sweet Evening 'tis:–Prithee, *Ned,* let's walk a little.–Look how lovingly the Trees are join'd, since thou wer't here, as if Nature had design'd this Walk for the private Shelter of forbidden Love. [*Several crossing the Stage.*] Look, here are some for making use of the Conveniency.

Lov. But, hark he, Friend, are the Women as tame and civil as they were before I left the Town? Can they endure the Smell of Tobacco, or vouchsafe a Man a Word with a dirty Cravat on?

Y. Wor. Ay, that they will; for Keeping is almost out of Fashion: So that now an honest Fellow, with a promising Back, need not fear a Night's Lodging for bare good Fellowship.

Lov. If Whoring be so poorly encourag'd, methinks the Women shou'd turn honest in their own Defence.

Y. Wor. Faith, I don't find there's a Whore the less for it; the Pleasure of Fornication is still the same; all the difference is, Lewdness is not so barefac'd as heretofore.–Virtue is as much debased as our Money; for Maidenheads are as scarce as our mill'd half Crowns; and faith, *Dei Gratia* is as hard to be found in a Girl of Sixteen, as round the Brims of an old Shilling.

Lov. Well, I find, in spite of Law and Duty, the Flesh will get the better of the Spirit. But I see no Game yet.–Prithee, *Will,* let's go and take t'other Bumper to enliven Assurance, that we may come down-right to the Business.

Y. Wor. No, no; what we have in our Bellies already, by the help of a little fresh Air, will soon be in our *Pericraniums,* and work us to a right pitch to taste the Pleasures of the Night.

Lov. The Day, thou mean'st; my Day always breaks at Sun-set. We wise Fellows, that know the Use of Life, know too that the Moon lights Men to more Pleasures than the Sun;—the Sun was meant for dull Souls of Business, and poor Rogues that have a mind to save Candles.

Y. Wor. Nay, the Night was always a Friend to Pleasure, and that made *Diana* run a Whoring by the light of her own Horns.

Lov. Right: And, prithee, what made *Daphne* run away from *Apollo,* but that he wore so much Day-light about his Ears?

Y. Wor. Ha! Look out, *Ned,* there's the Enemy before you!

Lov. Why then, as *Cæsar* said, Come follow me. [*Exit* Loveless.

Y. Wor. I hope 'tis his Wife, whom I desir'd to meet me here, that she might take a View of her Soldier before she new-mounted him. [*Exit.*

Enter Mrs. Flareit *and her Maid.*

Ma. I wonder, Madam, Sir *Novelty* don't come yet: I am so afraid he shou'd see *Narcissa,* and find out the trick of your Letter.

Fla. No! no! *Narcissa* is out of the way: I am sure he won't be long; for I heard the Hautboys, as they pass'd by me, mention his Name; I suppose, to make the Intrigue more fashionable, he intends to give me the Musick.

Ma. Suppose he take you for *Narcissa,* what Advantage do you propose by it?

Fla. I shall then have a just Occasion to quarrel with him for his Perfidiousness, and so force his Pocket to make his Peace with me: Beside, my Jealousy will not let me rest till I am reveng'd.

Ma. Jealousy! why, I have often heard you say, you loath'd him.

Fla. 'Tis my Pride, not Love, that makes me jealous: For, tho' I don't love him, yet I am incens'd to think he dares love another.

Ma. See! Madam, here he is, and the Musick with him.

Fla. Put on your Mask, and leave me.— [*They Mask.*

Enter Sir Novelty *with the Musick.*

Sir Nov. Here, Gentlemen, place your selves on this Spot, and pray oblige me with a Trumpet *Sonata.*—This taking a Man at his first Word, is a very new way of preserving Reputation, stop my

Vitals,—nay, and a secure one too; for now may we enjoy and grow weary of one another, before the Town can take any notice of us. [Flareit *making towards him.*] Ha! this must be she.—I suppose, Madam, you are no Stranger to the Contents of this Letter.

Fla. Dear Sir, this Place is too publick for my Acknowledgment, if you please to withdraw to a more private Conveniency. [*Exeunt.*

[*The Musick prepare to play, and all sorts of People gather about it.*

Enter at one Door Narcissa, Hillaria, Amanda, Elder Worthy, *and* Young Worthy; *at another,* Loveless *and* Snap, *who talk to the Masks.*

El. Wor. What say you, Ladies, shall we walk homewards? It begins to be dark.

Y. Wor. Prithee don't be so impatient, it's light enough to hear the Musick, I'll warrant ye.

Am. Mr. *Worthy,* you promis'd me a Sight I long for: Is Mr. *Loveless* among all those?

Y. Wor. That's he, Madam, surveying that masked Lady.

Am. Ha! Is't possible! Methinks I read his Vices in his Person! Can he be insensible, ev'n to the smart of pinching Poverty? Pray, Sir, your Hand:—I find my self disorder'd. It troubles me to think I dare not speak to him after so long a Separation.

Y. Wor. Madam, your staying here may be dangerous, therefore let me advise you to go home, and get all things in order to receive him: About an hour hence will be a convenient time to set my Design a-going; 'till then, let me beg you to have a little Patience: Give me leave, Madam, to see you to your Coach.

Am. I'll not trouble you, Sir; yonder's my Cousin *Welbred,* I'll beg his Protection. [*Exit.*

[*The Musick plays; after which* Narcissa *speaks.*

Nar. I vow it's very fine, considering what dull Souls our Nation are; I find 'tis an harder matter to reform their Manners, than their Government or Religion.

El. Wor. Since the one has been so happily accomplish'd, I know no reason why we should despair of the other; I hope in a little time to see our Youth return from Travel, big with Praises of their own Country. But come, Ladies, the Musick's done, I suppose; shall we walk?

Nar. Time enough; why you have no Taste of the true Pleasure of the Park: I'll warrant you hate as much to ridicule others, as to hear your self prais'd: For my part, I think a little harmless Railing's half the Pleasure of one's Life.

El. Wor. I don't love to create my self Enemies, by observing the Weakness of other People; I have more Faults of my own than I know how to mend.

Nar. Protect me! How can you see such a Medley of human Stuff as are here, without venting your Spleen?—Why look there now; is not it comical, to see that wretched Creature there with her autumnal Face, dress'd in all the Colours of the Spring?

El. Wor. Pray, who is she, Madam?

Nar. A Thing that won't believe her self out of date, tho' she was a known Woman at the *Restauration.*

Y. Wor. O! I know her, 'tis Mrs. *Holdout,* one that is proud of being an Original of fashionable Fornication, and values her self mightily for being one of the first Mistresses that ever kept her Coach publickly in *England.*

Hil. Pray who's that impudent young Fellow there?

El. Wor. Oh! that's an eternal Fan-tearer, and a constant Persecutor of Womankind: He had a great Misfortune lately.

Nar. Pray, what was it?

El. Wor. Why, impudently presuming to cuckold a *Dutch* Officer, he had his Fore-teeth kick'd out.

Omnes. Ha, ha, ha!

Nar. There's another too, Mr. *Worthy,* Do you know him?

Y. Wor. That's Beau *Noisy;* one that brags of Favours from my Lady, tho' refused by her Woman; that sups with my Lord, and borrows his Club of his Footmen; that beats the Watch, and is kick'd by his Companions; that is one Day at Court, and the next in Gaol; that goes to Church without Religion, is Valiant without Courage, Witty without Sense, and Drunk without Measure.

El. Wor. A very compleat Gentleman.

Hil. Prithee, Cousin, who's that over-shy Lady there, that won't seem to understand what that brisk young Fellow says to her?

Nar. Why, that's my Lady *Slylove:* The other ceremonious Gentleman is her Lover. She is so over-modest, that she makes it a Scruple of shifting her self before her Woman, but afterwards makes none of doing it before her Gallant.

Y. Wor. Hang her, she's a Jest to the whole Town: For tho' she has been the Mother of two By-blows, she endeavours to appear as ignorant in all Company, as if she did not know the Distinction of Sexes.

Nar. Look, look! Mr. *Worthy,* I vow, there's the Countess of *Incog.* out of her Dishabillee, in a high Head, I protest!

Y. Wor. 'Tis as great a Wonder to see her out of an Hackney-Coach, as out of Debt, or—

Nar. Or out of Countenance.

Y. Wor. That, indeed, she seldom changes; for she is never out of a Mask, and is so well known in't, that when she has a mind to be private, she goes barefac'd.

Nar. But come, Cousin, now let's see what Monsters the next Walk affords.

El. Wor. With all my Heart; 'tis in our way home.

Y. Wor. Ladies, I must beg your Pardon for a Moment, yonder comes one I have a little Business with, I'll dispatch it immediately, and follow you.

Hil. No, no; we'll stay for you.

Nar. You may, if you please, Cousin; but, I suppose, he will hardly thank you for't.

Hil. What, then you conclude 'tis a Woman's Business, by his promising a quick Dispatch?

Y. Wor. Madam, in three Minutes you shall know the Business: If it displease you, condemn me to an eternal Absence.

El. Wor. Come, Madam, let me be his Security.

Nar. I dare take your Word, Sir.—

[*Exeunt* Elder Worthy, Hillaria, *and* Narcissa.

Enter Sly, *Servant to* Young Worthy.

Y. Wor. Well! how goes Matters? Is she in a Readiness to receive him?

Sly. To an Hair, Sir; every Servant has his Cue, and all are impatient till the Comedy begins.

Y. Wor. Stand aside a little, and let us watch our Opportunity.

Snap. [*to a Mask.*] Enquire about half an Hour hence for Number *Two,* at the *Gridiron.*

Mask. To-morrow with all my Heart, but To-night I am engaged to the Chaplain of Colonel *Thunder*'s Regiment.

Snap. What, will you leave me for a Mutton-chop? for that's all he'll give you, I'm sure.

Mask. You are mistaken, faith, he keeps me.

Snap. Not to himself, I'll engage him: Yet he may too, if no body likes you no better than I do. Hark you, Child, prithee, when was your Smock wash'd?

Mask. Why, do'st thou pretend to fresh Linen, that never wore a clean Shirt but of thy Mother's own washing? [*Goes from him.*

Lov. What, no Adventure, no Game, *Snap?*

Snap. None, none, Sir; I can't prevail with any, from the Point Head-Cloths to the Horse-Guard Whore.

Lov. What a Pox! sure the Whores can't smell an empty Pocket?

Snap. No, no, that's certain, Sir, they must see it in our Faces.

Sly. [*to* Loveless.] My dear Boy, How is't? I'gad, I am glad thou art come to Town: My Lady expected you above an Hour ago, and I am overjoy'd I have found thee: Come, come, come along, she's impatient till she sees you.

Snap. Odsbud, Sir, follow him, he takes you for another.

Lov. I'gad, it looks with the face of an Intrigue,—I'll humour him:—Well, what, shall we go now?

Sly. Ay, ay, now it's pure and dark, you may go undiscover'd.

Lov. That's what I would do.

Sly. Odsheart, she longs to see thee; and she is a curious fine Creature, ye Rogue! such Eyes! such Lips!—and such a Tongue between 'em! ah, the Tip of it will set a Man's Soul on fire!

Lov. [*Aside.*] The Rogue makes me impatient!

Sly. Come, come, the Key, the Key, the Key, you dear Rogue!

Snap. O Lord! the Key, the Key! [*Aside.*

Lov. The Key: Why sh—sh—sh—shou'd yo—yo—you have it?

Sly. Ay, ay! quickly, give's it!

Lov. Why,—what the Devil,—sure I ha'n't lost it: Oh! no Gad, it is not there;—What shall we do!

Sly. Oon's, ne'er stand fumbling; if you have lost it, we must shoot the Lock, I think.

Lov. I'gad, and so we must, for I ha'n't it.

Sly. Come, come along, follow me.

Lov. *Snap,* stand by me, you Dog.

Snap. Ay, ay, Sir. [*Exeunt* Sly, Loveless, *and* Snap.

Y. Wor. Ha! ha! the Rogue managed him most dexterously: How greedily he chopt at the Bait? What the Event will be, Heav'n knows! but thus far 'tis pleasant; and since he is safe, I'll venture to divert my Company with the Story. Poor *Amanda,* thou well deserv'st a better Husband: Thou wer't never wanting in thy Endeavours to reclaim him: And, faith, considering how long a Despair has worn thee,

'Twere Pity now thy Hopes shou'd not succeed;
This new Attempt is Love's Last Shift *indeed.*

ACT IV. SCENE I.

The SCENE *continues.*

Enter Elder Worthy, Young Worthy, Hillaria, *and* Narcissa.

El. Wor. Well, Ladies, I believe 'tis time for us to be walking.

Hil. No, pray let me engage you to stay a little longer: Yonder comes Sir *Novelty* and his Mistress, in pursuance of the Design I told you of; pray have a little Patience, and you will see the Effects on't.

El. Wor. With all my Heart, Madam. [*They stand aside.*

Enter Sir Novelty, *embracing* Flareit, *mask'd.*

Sir Nov. Generous Creature! this is an unexampled Condescension, to meet my Passion with such early Kindness: Thus let me pay my soft Acknowledgments. [*Kisses her Hand.*

Hil. You must know, he has mistaken her for another.

Fla. For Heav'ns sake let me go; if *Hillaria* shou'd be at home before me, I am ruin'd for ever.

Nar. Hillaria! what does she mean?

Sir Nov. Narcissa's Reputation shall be ever safe, while my Life and Fortune can protect it.

Nar. O Gad, let me go: Does the impudent Creature take my Name upon her?—I'll pull off her Head-cloths.

Hil. Oh! fie! Cousin, what an ungenteel Revenge wou'd that be! Have a little Patience.

Nar. Oh! I am in a Flame.

Fla. But will you never see that common Creature *Flareit* more?

Sir Nov. Never! never! feed on such homely Fare, after so rich a Banquet!

Fla. Nay, but you must hate her too.

Sir Nov. That I did long ago. 'Tis true, I have been led away; but I detest a Strumpet: I am informed she keeps a Fellow under my Nose, and for that reason I wou'd not make the Settlement I lately gave her some Hopes of: But e'en let her please her self, for now I am wholly yours.

Fla. Oh, now you charm me! But will you love me ever?

Sir Nov. Will you be ever kind?

Fla. Be sure you never see *Flareit* more.

Sir Nov. When I do, may this soft Hand revenge my Perjury.

Fla. So it shall, Villain!

[*Strikes him a Box on the Ear, and unmasks.*

Omnes. Ha! ha! ha!

Sir Nov. Flareit, the Devil!

Fla. What, will nothing but a Maid go down with you! thou miserable conceited Wretch.—Foh! I'm a homely Puss! a Strumpet, not worth your Notice! Devil, I'll be reveng'd.

Sir Nov. Damn your Revenge, I'm sure I feel it.

[*Holding his Cheek.*

Nar. Really, Sir *Novelty,* I am oblig'd to you for your kind Thoughts of me, and your extraordinary Care of my Reputation.

Sir Nov. S'Death, she here! expos'd to half the Town!—Well, I must brazen it out however! [*Walks unconcern'd.*

Fla. What! no Pretence! no Evasion now!

Sir Nov. There's no occasion for any, Madam.

Fla. Come, come, swear you knew me all this while.

Sir Nov. No, faith, Madam, I did not know you: For if I had, you wou'd not have found me so furious a Lover.

Fla. Furies and Hell! Dares the Monster own his Guilt! This is beyond all Sufferance! Thou Wretch, thou Thing, thou Animal, that I (to the everlasting forfeiture of my Sense and Understanding) have made a Man. For till thou knewest me, 'twas doubted if thou wer't of human Kind. And do'st thou think I'll suffer such a Worm as thee to turn against me? No! when I do, may I be curs'd to thy Embraces all my Life, and never know a Joy beyond thee.

Sir Nov. Why—wh—wh—what will your Ladyship's Fury do, Madam? [*Smiling.*

Fla. Only change my Lodging, Sir.

Sir Nov. I shall keep mine, Madam, that you may know where to find me when your Fury is over.—You see I am good-natur'd.

[*Walks by her.*

Fla. This Bravery's affected: I know he loves me; and I'll pierce him to the Quick: I have yet a surer way to fool him. [*Aside.*

Hil. Methinks the Knight bears it bravely.

Nar. I protest the Lady weeps.

Y. Wor. She knows what she does, I'll warrant you.

El. Wor. Ay, ay, the Fox is a better Politician than the Lion.

Fla. [*with Tears in her Eyes.*] Now, Woman. [*Aside.*] Sir *Novelty*, pray, Sir, let me speak with you.

Sir Nov. Ay, Madam.

Fla. Before we part, (for I find I have irrecoverably lost your Love) let me beg of you, that from this Hour, you ne'er will see me more, or make any new Attempts to deceive my easy Temper: For I find my Nature's such, I shall believe you, tho' to my utter Ruin.

Sir Nov. Pray Heav'n she be in earnest. [*Aside.*

Fla. One thing more, Sir: Since our first acquaintance, you have received several Letters from me; I hope you will be so much a Gentleman as to let me have 'em again: Those I have of yours shall be return'd To-morrow Morning. And now, Sir, wishing you as much Happiness in her you love, as you once pretended I cou'd give you,–I take of you my everlasting Leave.–Farewel, and may your next Mistress love you till I hate you. [*–Is going.*

Sir Nov. So! now must I seem to persuade her. Nay, prithee, my Dear! why do you struggle so? Whether wou'd you go?

Fla. Pray, Sir, give me leave to pass, I can't bear to stay. [*Crying.*

Sir Nov. What is't that frightens you?

Fla. Your barbarous Usage: Pray let me go.

Sir Nov. Nay, if you are resolv'd, Madam, I won't press you against your Will. Your humble Servant; [*Leaves her.*] and a happy Riddance, stop my Vitals! [Flareit *looks back.*

Fla. Ha! not move to call me back! So unconcerned! Oh! I cou'd tear my Flesh, stab every Feature in this dull, decaying Face, that wants a Charm to hold him! Damn him! I loath him too! But shall my Pride now fall from such an height, and bear the Torture unreveng'd? No, my very Soul's on Fire; and nothing but the Villain's Blood shall quench it. Devil, have at thee.

[*Snatches* Young Worthy'*s Sword, and runs at him.*

Y. Wor. Have a Care, Sir.

Sir Nov. Let her alone, Gentlemen, I'll warrant you.

[*Draws, and stands upon his Guard.*

[Young Worthy *takes the Sword from her, and holds her.*

Fla. Prevented. Oh! I shall choak with boiling Gall. Oh! oh! humh! Let me go; I'll have his Blood, his Blood, his Blood!

Sir Nov. Let her come, let her come, Gentlemen.

Fla. Death and Vengeance, am I become his Sport! He's pleas'd, and smiles to see me rage the more! But he shall find no Fiend in Hell can match the Fury of a disappointed Woman!—Scorned! slighted! dismissed without a parting Pang! O torturing Thought! May all the Racks Mankind e'er gave our easy Sex, neglected Love, decaying Beauty, and all the Dotage of undone Desire light on me, if e'er I cease to be the eternal Plague of his remaining Life, nay, after Death:

—When his, his black Soul lies howling in Despair,
I'd plunge to Hell, and be his Torment there. [Exit.

El. Wor. Sure, Sir *Novelty,* you never lov'd this Lady, if you are so indifferent at parting.

Sir Nov. Why, faith, *Tom,* to tell you the Truth, her Jealousy has been so troublesome and so expensive to me of late, that I have these three Months sought an Opportunity to leave her: But, faith, I had always more respect to my Life, than to let her know it before.

Hil. Methinks, Sir *Novelty,* you had very little respect to her Life, when you drew upon her.

Sir Nov. Why, what wou'd you have had me done, Madam, complemented her with my naked Bosom? No! no! Look ye, Madam, if she had made any Advances, I cou'd have disarm'd her in Second at the very first Pass.—But come, Ladies, as we walk, I'll beg your Judgments in a particular nice Fancy, that I intend to appear in, the very first Week the Court is quite out of Mourning.

El. Wor. With all my Heart, Sir *Novelty.*—Come, Ladies, I think 'twere Charity not to keep you up any longer. See the Coaches ready at St. *James*'s Gate. [*To his Servants.*

[*Exeunt.*

SCENE II.

Enter two Servants. The SCENE Amanda's *House.*

1st Serv. Come, come make haste: Is the Supper and the Musick ready?

2d Serv. It is, it is. Well! is he come?

1st Serv. Ay, ay, I came before to tell my Lady the News. That Rogue *Sly* manag'd him rarely; he has been this half Hour pretending to pick the Lock of the Garden-Door. Well, poor Lady! I wish her good Luck with him, for she's certainly the best Mistress living. Hark ye, Is the Wine strong, as she order'd? Be sure you ply him home; for he must have two or three Bumpers to qualify him for her Design. See here he comes: Away to your Post. [*Exeunt.*

Enter Loveless, *conducted by* Sly, Snap *stealing after them.*

Lov. Where the Devil will this Fellow lead me?—Nothing but Silence and Darkness!—Sure the House is haunted, and he has brought me to face the Spirit at his wonted Hour!

Sly. There, there; in, in.—Slip on your Night-Gown, and refresh your self: In the mean time I'll acquaint my Lady that you are here. [*Exit.*

Lov. Snap.

Snap. Ay, ay, Sir, I'll warrant you. [*Exeunt.*

SCENE III.

The SCENE *changes to an Anti-chamber, a Table, Light, a Night-Gown, and a Periwig lying by. They re-enter.*

Lov. Ha! what sweet Lodgings are here? Where can this end?

Snap. I'gad, Sir, I long to know.—Pray Heav'n we are not deluded hither to be starv'd.—Methinks I wish I had brought the Remnants of my Dinner with me.

Lov. Hark! I hear some body coming! Hide your self, Rascal; I wou'd not have you seen.

Snap. Well, Sir, I'll line this Trench, in case of your being in Danger. [*Gets under the Table.*

Lov. Ha! this Night-Gown and Peruke don't lie here for nothing.—I'll make my self agreeable.—I have baulk'd many a Woman in my Time for want of a clean Shirt.— [*Puts 'em on.*

Enter Servants with a Supper; after them, a Man, Woman.

Lov. Ha! a Supper! Heav'n send it be no Vision! If the Meat be real, I shall believe the Lady may prove Flesh and Blood.— Now am I damnably puzzled to know whether this be she, or not. Madam.— [*Bows.*

Wom. Sir, my Lady begs your Pardon for a Moment.

Lov. Humh! her Lady! Good!

Wom. She's unfortunately detained by some Female Visitors, which she will dispatch with all the haste imaginable: In the mean time, be pleased to refresh your self with what the House affords.—Pray, Sir, sit down.

Lov. Not alone; Madam, you must bear me Company.

Wom. To oblige you, Sir, I'll exceed my Commission.

Snap. [*under the Table.*] Was there ever so unfortunate a Dog? What the Devil put it in my Head to hide my self before Supper? Why this is worse than being lock'd into a Closet, while another Man's a Bed with my Wife! I suppose my Master will take as much Care of me too, as I should of him, if I were in his Place.

Wom. Sir, my humble Service to you. [*Drinks.*

Lov. Madam, your humble Servant: I'll pledge you. *Snap,* when there's any Danger, I'll call you: In the mean time lie still, d'ye hear? [*Aside to* Snap.

Snap. I'gad, I'll shift for my self then. [*Snatches a Flask unseen.*] So, now I am arm'd, Defiance to all Danger.

Lov. Madam, your Lady's Health.

Snap. Ay, ay, let it go round, I say. [*Drinks.*

Wom. Well, really, Sir, my Lady's very happy, that she has got loose from her Relations: For they were always teizing her about you: But she defies 'em all now.—Come, Sir, Success to both your Wishes. [*Drinks.*

Lov. Give me a Glass: Methinks this Health inspires me.—My Heart grows lighter for the weight of Wine.—Here, Madam,—Prosperity to the Man that ventures most to please her.

Wom. What think you of a Song to support this Gaity?

Lov. With all my Heart.

A Song here.

Lov. You have oblig'd me, Madam: I'gad, I like this Girl! She takes off her Glass so feelingly, I am half persuaded she's of a thirsty Love: If her Lady don't make a little haste, I find I shall present my humble Service to her.

Enter a Servant, who whispers Amanda's *Woman.*

Wom. Sir, I ask your Pardon: My Lady has some Commands for me; I will return immediately.

Lov. Your Servant.—Methinks this is a very new Method of Intriguing!

Snap. Pray Heav'n it be new! for the old Way commonly ended in a good Beating: But a Pox of Danger, I say; and so here's good Luck to you, Sir.

Lov. Take heed, Rogue, you don't get drunk, and discover your self.

Snap. It must be with a fresh Flask then; for this is expired, *Supernaculum.*

Lov. Lie close, you Dog; I hear some body coming: I am impatient till I see this Creature. This Wine has arm'd me against all Thoughts of Danger! Pray Heav'n she be young, for then she can't want Beauty. Ha! here she comes! Now! never-failing Impudence assist me.

Enter Amanda *loosely dress'd.*

Am. Where's my Love? O, let me fly into his Arms, and live for ever there.

Lov. My Life, my Soul! [*Runs, and embraces her.*] By Heav'n, a tempting Creature! Melting, soft, and warm,—as my Desire,—Oh, that I cou'd hide my Face for ever thus, that, undiscover'd, I might reap the Harvest of a ripe Desire, without the lingring Pains of growing Love. [*Kisses her Hand.*

Am. Look up, my Lord, and bless me with a tender Look; and let my talking Eyes inform thee how I have languish'd for thy Absence.

Lov. Let's retire, and chase away our fleeting Cares with the Raptures of untir'd Love.

Am. Bless me! your Voice is strangely alter'd! Ha! defend me! Who's this? Help! help! within there?

Lov. So! I am discover'd! A Pox on my Tatling! that I cou'd not hold my Tongue till I got to her Bed-Chamber.

Enter Sly, *and other Servants.*

Sly. Did your Ladyship call Help, Madam? What's the Matter?

Am. Villain! Slave! who's this? What Ruffian have you brought here.—Dog, I'll have you murder'd. [Sly *looks in his Face.*

Sly. Bless me! O Lord! Dear Madam, I beg your Pardon: As I hope to be saved, Madam, 'tis a Mistake: I took him for Mr.—

Am. Be dumb! eternal Blockhead.—Here! take this Fellow, toss him in a Blanket, and let him be turn'd out of my Doors immediately.

Sly. O pray! dear Madam; for Heav'ns sake; I am a ruin'd Man.—

Snap. Ah! *Snap,* what will become of thee? Thou art fall'n into the Hand of a Tygress that has lost her Whelp: I have no Hopes, but in my Master's Impudence! Heaven strengthen it!

Am. I'll hear no more! Away with him! [*Exeunt the Servants with* Sly.] Now, Sir, for you: I expected—

Lov. A Man, Madam, did you not?

Am. Not a Stranger, Sir: But one that has a Right and Title to that Welcome, which by Mistake has been given to you.

Lov. Not an Husband, I presume? He wou'd not have been so privately conducted to your Chamber, and in the dark too!

Am. Whoever it was, Sir, is not your Business to examine: But, if you wou'd have civil Usage, pray be gone.

Lov. To be used civilly, I must stay, Madam: There can be no Danger in so fair a Creature!

Am. I doubt you are mad, Sir.

Lov. While my Senses have such luscious Food before 'em, no wonder if they are in some Confusion, each striving to be foremost at the Banquet; and sure my greedy Eyes will starve the rest. [*Approaching her.*

Am. Pray, Sir, keep your Distance, lest your Feeling too be gratify'd.

Snap. O Lord! wou'd I were hundred Leagues off at Sea!

Lov. Then briefly thus, Madam: Know, I like and love you: Now if you have so much Generosity as to let me know what Title my pretended Rival has to your Person, or your Inclinations; perhaps the little Hopes I then may have of supplanting him, may make me leave your House: If not, my Love shall still pursue you, tho' to the hazard of my Life; which I shall not easily resign, while this Sword can guard it.

Am. Oh, were this Courage shewn but in a better Cause, how worthy were the Man that own'd it! [*Aside.*] What is it, Sir, that you purpose, by this unnecessary Trifling? Know then, that I did expect a Lover; a Man, perhaps, more brave than you: One, that if present, wou'd have given you a shorter Answer to your Question.

Lov. I am glad to hear he's Brave, however: It betrays no Weakness in your Choice. But if you'd still preserve or raise the Joys of Love, remove him from your Thoughts a Moment, and in his room receive a warmer Heart; a Heart that must admire you more than he, because my Passion's of a fresher Date.

Am. What d'ye take me for?

Lov. A Woman, and the most Charming of your Sex: One, whose pointed Eyes declare you form'd for Love. And tho' your Words are flinty, your every Look and Motion all confess there's a secret Fire within you, which must sparkle, when the Steel of Love provokes it. Come, now pull away your Hand, to make me hold it faster.

Am. Nay, now you are rude, Sir.

Lov. If Love be Rudeness, let me be Impudent: When we are familiar, Rudeness will be Love. No Woman ever thought a Lover rude, after she had once granted him the Favour.

Am. Pray, Sir, forbear.

Lov. How can I, when my Desire's so violent? Oh, let me snatch the rosy Dew from those distilling Lips; and as you see your Power to charm, so chide me with your Pity. Why do you thus cruelly turn away your Face? I own the Blessing's worth an Age's Expectation; but if refused till merited, 'tis esteemed a Debt. Wou'd you oblige your Lover, let loose your early Kindness.

Am. I shall not take your Counsel, Sir, while I know a Woman's early Kindness is as little sign of her Generosity, as her Generosity is a sign of her Discretion: Nor wou'd I have you believe I am so ill provided for, that I need listen to any Man's first Addresses.

Lov. Why, Madam, wou'd not you drink the first time you had a Thirst?

Am. Yes; but not before I had.

Lov. If you can't drink, yet you may kiss the Cup; and that may give you Inclination.

Am. Your Pardon, Sir; I drink out of no body's Glass but my own: As the Man I love confines himself to me, so my Inclination keeps me true to him.

Lov. That's a Cheat imposed upon you, by your own Vanity: For when your Back's turn'd, your very Chamber-Maid sips of your Leavings, and becomes your Rival. Constancy in Love is all a Cheat; Women of your Understanding know it. The Joys of Love are only great when they are new; and to make 'em lasting, we must often change.

Am. Suppose 'twere a fresh Lover I now expected?

Lov. Why then, Madam, your Expectation's answer'd: For I must confess, I don't take you for an old Acquaintance, tho' somewhere I have seen a Face not much unlike you. Come, your Arguments are vain; for they are so charmingly deliver'd, they but inspire me the more, as Blows in Battle raise the brave Man's Courage. Come, every thing pleads for me; your Beauty, Wit, Time, Place, Opportunity, and my own Excess of burning Passion.

Am. Stand off, distant as the Globes of Heaven and Earth, that like a falling Star I may shoot with greater Force into your Arms, and think it Heaven to lie expiring there. [*Runs into his Arms.*

Snap. Ah! ah! ah! Rogue, the Day's our own.

Lov. Thou sweetest, softest Creature Heav'n e'er form'd: Thus let me twine my self about thy beauteous Limbs, till struggling with the Pangs of painful Bliss, motionless and mute we yield to conquering Love; both vanquish'd, and both Victors.

Am. Can all this Heat be real? Oh, why has hateful Vice such Power to charm, while poor abandon'd Virtue lies neglected? [*Aside.*

Lov. Come, let us surfeit on our new-born Raptures; let's waken sleeping Nature with Delight, till we may justly say, Now! now! we live!

Am. Come on; let's indulge the Transports of our present Bliss, and bid Defiance to our future Change of Fate. Who waits there?

Enter Amanda*'s Woman.*

Am. Bring me Word immediately if my Apartment's ready, as I order'd it. O, I am charm'd, I have found the Man to please me now: One that can, and dares maintain the noble Rapture of a lawless Love: I own my self a Libertine, a mortal Foe to that dull Thing call'd Virtue, that mere Disease of sickly Nature. Pleasure's the End of Life; and while I'm Mistress of my self, and Fortune, I will enjoy it to the Height. Speak freely then, (not that I love, like other Women, the nauseous Pleasure of a little Flattery) but answer me like a Man that scorns a Lye: Does my Face invite you, Sir? May I, from what you see of me, propose a Pleasure to my self in pleasing you?

Lov. By Heaven you may: I have seen all the Beauties that the Sun shines on, but never saw the Sun out-shin'd before: I have measur'd half the World in search of Pleasure; but not returning home, had ne'er been happy.

Am. Spoken like the Man I wish might love me.—Pray Heaven his Words prove true. [*Aside.*] Be sure you never flatter me; and when my Person tires you, confess it freely: For change whene'er you will, I'll change as soon: But while we chance to meet, still let it be with raging Fire: No matter how soon it dies, provided the small time it lasts, it burns the fiercer.

Lov. O! wou'd the blinded World, like us, agree to change, how lasting might the Joys of Love be? For thus Beauty, tho' stale to one, might somewhere else be new; and while this Man were blest in leaving what he loath'd, another were new-blest in receiving what he ne'er enjoy'd.

Re-enter Amanda*'s Woman.*

Wom. Madam, every thing is according to your Order.

Lov. Oh! lead me to the Scene of unsupportable Delight; rack me with Pleasures never known before, till I lie gasping with convulsive Passion: This Night let us be lavish to our unbounded Wishes.

Give all our Stock at once to raise the Fire,

And revel to the height of loose Desire. [Exeunt.

Wom. Ah! what an happy Creature's my Lady now? There's many an unsatisfy'd Wife about Town wou'd be glad to have her Husband as wicked as my Master, upon the same Terms my Lady has him. Few Women, I'm afraid, wou'd grudge an Husband the laying out his Stock of Love, that cou'd receive such considerable Interest for it! Well!—Now sha'n't I take one wink of Sleep, for thinking how they'll employ their time to Night.—Faith, I must listen, if I were to be hang'd for't. [*Listens at the Door.*

Snap. So! my Master's provided for, therefore it's time for me to take care of my self: I have no mind to be lock'd out of my Lodging; I fancy there's room for two in the Maid's Bed, as well as my Lady's.—This same Flask was plaguy strong Wine:—I find I shall storm, if she don't surrender fairly. By your leave, Damsel.

Wom. Bless me! who's this? O Lord what wou'd you have? Who are you?

Snap. One that has a Right and Title to your Body; my Master having already taken Possession of your Lady's.

Wom. Let me go, or I'll cry out.

Snap. Ye lye; ye dare not disturb your Lady: But the better to secure you, thus I stop your Mouth. [*Kisses her.*

Wom. Humh!—Lord bless me! is the Devil in you, tearing one's Things!

Snap. Then shew me your Bed-Chamber.

Wom. The Devil shall have you first.

Snap. A' shall have us both together then: Here will I fix, [*takes her about the Neck.*] just in this Posture till To-morrow Morning. In the mean time, when you find your Inclination stirring, prithee give me a Call, for at present I am very sleepy. [*Seems to sleep.*

Wom. Foh! how he stinks. Ah! what a Whiff was there:—The Rogue's as drunk as a Sailor with a Twelve-month's Arrears in his Pocket; or a *Jacobite* upon a Day of ill News. I'll ha' nothing to say to him,—Let me see, how shall I get rid of him?—O! I have it! I'll soon make him sober I'll warrant him: So-ho! Mr. What d'ye call 'um, Where do you intend to lie to Night?

Snap. Humh! why where you lay last Night, unless you change your Lodging.

Wom. Well, for once I'll take Pity of you! make no Noise, but put out the Candles, and follow me softly, for fear of disturbing my Lady.

Snap. I'll warrant ye, there's no fear of spoiling her Musick, while we are playing the same Tune.

SCENE IV.

The SCENE *changes to a dark Entry, and they re-enter.*

Wom. Where are you? Lend me your Hand.

Snap. Here! here! Make haste, my dear Concupiscence.

Wom. Hold! stand there a little, while I open the Door gently, without waking the Footmen.

[*She feels about, and opens a Trap-door.*

Wom. Come along softly this way!

Snap. Whereabouts are you?

Wom. Here, here, come strait forward.

[*He goes forward, and falls into the Cellar.*

Snap. O Lord! O Lord! I have broke my Neck.

Wom. I am glad to hear him say so, however I shou'd be loth to be hang'd for him. How d'ye, Sir?

Snap. D'ye, Sir! I am a League under Ground.

Wom. Whereabouts are you?

Snap. In Hell, I think.

Wom. No! no! you are but in the Road to it, I dare say. Ah, dear! why will you follow lewd Women at this rate, when they lead you to the very Gulph of Destruction? I knew you wou'd be swallow'd up at last. Ha! ha! ha! ha!

Snap. Ah, ye sneering Whore!

Wom. Shall I fetch you a Prayer-Book, Sir, to arm you against the Temptations of the Flesh?

Snap. No! you need but shew your damn'd ugly Face to do that.— Hark ye, either help me out, or I'll hang my self, and swear you murder'd me.

Wom. Nay, if you are so bloody-minded, good Night to ye, Sir.

[*She offers to shut the Door over him, and he catches hold on her.*

Snap. Ah! ah! ah! have I caught you? I'gad, we'll pig together now.

Wom. O Lord! pray let me go, and I'll do any thing.

Snap. And so you shall, before I part with you.

[*Pulls her in to him.*

And now, Master, my humble Service to you.

[*He pulls the Door over them.*

ACT V. SCENE I.

The SCENE *Sir* William Wisewoud*'s House.*

Enter Elder Worthy, Young Worthy, *and a Lawyer with a Writing.*

El. Wor. Are the Ladies ready?

Y. Wor. Hillaria is just gone up to hasten her Cousin, and Sir *William* will be here immediately.

El. Wor. But hark you, Brother! I have consider'd of it, and pray let me oblige you not to pursue your Design on his five thousand Pound: For, in short, 'tis no better than a Cheat, and what a Gentleman shou'd scorn to be guilty of. Is it not sufficient that I consent to your wronging him of his Daughter?

Y. Wor. Your Pardon, Brother, I can't allow that a Wrong: For his Daughter loves me: Her Fortune, you know, he has nothing to do with; and its a hard case a young Woman shall not have the disposal of her Heart. Love's a Fever of the Mind, which nothing but our own Wishes can aswage; and I don't question but we shall find Marriage a very cooling Cordial.—And as to the five thousand Pound, 'tis no more than what he has endeavour'd to cheat his Niece of.

El. Wor. What d'ye mean? I take him for an honest Man!

Y. Wor. Oh! very honest! As honest as an old Agent to a new-rais'd Regiment.—No, faith, I'll say that for him, he will not do an ill thing, unless he gets by it. In a word, this so very honest Sir *William,* as you take him to be, has offer'd me the Refusal of your Mistress; and upon Condition I will secure him five thousand Pound upon my Day of Marriage with her, he will secure me her Person, and ten thousand Pound, the remaining part of her Fortune! There's a Guardian for ye! What think ye now, Sir?

El. Wor. Why, I think he deserves to be serv'd in the same kind! I find Age and Avarice are inseparable! therefore e'en make what you can of him, and I will stand by you. But hark you, Mr. *Forge,* are you sure it will stand good in Law, if Sir *William* signs the Bond?

Law. In any Court in *England,* Sir.

El. Wor. Then there's your fifty Pieces; and if it succeeds, here are as many more in the same Pocket to answer 'em: But, mum,— here comes Sir *William,* and the Ladies.

Enter Sir William Wisewoud, Hillaria, *and* Narcissa.

Sir Wil. Good-morrow, Gentlemen! Mr. *Worthy,* I give you Joy! Odso! if my Heels were as light as my Heart, I shou'd ha' much ado to forbear dancing.— Here, here, take her, Man, [*Gives him* Narcissa*'s Hand.*] she's yours, and so is her thousand Pounds a Year, and my five thousand Pounds shall be yours too.

Y. Wor. You must ask me leave, first. [*Aside.*

Sir Wil. Odso! Is the Lawyer come?

El. Wor. He is, and all the Writings are ready, Sir.

Sir Wil. Come, come, let's see, Man! What's this? Odd! this Law is a plaguy troublesome thing; for now-a-days it won't let a Man give away his own, without repeating the Particulars five hundred times over; when in former Times a Man might have held his Title to twenty thousand Pounds a Year, in the compass of an Horn-book.

Law. That is, Sir, because there are more Knaves now-a-days, and this Age is more treacherous and distrustful than heretofore.

Sir Wil. That is, Sir, because there are more Lawyers than heretofore. But, come, What's this, prithee?

Law. These are the old Writings of your Daughter's Fortune; this is Mr. *Worthy*'s Settlement upon her;—and this, Sir, is your Bond for five thousand Pounds to him: There wants nothing but filling up the Blanks with the Parties Names; if you please, Sir, I'll do't immediately.

Sir Wil. Do so.

Law. May I crave your Daughter's Christian Name? the rest I know, Sir.

Sir Wil. Narcissa, Prithee make haste.—

Y. Wor. You know your Business.— [*Aside to the Lawyer.*

Law. I'll warrant you, Sir. [*Sits to write.*

Sir Wil. Mr. *Worthy,* methinks your Brother does not relish your Happiness as he shou'd do: Poor Man! I'll warrant he wishes himself in his Brother's Condition!

Y. Wor. Not I, I'll assure you, Sir.

Sir Wil. Niece! Niece! have you no Pity? Prithee look upon him a little! Odd! he's a pretty young Fellow:–I am sure he loves you, or he wou'd not have frequented my House so often! D'ye think his Brother cou'd not tell my Daughter his own Story, without your Assistance? Pshaw-waw! I tell you, you were the Beauty that made him so assiduous: Come, come, give him your Hand, and he'll soon creep into your Heart, I'll warrant you: Come, say the Word, and make him happy.

Hil. What, to make my self miserable, Sir! marry a Man without an Estate!

Sir Wil. Hang an Estate! true Love's beyond all Riches! 'Tis all Dirt,–mere Dirt!–Beside, ha'n't you fifteen thousand Pounds to your Portion?

Hil. I doubt, Sir, you wou'd be loth to give him your Daughter, tho' her Fortune's larger.

Sir Wil. Odd, if he lov'd her but half so well as he loves you, he shou'd have her for a Word speaking.

Hil. But, Sir, this asks some Consideration.–

Nar. You see, Mr. *Worthy,* what an extraordinary Kindness my Father has for you!

Y. Wor. Ay, Madam, and for your Cousin too: But I hope, with a little of your Assistance, we shall be both able, very shortly, to return it.

Nar. Nay, I was always ready to serve *Hillaria:* For Heav'n knows, I only marry to revenge her Quarrel to my Father: I cannot forgive his off'ring to fell her.

Y. Wor. Oh, you need not take such Pains, Madam, to conceal your Passion for me; you may own it without a Blush, upon your Wedding-Day.

Nar. My Passion! When did you hear me acknowledge any? If I thought you cou'd believe me guilty of such a Weakness, tho' after I had marry'd you, I wou'd never look you in the Face.

Y. Wor. A very pretty Humour this, faith! [*Aside.*] What a world of unnecessary Sins have we two to answer for! For she has told more Lyes to conceal her Love, than I have sworn false Oaths to promote it. Well, Madam, at present I'll content my self with your giving me leave to love.

Nar. Which if I don't give, you'll take, I suppose.

Hil. Well, Uncle, I won't promise you, but I'll go to Church and see them marry'd; when we come back, 'tis ten to one but I surprize you where you least think on.

Sir Wil. Why, that's well said!—Mr. *Worthy,* now! now's your Time: Odd! I have so fir'd her, 'tis not in her Power to deny you, Man.—To her! to her! I warrant her thy own, Boy! You'll keep your Word; five thousand Pound upon the Day of Marriage.

Y. Wor. I'll give you my Bond upon demand, Sir.

Sir Wil. O! I dare take your Word, Sir.—Come, Lawyer, have you done? Is all ready?

Law. All, Sir! This is your Bond to Mr. *Worthy:* Will you be pleased to sign that first, Sir?

Sir Wil. Ay, ay; let's see: *The Condition of this Obligation.* [Reads.] Hum, um,—Come, lend me the Pen.—There,—Mr. *Worthy,* I deliver this as my Act and Deed to you, and Heaven send you a good Bargain.—Niece, will you witness it? [*Which she does.*]—Come, Lawyer, your Fist too. [*Lawyer witnesses it.*

Law. Now, Sir, if you please to sign the Jointure.

El. Wor. Come on.—Sir *William,* I deliver this to you for the Use of your Daughter. Madam, will you give your self the trouble once more? [Hillaria *sets her Hand.*] Come, Sir,—[*The Lawyer does the same.*] So, now let a Coach be called as soon as you please, Sir.

Sir Wil. You may save that Charge, I saw your own at the Door.

El. Wor. Your Pardon, Sir, that wou'd make our Business too publick: For which Reason, Sir *William,* I hope you will excuse our not taking you along with us. [*Exit Servant.*

Sir Wil. Ay, ay, with all my Heart; the more Privacy, the less Expence. But pray, what time may I expect you back again? For *Amanda* has sent to me for the Writings of her Husband's Estate: I suppose she intends to redeem the Mortgage, and I am afraid she will keep me there till Dinner-time.

Y. Wor. Why, about that time she has obliged me to bring some of her nearest Friends to be Witnesses of her good or evil Fortune with her Husband: Methinks I long to know of her Success; if you please, Sir *William,* we'll meet you there.

Sir Wil. With all my Heart.—[*Enter a Servant.*] Well, Is the Coach come?

Serv. It is at the Door, Sir.

Sir Wil. Come, Gentlemen, no Ceremony; your time's short.

El. Wor. Your Servant, Sir *William*.

[*Exeunt* Elder Worthy, Young Worthy, Narcissa, *and* Hillaria.

Sir Wil. So! here's five thousand Pounds got with a wet Finger! This 'tis to read Mankind! I knew a young Lover wou'd never think he gave too much for his Mistress! Well! if I don't suddenly meet with some Misfortune, I shall never be able to bear this Tranquillity of Mind. [*Exit.*

SCENE II.

The SCENE *changes to* Amanda'*s House.*

Enter Amanda *sola.*

Am. Thus far my Hopes have all been answer'd, and my Disguise of vicious Love has charm'd him ev'n to a Madness of impure Desire:—But now I tremble to pull off the Mask, lest barefac'd Virtue shou'd fright him from my Arms for ever. Yet sure, there are Charms in Virtue, nay, stronger and more pleasing far than hateful Vice can boast of! else why have holy Martyrs perish'd for its sake? While Lewdness ever gives severe Repentance, and unwilling Death.—Good Heav'n inspire my Heart, and hang upon my Tongue the force of Truth and Eloquence, that I may lure this wandring Falcon back to Love and Virtue.—He comes, and now my dreaded Task begins!

Enter Loveless *in new Cloaths.*

Am. How fare you, Sir? D'ye not already think your self confin'd? Are you not tired with my easy Love?

Lov. O! never! never! you have so fill'd my Thoughts with Pleasures past, that but to reflect on 'em, is still new Rapture to my Soul, and the Bliss must last while I have Life or Memory.

Am. No Flattery, Sir! I lov'd you for your Plain-dealing; and to preserve my good Opinion, tell me, what think you of the Grapes persuading Juice? Come, speak freely, wou'd not the next Tavern-Bush put all this out of your Head?

Lov. Faith, Madam, to be free with you, I am apt to think you are in the right on't: For tho' Love and Wine are two very fine

Tunes, yet they make no Musick, if you play them both together; separately, they ravish us: Thus the Mistress ought to make room for the Bottle, the Bottle for the Mistress, and both to wait the Call of Inclination.

Am. That's generously spoken—I have observ'd, Sir, in all your Discourse, you confess something of a Man that has throughly known the World.—Pray give me leave to ask you, of what Condition you are, and whence you came?

Lov. Why, in the first place, Madam,—by Birth I am a Gentleman; by ill Friends, good Wine, and false Dice, almost a Beggar: But by your Servant's mistaking me, the happiest Man that ever Love and Beauty smil'd on.

Am. One thing more, Sir! Are you marry'd?—Now my Fears. [*Aside.*

Lov. I was, but very young.

Am. What was your Wife?

Lov. A foolish loving Thing, that built Castles in the Air, and thought it impossible for a Man to forswear himself when he made Love.

Am. Was she not virtuous?

Lov. Umph! Yes, faith, I believe she might, I was ne'er jealous of her.

Am. Did you ne'er love her?

Lov. Ah, most damnably at first, for she was within two Women of my Maidenhead.

Am. What's become of her?

Lov. Why, after I had been from her beyond Sea, about seven or eight Years, like a very loving Fool she dy'd of the Pip, and civilly left me the World to range in.

Am. Why did you leave her?

Lov. Because she grew stale, and I cou'd not whore in quiet for her: Besides, she was always exclaiming against my Extravagancies, particularly my Gaming, which she so violently oppos'd, that I fancy'd a Pleasure in it, which since I never found; for in one Month I lost between eight and ten thousand Pounds, which I had just before call'd in to pay my Debts. This Misfortune made my Creditors come so thick upon me, that I was forc'd to mortgage the remaining part of my Estate to purchase new Pleasure; which I knew I cou'd not do on this side of the Water, amidst the Clamours of insatiate Duns, and the more hateful Noise of a complaining Wife.

Am. Don't you wish you had taken her Counsel, tho'?

Lov. Not I, faith, Madam.

Am. Why so?

Lov. Because 'tis to no purpose: I am Master of more Philosophy, than to be concern'd at what I can't help.–But now, Madam,–pray give me leave to inform my self as far in your Condition.

Am. In a word, Sir, till you know me throughly, I must own my self a perfect Riddle to you.

Lov. Nay, nay, I know you are a Woman: But in what Circumstances, Wife, or Widow?

Am. A Wife, Sir; a true, a faithful, and a virtuous Wife.

Lov. Humh! truly, Madam, your Story begins something like a Riddle: A virtuous Wife, say you? What, and was you never false to your Husband?

Am. I never was, by Heav'n! for him, and only him, I still love above the World.

Lov. Good agen! Pray, Madam, don't your Memory fail you sometimes? because I fancy you don't remember what you do over Night!

Am. I told you, Sir, I shou'd appear a Riddle to you: But if my Heart will give me leave, I'll now unloose your fetter'd Apprehension:–But I must first amaze you more;–Pray, Sir, satisfy me in one Particular:–'Tis this,–What are your undissembled Thoughts of Virtue? Now, if you can, shake off your lose unthinking Part, and summon all your force of manly Reason to resolve me.

Lov. Faith, Madam, methinks this is a very odd Question for a Woman of your Character. I must confess you have amaz'd me.

Am. It ought not to amaze you! Why shou'd you think I make a mock of Virtue? But last Night you allow'd my Understanding greater than is usual in our Sex: If so, can you believe I have no farther Sense of Happiness, than what this empty, dark, and barren World can yield me? No, I have yet a Prospect of a sublimer Bliss, an Hope that carries me to the bright Regions of eternal Day.

Lov. Humh! I thought her last Night's Humour was too good to hold. I suppose, by and by she will ask me to go to Church with her.—Faith, Madam, in my Mind this Discourse is a little out of the way. You told me I should be acquainted with your Condition, and at present that's what I had rather be inform'd of.

Am. Sir, you shall: But first, this Question must be answer'd: Your Thoughts of Virtue, Sir?—By all my Hopes of Bliss hereafter, your answering this, pronounces half my good or evil Fate for ever: But on my Knees I beg you, do not speak till you have weigh'd it well:—Answer me with the same Truth and Sincerity, as you would answer Heav'n at your latest Hour.

Lov. Your Words confound me, Madam; some wondrous Secret sure lies ripen'd in your Breast, and seems to struggle for its fatal Birth! What is it I must answer you?

Am. Give me your real Thoughts of Virtue, Sir: Can you believe there ever was a Woman truly Mistress of it, or is it only Notion?

Lov. Let me consider, Madam. [*Aside.*] What can this mean? Why is she so earnest in her Demands, and begs me to be serious, as if her Life depended upon my Answer?—I will resolve her as I ought, as Truth, and Reason, and the strange Occasion seems to press me.—Most of your Sex confound the very Name of Virtue; for they wou'd seem to live without Desires; which, cou'd they do, that were not Virtue, but the defect of unperforming Nature, and no Praise to them: For who can boast a Victory when they have no Foe to conquer? Now she alone gives the fairest Proofs of Virtue, whose Conscience, and whose force of Reason can curb her warm Desires, when Opportunity wou'd raise 'em: That such a Woman may be found, I dare believe.

Am. May I believe that from your Soul you speak this undissembled Truth?

Lov. Madam, you may. But still you rack me with an Amazement! Why am I ask'd so strange a Question?

Am. I'll give you ease immediately.—Since then you have allow'd a Woman may be virtuous,—How will you excuse the Man who leaves the Bosom of a Wife so qualify'd, for the abandon'd Pleasures of deceitful Prostitutes? ruins her Fortune! contemns her Counsel! loaths her Bed, and leaves her to the lingring Miseries of Despair and Love: While, in return of all these Wrongs, she, his poor forsaken Wife meditates no Revenge but what her piercing Tears, and secret Vows to Heav'n for his Conversion, yield her:

Yet still loves on, is constant and unshaken to the last! Can you believe that such a Man can live without the Stings of Conscience, and yet be Master of his Senses! Conscience! did you ne'er feel the Checks of it? Did it never, never tell you of your broken Vows?

Lov. That you shou'd ask me this, confounds my Reason:—And yet your Words are utter'd with such a powerful Accent, they have awaken'd my Soul, and strike my Thoughts with Horror and Remorse.— [*Stands in a fix'd Posture.*

Am. Then let me strike you nearer, deeper yet:—But arm your Mind with gentle Pity first, or I am lost for ever.

Lov. I am all Pity, all Faith, Expectation, and confus'd Amazement: Be kind, be quick, and ease my Wonder.

Am. Look on me well: Revive your dead Remembrance: And oh! for Pity's sake, [*Kneels.*] hate me not for loving long; faithfully forgive this innocent Attempt of a despairing Passion, and I shall die in quiet.

Lov. Hah! speak on! [*Amazed.*

Am. It will not be!—The Word's too weighty for my faultring Tongue, and my Soul sinks beneath the fatal Burthen. Oh!— [*Falls on the Ground.*

Lov. Ha! she faints! Look up, fair Creature! behold a Heart that bleeds for your Distress, and fain wou'd share the weight of your oppressing Sorrows! Oh! thou hast ras'd a Thought within me, that shocks my Soul.

Am. 'Tis done! [*rising.*] The Conflict's past, and Heav'n bids me speak undaunted. Know then, ev'n all the boasted Raptures of your last Night's Love, you found in your *Amanda's* Arms:—I am your Wife.

Lov. Hah!

Am. For ever blest or miserable, as your next Breath shall sentence me.

Lov. My Wife! impossible! Is she not dead? How shall I believe thee?

Am. How Time and my Afflictions may have alter'd me, I know not: But here's an indelible Confirmation. [*Bares her Arm.*] These speaking Characters, which in their cheerful Bloom our early Passions mutually recorded.

Lov. Hah! 'tis here;—'tis no Illusion, but my real Name; which seems to upbraid me as a Witness of my perjur'd Love:—Oh, I am confounded with my Guilt, and tremble to behold thee.—Pray give me leave to think. [*Turns from her.*

Am. I will: [*kneels.*] But you must look upon me: For only Eyes can hear the Language of the Eyes, and mine have sure the tenderest Tale of Love to tell, that ever Misery, at the dawn of rising Hope, cou'd utter.

Lov. I have wrong'd you. Oh! rise! basely wrong'd you! And can I see your Face?

Am. One kind, one pitying Look cancels those Wrongs for ever: And oh! forgive my fond presuming Passion; for from my Soul I pardon and forgive you all: All, all but this, the greatest, your unkind Delay of Love.

Lov. Oh! seal my Pardon with thy trembling Lips, while with this tender Grasp of fond reviving Love I seize my Bliss, and stifle all thy Wrongs for ever. [*Embraces her.*

Am. No more; I'll wash away their Memory in Tears of flowing Joy.

Lov. Oh! thou hast rouz'd me from my deep Lethargy of Vice! For hitherto my Soul has been enslav'd to loose Desires, to vain deluding Follies, and Shadows of substantial Bliss: But now I wake with Joy, to find my Rapture real.—Thus let me kneel and pay my Thanks to her, whose conqu'ring Virtue has at last subdu'd me. Here will I fix, thus prostrate, sigh my Shame, and wash my Crimes in never-ceasing Tears of Penitence.

Am. O rise! this Posture heaps new Guilt on me! Now you overpay me.

Lov. Have I not used thee like a Villain? For almost ten long Years depriv'd thee of my Love, and ruin'd all thy Fortune! But I will labour, dig, beg, or starve to give new Proofs of my unfeign'd Affection.

Am. Forbear this Tenderness, lest I repent of having mov'd your Soul so far. You shall not need to beg, Heav'n has provided for us beyond its common Care: 'Tis now near two Years since my Uncle Sir *William Wealthy* sent you the News of my pretended Death; knowing the extravagance of your Temper, he thought it fit you shou'd believe no other of me; and about a Month after he had sent you that Advice, poor Man, he dy'd, and left me in full Possession of two thousand Pounds a Year, which I now cannot offer as a Gift, because my Duty, and your lawful Right, makes you the undisputed Master of it.

Lov. How have I labour'd for my own undoing; while, in despite of all my Follies, kind Heav'n resolv'd my Happiness!

Enter a Servant to Amanda.

Serv. Madam, Sir *William Wisewoud* has sent your Ladyship the Writings you desir'd him, and says he'll wait on you immediately.

Am. Now, Sir, if you please to withdraw a while, you may inform your self how fair a Fortune you are Master of.

Lov. None, none that can outweigh a virtuous Mind; while in my Arms I thus can circle thee, I grasp more Treasure, than in a Day the posting Sun can travel o'er. Oh! why have I so long been blind to the Perfections of thy Mind and Person? Not knowing thee a Wife, I found thee charming beyond the Wishes of luxurious Love. Is it then a Name, a Word shall rob thee of thy Worth? Can Fancy be a surer Guide to Happiness than Reason? Oh! I have wander'd like a benighted Wretch, and lost my self in Life's unpleasing Journey.

'Twas heedless Fancy first, that made me stray,
But Reason now breaks forth, and lights me on my Way.

[Exeunt.

SCENE III.

The SCENE *changes to an Entry.*

Enter three or four Servants.

1st Serv. Prithee, *Tom,* make haste below there; my Lady has order'd Dinner at half an Hour after One, precisely. Look out some of the Red that came in last.

[*Two of the Servants hawl* Snap *and* Amanda'*s Woman out of the Cellar.*

2d Serv. Come, Sir, come out here, and shew your Face.

Wom. Oh, I am undone; ruin'd!

2d Serv. Pray, Sir, who are you, and what was your Business, and how in the Devil's Name, came you here?

Snap. Why truly, Sir, the Flesh led me to the Cellar-Door; but I believe the Devil push'd me in.—That Gentlewoman can inform you better.

3d Serv. Pray, Mrs. *Anne,* how came you two together in the Cellar?

Wom. Why, he— he— pu— pu— pull'd me in. [*Sobbing.*

3d Serv. But how the Devil came he in?

Wom. He fe— fe— fe— fell in.

2d Serv. How came he into the House?

Wom. I don— do— don't know.

2d Serv. Ah! you are a Crocodile; I thought what was the Reason I cou'd never get a good Word from you! What in a Cellar too! But come, Sir, we will take care of you, however. Bring him along, we will first carry him before my Lady, and then toss him in a Blanket.

Snap. Nay, but Gentlemen! dear Gentlemen. [*Exeunt.*

Enter Loveless, Amanda, Elder Worthy, Young Worthy, Narcissa, *and* Hillaria.

El. Wor. This is indeed a joyful Day; we must all congratulate your Happiness.

Am. Which while our Lives permit us to enjoy, we must still reflect with Gratitude on the generous Author of it. Sir, we owe you more than Words can pay you.

Lov. Words are indeed too weak, therefore let my Gratitude be dumb till it can speak in Actions.

Y. Wor. The Success of the Design I thought on, sufficiently rewards me.

Hil. When I reflect upon *Amanda*'s past Afflictions, I cou'd almost weep to think of her unexpected Change of Fortune.

El. Wor. Methinks her fair Example shou'd persuade all constant Wives ne'er to repine at unrewarded Virtue. Nay, ev'n my Brother being the first Adviser of it, has aton'd for all the Looseness of his Character.

Lov. I never can return his Kindness.

Nar. In a short time, Sir, I suppose you'll meet with an Opportunity, if you can find a Receipt to preserve Love, after his Honey-Moon's over.

Lov. The Receipt is easily found, Madam; Love's a tender Plant which can't live out of a warm Bed: You must take care, with undissembled Kindness, to keep him from the Northern Blast of Jealousy.

Nar. But I have heard, your experienc'd Lovers make use of Coldness, and that's more agreeable to my Inclination.

Lov. Coldness, Madam, before Marriage, like throwing a little Water upon a clear Fire, makes it burn the fiercer; but after Marriage, you must still take care to lay on fresh Fuel.

Nar. Oh fye, Sir! How many Examples have we of Mens hating their Wives for being too fond of 'em?

Lov. No Wonder, Madam: You may stifle a Flame, by heaping on too great a Load.

Nar. Nay, Sir, if there be no other way of destroying his Passion, for me, he may love till Doomsday.

El. Wor. Humph! don't you smell Powder, Gentlemen? Sir *Novelty* is not far off.

Lov. What, not our Fellow-Collegian, I hope, that was expell'd the University for beating the Proctor?

El. Wor. The same.

Lov. Does that Weed grow still?

El. Wor. Ay, faith, and as rank as ever, as you shall see; for here he comes.

Enter Sir Novelty.

Sir Nov. Ladies, your humble Servant. Dear *Loveless,* let me embrace thee, I am o'erjoy'd at thy good Fortune: Stop my Vitals,—the whole Town rings of it already—My Lady *Tattle-tongue* has tir'd a pair of Horses in spreading the News about. Hearing, Gentlemen, that you were all met upon an extraordinary good Occasion, I cou'd not resist this Opportunity of joining my Joy with yours: For you must know I am—

Nar. Marry'd, Sir!

Sir Nov. To my Liberty, Madam! I have just parted from my Mistress.

Nar. And pray, Sir, how do you find your self after it?

Sir Nov. The happiest Man alive, Madam; Pleasant! Easy! Gay! Light! and Free as Air: Hah; [*Capers.*] I beg your Ladyship's Pardon, Madam, but upon my Soul I cannot confine my Rapture.

Nar. Are you so indifferent, Sir?

Sir Nov. Oh! Madam, she's engag'd already to a Temple Beau! I saw 'em in a Coach together, so fond! and bore it with as unmov'd a Countenance, as *Tom Worthy* does a thund'ring Jest in a Comedy, when the whole House roars at it.

Y. Wor. Pray, Sir, what occasion'd your Separation?

Sir Nov. Why this, Sir:—You must know, she being still possess'd with a Brace of implacable Devils, call'd Revenge and Jealousy, dogg'd me this Morning to the Chocolate-house, where I was oblig'd to leave a Letter for a young foolish Girl, that—(you'll excuse me, Sir;) which I had no sooner deliver'd to the Maid of the House, but whip! she snatches it out of her Hand, flew at her like a Dragon, tore off her Headcloths, flung down three or four Sets of Lemonade-Glasses, dash'd my Lord *Whiffle*'s Chocolate in his Face, cut him over the Nose, and had like to have strangled me in my own Steinkirk.

Lov. Pray, Sir, how did this end?

Sir Nov. Comically, stop my Vitals! for in the Cloud of Powder that she had batter'd out of the Beaux' Periwigs, I stole away: After which, I sent a Friend to her with an Offer, which she readily accepted (three hundred Pounds a Year during Life) provided she wou'd renounce all Claims to me, and resign my Person to my own Disposal.

El. Wor. Methinks, Sir *Novelty*, you were a little too extravagant in your Settlement, considering how the Price of Women is fallen.

Sir Nov. Therefore I did it,—to be the first Man shou'd raise their Price: For the Devil take me, the Women of the Town now come down so low, that my very Footman, while he kept my Place t'other Day at the Play-house, carry'd a Mask out of the Side-Box with him, and, stop my Vitals, the Rogue is now taking Physick for't.

Enter the Servants with Snap.

1st Serv. Come, bring him along there.

Lov. How now! hah! *Snap* in hold? Pray let's know the Business; release him, Gentlemen.

1st Serv. Why, an't please you, Sir, this Fellow was taken in the Cellar with my Lady's Woman: She says he kept her in by Force, and was rude to her: She stands crying here without, and begs her Ladyship to do her Justice.

Am. Mr. *Loveless,* we are both the Occasion of this Misfortune; and for the poor Girl's Reputation-sake, something shou'd be done.

Lov. Snap, answer me directly; have you lain with this poor Girl?

Snap. Why truly, Sir, imagining you were doing little less with my Lady, I must confess I did commit Familiarity with her, or so, Sir.

Lov. Then you shall marry her, Sir! No Reply, unless it be your Promise.

Snap. Marry her! O Lord, Sir, after I have lain with her? Why, Sir! how the Devil can you think a Man can have any Stomach to his Dinner, after he has had three or four Slices off the Spit?

Lov. Well, Sirrah! to renew your Appetite, and because thou hast been my old Acquaintance, I'll give thee an 100 *l.* with her, and thirty Pounds a Year during Life, to set you up in some honest Employment.

Snap. Ah! Sir, now I understand you: Heav'n reward you! Well, Sir, I partly find that the gentile Scenes of our Lives are pretty well over; and I thank Heav'n, that I have so much Grace left, that I can repent, when I have no more Opportunities of being wicked.— Come, Spouse. [*She enters.*] here's my Hand, the rest of my Body shall be forth-coming. Ah! little did my Master and I think last Night that we were robbing our own Orchards. [*Exeunt.*

El. Wor. Brother, stand upon your Guard; here comes Sir *William.*

Enter Sir William Wisewoud.

Sir Wil. Joy, Joy to you all. Madam, I congratulate your good Fortune. Well, my dear Rogue, must not I give thee Joy too? ha!

Y. Wor. If you please, Sir: But I confess I have more than I deserve already.

Sir Wil. And art thou marry'd?

Y. Wor. Yes, Sir, I am marry'd.

Sir Wil. Odso, I am glad on't: I dare swear thou do'st not grudge me the 5000 *l.*

Y. Wor. Not I, really Sir: You have given me all my Soul could wish for, but the Addition of a Father's Blessing.

[*Kneels with* Narcissa.

Sir Wil. Humh! what do'st thou mean? I am none of thy Father.

Y. Wor. This Lady is your Daughter, Sir, I hope.

Sir Wil. Prithee get up! prithee get up! thou art stark mad! True, I believe she may be my Daughter: Well, and so, Sir!

Y. Wor. If she be not, I'm certain she's my Wife, Sir.

Sir Wil. Humh! Mr. *Worthy,* pray, Sir, do me the Favour to help me to understand your Brother a little:—Do you know any thing of his being marry'd?

El. Wor. Then, without any Abuse, Sir *William,* he marry'd your Daughter this very Morning, not an Hour ago, Sir.

Sir Wil. Pray, Sir, whose Consent had you? Who advis'd you to it?

Y. Wor. Our mutual Love, and your Consent, Sir, with these Writings entitling her to a thousand Pounds a Year, and this Bond, whereby you have oblig'd your self to pay me five thousand Pounds on our Day of Marriage, are sufficient Proofs of.

Sir Wil. He, he; I gave your Brother such a Bond, Sir?

Y. Wor. You did so; but the Obligation is to me: Look there, Sir.

Sir Wil. Very good! this is my Hand, I must confess Sir: And what then?

Y. Wor. Why then, I expect my five thousand Pounds, Sir: Pray, Sir, do you know my Name?

Sir Wil. I am not drunk, Sir; I am sure it was *Worthy,* and *Jack,* or *Tom,* or *Dick,* or something.

Y. Wor. No, Sir, I'll shew you,—'tis *William;* look you there, Sir: You shou'd have taken more care of the Lawyer, Sir, that fill'd up the Blank.

El. Wor. So, now his Eyes are open.

Sir Wil. And have you marry'd my Daughter against my Consent, and trickt me out of five thousand Pounds, Sir?

Hil. His Brother, Sir, has marry'd me too with my Consent, and I am not trickt out of five thousand Pounds.

Sir Wil. Insulting Witch! Look ye, Sir, I never had a substantial Cause to be angry in my Life before: But now I have Reason on my side, I will indulge my Indignation most immoderately: I must confess, I have not Patience to wait the slow Redress of a tedious Law-Suit; therefore am resolv'd to right my self the nearest way;—Draw, draw, Sir: You must not enjoy my five thousand Pounds, tho' I fling as much more after it, in procuring a Pardon for killing you. [*They hold him.*] Let me come at him! I'll murder him! I'll cut him! I'll tear him, I'll broil him, and eat him! a Rogue! a Dog! a cursed Dog! a cut-throat, murdering Dog!

El. Wor. O fye, Sir *William,* how monstrous is this Passion?

Sir Wil. You have disarm'd me, but I shall find a time to poison him.

Lov. Think better on't, Sir *William,* your Daughter has marry'd a Gentleman, and one whose Love entitles him to her Person.

Sir Wil. Ay, but the five thousand Pounds, Sir! Why the very Report of his having such a Fortune, will ruin him. I'll warrant you, within this Week he will have more Duns at his Chamber in a Morning, than a gaming Lord after a good Night at the Groom-Porter's, or a Poet upon the fourth Day of his new Play. I shall never be pleased with paying it against my own Consent, Sir.

Hil. Yet you wou'd have had me done it, Sir *William:* But, however, I heartily wish you wou'd as freely forgive Mr. *Worthy,* as I do you, Sir.

Sir Wil. I must confess, this Girl's good Nature makes me asham'd of what I have offer'd: But, Mr. *Worthy,* I did not expect such Usage from a Man of your Character; I always took you for a Gentleman.

El. Wor. You shall find me no other, Sir. Brother, a Word with you.

Lov. Sir *William,* I have some Obligations to this Gentleman, and have so great a Confidence in your Daughter's Merit, and his Love, that I here promise to return you your five thousand Pounds, if after the Expiration of one Year, you are then dissatisfy'd in his being your Son-in-Law.

Y. Wor. But see, Brother, he has forestall'd your Purpose.

El. Wor. Mr. *Loveless,* you have been before-hand with me, but you must give me leave to offer Sir *William* my joint Security for what you promised him.

Lov. With all my Heart, Sir: Dare you take our Bonds, Sir *William?*

Y. Wor. Hold, Gentlemen! I shou'd blush to be oblig'd to that degree: Therefore, Sir *William,* as the first Proof of that Respect and Duty I owe a Father, I here, unask'd, return your Bond, and will henceforth expect nothing from you, but as my Conduct shall deserve it.

Am. This is indeed a generous Act; methinks 'twere pity it shou'd go unrewarded.

Sir Wil. Nay, now you vanquish me; after this, I can't suspect your future Conduct: There, Sir, 'tis yours, I acknowledge the Bond, and wish you all the Happiness of a bridal Bed. Heav'n's Blessing on you both: Now rise my Boy; and let the World know 'twas I set you upon your Legs again.

Y. Wor. I'll study to deserve your Bounty, Sir.

Lov. Now, Sir *William,* you have shewn your self a Father. This prudent Action has secur'd your Daughter from the usual Consequence of a stol'n Marriage, a Parent's Curse. Now she must be happy in her Love, while you have such a tender care on't.

Am. This is indeed a happy Meeting: We all of us have drawn our several Prizes in the Lottery of human Life; therefore I beg our Joys may be united: Not one of us must part this Day. The Ladies I'll intreat my Guests.

Lov. The rest are mine, and I hope will often be so.

Am. 'Tis yet too soon to dine; therefore, to divert us in the mean time, what think you of a little Musick? the Subject perhaps not improper to this Occasion.

El. Wor. 'Twill oblige us, Madam; we are all Lovers of it.

SCENE IV.

The SCENE draws, and discovers LOVE seated on a Throne, atended with a CHORUS.

FAME.

HAIL! hail! victorious Love!
To whom all Hearts below,
With no less Pleasure bow,

Than to the thundring Jove,
The happy Souls above.

Cho. Hail! *&c.*

Enter REASON.

REASON.

Cease, cease, fond Fools, your empty Noise,
And follow not such idle Joys:
Love gives you but a short-liv'd Bliss,
But I bestow immortal Happiness.

LOVE.

Rebellious Reason, *talk no more;*
Of all my Slaves, I thee abhor:
But thou, alas! do'st strive in vain
To free the Lover from a pleasing Chain:
In spite of Reason, Love *shall live and reign,*

Cho. In spite, *&c.*

A Martial Symphony.

Enter HONOUR.

What Wretch wou'd follow Love's *Alarms,*
When Honour's *Trumpet sounds to Arms!*
Hark! how the warlike Notes inspire
In ev'ry Breast a glowing Fire!

LOVE.

Hark! how it swells with Love and soft Desire!

HONOUR.

Behold, behold the marry'd State,
By thee too soon betray'd,
Repenting now too late.

Enter MARRIAGE *with his Yoke.*

MARRIAGE.

O! tell me cruel God of Love,
Why didst thou my Thoughts possess
With an eternal Round of Happiness?

And yet alas! I lead a wretched Life,
Doom'd to this galling Yoke,—the Emblem of a Wife!

LOVE.

Ungrateful Wretch! how dar'st thou Love *upbraid?*
I gave thee Raptures in the bridal Bed.

MARRIAGE.

Long since, alas! the airy Vision's fled,
And I, with wandring Flames, my Passion feed.
O! tell me, pow'rful God,
Where I shall find
My former Peace of Mind?

LOVE.

Where first I promis'd thee a happy Life,
There thou shalt find it in a virtuous Wife.

LOVE and FAME.

Go home, unhappy Wretch, and mourn
For all thy guilty Passion past;
There thou shalt those Joys return,
Which shall for ever, ever last.

End with the first *Chorus.*

Lov. 'Twas generously design'd, and all my Life to come shall shew how I approve the Moral. Oh! *Amanda!* once more receive me to thy Arms; and while I am there, let all the World confess my Happiness. By my Example taught, let every Man, whose Fate has bound him to a marry'd Life, beware of letting loose his wild Desires: For if Experience may be allow'd to judge, I must proclaim the Folly of a wandring Passion. The greatest Happiness we can hope on Earth,

And sure the nearest to the Joys above,
Is the chaste Rapture of a virtuous Love.

EPILOGUE,

Spoken by Miss *Cross,* (who sung CUPID.)

NOW, Gallants, for the Author. First, To you
Kind City-Gentlemen o'th'middle Row;
He hopes you nothing to his Charge can lay,
There's not a Cuckold made in all his Play.
Nay, you must own, if you believe your Eyes,
He draws his Pen against your Enemies:
For he declares, to Day, he merely strives
To maul the Beaux—because they maul your Wives.
Now, Sirs, To you whose sole Religion's Drinking,
Whoring, Roaring, without the Pain of Thinking,
He fears he's made a Fault you'll ne'er forgive,
A Crime beyond the Hopes of a Reprieve:
An honest Rake forego the Joys of Life!
His Whores, and Wine! t'Embrace a dull chaste Wife.
Such out-of-fashion Stuff! But then again,
He's lew'd for above four Acts, Gentlemen!
For faith, he knew, when once he'd chang'd his Fortune,
And reform'd his Vice, 'twas time—to drop the Curtain.
Four Acts for your course Palates were design'd,
But then the Ladies Taste is more refin'd,
They, for Amanda's *Sake, will sure be kind.*
Pray let this Figure once your Pity move:
Can you resist the pleading God of Love!
In vain my Pray'rs the other Sex pursue,
Unless your conq'ring Smiles their stubborn Hearts subdue.

THE

The Carelefs HUSBAND.

A

COMEDY.

As it is now Acted at the

THEATRE ROYAL
In *DRURY-LANE.*

By His MAJESTY's Servants.

By *C. CIBBER.*

Yet none Sir FOPLING *Him, or Him can call;*
He's Knight o'th' Shire, and Reprefents you All.
Prol. to Sir FOP.

Qui capit, ille facit.

LONDON:
Printed in the Year M.DCC.XXI.

To the Most Illustrious
JOHN,
DUKE of ARGYLE.

This Play, at last, through many Difficulties, has made way to throw it self at your Grace's Feet: And considering what well-meant Attempts were made to intercept it in its Course to so great an Honour, I have had reason not to think it intirely successful, till (where my Ambition always design'd it) I found it safe in your Protection: Which, when several Means had fail'd of making it less worthy of, the Spleen ended with the Old Good-nature that was offer'd to my First Play, *viz.* That it was none of my own. But that's a Praise I have indeed some reason to be proud of, since your Grace, from Evincing Circumstances, is able to divide the Malice from the Compliment.

The best Criticks have long and justly complain'd, that the Coarsness of most Characters in our late Comedies have been unfit Entertainments for People of Quality, especially the Ladies: And therefore I was long in hopes, that some able Pen (whose Expectation did not hang upon the Profits of Success) wou'd generously attempt to reform the Town into a better Taste than the World generally allows 'em: But nothing of that kind having lately appear'd, that would give me an Opportunity of being wise at another's Expence, I found it impossible any longer to resist the secret Temptation of my Vanity, and so e'en struck the first Blow my self: And the Event has now convinc'd me, that whoever sticks closely to Nature, can't easily write above the Understanding of the Galleries, tho' at the same time he may possibly deserve Applause of the Boxes.

This Play, before its Tryal on the Stage, was examined by several People of Quality, that came into your Grace's Opinion of its being a just, proper, and diverting Attempt in Comedy; but few of 'em carry'd the Compliment beyond their private Approbation: For when I was wishing for a little farther Hope, they stopt short of your Grace's Penetration, and only kindly wisht me what they seem'd to fear, and you assur'd me of, a General Success.

But your Grace has been pleas'd, not only to encourage me with your Judgment; but have likewise by your Favourable Influence in the Bounties that were rais'd for me the Third and Sixth Day, defended me against any Hazards of an entire Disappointment from so bold an Undertaking: And therefore, whatever the World may think of me, as one they call a *Poet;* yet I am confident, as your Grace understands me, I shall not want your Belief, when I assure you that this *Dedication* is the Result of a profound Acknowledgment, an Artless Inclination, proudly Glad, and Grateful.

And if the Dialogue of the following Scenes flows with more easie turn of Thought and Spirit, than what I have usually produc'd; I shall not yet blame some People for saying 'tis not my own, unless they knew at the same time I owe most of it to the many stollen Observations I have made from your Grace's manner of Conversing.

And if ever the Influence of your Grace's more shining Qualities should persuade me to attempt a *Tragedy,* I shall then with the same Freedom borrow all the Ornamental Virtues of my Hero, where now I only am indebted for part of the Fine Gentleman. Greatness of Birth and Mind, Sweetness of Temper, flowing from the fixt and Native Principles of Courage and of Honour, are Beauties that I reserve for a farther Opportunity of expressing the Zeal and Gratitude of,

My LORD,

Your GRACE'*s Most Obedient,*
Most Obliged and Humble Servant,
COLLEY CIBBER.

THE PROLOGUE.

Of all the various Vices of the Age,
And Shoals of Fools expos'd upon the Stage,
How few are lasht that call for Satyr's Rage!
What can you think, to see our Plays so full
Of Madmen, Coxcombs, and the driveling Fool;
Of Citts, of Sharpers, Rakes and roaring Bullies,
Of Cheats, of Cuckolds, Aldermen and Cullies?
Wou'd not one swear, 'twere taken for a Rule,
That Satyr's Rod in the Dramatick School
Was only meant for the Incorrigible Fool?
As if too Vice and Folly were confin'd
To the vile Scum alone of Human Kind;
Creatures a Muse should Scorn, such abject Trash
Deserve not Satyr's, but the Hangman's Lash.
Wretches so far shut out from Sense of Shame
Newgate *or* Bedlam *only shou'd reclaim;*
For Satyr ne'er was meant to make wild Monsters tame.
No, Sirs—
We rather think the Persons fit for Plays,
Are they whose Birth and Education says
They've ev'ry Help that shou'd improve Mankind,
Yet still live Slaves to a vile tainted Mind;
Such as in Wit are often seen t'abound
And yet have some weak Part, where Folly's found:
For Follies sprout like Weeds, highest in Fruitful Ground.
And 'tis observ'd, the Garden of the Mind
To no infestive Weed's so much inclin'd,
As the rank Pride that some from Affectation find.
A Folly too well known to make its Court

With most Success among the better Sort.
Such are the Persons we to day provide,
And Nature's Fools for once are laid aside.
This is the Ground on which our Play we build;
But in the Structure must to Judgment yield:
And where the Poet fails in Art, or Care,
We bet your wonted Mercy to the Player.

PROLOGUE

Upon the last Campaign.

Written by a Person of Quality; design'd for the Sixth Day, but not spoken.

A Paying Nation hates the Fighting Trade,
And Lingring War in usual Methods made:
When Armies walk about from Wood to River,
And Threescore Thousand only get together
To Eat, and Drink, consult, and find the way
How without Fighting they may earn their Pay;
When prudent Generals get, by Safeguard giving,
An honest, quiet, comfortable Living;
But never fight it up to a Thanksgiving.
These manage War with the Physicians Skill,
And use such means as neither Cure, nor Kill:
Like the wise Doctors, safe by their Degrees,
They give weak Doses, but take swinging Fees.
The Trade continuing, which can never end,
While the sick State has any thing to spend.
Thanks then to him who strikes at the Disease,
And bravely tries to set the World at Ease:
For if such Fighting last but one Year more,
Two Danube *Victories will quit the score,*
And soon recruit our almost lavish'd Store.
A happy Peace regains our Treasure lost,
Our own the Glory, and our Foes the Cost.
No Favour let the Homebred Sparks expect
But Scorn from Men, and from the Fair Neglect.
Beaux, that spend all their Time in soft Love-making;
Those tender Souls, whose Hearts are always aking,
Shun 'em, ye Fair, prevent their Am'rous Boasting;

Nor poorly yield to idle Talk, and Toasting.
If you have Favours, which you must bestow,
Give 'em the Soldiers, they deserve 'em now;
Who make proud Tyrants stoop, should only Kneel to you.
Minerva *guides our General to Fame,*
No Cruelties in War affect his Name,
Mild in the Camp, by no Success made vain.
A Gentle Goddess animates his Mind;
Bold for his Friends, to Conquer'd Foes as Kind,
Design'd by Heav'n for Anna's *happy Reign,*
Whose generous Soul seeks only to restrain
Unbounded Tyranny, and lawless Might,
Revenge Oppression, and restore the Right:
War not her Choice, but necessary Fence,
Truth to promote, and humble Insolence.
Where-e'er her Influence flys, it Joy creates,
And Peace and Safety brings to distant States:
With such Success her Chief begins his Race,
That his first Battel brightly does efface
The Tedious Labours of our Modern Wars;
Out-does at once old Soldiers, and the Tars.
In him no sauntring in the Field we find,
No Doubt remains where Victory inclin'd.
His Sword decides, no double Praise is giv'n,
Where neither side is pleas'd, yet both thank Heav'n.
From War he quickly Kingdoms will release:
Rapine and Rage soon turn to Joy and Peace,
And by Destruction make Destruction cease.

Dramatis Personae.

MEN.

Lord Morelove,	Mr. *Powel.*
Lord Foppington,	Mr. *Cibber.*
Sir Charles Easy,	Mr. *Wilks.*

WOMEN.

Lady Betty Modish,	Mrs. *Oldfield.*
Lady Easy,	Mrs. *Knight.*
Lady Graveairs,	Mrs. *More.*
Mrs. Edging, *Woman to Lady* Easy,	Mrs. *Lucas.*

SCENE, *WINDSOR.*

THE

Careless HUSBAND.

ACT I. SCENE I.

SCENE, *Sir* Charles Easy*'s Lodgings.*

Enter Lady Easy *alone.*

Lady Ea. Was ever Woman's Spirit, by an injurious Husband, broke like mine? A vile, licentious Man! must he bring home his Follies too? Wrong me with my very Servant! O! how tedious a Relief is Patience! and yet in my Condition 'tis the only Remedy: For to reproach him with my Wrongs, is taking on my self the Means of a Redress, bidding Defiance to his Falshood, and naturally but provokes him to undo me. Th' uneasy Thought of my continual Jealousy may teaze him to a fixt Aversion; and hitherto, though he neglects, I cannot think he hates me.—It must be so; since I want Power to please him, he never shall upbraid me with an Attempt of making him uneasy—My Eyes and Tongue shall yet be blind and silent to my Wrongs; nor would I have him think my Virtue cou'd suspect him, till by some gross, apparent Proof of his Misdoing, he forces me to see,—and to forgive it.

Enter Edging *hastily.*

Edg. O Madam!

Lady Ea. What's the matter?

Edg. I have the strangest thing to shew your Ladyship—such a Discovery—

Lady Ea. You are resolv'd to make it without much Ceremony, I find—What's the Business, pray?

Edg. The Business, Madam! I have not Patience to tell you, I am out of Breath at the very Thoughts on't, I shall not be able to speak this half Hour.

Lady Ea. Not to the Purpose, I believe; but methinks you talk impertinently with a great deal of Ease.

Edg. Nay, Madam, perhaps not so impertinent as your Ladyship thinks; there's that will speak to the purpose, I am sure—A base Man— [*Gives a Letter.*

Lady Ea. What's this, an open Letter? Whence comes it?

Edg. Nay, read it, Madam, you'll soon guess—If these are the Tricks of Husbands, keep me a Maid still, say I.

Lady Ea. [*Looking on the Superscription.*] To Sir *Charles Easy!* Ha! Too well I know this hateful hand—O my Heart? But I must veil my Jealousy which 'tis not fit this Creature should suppose I am acquainted with [*Aside.*]—This Direction is to your Master, how came you by it?

Edg. Why, Madam, as my Master was lying down, after he came in from Hunting, he sent me into his Dressing Room to fetch his Snuff-Box out of his Wastcoat-Pocket; and so, as I was searching for the Box, Madam, there I found this wicked Letter from a Mistress; which I had no sooner read, but, I declare it, my very Blood rose at him again, methought I could have torn him and her to pieces.

Lady Ea. Intolerable! This odious Thing's jealous of him her self, and wants me to join with her in a Revenge upon him—Sure I am fallen indeed! But 'twere to make me lower yet, to let her think I understand her. [*Aside.*

Edg. Nay, pray, Madam, read it; you'll be out of Patience at it.

Lady Ea. You are bold, Mistress; has my Indulgence of your Master's good Humour flatter'd you into the Assurance of reading his Letters?—A Liberty I never gave my self.—Here—lay it where you had it immediately—Shou'd he know of your Sauciness, 'twou'd not be my Favour cou'd protect you. [*Exit Lady* Easy.

Edg. Your Favour! Marry come up! Sure I don't depend upon your Favour!—'Tis not come to that, I hope—Poor Creature!—don't you think I am my Master's Mistress for nothing—you shall find, Madam, I won't be snapt up as I have been—Not but it vexes me to think she shou'd not be as uneasy as I. I am sure he's a base Man to me, and I could cry my Eyes out that she shou'd not think him as bad to her every jot. If I am wrong'd, sure she may very well expect it, that is but his Wife—A conceited Thing—she need not be so easy neither—I am as handsom as she, I hope—Here's my Master,—I'll try whether I am to be huff'd by her, or no. [*Walks behind.*

Enter Sir Charles Easy.

Sir Cha. So! the Day is come again—Life but rises to another Stage, and the same dull Journey is before us—How like Children do we judge of Happiness! When I was stinted in my Fortune, almost every thing was a Pleasure to me, because most things then being out of my Reach, I had always the Pleasure of hoping for 'em; now Fortune's in my hand, she's as insipid as an old Acquaintance—It's mighty silly, Faith—Just the same thing by my Wife too; I am told she's extreamly handsom—nay, and I have heard a great many People say she is certainly the best Woman in the World—why, I don't know but she may; yet I could never find that her Person, or good Qualities, gave me any Concern—In my Eye the Woman has no more Charms than my Mother.

Edg. Hum!—he takes no Notice of me yet—I'll let him see, I can take as little Notice of him. [*She walks by him gravely, he turns her about and holds her, she struggles.*] Pray, Sir.

Sir Cha. A pretty pert Air that—I'll humour it—What's the matter, Child? Are you not well? Kiss me, Hussy.

Edg. No, the Duce fetch me, if I do.

Sir Cha. Has any thing put thee out of Humour, Love?

Edg. No, Sir, 'tis not worth my being out of Humour at—tho' if ever you have any thing to say to me again, I'll be burn'd.

Sir Cha. Some body has bely'd me to thee.

Edg. No, Sir, 'tis you have bely'd your self to me—did not I ask you, when you first made a Fool of me, if you would be always constant to me, and did not you say, I might be sure you wou'd? And here, instead of that, you are going on in your old Intrigue with my Lady *Graveairs*—

Sir Cha. So—

Edg. Beside, don't you suffer my Lady to huff me every day, as if I were her Dog, or had no more Concern with you—I declare I won't bear it, and she shan't think to huff me—for ought I know, I am as agreeable as she; and tho' she dares not take any Notice of your Baseness to her, you shan't think to use me so—and so pray take your nasty Letter—I know the Hand well enough. For my part, I won't stay in the Family to be abus'd at this rate—I that have refus'd Lords and Dukes for your sake—I'd have you to know, Sir, I have had as many Blue and Green Ribbons after me, for ought I know, as would have made me a Falbala Apron.

Sir Cha. My Lady *Graveairs!* my nasty Letter! and I won't stay in the Family!—Death! I'm in a pretty Condition—What an unlimited Privilege has this Jade got from being a Whore?

Edg. I suppose, Sir, you think to use every body as you do your Wife.

Sir Cha. My Wife, hah! Come hither, Mrs. *Edging;* hark you, Drab. [*Seizing her by the Shoulder.*

Edg. Oh!

Sir Cha. When you speak of my Wife, you are to say your Lady, and you are never to speak of your Lady to me in any regard of her being my Wife—for look you, Child, you are not Her Strumpet, but Mine, therefore I only give you leave to be saucy with me;—in the next place, you are never to suppose there is any such Person as my Lady *Graveairs;* and lastly, my pretty one, how came you by this Letter?

Edg. It's no matter, perhaps.

Sir Cha. Ay, but if you should not tell me quickly, how are you sure I won't take a great Piece of Flesh out of your Shoulder?—My Dear. [*Shakes her.*

Edg. O lud! O lud! I will tell you, Sir.

Sir Cha. Quickly then— [*Again.*

Edg. Oh! I took it out of your Pocket, Sir.

Sir Cha. When?

Edg. Oh! this Morning, when you sent me for your Snuff-box.

Sir Cha. And your Ladyship's pretty Curiosity has look'd it over, I presume—ha— [*Again.*

Edg. O lud! dear Sir, don't be angry—indeed I'll never touch one again.

Sir Cha. I don't believe you will, and I'll tell you how you shall be sure you never will.

Edg. Yes, Sir.

Sir Cha. By stedfastly believing that the next time you offer it, you will have your pretty white Neck twisted behind you.

Edg. Yes, Sir. [*Curtesing.*

Sir Cha. And you will be sure to remember every thing I have said to you?

Edg. Yes, Sir.

Sir Cha. And now, Child, I was not angry with your Person, but your Follies; which since I find you are a little sensible of—don't be wholly discourag'd—for I believe I—I shall have Occasion for you again—

Edg. Yes, Sir.

Sir Cha. In the mean time let me hear no more of your Lady, Child.

Edg. No, Sir.

Sir Cha. Here she comes, be gone.

Edg. Yes, Sir—Oh! I was never so frighten'd in my Life. [*Exit.*

Sir Cha. So! good Discipline makes good Soldiers—It often puzzles me to think, from my own Carelessness, and my Wife's continual good Humour, whether she really knows any thing of the strength of my Forces—I'll sift her a little.

Enter Lady Easy.

My Dear, how do you do? You are dress'd very early to Day; are you going out?

Lady Ea. Only to Church, my Dear.

Sir Cha. Is it so late then?

Lady Ea. The Bell has just rung.

Sir Cha. Well, Child, how does *Windsor* Air agree with you? Do you find your self any better yet? or have you a mind to go to *London* again?

Lady Ea. No, indeed, my Dear; the Air's so very pleasant, that if it were a Place of less Company, I could be content to end my Days here.

Sir Cha. Prithee, my Dear, what sort of Company would most please you?

Lady Ea. When Business wou'd permit it, Yours; and in your Absence a sincere Friend, that were truly happy in an honest

Husband, to sit a chearful Hour, and talk in mutual Praise of our Condition.

Sir Cha. Are you then really very happy, my Dear?

Lady Ea. Why shou'd you question it? [*Smiling on him.*

Sir Cha. Because I fancy I am not so good to you as I shou'd be.

Lady Ea. Pshah!

Sir Cha. Nay, the Duce take me if I don't really confess my self so bad, that I have often wonder'd how any Woman of your Sense, Rank and Person, could think it worth her while to have so many useless good Qualities.

Lady Ea. Fie, my Dear.

Sir Cha. By my Soul, I'm serious.

Lady Ea. I can't boast of my good Qualities; nor if I could, do I believe you think 'em useless.

Sir Cha. Nay, I submit to you–Don't you find 'em so? Do you perceive that I am one Tittle the better Husband for your being so good a Wife?

Lady Ea. Pshah! you jest with me.

Sir Cha. Upon my Life I don't.–Tell me truly, was you never jealous of me?

Lady Ea. Did I ever give you any Sign of it?

Sir Cha. Um–that's true–but do you really think I never gave you Occasion?

Lady Ea. That's an odd question–but suppose you had?

Sir Cha. Why then, what good has your Virtue done you, since all the good Qualities of it could not keep me to your self?

Lady Ea. What Occasion have you given me to suppose I have not kept you to my self?

Sir Cha. I given you Occasion–Fie! my Dear–you may be sure I–I–look you, that is not the thing; but still a–(Death! what a Blunder have I made!)–a still, I say, Madam, you shan't make me believe you have never been jealous of me; not that you ever had any real Cause, but I know Women of your Principles have more Pride than those that have no Principles at all; and where there is Pride, there must be some Jealousy–so that if you are jealous, my Dear, you know you wrong me, and–

Lady Ea. Why then upon my Word, my Dear, I don't know that ever I wrong'd you that way in my Life.

Sir Cha. But suppose I had given you a real Cause to be jealous; how would you do then?

Lady Ea. It must be a very substantial one that makes me jealous.

Sir Cha. Say it were a substantial one; suppose now I were well with a Woman of your own Acquaintance, that under pretence of frequent Visits to you, shou'd only come to carry on an Affair with me—Suppose now my Lady *Graveairs* and I were great—

Lady Ea. Wou'd I could not suppose it. [*Aside.*

Sir Cha. If I come off here, I believe I am pretty safe—[*Aside.*] Suppose, I say, my Lady and I were so very familiar, that not only your self, but half the Town should see it.

Lady Ea. Then I should cry my self sick in some dark Closet, and forget my Tears when you spoke kindly to me.

Sir Cha. The most convenient piece of Virtue sure that ever Wife was Mistress of. [*Aside.*

Lady Ea. But pray, my Dear, did you ever think that I had any ill Thoughts of my Lady *Graveairs?*

Sir Cha. O Fie! Child, only you know she and I us'd to be a little free sometimes, so I had a Mind to see if you thought there was any harm in it: But since I find you very easy, I think my self oblig'd to tell you, that upon my Soul, my Dear, I have so little regard to her Person, that the Duce take me, if I would not as soon have an Affair with thy own Woman.

Lady Ea. Indeed, my Dear, I should as soon suspect you with one as t'other.

Sir Cha. Poor Dear—shou'dst thou—give me a Kiss.

Lady Ea. Pshah! you don't care to kiss me.

Sir Cha. By my Soul I do—I wish I may die, if I don't think you are a very fine Woman.

Lady Ea. I only wish you wou'd think me a good Wife. [*Kisses her.*] But pray, my Dear, what has made you so strangely Inquisitive?

Sir Cha. Inquisitive—Why—a—I don't know, one's always saying one foolish thing or another—Toll le roll. [*Sings and talks.*] My Dear, what! are we never to have any Ball here? Toll le roll. I fancy I could recover my Dancing again, if I would but practise, Toll loll loll!

Lady Ea. This Excess of Carelessness to me excuses half his Vices, if I can make him once think seriously—Time yet may be my Friend.

Enter a Servant.

Serv. Sir, my Lord *Morelove* gives his Service—

Sir Cha. Lord *Morelove!* where is he?

Serv. At the Chocolate-House; he call'd me to him as I went by, and bid me tell your Honour he'll wait upon you presently.

Lady Ea. I thought you had not expected him here again this Season, my Dear.

Sir Cha. I thought so too; but you see there's no depending upon the Resolution of a Man that's in Love.

Lady Ea. Is there a Chair?

Serv. Yes, Madam. [*Exit Servant.*

Lady Ea. I suppose Lady *Betty Modish* has drawn him hither.

Sir Cha. Ay, poor Soul, for all his Bravery, I am afraid so.

Lady Ea. Well, my Dear, I han't time to ask my Lord how he does now; you'll excuse me to him, but I hope you'll make him Dine with us.

Sir Cha. I'll ask him; if you see Lady *Betty* at Prayers, make her Dine too; but don't take any notice of my Lord's being in Town.

Lady Ea. Very well! if I should not meet her there, I'll call at her Lodgings.

Sir Cha. Do so.

Lady Ea. My Dear, your Servant. [*Exit Lady* Easy.

Sir Cha. My Dear, I'm yours. Well! one way or other this Woman will certainly bring about her Business with me at last; for tho' she can't make me happy in her own Person, she lets me be so intolerably easie with the Women that can, that she has at least brought me into a fair way of being as weary of them too.

Enter Servant and Lord Morelove.

Serv. Sir, my Lord's come.

Lord Mo. Dear *Charles!*

Sir Cha. My dear Lord! this is an Happiness undreamt of; I little thought to have seen you at *Windsor* again this Season; I concluded of course, that Books and Solitude had secur'd you till Winter.

Lord Mo. Nay, I did not think of coming my self; but I found my self not very well in *London,* so I thought—a—little Hunting, and this Air—

Sir Cha. Ha! ha! ha!

Lord Mo. What do you laugh at?

Sir Cha. Only because you should not go on with your Story: If you did but see how sillily a Man fumbles for an Excuse, when he's a little asham'd of being in Love, you would not wonder what I laugh at, ha! ha!

Lord Mo. Thou art a very happy Fellow—nothing touches thee—always easy—Then you conclude I follow Lady *Betty* again?

Sir Cha. Yes, Faith do I; and to make you easy, my Lord, I cannot see why a Man that can ride fifty Miles after a poor Stag, should be asham'd of running twenty in chase of a fine Woman, that, in all Probability, will make him so much the better Sport too. [*Embracing.*

Lord Mo. Dear *Charles,* don't flatter my Distemper; I own I still follow her: Do you think her Charms have Power to excuse me to the World!

Sir Cha. Ay! ay! a fine Woman's an Excuse for any thing; and the Scandal of being her Jest, is a Jest it self; we are all forc'd to be their Fools, before we can be their Favourites.

Lord Mo. You are willing to give me hope, but I can't believe she has the least degree of Inclination for me.

Sir Cha. I don't know that—I'm sure her Pride likes you, and that's generally your fine Lady's darling Passion.

Lord Mo. Do you suppose if I could grow indifferent, it wou'd touch her?

Sir Cha. Sting her to the Heart—Will you take my Advice?

Lord Mo. I have no Relief but that; had I not thee now and then to talk an Hour, my Life were insupportable.

Sir Cha. I am sorry for that, my Lord—but mind what I say to you—But hold, first let me know the Particulars of your late Quarrel with her.

Lord Mo. Why—about three Weeks ago, when I was last here at *Windsor,* she had for some Days treated me with a little more Reserve, and another with more Freedom, than I found my self easy at.

Sir Cha. Who was that other?

Lord Mo. One of my Lord *Foppington*'s Gang, the pert Coxcomb that's just come to a small Estate, and a great Perriwig—he that Sings himself among the Women—What d'ye call him?—He won't speak to a Commoner, when a Lord's in Company—You always see him with a Cane dangling at his Button, his Breast open, no Gloves, one Eye tuck'd under his Hat, and a Tooth-pick—*Startup,* that's his Name.

Sir Cha. O! I have met him in a Visit—but pray go on.

Lord Mo. So, disputing with her about the Conduct of Women, I took the liberty to tell her, how far I thought she err'd in hers; she told me I was rude, and that she would never believe any Man could love a Woman, that thought her in the wrong in any thing she had a mind to, at least, if he dar'd to tell her so—This provok'd me into her whole Character, with as much Spite and civil Malice, as I have seen her bestow upon a Woman of true Beauty, when the Men first toasted her; so in the middle of my Wisdom, she told me, she desir'd to be alone, that I would take my odious proud Heart along with me, and trouble her no more—I—bow'd very low, and as I left the Room, vow'd I never wou'd, and that my proud Heart should never be humbled by the Outside of a fine Woman—About an Hour after, I whipp'd into my Chaise for *London,* and have never seen her since.

Sir Cha. Very well, and how did you find your proud Heart by that time you got to *Hounslow?*

Lord Mo. I'm almost asham'd to tell you—I found her so much in the right, that I curs'd my Pride for contradicting her at all, and began to think, according to her Maxim, that no Woman could be in the wrong to a Man that she had in her Power.

Sir Cha. Ha! ha! well, I'll tell you what you shall do. You can see her without trembling, I hope.

Lord Mo. Not if she receives me well.

Sir Cha. If she receives you well, you will have no occasion for what I am going to say to you—First, you shall dine with her.

Lord Mo. How! where! when!

Sir Cha. Here! here! at two a Clock.

Lord Mo. Dear *Charles!*

Sir Cha. My Wife's gone to invite her; when you see her first, be neither too humble, nor too stubborn; let her see by the Ease in your Behaviour, you are still pleas'd in being near her, while she is upon reasonable Terms with you. This will either open the Door of an *Ecclarcisement,* or quite shut it against you—and if she is still resolv'd to keep you out—

Lord Mo. Nay, if she insults me then, perhaps I may recover Pride enough to rally her by an over-acted Submission.

Sir Cha. Why you improve, my Lord; this is the very thing I was going to propose to you.

Lord Mo. Was it, Faith! Hark you, dare you stand by me?

Sir Cha. Dare I! ay, to my last drop of Assurance, against all the insolent Airs of the proudest Beauty in *Christendom.*

Lord Mo. Nay, then Defiance to her—We two—Thou hast inspir'd me, I find my self as valiant as a flatter'd Coward.

Sir Cha. Courage, my Lord—I'll warrant we beat her.

Lord Mo. My Blood stirs at the very thought on't; I long to be engag'd.

Sir Cha. She'll certainly give Ground, when she once sees you are thoroughly provok'd.

Lord Mo. Dear *Charles,* thou art a Friend indeed.

Enter a Servant.

Serv. Sir, my Lord *Foppington* gives his Service, and if your Honour's at Leisure, he'll wait on you as soon as he is dress'd.

Lord Mo. Lord *Foppington!* is he in Town?

Sir Cha. Yes—I heard last Night he was come. Give my Service to his Lordship, and tell him, I shall be glad he'll do me the Honour of his Company here at Dinner. [*Exit Servant.*] We may have Occasion for him in our Design upon Lady *Betty.*

Lord Mo. What Use can we make of him?

Sir Cha. We'll see when he comes; at least there's no Danger in him; not but I suppose you know he's your Rival.

Lord Mo. Pshah! a Coxcomb.

Sir Cha. Nay, don't despise him neither—he's able to give you Advice; for tho' he's in Love with the same Woman, yet to him she has not Charms enough to give a Minute's Pain.

Lord Mo. Prithee, what Sense has he of Love?

Sir Cha. Faith very near as much as a Man of Sense ought to have. I grant you, he knows not how to value a Woman truly deserving, but he has a pretty just Esteem for most Ladies about Town.

Lord Mo. That he follows, I grant you—for he seldom visits any of extraordinary Reputation.

Sir Cha. Have a care, I have seen him at Lady *Betty Modish*'s.

Lord Mo. To be laugh'd at.

Sir Cha. Don't be too confident of that; the Women now begin to laugh *with* him, not *at* him: For he really sometimes rallies his own Humour with so much Ease and Pleasantry, that a great many Women begin to think he has no Follies at all; and those he has, have been as much owing to his Youth, and a great Estate, as want of natural Wit: Tis true, he's often a Bubble to his Pleasures, but he has always been wisely vain enough to keep himself from being too much the Ladies humble Servant in Love.

Lord Mo. There indeed I almost envy him.

Sir Cha. The Easiness of his Opinion upon the Sex, will go near to pique you—We must have him.

Lord Mo. As you please—but what shall we do with our selves till Dinner?

Sir Cha. What think you of a Party at Picquet?

Lord Mo. O! you are too hard for me.

Sir Cha. Fie! fie! what, when you play with his Grace?

Lord Mo. Upon my Soul, he gives me three Points.

Sir Cha. Does he? why then you shall give me but two—Here, Fellow, get Cards. *Allons.* [*Exeunt.*

ACT II. SCENE I.

The SCENE, *Lady* Betty Modish's *Lodgings.*

Enter Lady Betty, *and Lady* Easy, *meeting.*

Lady Bet. Oh! my Dear! I am overjoy'd to see you! I am strangely happy to day; I have just receiv'd my new Scarf from *London,* and you are most critically come to give me your Opinion of it.

Lady Ea. O! your Servant, Madam, I am a very indifferent Judge, you know: What is it with Sleeves?

Lady Bet. O! 'tis impossible to tell you what it is—'Tis all Extravagance both in Mode and Fancy; my Dear, I believe there's Six Thousand Yards of Edging in it—Then such an enchanting Slope from the Elbow—something so New, so Lively, so Noble, so Coquet and Charming—but you shall see it, my Dear—

Lady Ea. Indeed I won't, my Dear; I am resolv'd to mortify you for being so wrongly fond of a Trifle.

Lady Bet. Nay now, my Dear, you are Ill-natur'd.

Lady Ea. Why truly I'm half angry, to see a Woman of your Sense so warmly concern'd in the Care of her Outside; for when we have taken our best Pains about it, 'tis the Beauty of the Mind alone that gives us lasting Value.

Lady Bet. Ah! my Dear, my Dear! you have been a married Woman to a fine purpose indeed, that know so little of the Taste of Mankind: Take my Word, a new Fashion, upon a fine Woman, is often a greater Proof of her Value, than you are aware of.

Lady Ea. That I can't comprehend; for you see, among the Men, nothing's more ridiculous than a new Fashion, those of the first Sense are always the last that come into 'em.

Lady Bet. That is, because the only Merit of a Man is his Sense; but doubtless the greatest Value of a Woman is her Beauty. An homely Woman at the Head of a Fashion, would not be allow'd in it by the Men, and consequently not follow'd by the Women: So that to be successful in one's Fancy, is an evident sign of one's being admir'd, and I always take Admiration for the best Proof of

Beauty, and Beauty certainly is the Source of Power, as Power in all Creatures is the heighth of Happiness.

Lady Ea. At this rate you had rather be thought Beautiful than Good.

Lady Bet. As I had rather Command than Obey: The wisest homely Woman can't make a Man of Sense of a Fool, but the veriest Fool of a Beauty, shall make an Ass of a Statesman; so that in short, I can't see a Woman of Spirit has any Business in this World but to dress–and make the Men like her.

Lady Ea. Do you suppose this is a Principle the Men of Sense will admire you for?

Lady Bet. I do suppose, that when I suffer any Man to like my Person, he shan't dare to find Fault with my Principle.

Lady Ea. But Men of Sense are not so easily humbled.

Lady Bet. The easiest of any; one has ten thousand times the Trouble with a Coxcomb.

Lady Ea. Nay, that may be; for I have seen you throw away more good Humour in hopes of a *Tendresse* from my Lord *Foppington,* who loves all Women alike, than would have made my Lord *Morelove* perfectly happy, who loves only you.

Lady Bet. The Men of Sense, my Dear, make the best Fools in the World; their Sincerity and good Breeding throws 'em so entirely into one's Power, and gives one such an agreeable Thirst of using 'em ill, to shew that Power–'tis impossible not to quench it.

Lady Ea. But methinks, my Lord *Morelove*'s Manner to you might move any Woman to a kinder Sense of his Merit.

Lady Bet. Ay! but would it not be hard, my Dear, for a poor weak Woman to have a Man of his Quality and Reputation in her Power, and not let the World see him there? Wou'd any Creature sit New dress'd all day in her Closet? Cou'd you bear to have a sweet-fancy'd Suit, and never shew it at the Play, or the Drawing-Room?

Lady Ea. But one wou'd not ride in it, methinks, or harrass it out when there's no occasion.

Lady Bet. Pooh! my Lord *Morelove*'s a meer *Indian* Damask, one can't wear him out; o' my Conscience I must give him to my Woman at last, I begin to be known by him: Had not I best leave him off, my Dear? For (poor Soul) I believe I have a little fretted him of late.

Lady Ea. Now 'tis to me amazing, how a Man of his Spirit can bear to be us'd like a Dog for Four or Five Years together—but nothing's a Wonder in Love; yet pray, when you found you could not like him at first, why did you ever encourage him?

Lady Bet. Why, what wou'd you have one do? For my part, I could no more chuse a Man by my Eye, than a Shoe; one must draw 'em on a little to see if they are right to one's Foot.

Lady Ea. But I'd no more fool on with a Man I could not like, than I'd wear a Shoe that pinch'd me.

Lady Bet. Ay, but then a poor Wretch tells one, he'll widen 'em, or do any thing, and is so civil and silly, that one does not know how to turn such a Trifle as a pair of Shoes, or an Heart, upon a Fellow's Hands again.

Lady Ea. Well! I confess you are very happily distinguish'd among most Women of Fortune, to have a Man of my Lord *More-love*'s Sense and Quality so long and honourably in Love with you: For now-a-days one hardly ever hears of such a thing as a Man of Quality in Love with the Woman he wou'd marry: To be in Love now, is only having a Design upon a Woman, a modish way of declaring War against her Virtue, which they generally attack first, by toasting up her Vanity.

Lady Bet. Ay! but the World knows, that is not the case between my Lord and me.

Lady Ea. Therefore I think you happy.

Lady Bet. Now I don't see it; I'll swear I'm better pleas'd to know there are a great many foolish Fellows of Quality that take Occasion to toast me frequently.

Lady Ea. I vow I should not thank any Gentleman for toasting me; and I have often wonder'd how a Woman of your Spirit cou'd bear a great many other Freedoms I have seen some Men take with you.

Lady Bet. As how, my Dear? Come, prithee be free with me; for you must know, I love dearly to hear my Faults—Who is't you have observ'd to be too free with me?

Lady Ea. Why there's my Lord *Foppington;* cou'd any Woman but you, bear to see him with a respectful Fleer stare full in her Face, draw up his Breath, and cry—Gad, you're handsome?

Lady Bet. My Dear, fine Fruit will have Flies about it; but, poor things, they do it no harm: For, if you observe, People are generally most apt to chuse that that the Flies have been busy with, ha! ha!

Lady Ea. Thou art a strange giddy Creature.

Lady Bet. That may be from so much Circulation of Thought, my Dear.

Lady Ea. But my Lord *Foppington*'s married, and one wou'd not fool with him for his Lady's sake; it may make her uneasy, and—

Lady Bet. Poor Creature, her Pride indeed makes her carry it off without taking any Notice of it to me; tho' I know she hates me in her Heart, and I can't endure malicious People; so I us'd to dine there once a Week, purely to give her Disorder; if you had but seen, when my Lord and I fool'd a little, the Creature look'd so ugly!

Lady Ea. But I should not think my Reputation safe; my Lord *Foppington*'s a Man that talks often of his Amours, but seldom speaks of Favours that are refus'd him.

Lady Bet. Pshah! will any thing a Man says make a Woman less agreeable? Will his talking spoil one's Complexion, or put one's Hair out of Order?—and for Reputation, look you, my Dear, take it for a Rule, that as amongst the lower Rank of People, no Woman wants Beauty that has Fortune; so amongst People of Fortune, no Woman wants Virtue that has Beauty: But an Estate and Beauty join'd, is of an unlimited, nay, a Power Pontifical, makes one not only Absolute, but Infallible—A fine Woman's never in the wrong, or if we were, 'tis not the strength of a poor Creature's Reason that can unfetter him—O! how I love to hear a Wretch curse himself for loving on, or now and then coming out with a—

"Yet for the Plague of human Race,
"This Devil has an Angel's Face.

Lady Ea. At this rate, I don't see you allow Reputation to be at all Essential to a fine Woman.

Lady Bet. Just as much as Honour to a great Man: Power always is above Scandal: Don't you hear People say, the King of *France* owes most of his Conquests to breaking his Word? and wou'd not the Confederates have a fine time on't, if they were only to go to War with Reproaches? Indeed, my Dear, that Jewel Reputation is a very fanciful Business; one shall not see an homely Creature in Town, but wears it in her Mouth as monstrously as the *Indians* do Bobs at their Lips, and it really becomes 'em just alike.

Lady Ea. Have a care, my Dear, of trusting too far to Power alone: For nothing is more ridiculous than the Fall of Pride; and Woman's Pride at best may be suspected to be more a Distrust, than a real Contempt of Mankind: For when we have said all we can, a deserving Husband is certainly our best Happiness; and I don't question but my Lord *Morelove*'s Merit, in a little time, will make you think so too; for whatever Airs you give your self to the World, I am sure your Heart don't want good Nature.

Lady Bet. You are mistaken, I am very ill-natur'd, tho' your good Humour won't let you see it.

Lady Ea. Then to give me a Proof on't let me see you refuse to go immediately and Dine with me, after I have promis'd Sir *Charles* to bring you.

Lady Bet. Pray don't ask me.

Lady Ea. Why?

Lady Bet. Because, to let you see I hate good Nature, I'll go without asking, that you mayn't have the Malice to say I did you a Favour.

Lady Ea. Thou art a mad Creature. [*Exeunt Arm in Arm.*

SCENE II.

The SCENE *changes to Sir* Charles*'s Lodgings. Lord* Morelove *and Sir* Charles *at Picquet.*

Sir Cha. Come, my Lord, one single Game for the Tout, and so have done.

Lord Mo. No, hang 'em, I have enough of 'em: Ill Cards are the dullest Company in the World—How much is it?

Sir Cha. Three Parties.

Lord Mo. Fifteen Pound—very well.

[*While Lord* Morelove *counts out his Money, a Servant gives Sir* Charles *a Letter, which he reads to himself.*

Sir Cha. [*To the Servant.*] Give my Service, say, I have Company dines with me; if I have time, I'll call there in the Afternoon—ha! ha! ha! [*Exit Servant.*

Lord Mo. What's the Matter—There— [*Paying the Money.*

Sir Cha. The old Affair—my Lady *Graveairs.*

Lord Mo. O! prithee, how does that go on?

Sir Cha. As agreeably as a *Chancery* Suit: For now it's come to the intolerable Plague of my not being able to get rid on't; as you may see— [*Giving the Letter.*

Lord Mo. [*Reads.*] "Your Behaviour since I came to *Windsor* has
"convinc'd me of your Villainy without my being surpriz'd,
"or angry at it: I desire you would let me see you at my
"Lodgings immediately, where I shall have a better Oppor-
"tunity to convince you, that I never can, or positively will
"be, as I have been, Yours, &c.

A very whimsical Letter!—Faith, I think she has hard luck with you. If a Man were oblig'd to have a Mistress, her Person and Condition seem to be cut out for the Ease of a Lover: For she's a Young, Handsom, Wild, Well-jointured Widow—But what's your Quarrel?

Sir Cha. Nothing—she sees the Coolness happens to be first on my side; and her Business with me now, I suppose, is to convince me, how heartily she's vex'd, that she was not before-hand with me.

Lord Mo. Her Pride and your Indifference must occasion a pleasant Scene sure; what do you intend to do?

Sir Cha. Treat her with a cool Familiar Air, till I pique her to forbid me her sight, and then take her at her Word.

Lord Mo. Very Gallant and provoking! [*Enter a Servant.*

Serv. Sir, my Lord *Foppington!*— [*Exit.*

Sir Cha. O—now, my Lord, if you have a mind to be let into the Mystery of making Love without Pain,—here's one that's a Master of the Art, and shall declaim to you—

Enter Lord Foppington.

My dear Lord *Foppington!*

Lord Fop. My Dear Agreeable! *Que Je t'embrasse! Pardi! Il y a Cent Anns que Je ne T'ay veu*—My Lord, I am your Lordship's most Obedient Humble Servant.

Lord Mo. My Lord, I kiss your Hands—I hope we shall have you here some Time; you seem to have laid in a Stock of Health to be in at the Diversions of the Place—You look extremely well.

Lord Fop. To see one's Friends look so, may easily give a *Vermeile* to one's Complexion.

Sir Cha. Lovers in hope, my Lord, always have a visible *Brillant* in their Eyes and Air.

Lord Fop. What dost thou mean, *Charles!*

Sir Cha. Come, come, confess what really brought you to *Windsor,* now you have no Business there.

Lord Fop. Why two Hours, and Six of the best Nags in Christendom, or the Devil drive me.

Lord Mo. You make haste, my Lord.

Lord Fop. My Lord, I always fly when I pursue—But they are well kept, indeed—I love to have Creatures go as I bid 'em; you have seen 'em, *Charles,* but so has all the World: *Foppington's* Long-tails are known in every Road in *England.*

Sir Cha. Well, my Lord, but how came they to bring you this Road? You don't use to take these irregular Jaunts without some Design in your Head of having more than Nothing to do.

Lord Fop. Pshah! Pox! prithee *Charles,* thou know'st I am a Fellow *sans Consequence,* be where I will.

Sir Cha. Nay, nay, this is too much among Friends, my Lord; come, come—we must have it, your Real Business here?

Lord Fop. Why then, *Entre Nous,* there is a certain *Fille de Joye* about the Court here, that loves winning at Cards better than all the fine things I have been able to say to her,—so I have brought an odd Thousand Bill in my Pocket, that I design *Tete a Tete,* to play off with her at Picquet, or so; and now the Business is out.

Sir Cha. Ah! and a very good Business too, my Lord.

Lord Fop. If it be well done, *Charles—.*

Sir Cha. That's as you manage your Cards, my Lord.

Lord Mo. This must be a Woman of Consequence, by the Value you set upon her Favours.

Sir Cha. O! Nothing's above the Price of a Fine Woman.

Lord Fop. Nay, look you, Gentlemen, the Price may not happen to be altogether so high neither—For I fancy I know enough of the Game, to make it but an even Bet I get her for nothing?

Lord Mo. How so, my Lord?

Lord Fop. Because, if she happen to lose a good Sum to me, I shall buy her with her own Money.

Lord Mo. That's new, I confess.

Lord Fop. You know, *Charles,* 'tis not impossible but I may be five Hundred Pound deep with her—then Bills may fall short, and the Devil's in't if I want Assurance to ask her to pay me some way or other.

Sir Cha. And a Man must be a Churl indeed that won't take a Lady's Personal Security; hah! hah! hah!

Lord Fop. Heh! heh! heh! thou art a Devil, *Charles.*

Lord Mo. Death! how happy is this Coxcomb? [*Aside.*

Lord Fop. But to tell you the Truth, Gentlemen—I had another pressing Temptation that brought me hither, which was—my Wife.

Lord Mo. That's kind indeed, my Lady has been here this Month, she'll be glad to see you.

Lord Fop. That I don't know; for I design this Afternoon to send her to *London.*

Lord Mo. What! the same Day you come, my Lord? that would be cruel.

Lord Fop. Ay, but it will be mighty convenient; for she is positively of no manner of Use in my Amours.

Lord Mo. That's your Fault; the Town thinks her a very deserving Woman.

Lord Fop. If she were a Woman of the Town, perhaps I shou'd think so too: But she happens to be my Wife; and when a Wife is once given to deserve more than her Husband's Inclinations can pay, in my Mind she has no Merit at all.

Lord Mo. She's extremely well bred, and of a very prudent Conduct.

Lord Fop. Um—ay—the Woman's proud enough.

Lord Mo. Add to this, all the World allows her handsom.

Lord Fop. The World's extremely civil, my Lord; and I should take it as a Favour done to me, if they cou'd find an Expedient to unmarry the poor Woman from the only Man in the World that can't think her handsom.

Lord Mo. I believe there are a great many in the World that are sorry 'tis not in their Power to unmarry her.

Lord Fop. I am a great many in the World's very Humble Servant, and whenever they find 'tis in their Power, their High and Mighty Wisdoms may command me at a quarter of an Hour's Warning.

Lord Mo. Pray, my Lord, what did you marry for?

Lord Fop. To pay my Debts at Play, and disinherit my younger Brother.

Lord Mo. But there are some things due to a Wife.

Lord Fop. And there are some Debts I don't care to pay—to both which I plead Husband, and my Lord.

Lord Mo. If I shou'd do so, I shou'd expect to have my own Coach stopt in the Street, and to meet my Wife with the Windows up in a Hackney.

Lord Fop. Then wou'd I put in Bail, and order a separate Maintenance.

Lord Mo. So pay double the Sum of the Debt, and be married for nothing.

Lord Fop. Now I think deferring a Dun, and getting rid of one's Wife, are two the most agreeable Sweets in the Liberties of an *English* Subject.

Lord Mo. If I were married, I would as soon part from my Estate, as my Wife.

Lord Fop. Now I wou'd not, Sun-burn me if I wou'd.

Lord Mo. Death! But since you are thus indifferent, my Lord, why wou'd you needs marry a Woman of so much Merit? Could not you have laid out your Spleen upon some Ill-natur'd Shrew, that wanted the Plague of an Ill Husband, and have let her alone to some plain, honest Man of Quality that wou'd have deserv'd her?

Lord Fop. Why faith, my Lord, that might have been consider'd; but I really grew so passionately fond of her Fortune, that, Curse catch me, I was quite blind to the rest of her good Qualities: For to tell you the Truth, if it had been possible the old Putt of a Peer cou'd have toss'd me in t'other five Thousand for 'em, by my Consent, she shou'd have relinquisht her Merit and Virtues to any of her younger Sisters.

Sir Cha. Ay, ay, my Lord, Virtues in a Wife are good for nothing but to make her Proud, and put the World in Mind of her Husband's Faults.

Lord Fop. Right, *Charles:* And strike me Blind but the Women of Virtue are now grown such Ideots in Love, they expect of a Man, just as they do of a Coach-Horse, that one's Appetite, like t'other's Flesh, should increase by Feeding.

Sir Cha. Right, my Lord, and don't consider, that *Toutjours Chapons Bouilles* will never do with an *English* Stomach.

Lord Fop. Ha! ha! ha! To tell you the Truth, *Charles,* I have known so much of that sort of Eating, that I now think, for an hearty Meal, no Wild-Fowl in *Europe* is comparable to a Joint of *Banstead* Mutton.

Lord Mo. How do you mean?

Lord Fop. Why, that for my part, I had rather have a plain Slice of my Wife's Woman, than my Guts full of e'er an Ortolan Duchess in Christendom.

Lord Mo. But I thought, my Lord, your chief Business now at *Windsor* had been your Design upon a Woman of Quality.

Lord Fop. That's true, my Lord; tho' I don't think your fine Lady the best Dish my self, yet a Man of Quality can't be without such Things at his Table.

Lord Mo. O! then you only desire the Reputation of an Affair with her?

Lord Fop. I think the Reputation is the most inviting Part of an Amour with most Women of Quality.

Lord Mo. Why so, my Lord?

Lord Fop. Why who the Devil would run thro' all the Degrees of Form and Ceremony, that lead one up to the last Favour, if it were not for the Reputation of Understanding the nearest Way to get over the Difficulty?

Lord Mo. But, my Lord, does not the Reputation of your being so general an Undertaker frighten the Women from engaging with you? for they say, no Man can love but One at a time.

Lord Fop. That's just one more than ever I came up to: For, stop my Breath, if ever I lov'd one in my Life.

Lord Mo. How do you get 'em then?

Lord Fop. Why sometimes as they get other People; I dress, and let 'em get me; or, if that won't do, as I got my Title, I buy 'em.

Lord Mo. But how can you, that profess Indifference, think it worth your while to come so often up to the Price of a Woman of Quality?

Lord Fop. Because you must know, my Lord, that most of them begin now to come down to Reason; I mean, those that are to be had, for some die Fools: But with the Wiser sort, 'tis not of late so very Expensive; now and then a *Partie Quarrie,* a Jaunt or two in a Hack to an *Indian* House, a little *China,* an Odd Thing for a Gown, or so, and in Three Days after you meet her at the Conveniency of trying it *Chez Mademoiselle D'Epingle.*

Sir Cha. Ay, ay, my Lord, and when you are there, you know, what between a little Chat, a Dish of Tea, *Mademoiselle*'s good Humour, and a *Petit Chanson,* or two; the Devil's in't if a Man can't fool away the Time, till he sees how it looks upon her by Candle-light.

Lord Fop. Heh! heh! well said, *Charles;* I'gad, I fancy thee and I have unlac'd many a Reputation there—Your great Lady is as soon undrest as her Woman.

Lord Mo. I cou'd never find it so—the Shame, or Scandal of a Repulse, always made me afraid of attempting a Woman of Condition.

Sir Cha. Ha! ha! I'gad, my Lord, you deserve to be ill us'd, your Modesty's enough to spoil any Woman in the World; but my Lord and I understand the Sex a little better, we see plainly that Women are only Cold, as some Men are Brave, from the Modesty or Fear of those that attack 'em.

Lord Fop. Right, *Charles*—a Man shou'd no more give up his Heart to a Woman, than his Sword to a Bully; they are both as insolent as the Devil after it.

Sir Cha. How do you like that, my Lord?

[*Aside to Lord* Morelove.

Lord Mo. Faith, I envy him—But, my Lord, suppose your Inclination shou'd stumble upon a Woman truly Virtuous, wou'd not a severe Repulse from such an one put you strangely out of Countenance?

Lord Fop. Not at all, my Lord—for if a Man don't mind a Box o'the Ear in a fair Struggle with a fresh Country Girl, why the Duce shou'd he be concern'd at an Impertinent Frown for an Attack upon a Woman of Quality?

Lord Mo. Then you have no Notion of a Lady's Cruelty?

Lord Fop. Ha! ha! let me Blood, if I think there's a greater Jest in Nature. I am ready to crack my Guts with laughing, to see a senseless Flirt, because the Creature happens to have a little Pride that she calls Virtue about her, give her self all the Insolent Airs of Resentment and Disdain to an honest Fellow, that all the while does not care three Pinches of Snuff, if she and her Virtue were to run with their last Favours through the first Regiment of Guards—Ha! ha!—it puts me in mind of an Affair of mine, so Impertinent—

Lord Mo. O! that's impossible, my Lord,—pray let's hear it.

Lord Fop. Why I happen'd once to be very well in a certain Man of Quality's Family, and his Wife lik'd me.

Lord Mo. How do you know she lik'd you?

Lord Fop. Why, from the very Moment I told her I lik'd her, she never durst trust her self at the end of a Room with me.

Lord Mo. That might be her not liking you.

Lord Fop. My Lord—Women of Quality don't use to speak the thing plain—but to satisfie you I did not want Encouragement, I never came there in my Life, but she did immediately Smile, and borrow my Snuff-box.

Lord Mo. She lik'd your Snuff at least—Well, but how did she use you?

Lord Fop. By all that's Infamous she Jilted me.

Lord Mo. How! Jilt you?

Lord Fop. Ay, Death's Curse, she Jilted me.

Lord Mo. Pray let's hear.

Lord Fop. For when I was pretty well convinc'd she had a Mind to me, I one Day made her a Hint of an Appointment; upon which, with an insolent Frown in her Face (that made her look as ugly as the Devil) she told me, that if ever I came thither again, her Lord should know that she had forbidden me the House before—Did you ever hear of such a Slut?

Sir Cha. Intolerable!

Lord Mo. But how did her Answer agree with you?

Lord Fop. O, Passionately well! For I star'd full in her Face, and burst out a laughing; at which she turn'd upon her Heel, gave a crack with her Fan like a Coach-whip, and Bridl'd out of the Room with the Air and Complexion of an incens'd Turkey-Cock.

[*A Servant whispers Sir* Charles.

Lord Mo. What did you then?

Lord Fop. I—look'd after her, gap'd, threw up the Sash, and fell a singing out of the Window—so that you see, my Lord, while a Man is not in Love, there's no great Affliction in missing one's way to a Woman.

Sir Cha. Ay, ay, you talk this very well, my Lord; but now let's see how you dare behave your self upon Action—Dinner's serv'd, and the Ladies stay for us—There's one within has been too hard for as brisk a Man as your self.

Lord Mo. I guess who you mean—Have a Care, my Lord, she'll prove your Courage for you.

Lord Fop. Will she! then she's an undone Creature. For let me tell you, Gentlemen, Courage is the whole Mystery of making Love, and of more Use than Conduct is in War; for the bravest Fellow in *Europe* may beat his Brains out against the stubborn Walls of a Town—But

— "Women, Born to be Controll'd
"Stoop to the Forward, and the Bold. [*Exeunt.*

ACT III. SCENE I.

The SCENE *continues.*

Enter Lord Morelove *and Sir* Charles.

Lord Mo. So! Did not I bear up bravely?

Sir Cha. Admirably! with the best bred Insolence in Nature! You insulted like a Woman of Quality, when her Country-bred Husband's jealous of her in the wrong Place.

Lord Mo. Ha! ha! Did you observe, when I first came into the Room, how carelessly she brush'd her Eyes over me, and when the Company saluted me, stood all the while with her Face to the Window? ha! ha!

Sir Cha. What astonish'd Airs she gave her self, when you ask'd her, what made her so grave upon her old Friends?

Lord Mo. And whenever I offer'd any thing in Talk, what affected Care she took to direct her Observations of it to a third Person?

Sir Cha. I observ'd she did not eat above the Rump of a Pigeon all Dinner Time.

Lord Mo. And how she colour'd when I told her, her Ladyship had lost her Stomach.

Sir Cha. If you keep your Temper she's undone.

Lord Mo. Provided she sticks to her Pride, I believe I may.

Sir Cha. Ah! never fear her; I warrant in the Humour she is in, she wou'd as soon part with her Sense of Feeling.

Lord Mo. Well! what's to be done next?

Sir Cha. Only observe her Motions; for by her Behaviour at Dinner, I am sure she designs to gall you with my Lord *Foppington;* if so, you must even stand her Fire, and then play my Lady *Graveairs* upon her, whom I'll immediately Pique and prepare for your purpose.

Lord Mo. I understand you—the properest Woman in the World too, for she'll certainly encourage the least Offer from me, in hopes of Revenging her Slights upon you.

Sir Cha. Right; and the very Encouragement she gives you, at the same time will give me a Pretence to widen the Breach of my Quarrel to her.

Lord Mo. Besides, *Charles,* I own I am fond of any Attempt that will forward a Misunderstanding there, for your Lady's sake: A Woman so truly good in her Nature, ought to have something more from a Man, than bare Occasions to prove her Goodness.

Sir Cha. Why then upon Honour, my Lord, to give you Proof that I am positively the best Husband in the World, my Wife—never yet found me out.

Lord Mo. That may be her being the best Wife in the World: She, may be, won't find you out.

Sir Cha. Nay, if she won't tell a Man of his Faults, when she sees 'em, how the Duce should he mend 'em? But however, you see I am going to leave 'em off as fast as I can.

Lord Mo. Being tir'd of a Woman is indeed a pretty tolerable Assurance of a Man's not designing to fool on with her—Here she comes, and if I don't mistake, Brim full of Reproaches—You can't take her in a better time—I'll leave you.

Enter Lady Graveairs.

Your Ladyship's most Humble Servant, is the Company broke up, pray?

Lady Gra. No, my Lord, they are just talking of Basset; my Lord *Foppington* has a mind to Tally, if your Lordship would encourage the Table.

Lord Mo. O Madam, with all my Heart! But Sir *Charles,* I know, is hard to be got to it; I'll leave your Ladyship to prevail with him. [*Exit Lord* Morelove.

[*Sir* Charles *and Lady* Graveairs *salute coldly, and trifle some time before they speak.*

Lady Gra. Sir *Charles,* I sent you a Note this Morning—

Sir Cha. Yes, Madam, but there were some Passages I did not expect from your Ladyship; you seem'd to tax me with Things that—

Lady Gra. Look you, Sir, 'tis not at all material, whether I tax'd you with any thing, or no: I don't in the least desire to hear you clear your self, upon my Word, you may be very easy as to that

Matter; for my part, I am mighty well satisfy'd, things are as they are; all I have to say to you is, that you need not give your self the Trouble to call at my Lodgings this Afternoon, if you should have Time, as you were pleas'd to send me Word—and so your Servant, Sir,—that's all— [*Going.*

Sir Cha. Hold, Madam.

Lady Gra. Look you, Sir *Charles,* 'tis not your calling me back that will signify any thing, I can assure you.

Sir Cha. Why this extraordinary Haste, Madam?

Lady Gra. In short, Sir *Charles,* I have taken a great many things from you of late, that you know I have often told you I would positively bear no longer:—But I see things are in vain, and the more People strive to oblige the People, the less they are thank'd for't: And since there must be an end of one's Ridiculousness one time or other, I don't see any time so proper as the present, and therefore, Sir, I desire you would think of things accordingly—your Servant— [*Going, he holds her.*

Sir Cha. Nay, Madam, let's start fair, however; you ought at least to stay till I am as ready as your Ladyship; and then,—if we must part—

Affectedly.]
Adieu, ye silent Grots, and shady Groves;
Ye soft Amusements of our growing Loves:
Adieu, ye whisper'd Sighs, that fann'd the Fire,
And all the Thrilling Joys of young Desire.

Lady Gra. O mighty well, Sir: I am very glad we are at last come to a right Understanding, the only way I have long wish'd for; not but I'd have you to know, I see your Design through all your painted Ease of Resignation; I know, you would give your Soul to make me uneasy now.

Sir Cha. O fie, Madam! upon my Word, I wou'd not make you uneasie, if it were in my Power.

Lady Gra. O dear Sir, you need not take such Care, upon my Word; you'll find I can part with you without the least Disorder—I'll try at least, and so once more, and for ever, Sir, your Servant: Not but you must give me leave to tell you, as my last Thought of you too, that I do think—you are a Villain— [*Exit hastily.*

Sir Cha. O your very humble Servant, Madam—[*Bowing low.*]

What a charming Quality is a Woman's Pride, that's strong enough to refuse a Man her Favours when he's weary of 'em—Ah!

[*Lady* Graveairs *returns.*

Lady Gra. Look you, Sir *Charles*—don't presume upon the Easiness of my Temper: For to convince you that I am positively in earnest in this matter, I desire you would let me have what Letters you have had of mine since you came to *Windsor,* and I expect you'll return the rest, as I will yours, as soon as we come to *London.*

Sir Cha. Upon my Faith, Madam, I never keep any, I always put Snuff in 'em, and so they wear out.

Lady Gra. Sir *Charles,* I must have 'em; for positively I won't stir without 'em.

Sir Cha. Ha! then I must be civil, I see. [*Aside.*] Perhaps, Madam, I have no mind to part with them—or you.

Lady Gra. Look you, Sir, all those sort of things are in vain, now there's an End of every thing between us—If you say you won't give 'em, I must e'en get 'em as well as I can.

Sir Cha. Hah! that won't do then, I find. [*Aside.*

Lady Gra. Who's there? Mrs. *Edging?*—Your keeping a Letter, Sir, won't keep me, I'll assure you.

Enter Edging.

Edg. Did your Ladyship call me, Madam?

Lady Gra. Ay, Child; pray do me the Favour to fetch my Scarf out of the Dining-Room.

Edg. Yes, Madam—

Sir Cha. O! then there's Hope again. [*Aside.*

Edg. Ha! she looks as if my Master had quarrell'd with her; I hope she's going away in a Huff—she shan't stay for her Scarf, I warrant her—This is pure. [*Aside. Exit smiling.*

Lady Gra. Pray, Sir *Charles,* before I go, give me leave now, after all, to ask you—why you have us'd me thus?

Sir Cha. What is't you call Usage, Madam?

Lady Gra. Why then, since you will have it, how comes it you have been so grossly careless and neglectful of me of late? Only tell me seriously wherein I have deserv'd this?

Sir Cha. Why then seriously, Madam—

Re-enter Edging *with a Scarf.*

We are interrupted—

Edg. Here's your Ladyship's Scarf, Madam.

Lady Gra. Thank you, Mrs. *Edging*—O law! pray will you let some body get me a Chair to the Door.

Edg. Humh! she might have told me that before, if she had been in such haste to go— [*Exit.*

Lady Gra. Now, Sir.

Sir Cha. Then seriously, I say, I am of late grown so very lazy in my Pleasures, that I had rather lose a Woman, than go through the Plague and Trouble of having or keeping her; and to be free, I have found so much, even in my Acquaintance with you, whom I confess to be a Mistress in the Art of Pleasing, that I am from henceforth resolv'd to follow no Pleasure that rises above the Degree of Amusement—and that Woman that expects I should make her my Business; why—like my Business, is then in a fair way of being forgot:—When once she comes to reproach me with Vows, and Usage, and Stuff,—I had as lief hear her talk of Bills, Bonds, and Ejectments; her Passion becomes as troublesome as a Law-Suit, and I would as soon converse with my Sollicitor—In short, I shall never care Six Pence for any Woman that won't be Obedient—

Lady Gra. I'll swear, Sir, you have a very free way of treating People; I am glad I am so well acquainted with your Principles however—and you'd have me Obedient?

Sir Cha. Why not? my Wife's so, and I think she has as much Pretence to be proud, as your Ladyship.

Lady Gra. Lard! is there no Chair to be had, I wonder?

Enter Edging.

Edg. Here's a Chair, Madam.

Lady Gra. 'Tis very well, Mrs. *Edging*—Pray will you let some body get me a Glass of fair Water.

Edg. Humh! her Huff's almost over, I suppose—I see he is a Villain still. [*Exit.*

Lady Gra. Well, that was the prettiest Fancy about Obedience sure that ever was! Certainly a Woman of Condition must be infinitely happy under the Dominion of so generous a Lover! But how came you to forget Kicking and Whipping all this while? methinks you should not have left so fashionable an Article out of your Scheme of Government.

Sir Cha. Um!–No, there's too much Trouble in that; though I have known 'em of admirable Use in the Reformation of some humoursome Gentlewomen.

Lady Gra. But one thing more, and I have done–Pray what degree of Spirit must the Lady have, that is to make her self happy under so much Freedom, Order, and Tranquillity?

Sir Cha. O! she must at least have as much Spirit as your Ladyship, or she'd give me no Pleasure in breaking it.

Lady Gra. No; that would be troublesome–You had better take one that's broken to your Hand–there are such Souls to be hir'd, I believe; things that will rub your Temples in an Evening till you fall fast a-sleep in their Laps, Creatures too that think their Wages their Reward; I fancy at last, that will be the best Method for the lazy Passion of a marry'd Man, that has outliv'd his any other Sense of Gratification.

Sir Cha. Look you, Madam–I have lov'd you very well a great while; now you would have me love you better and longer, which is not in my Power to do; and I don't think there's any Plague upon Earth like a Dun that comes for more Money than one's ever likely to be able to pay.

Lady Gra. A Dun! do you take me for a Dun, Sir? do I come a Dunning to you? [*Walks in an Heat.*

Sir Cha. H'st! Don't expose your self–here's Company–

Lady Gra. I care not–A Dun!–You shall see, Sir, I can revenge an Affront, though I despise the Wretch that offers it–A Dun!–O! I could die with laughing at the Fancy. [*Exit.*

Sir Cha. So! she's in admirable Order–Here comes my Lord, and I'm afraid in the very Nick of his Occasion for her.

Enter Lord Morelove.

Lord Mo. O *Charles!* undone again! all's lost and ruin'd.

Sir Cha. What's the matter now?

Lord Mo. I have been playing the Fool yonder even to Contempt; my senseless Jealousy has confess'd a Weakness I never shall forgive my self—She has insulted on it to that Degree too—I can't bear the Thought—O *Charles!* this Devil still is Mistress of my Heart, and I could dash my Brains to think how grossly too I have let her know it.

Sir Cha. Ah! how it would tickle her if she saw you in this Condition: Ha! ha! ha!

Lord Mo. Prithee don't torture me: Think of some present Ease, or I shall burst—

Sir Cha. Well, well, let's hear, pray—what has she done to you? ha! ha!

Lord Mo. Why, ever since I left you, she treated me with so much Coolness and ill Nature, and that thing of a Lord with so much laughing Ease, such an acquainted, such a spiteful Familiarity, that at the last she saw and triumph'd in my Uneasiness.

Sir Cha. Well! and so you left the Room in a Pet? ha!

Lord Mo. O worse, worse still! for at last, with half Shame and Anger in my Looks, I thrust my self between my Lord and her, press'd her by the Hand, and in a Whisper, trembling, begg'd her in Pity of her self and me, to shew her good Humour only where she knew it was truly valued; at which she broke from me with a cold Smile, sat her down by the Peer, whisper'd him, and burst into a loud Laughter in my Face.

Sir Cha. Ha! ha! then would I have given fifty Pound to have seen your Face: Why what, in the Name of Common Sense, had you to do with Humility? Will you never have enough on't? Death! 'Twas setting a lighted Match to Gun-powder to blow your self up.

Lord Mo. I see my Folly now, *Charles*—But what shall I do with the small Remains of Life that she has left me?

Sir Cha. O, throw it at her Feet by all means, put on your Tragedy Face, catch fast hold of her Petticoat, whip out your Handkerchief, and in point Blank Verse, desire her, one way or other, to make an end of the Business. [*In a whining Tone.*

Lord Mo. What a Fool dost thou make me?

Sir Cha. I only shew you, as you come out of her Hands, my Lord.

Lord Mo. How contemptibly have I behav'd my self?

Sir Cha. That's according as you bear her Behaviour.

Lord Mo. Bear it! no: I thank thee, *Charles*—thou hast wak'd me now; and if I bear it—What have you done with my Lady *Graveairs?*

Sir Cha. Your Business, I believe—She's ready for you, she's just gone down Stairs, and if you don't make haste after her, I expect her back again with a Knife or a Pistol, presently.

Lord Mo. I'll go this Minute.

Sir Cha. No, stay a little, here comes my Lord: We'll see what we can get out of him first.

Lord Mo. Methinks I now could laugh at her.

Enter Lord Foppington.

Lord Fop. Nay, prithee, Sir *Charles,* let's have a little of thee—We have been so *Chagrin* without thee, that, stap my Breath, the Ladies are gone half asleep to Church for want of thy Company.

Sir Cha. That's hard indeed, while your Lordship was among 'em: Is Lady *Betty* gone too?

Lord Fop. She was just upon the Wing—But I caught her by the Snuff-box, and she pretends to stay to see if I'll give it her again, or no.

Lord Mo. Death! 'tis that I gave her, and the only Present she ever would receive from me—Ask him how he came by it.

[*Aside to Sir* Charles.

Sir Cha. Prithee don't be uneasy—Did she give it you, my Lord?

Lord Fop. Faith, *Charles,* I can't say she did, or she did not, but we were playing the Fool, and I took it—*a la*—Pshah! I can't tell thee in *French* neither, but *Horace* touches it to a Nicety—'twas *Pignus Direptum Male Pertinaci.*

Lord Mo. So! but I must bear it—If your Lordship has a Mind to the Box, I'll stand by you in the keeping of it.

Lord Fop. My Lord, I am passionately oblig'd to you, but I am afraid I can't answer your hazarding so much of the Lady's Favour.

Lord Mo. Not at all, my Lord: 'Tis possible I may not have the same Regard to her Frown that your Lordship has.

Lord Fop. That's Bite, I'm sure—he'd give a Joint of his little Finger to be as well with her as I am. [*Aside.*] But here she comes! *Charles,* stand by me—Must not a Man be a vain Coxcomb now, to think this Creature follow'd one?

Sir Cha. Nothing so plain, my Lord.

Lord Fop. Flattering Devil!

Enter Lady Betty.

Lady Bet. Pshah! my Lord *Foppington!* Prithee don't play the Fool now, but give me my Snuff-box—Sir *Charles,* help me to take it from him.

Sir Cha. You know, I hate Trouble, Madam.

Lady Bet. Pooh! you'll make me stay till Prayers are half over now.

Lord Fop. If you'll promise me not to go to Church, I'll give it you.

Lady Bet. I'll promise nothing at all, for positively I will have it. [*Struggles with him.*

Lord Fop. Then comparatively I won't part with it—ha! ha! [*Struggling with her.*

Lady Bet. O you Devil! you have kill'd my Arm! Oh! Well—if you'll let me have it, I'll give you a better.

Lord Mo. O *Charles!* that has a View of distant Kindness in it. [*Aside to Sir* Charles.

Lord Fop. Nay, now I keep it superlatively—I find there's a secret Value in it.

Lady Bet. O dismal! upon my Word, I am only asham'd to give it you? Do you think I wou'd offer such an odious-fancy'd Thing to any body I had the least Value for?

Sir Cha. Now it comes a little nearer, methinks it does not seem to be any Kindness at all. [*Aside to Lord* Morelove.

Lord Fop. Why really, Madam, upon second View, it has not extreamly the Mode of a Lady's Utensil; are you sure it never held any thing but Snuff?

Lady Bet. O! you Monster!

Lord Fop. Nay, I only ask, because it seems to me to have very much the Air and Fancy of Monsieur *Smoakandsot's* Tobacco-box.

Lord Mo. I can bear no more.

Sir Cha. Why don't then; I'll step into the Company, and return to your Relief immediately. [*Exit.*

Lord Mo. [*To Lady* Betty.] Come, Madam, will your Ladyship give me leave to end the Difference?—Since the Slightness of the Thing may let you bestow it without any Mark of Favour, shall I beg it of your Ladyship?

Lady Bet. O my Lord, no body sooner—I beg you give it my Lord.

[*Looking earnestly on Lord* Foppington *who smiling gives it to Lord* Morelove *and then bows gravely to her.*

Lord Mo. Only to have the Honour of restoring it to your Lordship; and if there be any other Trifle of mine your Lordship has a Fancy to, tho' it were a Mistress, I don't know any Person in the World that has so good a Claim to my Resignation.

Lord Fop. O my Lord, this Generosity will distract me.

Lord Mo. My Lord, I do you but common Justice: But from your Conversation, I had never known the true Value of the Sex: You positively understand 'em the best of any Man breathing, therefore I think every one of common Prudence ought to resign to you.

Lord Fop. Then positively your Lordship's the most obliging Person in the World, for I'm sure your Judgment can never like any Woman that is not the finest Creature in the Universe.

[*Bowing to Lady* Betty.

Lord Mo. O! your Lordship does me too much Honour, I have the worst Judgment in the World, no Man has been more deceiv'd in it.

Lord Fop. Then your Lordship, I presume, has been apt to chuse in a Mask, or by Candle-light.

Lord Mo. In a Mask, indeed, my Lord, and of all Masks the most dangerous.

Lord Fop. Pray, what's that, my Lord?

Lord Mo. A bare Face.

Lord Fop. Your Lordship will pardon me, if I don't so readily comprehend how a Woman's bare Face can hide her Face.

Lord Mo. It often hides her Heart, my Lord, and therefore I think it sometimes a more dangerous Mask than a Piece of Velvet: That's rather a Mark than a Disguise of an ill Woman: But the Mischiefs skulking behind a Beauteous Form, give no Warning, they are always Sure, Fatal, and Innumerable.

Lady Bet. O barbarous Aspersion! my Lord *Foppington,* have you nothing to say for the poor Women?

Lord Fop. I must confess, Madam, nothing of this nature ever happen'd in my Course of Amours: I always Judge the Beauteous Form of a Woman to be the most agreeable Part of her Composition, and when once a Lady does me the Honour to toss that into my Arms, I think my self obliged in good Nature not to quarrel about the rest of her Equipage.

Lady Bet. Why ay, my Lord, there's some good Humour in that now.

Lord Mo. He's happy in a plain *English* Stomach, Madam; I could recommend a Dish that's perfectly to your Lordship's Goust, where Beauty is the only Sauce to it.

Lady Bet. So!

Lord Fop. My Lord, when my Wine's right, I never care it should be Zested.

Lord Mo. I know some Ladies would thank you for that Opinion.

Lady Bet. My Lord *Morelove*'s really grown such a Churl to the Women, I don't only think he is not, but can't conceive how he ever cou'd be in Love.

Lord Mo. Upon my Word, Madam, I once thought I was. [*Smiling.*

Lady Bet. Fie! fie! how cou'd you think so? I fancy now you had only a Mind to Domineer over some poor Creature, and so you thought you were in Love, ha! ha!

Lord Mo. The Lady I lov'd, Madam, grew so unfortunate in her Conduct, that she at last brought me to treat her with the same Indifference and Civility as I now pay your Ladyship.

Lady Bet. And ten to one, just at that time she never thought you such tolerable Company.

Lord Mo. That I can't say, Madam, for at that time she grew so affected, there was no judging of her Thoughts at all. [*Mimicking her.*

Lady Bet. What, and so you left the poor Lady? O you Inconstant Creature!

Lord Mo. No, Madam, to have lov'd her on had been Inconstancy for she was never Two Hours together the same Woman.

[*Lady* Betty *and Lord* Morelove *seem to talk.*

Lord Fop. [*Aside.*] Ha! ha! ha! I see he has a Mind to abuse her; so I'll e'en give him an Opportunity of doing his Business with her at once for ever—My Lord, I perceive your Lordship's going to be good Company to the Lady, and for her sake I don't think it good Manners in me to disturb you—

Enter Sir Charles.

Sir Cha. My Lord *Foppington!*

Lord Fop. O *Charles!* I was just wanting thee–Hark thee–I have three thousand Secrets for thee–I have made such Discoveries! to tell thee all in One Word–*Morelove's* as Jealous of me as the Devil: heh! heh! heh!

Sir Cha. Is't possible? has she given him any Occasion?

Lord Fop. Only rally'd him to Death upon my Account; she told me within just now, she'd use him like a Dog, and begg'd me to draw off for an Opportunity.

Sir Cha. O! keep in while the Scent lies, and she's your own, my Lord.

Lord Fop. I can't tell that, *Charles,* but I'm sure she's fairly unharbour'd, and when I once throw off my Inclinations, I usually follow 'em till the Game has enough on't; and between thee and I she's pretty well blown too, she can't stand long, I believe; for, Curse catch me, if I have not rid down half a Thousand Pound after her already.

Sir Cha. What do you mean?

Lord Fop. I have lost Five Hundred to her at Picquet since Dinner.

Sir Cha. You are a fortunate Man, faith; you are resolv'd not to be thrown out, I see.

Lord Fop. Hang it! What should a Man come out for, if he does not keep up to the Sport?

Sir Cha. Well push'd, my Lord.

Lord Fop. *Tayo!* Have at her–

Sir Cha. Down, down, my Lord–ah–'ware Hanches.

Lord Fop. Ay! *Charles.* [*Embracing him.*] Prithee let's observe a little; there's a foolish Cur, now I have run her to a Stand, has a Mind to be at her by himself, and thou shalt see she won't stir out of her Way for him. [*They stand aside.*

Lord Mo. Ha! ha! Your Ladyship's very grave of a sudden, you look as if your Lover had insolently recover'd his common Senses.

Lady Bet. And your Lordship is so very gay, and unlike your self, one would swear you were just come from the Pleasure of making your Mistress afraid of you.

Lord Mo. No, faith, quite contrary—For do you know, Madam, I have just found out, that upon your Account I have made my self One of the most ridiculous Puppies upon the Face of the Earth—I have, upon my faith!—nay, and so extravagantly such—ha! ha! ha! that it's at last become a Jest even to my self, and I can't help laughing at it for the Soul of me; ha! ha! ha!

Lady Bet. I want to cure him of that Laugh now. [*Aside.*] My Lord, since you are so generous, I'll tell you another Secret: Do you know too, that I still find (spite of all your great Wisdom, and my contemptible Qualities, as you are pleas'd now and then to call 'em:) Do you know, I say, that I see under all this, you still love me with the same helpless Passion; and can your vast Foresight imagine I won't use you accordingly, for these extraordinary Airs you are pleas'd to give your self?

Lord Mo. O by all means, Madam, 'tis fit you should, and I expect it, whenever it is in your Power—Confusion! [*Aside.*

Lady Bet. My Lord, you have talk'd to me this half Hour, without confessing Pain, [*Pauses, and affects to Gape.*] only remember it.

Lord Mo. Hell and Tortures?

Lady Bet. What did you say, my Lord?

Lord Mo. Fire and Furies!

Lady Bet. Ha! ha! he's disorder'd—Now I am easy—My Lord *Foppington,* have you a Mind to your Revenge at Picquet?

Lord Fop. I have always a Mind to an Opportunity of entertaining your Ladyship, Madam.

[*Lady* Betty *coquets with Lord* Foppington.

Lord Mo. O! *Charles*—The Insolence of this Woman might furnish out a thousand Devils.

Sir Cha. And your Temper is enough to furnish out a thousand such Women—Come away—I have Business for you upon the Terrace.

Lord Mo. Let me but speak one Word to her—

Sir Cha. Not a Syllable—the Tongue's a Weapon you'll always have the worst at: For I see you have no Guard, and she carries a Devilish Edge.

Lady Bet. My Lord, don't let any thing I have said frighten you away; for if you have the least Inclination to stay and rail, you know the old Conditions; 'tis but your asking me Pardon next Day, and you may give your Passion any liberty you think fit.

Lord Mo. Daggers and Death!

Sir Cha. Are you Mad?

Lord Mo. Let me speak to her now, or I shall burst–

Sir Cha. Upon Condition you'll speak no more of her to me, my Lord, do as you please.

Lord Mo. Prithee pardon me–I know not what to do.

Sir Cha. Come along–I'll set you to work I warrant you–Nay, nay, none of your parting Ogles–Will you go?

Lord Mo. Yes–and I hope for ever–

[*Exit Sir* Charles *pulling away Lord* Morelove.

Lord Fop. Ha! ha! ha! Did ever Mortal Monster set up for a Lover with such unfortunate Qualifications?

Lady Bet. Indeed, my Lord *Morelove* has something strangely singular in his Manner.

Lord Fop. I thought I should have burst to see the Creature pretend to Rally, and give himself the Airs of one of Us–But, run me through, Madam, your Ladyship push'd like a Fencing-Master; that last Thrust was a *Coup de Grace,* I believe–I am afraid his Honour will hardly meet your Ladyship in haste again.

Lady Bet. Not unless his Second, Sir *Charles,* keeps him better in Practice, perhaps.–Well, the Humour of this Creature has done me signal Service to Day, I must keep it up, for fear of a second Engagement. [*Aside.*

Lord Fop. Never was poor Wit so foil'd at his own Weapon, sure.

Lady Bet. Wit! had he ever any Pretence to it?

Lord Fop. Ha! ha! he has not much in Love, I think, though he wears the Reputation of a very pretty young Fellow, among some sort of People; but, strike me stupid, if ever I could discover Common Sense in all the Progress of his Amours: He expects a Womân should like him for endeavouring to convince her, that she has not one good Quality belonging to the whole Composition of her Soul and Body.

Lady Bet. That, I suppose, is only in a modest hope, that she'll mend her Faults, to qualify her self for his vast Merit, ha! ha!

Lord Fop. Poor *Morelove,* I see she can't endure him. [*Aside.*

Lady Bet. Or if one really had all those Faults, he does not consider, that Sincerity in Love is as much out of Fashion as sweet Snuff; no body takes it now.

Lord Fop. O! no Mortal, Madam, unless it be here and there a Squire, that's making his lawful Court to the Cherry-cheek Charms of my Lord Bishop's great fat Daughter in the Country.

Lady Bet. O! what a surfeiting Couple has he put together— [*Throwing her Hand carelessly upon his.*

Lord Fop. Fond of me, by all that's tender—Poor Fool, I'll give thee Ease immediately. [*Aside.*] —But, Madam, you were pleas'd just now to offer me my Revenge at Picquet—Now here's no body within, and I think we can't make use of a better Opportunity.

Lady Bet. O! no: Not now, my Lord—I have a Favour I would fain beg of you first.

Lord Fop. But Time, Madam, is very precious in this Place, and I shall not easily forgive my self if I don't take him by the Forelock.

Lady Bet. But I have a great mind to have a little more Sport with my Lord *Morelove* first, and would fain beg your Assistance.

Lord Fop. O! with all my Heart; and, upon second Thoughts, I don't know but piquing a Rival in Publick may be as good Sport, as being well with a Mistress in private: For, after all, the Pleasure of a fine Woman is like that of her own Virtue, not so much in the Thing, as the Reputation of having it. [*Aside.*] —Well, Madam, but how can I serve you in this Affair?

Lady Bet. Why, methought, as my Lord *Morelove* went out, he shew'd a stern Resentment in his Look, that seem'd to threaten me with Rebellion, and downright Defiance: Now I have a great Fancy that you and I should follow him to the Terrace, and laugh at his Resolution before he has time to put it in Practice.

Lord Fop. And so punish his Fault before he commits it! ha! ha! ha!

Lady Bet. Nay, we won't give him time, if his Courage should fail, to repent it.

Lord Fop. Ha! ha! ha! let me Blood, if I don't long to be at it! ha! ha!

Lady Bet. O! 'twill be such Diversion to see him bite his Lips, and broil within, only with seeing us ready to split our Sides in laughing at nothing, ha! ha!

Lord Fop. Ha! ha! I see the Creature does really like me. [*Aside.*] And then, Madam, to hear him hum a broken piece of a Tune in Affectation of his not minding us—'twill be so foolish, when we know he loves us to Death all the while, ha! ha!

Lady Bet. And if at last his sage Mouth should open in surly Contradiction of our Humour, then will we, in pure opposition to his, immediately fall foul upon every thing that is not Gallant and Fashionable; Constancy shall be the Mark of Age and Ugliness, Virtue a Jest, we'll rally Discretion out of Doors, lay Gravity at our Feet, and only Love, free Love, Disorder, Liberty and Pleasure be our standing Principles.

Lord Fop. Madam, you transport me: For if ever I was obliged to Nature for any one tolerable Qualification, 'twas positively the Talent of being exuberantly pleasant upon this Subject—I am impatient—my Fancy's upon the Wing already—let's fly to him.

Lady Bet. No, no; stay till I am just got out, our going together won't be so proper.

Lord Fop. As your Ladyship pleases, Madam—But when this Affair is over, you won't forget that I have a certain Revenge due.

Lady Bet. Ay! ay! after Supper I am for you—Nay, you shan't stir a Step, my Lord— [*Seeing her to the Door.*

Lord Fop. Only to tell you, you have fix'd me yours to the last Existence of my Soul's eternal Entity—

Lady Bet. O, your Servant— [*Exit.*

Lord Fop. Ha! ha! stark mad for me, by all that's Handsome! Poor *Morelove!* That a Fellow who has ever been abroad, shou'd think a Woman of her Spirit is to be taken as the Confederates do Towns, by a Regular Siege, when so many of the *French* Successes might have shewn him the surest way is to whisper the Governor—How can a Coxcomb give himself the Fatigue of Bombarding a Woman's Understanding, when he may with so much Ease make a Friend of her Constitution—I'll see if I can shew him a little *French* Play with Lady *Betty*—let me see—Ay, I'll make an end of it the old way, get her into Picquet at her own Lodgings—not mind one Tittle of my Play, give her every Game before she's half up, that she may judge the Strength of my Inclination by my haste of losing up to her Price; then of a sudden, with a familiar Leer cry—Rat Picquet—sweep Counters, Cards, and Money all upon the Floor, & *donc—l'Affaire est faite.* [*Exit.*

ACT IV. SCENE I.

SCENE, *The Castle Terrace.*

Enter Lady Betty *and Lady* Easy.

Lady Ea. My Dear, you really talk to me as if I were your Lover, and not your Friend; or else I am so dull, that by all you've said I can't make the least guess at your real Thoughts—Can you be serious for a Moment?

Lady Bet. Not easily: But I would do more to oblige you.

Lady Ea. Then pray deal ingenuously, and tell me without Reserve, are you sure you don't love my Lord *Morelove?*

Lady Bet. Then seriously—I think not—But because I won't be positive, you shall judge by the worst of my Symptoms—First, I own I like his Conversation, his Person has neither Fault nor Beauty—well enough—I don't remember I ever secretly wish'd my self married to him, or—that I ever seriously resolv'd against it.

Lady Ea. Well, so far you are tolerably safe:—But come—as to his manner of addressings to you, what Effect has that had?

Lady Bet. I am not a little pleas'd to observe few Men follow a Woman with the same Fatigue and Spirit, that he does me—am more pleas'd when he let's me use him ill; and if ever I have a favourable Thought of him, 'tis when I see he can't bear that Usage.

Lady Ea. Have a Care, that last is a dangerous Symptom—He pleases your Pride, I find.

Lady Bet. Oh! perfectly: In that—I own no Mortal ever can come up to him.

Lady Ea. But now, my Dear, now comes the main Point—Jealousy! are you sure you have never been touch'd with it? Tell me that with a safe Conscience, and then I pronounce you clear.

Lady Bet. Nay, then I defy him; for positively I was never jealous in my Life.

Lady Ea. How, Madam! have you never been stirr'd enough, to think a Woman strangely forward for being a little familiar in Talk with him? Or are you sure his Gallantry to another never gave you the least Disorder? Were you never, upon no Accident, in an Apprehension of losing him?

Lady Bet. Hah! Why, Madam—Bless me!—wh—wh—why sure you don't call this Jealousy, my Dear?

Lady Ea. Nay, nay, that is not the Business—Have you ever felt any thing of this Nature, Madam?

Lady Bet. Lord! don't be so hasty, my Dear—any thing of this Nature—O lud! I swear I don't like it: Dear Creature, bring me off here; for I am half frighted out of my Wits.

Lady Ea. Nay, if you can rally upon't, your Wound is not over deep, I'm afraid.

Lady Bet. Well, that's comfortably said, however.

Lady Ea. But come, to the Point—how far have you been jealous?

Lady Bet. Why—O bless me! He gave the Musick one Night to my Lady *Languish* here upon the Terrace; and (tho' she and I were very good Friends) I remember I could not speak to her in a Week for't—Oh!

Lady Ea. Nay, now you may laugh if you can; for, take my Word, the Marks are upon you—But come—what else?

Lady Bet. O nothing else, upon my Word, my Dear.

Lady Ea. Well, one Word more, and then I give Sentence: Suppose you were heartily convinc'd, that he actually follow'd another Woman?

Lady Bet. But pray, my Dear, what occasion is there to suppose any such thing at all?

Lady Ea. Guilty, upon my Honour.

Lady Bet. Pshah! I defy him to say, that ever I own'd any Inclination for him.

Lady Ea. No, but you have given him terrible Leave to guess it.

Lady Bet. If ever you see us meet again, you'll have but little Reason to think so, I can assure you.

Lady Ea. That I shall see presently; for here comes Sir *Charles,* and I am sure my Lord can't be far off.

Enter Sir Charles.

Sir Cha. Servant, Lady *Betty*—My Dear, how do you do?

Lady Ea. At your Service, my Dear—But pray what have you done with my Lord *Morelove?*

Lady Bet. Ay, Sir *Charles,* pray, how does your Pupil do? Have you any Hopes of him? Is he Docible?

Sir Cha. Well, Madam, to confess your Triumph over me, as well as him, I own my hopes of him are lost. I offer'd what I could to his Instruction, but he's incorrigibly yours, and undone—and the News, I presume, does not displease your Ladyship.

Lady Bet. Fie, fie, Sir *Charles,* you disparage your Friend, I am afraid you don't take Pains with him.

Sir Cha. Ha! I fancy, Lady *Betty,* your good Nature won't let you sleep a-Nights? Don't you love dearly to hurt People?

Lady Bet. O! your Servant; then without a Jest, the Man is so unfortunate in his want of Patience, that let me die, if I don't often pity him.

Sir Cha. Ha! strange Goodness—O that I were your Lover for a Month or two.

Lady Bet. What then?

Sir Cha. I wou'd make that pretty Heart's Blood of yours ake in a Fortnight.

Lady Bet. Hugh—I should hate you, your Assurance wou'd make your Address intolerable.

Sir Cha. I believe it wou'd, for I'd never Address you at all.

Lady Bet. O! you Clown you! [*Hitting him with her Fan.*

Sir Cha. Why, what to do? to feed a diseas'd Pride, that's Eternally breaking out in the Affectation of an ill Nature, that—in my Conscience I believe is but Affectation.

Lady Bet. You, nor your Friend have no great Reason to complain of my Fondness, I believe. Ha! ha! ha!

Sir Cha. [*Looking earnestly on her.*] Thou insolent Creature! How can you make a Jest of a Man, whose whole Life's but one continued Torment from your want of common Gratitude?

Lady Bet. Torment! for my part I really believe him as easy as you are.

Sir Cha. Poor intolerable Affectation! You know the contrary, you know him blindly yours, you know your Power, and the whole Pleasure of your Life's the poor and low Abuse of it.

Lady Bet. Pray how do I abuse it?—If I have any Power.

Sir Cha. You drive him to Extremes that make him mad, then punish him for acting against his Reason: You've almost turn'd his Brain, his common Judgment fails him; he's now, at this very Moment, driven by his Despair upon a Project, in hopes to free him from your Power, that I am sensible, and so must any one be that has his Sense, of course must ruin him with you, for ever: I almost blush to think of it, yet your unreasonable Disdain has forc'd him to it; and shou'd he now suspect I offer'd but a hint of it to you, as in Contempt of his Design, I know he'd call my Life to answer it: But I have no regard to Men in Madness, I rather chuse for once to trust in your good Nature, in hopes the Man, whom your unwary Beauty had made Miserable, your Generosity wou'd scorn to make Ridiculous.

Lady Bet. Sir *Charles,* you charge me very home, I never had it in my Inclination to make any thing ridiculous that did not deserve it. Pray, what is this Business you think so extravagant in him?

Sir Cha. Something so absurdly Rash and Bold, you'll hardly forgive ev'n me that tell it you.

Lady Bet. O fie! If it be a Fault, Sir *Charles,* I shall consider it as His, not Yours. Pray, what is it?

Lady Ea. I long to know, methinks.

Sir Cha. You may be sure he did not want my Dissuasions from it.

Lady Bet. Let's hear it.

Sir Cha. Why this Man, whom I have known to love you with such Excess of Generous Desire, whom I have heard in his Ecstatick Praises on your Beauty talk till from the soft Heat of his Distilling Thoughts the Tears have fall'n.

Lady Bet. O Sir *Charles*— [*Blushing.*

Sir Cha. Nay, grudge not, since 'tis past, to hear what was (tho' you contemn'd it) once his Merit: But now I own that Merit ought to be forgotten.

Lady Bet. Pray, Sir, be plain.

Sir Cha. This Man, I say, whose unhappy Passion has so ill succeeded with you, at last has forfeited all his Hopes (into which, pardon me, I confess my Friendship had lately flatter'd him) his Hopes of ev'n deserving now your lowest Pity or Regard.

Lady Bet. You amaze me—For I can't suppose his utmost Malice dares assault my Reputation—and what—

Sir Cha. No, but he maliciously presumes the World will do it for him; and indeed he has taken no unlikely means to make them busy with their Tongues: For he is this Moment upon the open Terrace, in the highest Publick Gallantry with my Lady *Graveairs.* And to convince the World and me, he said, he was not that tame Lover we fancied him, he'd venture to give her the Musick to Night: Nay, I heard him, before my Face, speak to one of the Hautboys, to engage the rest, and desir'd they would all take their Directions only from my Lady *Graveairs.*

Lady Bet. My Lady *Graveairs!* Truly I think my Lord's very much in the Right on't—for my part, Sir *Charles,* I don't see any thing in this that's so very ridiculous, nor indeed that ought to make me think either the better or worse of him for't.

Sir Cha. Pshah! Pshah! Madam, you and I know 'tis not in his Power to renounce you; this is but the poor Disguise of a resenting Passion vainly ruffled to a Storm, which the least gentle Look from you can reconcile at Will, and laugh into a Calm again.

Lady Bet. Indeed, Sir *Charles,* I shan't give my self that Trouble, I believe.

Sir Cha. So I told him, Madam; Are not all your Complaints, said I, already owing to her Pride, and can you suppose this publick Defiance of it (which you know you can't make good too) won't incense her more against you?—That's what I'd have, said he, starting wildly, I care not what becomes of me, so I but live to see her piqued at it.

Lady Bet. Upon my Word, I fancy my Lord will find himself mistaken—I shan't be piqued, I believe—I must first have a Value for the Thing I lose, before it piques me: Piqued! ha! ha! ha! [*Disorder'd.*

Sir Cha. Madam, you've said the very Thing I urg'd to him; I know her Temper so well, said I, that tho' she doated on you, if you once stood out against her, she'd sooner burst than shew the least Motion of Uneasiness.

Lady Bet. I can assure you, Sir *Charles,* my Lord won't find himself deceiv'd in your Opinion—Piqued!

Sir Cha. She has it! [*Aside.*

Lady Ea. Alas, poor Woman! how little do our Passions make us?

Lady Bet. Not, but I would advise him to have a little Regard to my Reputation in this Business: I would have him take heed of publickly affronting me.

Sir Cha. Right, Madam, that's what I strictly warn'd him of: for among Friends, whenever the World sees him follow another Woman, the malicious Tea-Tables will be very apt to be free with your Ladyship.

Lady Bet. I'd have him consider that, methinks.

Sir Cha. But alas! Madam, 'tis not in his Power to think with Reason, his mad Resentment has destroy'd even his Principles of common Honesty: He considers nothing but a senseless proud Revenge, which in this Fit of Lunacy 'tis impossible that either Threats or Danger can dissuade him from.

Lady Bet. What! does he defy me, threaten me! then he shall see, that I have Passions too, and know, as well as he, to stir my Heart against any Pride that dares insult me. Does he suppose I fear him? Fear the little Malice of a slighted Passion, that my own Scorn has stung into a despised Resentment! Fear him! O! it provokes me to think he dares have such a Thought!

Lady Ea. Dear Creature, don't disorder your self so.

Lady Bet. Let me but live to see him once more within my Power, and I'll forgive the rest of Fortune. [*Walking disorder'd.*

Lady Ea. Well! certainly I am very ill-natur'd; for though I see this News has disturb'd my Friend, I can't help being pleased with any Hopes of my Lady *Graveairs* being otherwise dispos'd of. [*Aside.*] My Dear, I am afraid you have provok'd her a little too far.

Sir Cha. Oh! not at all—You shall see—I'll sweeten her, and she'll cool like a Dish of Tea.

Lady Bet. I may see him with his complaining Face again—

Sir Cha. I am sorry, Madam, you so wrongly judge of what I've told you; I was in Hopes to have stirr'd your Pity, not your Anger; I little thought your Generosity wou'd punish him for Faults, which you your self resolv'd he shou'd commit—Yonder he comes, and all the World with him: Might I advise you, Madam, you shou'd not resent this thing at all—I wou'd not so much as stay to see him in his Fault; nay, I'd be the last that heard of it: Nothing can sting him more, or so justly punish his Folly, as your utter Neglect of it.

Lady Ea. Come, dear Creature, be persuaded, and go home with me, it will shew more Indifference to avoid him.

Lady Bet. No, Madam, I'll oblige his Vanity for once, and stay to let him see how strangely he has piqued me.

Sir Cha. [*Aside.*] O not at all to speak of; you had as good part with a little of that Pride of yours, or I shall yet make it a very troublesome Companion to you.

[*Goes from them, and whispers Lord* Morelove.

Enter Lord Foppington; *a little after, Lord* Morelove, *Lady* Graveairs, *and other Ladies.*

Lord Fop. Ladies, your Servant—O! we have wanted you beyond Reparation—such Diversion!

Lady Bet. Well! my Lord! have you seen my Lord *Morelove?*

Lord Fop. Seen him!—ha! ha! ha!—O, I have such things to tell you, Madam—you'll die—

Lady Bet. O pray, let's hear 'em, I was never in a better Humour to receive them.

Lord Fop. Hark you. [*They whisper.*

Lord Mo. So, she's engag'd already. [*To Sir* Charles.

Sir Cha. So much the better; make but a just Advantage of my Success, and she's undone.

Lord Fop.
Lady Bet. } Ha! ha! ha!

Sir Cha. You see already what ridiculous Pains she's taking to stir your Jealousy, and cover her own.

Lord Fop.
Lady Bet. } Ha! ha! ha!

Lord Mo. O never fear me; for, upon my Word, it now appears ridiculous ev'n to me.

Sir Cha. And hark you.— [*Whispers Lord* Morelove.

Lady Bet. And so the Widow was as full of Airs as his Lordship?

Sir Cha. Only observe that, and 'tis impossible you can fail. [*Aside.*

Lord Mo. Dear *Charles,* you have convinc'd me, and I thank you

Lady Gra. My Lord *Morelove!* What, do you leave us?

Lord Mo. Ten thousand Pardons, Madam, I was but just—

Lady Gra. Nay, nay, no Excuses, my Lord, so you will but let us have you again.

Sir Cha. [*Aside to Lady* Graveairs.] I see you have good Humour, Madam, when you like your Company.

Lady Gra. And you, I see, for all your mighty Thirst of Dominion, could stoop to be obedient, if one thought it worth one's while to make you so!

Sir Cha. Ha! Power would make her an admirable Tyrant. [*Aside.*

Lady Ea. [*Observing Sir* Charles *and Lady* Graveairs.] So! there's another Couple have quarrell'd too, I find—Those Airs to my Lord *Morelove,* look as if design'd to recover Sir *Charles* into Jealousy: I'll endeavour to join the Company, and it may be that will let me into the Secret. [*Aside.*] My Lord *Foppington,* I vow this is very uncomplaisant, to engross so agreeable a Part of the Company to your self.

Sir Cha. Nay, my Lord, that is not fair indeed to enter into Secrets among Friends!—Ladies, what say you? I think we ought to declare against it.

Ladies. O! no Secrets, no Secrets.

Lady Bet. Well, Ladies, I ought only to ask your Pardon: My Lord's excusable, for I would haul him into a Corner.

Lord Fop. I swear it's very hard ho! I observe two People of extreme Condition, can no sooner grow particular, but the Multitude of both Sexes are immediately up, and think their Properties invaded—

Lady Bet. Odious Multitude—

Lord Fop. Perish the *Canaille.*

Lady Gra. O, my Lord, we Women have all Reason to be jealous of Lady *Betty Modish*'s Power.

Lord Mo. [*To Lady* Betty.] As the Men, Madam, all have of my Lord *Foppington;* beside, Favourites of great Merit discourage those of an inferior Class for their Prince's Service; He has already lost you one of your Retinue, Madam.

Lady Bet. Not at all, my Lord, he has only made Room for another: One must sometimes make Vacancies, or there could be no Preferments.

Lord Fop. Ha! ha! Ladies Favours, my Lord, like Places at Court, are not always held for Life, you know.

Lady Bet. No indeed! if they were, the poor fine Women would be all us'd like their Wives; and no more minded than the Business of the Nation.

Lady Ea. Have a Care, Madam, an undeserving Favourite has been the Ruin of many a Prince's Empire.

Lord Fop. Ha! ha! Upon my Soul, Lady *Betty,* we must grow more discreet; for positively if we go on at this rate, we shall have the World throw you under the Scandal of Constancy, and I shall have all the Swords of Condition at my Throat for a Monopolist.

Lord Mo. O! there's no great Fear of that, my Lord; tho' the Men of Sense give it over, there will be always some idle Fellows vain enough to believe their Merit may succeed as well as your Lordship's.

Lady Bet. Or, if they should not, my Lord, Cast Lovers, you know need not fear being long out of Employment, while there are so many well-dispos'd People in the World—There are generally neglected Wives, Stale Maids, or Charitable Widows always ready to relieve the Necessities of a Disappointed Passion—and, by the way, Hark you, Sir *Charles.*

Lord Mo. [*Aside.*] So! she's stirr'd, I see; for all her Pains to hide it—she would hardly have glanc'd an Affront at a Woman she was not piqued at.

Lady Gra. [*Aside.*] That Wit was thrown at me, I suppose; but I'll return it.

Lady Bet. [*Softly to Sir* Charles.] Pray, how came you all this while to trust your Mistress so easily?

Sir Cha. One is not so apt, Madam, to be alarm'd at the Liberties of an Old Acquaintance, as perhaps your Ladyship ought to be at the Resentment of an Hard-us'd, Honourable Lover.

Lady Bet. Suppose I were alarm'd, how does that make you easy?

Sir Cha. Come, come, be wise at last; my trusting them together, may easily convince you, that (as I told you before) I know his Addresses to her are only outward, and 'twill be your Fault now, if you let him go on till the World thinks him in earnest; and a Thousand busy Tongues are set upon malicious Enquiries into your Reputation

Lady Bet. Why, Sir *Charles,* do you suppose while he behaves himself as he does, that I won't convince him of my Indifference?

Sir Cha. But hear me, Madam–

Lady Gra. [*Aside.*] The Air of that Whisper looks as if the Lady had a Mind to be making her Peace again; and 'tis possible, his Worship's being so busy in the Matter too, may proceed as much from his Jealousy of my Lord with me, as Friendship to her, at least I fancy so; therefore I'm resolv'd to keep her still piqued, and prevent it, tho' it be only to gall him–Sir *Charles,* that is not fair, to take a Privilege you just now declared against in my Lord *Foppington.*

Lord Mo. Well observ'd, Madam.

Lady Gra. Beside, it looks so affected to whisper, when every body guesses the Secret.

Lord Mo. Ha! ha! ha!

Lady Bet. O! Madam, your Pardon in particular: But 'tis possible you may be mistaken: The Secrets of People that have any Regard to their Actions, are not so soon guess'd, as theirs that have made a Confident of the whole Town.

Lord Fop. Ha! ha! ha!

Lady Gra. A *Coquete* in her Affected Airs of Disdain to a revolted Lover, I'm afraid must exceed your Ladyship in Prudence, not to let the World see at the same time, she'd give her Eyes to make her Peace with him: Ha! ha!

Lord Mo. Ha! ha! ha!

Lady Bet. 'Twou'd be a Mortification indeed, if it were in the Power of a fading Widow's Charms to prevent it; and the Man must be miserably reduc'd sure, that cou'd bear to live buried in Woollen, or take up with the Motherly Comforts of a Swan-skin Petticoat. Ha! ha!

Lord Fop. Ha! ha! ha!

Lady Gra. Widows, it seems, are not so squeamish to their Interest, they know their own Minds, and take the Man they like, though it happens to be one that a froward vain Girl has disoblig'd, and is pining to be Friends with.

Lord Mo. Nay, tho' it happens to be one, that confesses he once was fond of a piece of Folly, and afterwards asham'd on't.

Lady Bet. Nay, my Lord, there's no standing against two of you.

Lord Fop. No, faith, that's odds at Tennis, my Lord: Not but if your Ladyship pleases, I'll endeavour to keep your Back-hand a little: Tho' upon my Soul, you may safely set me up at the Line: For, knock me down, if ever I saw a Rest of Wit better play'd, than that last, in my Life—What say you, Madam, shall we engage?

Lady Bet. As you please, my Lord.

Lord Fop. Ha! ha! ha! *Allons! Tout de Bon, Joues mi lor.*

Lord Mo. O pardon me, Sir, I shall never think my self in any thing a Match for the Lady.

Lord Fop. To you, Madam.

Lady Bet. That's much, my Lord, when the World knows you have been so many Years teazing me to play the Fool with you.

Lord Fop. Ah! *Bien joue.* Ha! ha! ha!

Lord Mo. At that Game, I confess, your Ladyship has chosen a much properer Person to improve your Hand with.

Lord Fop. To me, Madam.—My Lord, I presume whoever the Lady thinks fit to play the Fool with, will at least be able to give as much Envy as the wise Person that had not Wit enough to keep well with her when he was so.

Lady Gra. O! my Lord! both Parties must needs be greatly happy for I dare swear, neither will have any Rivals to disturb 'em.

Lord Mo. Ha! ha!

Lady Bet. None that will disturb 'em, I dare swear.

Lord Fop. Ha! ha! ha!

Lord Mo.
Lady Gra. } Ha! ha! ha!
Lady Bet.

Sir Cha. I don't know, Gentlefolks—but you are all in extreme good Humour, methinks; I hope there's none of it affected.

Lady Ea. I should be loth to answer for any but my Lord *Foppington.* [*Aside.*

Lady Bet. Mine is not, I'll swear.

Lord Mo. Nor mine, I'm sure.

Lady Gra. Mine's sincere, depend upon't.

Lord Fop. And may the eternal Frowns of the whole Sex doubly dem me, if mine is not.

Lady Ea. Well, good People, I am mighty glad to hear it. You have all perform'd extremely well: But if you please, you shall ev'n give over your Wit now, while it is well.

Lady Bet. [*To her self.*] Now I see his Humour, I'll stand it out, if I were sure to die for't.

Sir Cha. You should not have proceeded so far with my Lord *Foppington,* after what I had told you. [*Aside to Lady* Betty.

Lady Bet. Pray, Sir *Charles,* give me leave to understand my self a little.

Sir Cha. Your Pardon, Madam, I thought a right Understanding would have been for both your Interests, and Reputation.

Lady Bet. For his, perhaps.

Sir Cha. Nay then, Madam, it's time for me to take care of my Friend.

Lady Bet. I never in the least doubted your Friendship to him in any thing that was to shew your self my Enemy.

Sir Cha. Since I see, Madam, you have so ungrateful a Sense of my Lord *Morelove*'s Merit, and my Service, I shall never be asham'd of using my Power henceforth to keep him intirely out of your Ladyship's.

Lady Bet. Was ever any thing so insolent! I could find in my Heart to run the hazard of a downright Compliance, if it were only to convince him, that my Power, perhaps, is not inferior to his. [*To her self.*

Lady Ea. My Lord *Foppington,* I think you generally lead the Company upon these Occasions. Pray, will you think of some prettier sort of Diversion for us, than Parties and Whisper?

Lord Fop. What say you, Ladies, shall we step and see what's done at the Basset-Table?

Lady Bet. With all my Heart; Lady *Easy*—

Lady Ea. I think 'tis the best thing we can do; and because we won't part to Night, you shall all Sup where you Din'd—What say you, my Lord?

Lord Mo. Your Ladyship may be sure of me, Madam.

Lord Fop. Ay, ay, we'll all come.

Lady Ea. Then pray let's change Parties a little. My Lord *Foppington,* you shall Squire me.

Lord Fop. O! you do me Honour, Madam.

Lady Bet. My Lord *Morelove,* pray let me speak with you.

Lord Mo. Me, Madam?

Lady Bet. If you please, my Lord.

Lord Mo. Ha! that Look shot thro' me! what can this mean? [*Aside.*

Lady Bet. This is no proper Place to tell you what it is; but there is one thing I'd fain be truly answer'd in: I suppose you'll be at my Lady *Easy* 's by and by; and if you'll give me leave there–

Lord Mo. If you please to do me that Honour, Madam, I shall certainly be there.

Lady Bet. That's all, my Lord.

Lord Mo. Is not your Ladyship for Walking?

Lady Bet. If your Lordship dares venture with me.

Lord Mo. O! Madam! [*Taking her Hand.*] How my Heart dances! what heav'nly Musick's in her Voice, when soften'd into Kindness! [*Aside.*

Lady Bet. Ha! his Hand trembles–Sir *Charles* may be mistaken.

Lord Fop. My Lady *Graveairs,* you won't let Sir *Charles* leave us?

Lady Gra. No, my Lord, we'll follow you–stay a little. [*To Sir* Charles.

Sir Cha. I thought your Ladyship design'd to follow 'em.

Lady Gra. Perhaps I'd speak with you.

Sir Cha. But, Madam, consider we shall certainly be observ'd.

Lady Gra. Lord, Sir! if you think it such a Favour. [*Exit hastily.*

Sir Cha. Is she gone? let her go, *&c.* [*Exit Singing.*

ACT V. SCENE I.

The SCENE *continues.*

Enter Sir Charles *and Lord* Morelove.

Sir Cha. Come a little this way—my Lady *Graveairs* had an Eye upon me as I stole off, and I'm apprehensive will make use of any Opportunity to talk with me.

Lord Mo. O! we are pretty safe here—well! you were speaking of Lady *Betty.*

Sir Cha. Ay, my Lord—I say, notwithstanding all this sudden Change of her Behaviour, I would not have you yet be too secure of her: For, between you and I, since, as I told you, I have profess'd my self an open Enemy to her Power with you, 'tis not impossible but this new Air of good Humour may very much proceed from a little Woman's Pride, of convincing me you are not yet out of her Power.

Lord Mo. Not unlikely: but still, can we make no Advantage of it?

Sir Cha. That's what I have been thinking of—look you—Death! my Lady *Graveairs!*

Lord Mo. Ha! she will have Audience I find.

Sir Cha. There's no avoiding her—the Truth is, I have ow'd her a little Good Nature a great while—I see there is but one way of getting rid of her—I must ev'n appoint her a Day of Payment at last. If you'll step into my Lodgings, my Lord, I'll just give her an Answer, and be with you in a Moment.

Lord Mo. Very well, I'll stay there for you.

[*Exit Lord* Morelove.

Enter Lady Graveairs *on the other side.*

Lady Gra. Sir *Charles!*

Sir Cha. Come, come, no more of these Reproachful Looks; you'll find, Madam, I have deserv'd better of you than your Jealousy imagines—Is it a Fault to be tender of your Reputation?—

fie, fie—This may be a proper time to Talk, and of my Contriving too—You see I just now shook off my Lord *Morelove* on purpose.

Lady Gra. May I believe you?

Sir Cha. Still doubting my Fidelity, and mistaking my Discretion for want of Good Nature.

Lady Gra. Don't think me troublesome—For I confess 'tis Death to think of parting with you: Since the World sees, for you I have neglected Friends and Reputation, have stood the little Insults of disdainful Prudes, that envy'd me perhaps your Friendship; have born the freezing Looks of near and general Acquaintance—Since this is so—don't let 'em ridicule me too, and say, my foolish Vanity undid me; don't let 'em point at me as a Cast Mistress.

Sir Cha. You wrong me to suppose the Thought; you'll have better of me when we meet: When shall you be at leisure?

Lady Gra. I confess, I wou'd see you once again; if what I have more to say prove ineffectual, perhaps it may convince me then, 'tis my Interest to part with you—Can you come to Night?

Sir Cha. You know we have Company, and I'm afraid they'll stay too late—Can't it be before Supper—What's a Clock now?

Lady Gra. It's almost Six.

Sir Cha. At Seven then be sure of me; till when, I'd have you go back to the Ladies to avoid Suspicion, and about that Time have the Vapours.

Lady Gra. May I depend upon you? [*Exit.*

Sir Cha. Depend on every thing—A very troublesome Business this—send me once fairly rid on't—if ever I'm caught in an *Honourable* Affair again!—A Debt now that a little ready Civility, and away, would satisfy, a Man might bear with; but to have a Rent-Charge upon one's Good Nature, with an unconscionable long Scroll of Arrears too, that wou'd eat out the Profits of the best Estate in Christendom—ah—intolerable!—Well! I'll ev'n to my Lord, and shake off the Thoughts on't. [*Exit.*

Enter Lady Betty *and Lady* Easy.

Lady Bet. I observe, my Dear, you have usually this great Fortune at Play, it were enough to make one suspect your good luck with an Husband.

Lady Ea. Truly I don't complain of my Fortune either way.

Lady Bet. Prithee tell me, you are often advising me to it, are there those real comfortable Advantages in Marriage, that our old Aunts and Grandmothers would persuade us of?

Lady Ea. Upon my Word, if I had the worst Husband in the World, I should still think so.

Lady Bet. Ay, but then the Hazard of not having a good one, my Dear.

Lady Ea. You may have a good one, I dare say, if you don't give Airs till you spoil him.

Lady Bet. Can there be the same dear, full Delight in giving Ease, as Pain? O! my Dear, the Thought of parting with one's Power is insupportable!

Lady Ea. And the keeping it, till it dwindles into no Power at all, is most rufully foolish.

Lady Bet. But still to marry before one's heartily in Love—

Lady Ea. Is not half so formidable a Calamity—but if I have any Eyes, my Dear, you'll run no great Hazard of that, in venturing upon my Lord *Morelove*—You don't know, perhaps, that within this half Hour the Tone of your Voice is strangely soften'd to him, ha! ha! ha!

Lady Bet. My Dear, you are positively, one or other, the most censorious Creature in the World—and so I see it's in vain to talk with you—Pray, will you go back to the Company?

Lady Ea. Ah! poor Lady *Betty*. [*Exeunt.*

SCENE II.

The SCENE *changes to Sir* Charles's *Lodgings.*

Enter Sir Charles *and Lord* Morelove.

Lord Mo. Charles! you have transported me! you have made my Part in the Scene so very easy too, 'tis impossible I should fail in it.

Sir Cha. That's what I consider'd: For now the more you throw your self into her Power, the more I shall be able to force her into yours.

Lord Mo. After all (begging the Ladies Pardon) your fine Women, like Bullies, are only stout where they know their Men: A Man of an honest Courage may fright 'em into any thing! Well, I am fully instructed, and will about it instantly—Won't you go along with me?

Sir Cha. That may not be so proper:—besides I have a little Business upon my Hands.

Lord Mo. O! your Servant, Sir—Good by to you—you shan't stir.

Sir Cha. My Lord, your Servant— [*Exit Lord* Morelove. So! now to dispose of my self, 'till 'tis time to think of my Lady *Graveairs*—Umph!—I have no great Maw to that Business, methinks —I don't find my self in Humour enough to come up to the Civil Things that are usually expected in the making up of an old Quarrel—[Edging *crosses the Stage.*] There goes a warmer Temptation by half—Ha! into my Wife's Bed-chamber too—I question if the Jade has any great Business there;—I have a Fancy she has only a mind to be taking the Opportunity of no body's being at home, to make her Peace with me—let me see—ay, I shall have time enough to go to her Ladyship afterwards—Besides I want a little Sleep, I find—Your young Fops may talk of their Women of Quality—but to me now, there's a strange agreeable Convenience in a Creature one is not oblig'd to say much to upon these Occasions. [*Going.*

Enter Edging.

Edg. Did you call me, Sir?

Sir Cha. Ha! all's Right—[*Aside.*]—Yes, Madam, I did call you. [*Sits down.*

Edg. What wou'd you please to have, Sir?

Sir Cha. Have! why, I wou'd have you grow a good Girl, and know when you are well us'd, Hussy.

Edg. Sir, I don't complain of any thing, not I.

Sir Cha. Well, don't be uneasy—I am not angry with you now—Come and Kiss me.

Edg. Lard, Sir!

Sir Cha. Don't be a Fool now—come hither.

Edg. Pshah— [*Goes to him.*

Sir Cha. No wry Faces—so—sit down. I won't have you look Grave neither. Let me see you smile, you Jade you.

Edg. Hah! hah! [*Laughs and blushes.*

Sir Cha. Ah! you melting Rogue!

Edg. Come, don't you be at your Tricks now—Lard! can't you sit still and talk with one? I'm sure there's ten times more Love in that, and fifty times the Satisfaction, People may say what they will.

Sir Cha. Well! now you're good, you shall have your own way.—I am going to lie down in the next Room; and, since you love a little Chat, come and throw my Night-Gown over me, and you shall talk me to sleep— [*Exit Sir* Charles.

Edg. Yes, Sir—for all his Way, I see he likes me still.

[*Exit after him.*

SCENE III.

The SCENE *changes to the Terrace.*

Enter Lady Betty, *Lady* Easy, *and Lord* Morelove.

Lord Mo. Nay, Madam, there you are too severe upon him; for, bating now and then a little Vanity, my Lord *Foppington* does not want Wit sometimes to make him a very tolerable Woman's Man.

Lady Bet. But such Eternal Vanity grows Tiresome.

Lady Ea. Come, if he were not so loose in his Morals, Vanity methinks might easily be excus'd, considering how much 'tis in Fashion: For pray observe, what's half the Conversation of most of the fine young People about Town, but a perpetual Affectation of appearing foremost in the Knowledge of Manners, new Modes, and Scandal? and in that I don't see any Body comes up to him.

Lord Mo. Nor I indeed—and here he comes—Pray, Madam, let's have a little more of him; no body shews him to more Advantage than your Ladyship.

Lady Bet. Nay, with all my Heart; you'll second me, my Lord.

Lord Mo. Upon Occasion, Madam—

Lady Ea. Engaging upon Parties, my Lord?

[*Aside, and smiling to Lord* Morelove.

Enter Lord Foppington.

Lord Fop. So, Ladies! what's the Affair now?

Lady Bet. Why you were, my Lord; I was allowing you a great many good Qualities; but Lady *Easy* says you are a perfect Hypocrite; and that whatever Airs you give your self to the Women, she's confident you value no Woman in the World equal to your own Lady.

Lord Fop. You see, Madam, how I am scandaliz'd upon your Account: But it's so natural for a Prude to be Malicious, when a Man endeavours to be well with any body but her self; did you never observe she was Piqu'd at that before? Ha! ha!

Lady Bet. I'll swear you are a provoking Creature.

Lord Fop. Let's be more familiar upon't, and give her Disorder: Ha! ha!

Lady Bet. Ha! ha! ha!

Lord Fop. Stap my Breath, but Lady *Easy* is an Admirable Discoverer–Marriage is indeed a Prodigious Security of one's Inclination: A Man's likely to take a World of Pains in an Employment, where he can't be turn'd out for his Idleness.

Lady Bet. I vow, my Lord, that's vastly Generous to all the Fine Women; you are for giving 'em a Despotick Power in Love, I see, to reward and punish as they think fit.

Lord Fop. Ha! ha! Right, Madam; what signifies Beauty without Power? And a fine Woman when she's Married makes as ridiculous a Figure, as a beaten General marching out of a Garrison.

Lady Ea. I'm afraid, Lady *Betty,* the greatest Danger in your Use of Power, wou'd be from a too heedless Liberality; you would more mind the Man than his Merit.

Lord Fop. Piqu'd again, by all that's Fretful–Well, certainly to give Envy is a Pleasure inexpressible. [*To Lady* Betty.

Lady Bet. Ha! ha! ha!

Lady Ea. Does not she shew him well, my Lord?

[*Aside to Lord* Morelove.

Lord Mo. Perfectly, and me too to my self–For now I almost blush to think I ever was uneasy at him. [*To Lady* Easy.

Lord Fop. Lady *Easy,* I ask ten thousand Pardons, I'm afraid I am Rude all this while.

Lady Ea. O not at all, my Lord, you are always good Company, when you please: not but in some things, indeed, you are apt to be like other fine Gentlemen, a little too loose in your Principles.

Lord Fop. O, Madam, never to the Offence of the Ladies; I agree in any Community with them; no body is a more constant Churchman, when the fine Women are there.

Lady Ea. O fie, my Lord, you ought not to go for their sakes at all. And I wonder you that are for being such a good Husband of your Virtues, are not afraid of bringing your Prudence into a Lampoon or a Play.

Lady Bet. Lampoons and Plays, Madam, are only things to be laugh'd at.

Lord Mo. Plays now indeed we need not be so much afraid of, for since the late short-sighted View of 'em, Vice may go on and prosper, the Stage dares hardly shew a Vicious Person speaking like himself, for fear of being call'd Prophane for exposing him.

Lady Ea. 'Tis hard indeed, when People won't distinguish between what's meant for Contempt, and what for Example.

Lord Fop. Od so! Ladies, the Court's coming home, I see; shall not we make our Bows?

Lady Bet. O! by all means.

Lady Ea. Lady *Betty,* I must leave you; for I'm oblig'd to write Letters, and I know you won't give me Time after Supper.

Lady Bet. Well, my Dear, I'll make a short Visit and be with you. [*Exit Lady* Easy.
Pray, what's become of my Lady *Graveairs?*

Lord Mo. Oh, I believe she's gone home, Madam, she seem'd not to be very well.

Lord Fop. And where's Sir *Charles,* my Lord?

Lord Mo. I left him at his own Lodgings.

Lady Bet. He's upon some Ramble, I'm afraid.

Lord Fop. Nay, as for that matter, a Man may ramble at Home sometimes—But here come the Chaises, we must make a little more Haste, Madam. [*Exeunt.*

SCENE IV.

The SCENE *changes to Sir* Charles's *Lodgings.*

Enter Lady Easy *and a Servant.*

Lady Ea. Is your Master come home?

Serv. Yes, Madam.

Lady Ea. Where is he?

Serv. I believe, Madam, he's laid down to sleep.

Lady Ea. Where's *Edging?* Bid her get me some Wax and Paper—stay, it's no matter, now I think on't—there's some above upon my Toilet. [*Exeunt severally.*

SCENE V.

The SCENE *opens, and discovers Sir* Charles *without his Periwig, and* Edging *by him, both asleep in two Easy Chairs.*

Then Enter Lady Easy, *who starts and trembles, some time unable to speak.*

Lady Ea. Ha!
Protect me Virtue, Patience, Reason!
Teach me to bear this killing Sight, or let
Me think my dreaming Senses are deceiv'd!
For sure a Sight like This might raise the Arm
Of Duty, even to the Breast of Love! At least
I'll throw this Vizor of my Patience off:
Now wake him in his Guilt,
And bare-fac'd front him with my Wrongs.
I'll talk to him till he blushes, nay 'till he—
Frowns on me, perhaps—and then
I'm lost again—The Ease of a few Tears
Is all that's left to me—
And Duty too forbids me to insult,
Where I have vow'd Obedience—Perhaps
The Fault's in me, and Nature has not form'd
Me with the Thousand little Requisites
That warm the Heart to Love—
Somewhere there is a Fault—
But Heav'n best knows what both of us deserve:
Ha! Bare-headed, and in so sound a Sleep!
Who knows, while thus expos'd to th' unwholsome Air,
But Heav'n offended may o'ertake his Crime,

And, in some languishing Distemper, leave him
A severe Example of its violated Laws—
Forbid it Mercy, and forbid it Love.
This may prevent it.

[*Takes a Steinkirk off her Neck, and lays it gently on his Head.*

And if he should wake offended at my too busy Care, let my heart-breaking Patience, Duty, and my fond Affection plead my Pardon.

[*Exit.*

[*After she has been out some Time, a Bell rings;* Edging *wakes, and stirs Sir* Charles.

Edg. Oh!

Sir Cha. How now! what's the Matter?

Edg. O! bless my Soul, my Lady's come home.

Sir Cha. Go, go then. [*Bell rings.*

Edg. O lud! my Head's in such a Condition too. [*Runs to the Glass.*] I am coming, Madam—O lud! here's no Powder neither—Here, Madam. [*Exit.*

Sir Cha. How now! [*Feeling the Steinkirk upon his Head.*] What's this? How came it here? [*Puts on his Wig.*] Did not I see my Wife wear this to Day?—Death! she can't have been here, sure! —It could not be Jealousy that brought her home—for my coming was accidental—so too, I fear, might hers.—How careless have I been?—Not to secure the Door neither—'Twas foolish—It must be so! She certainly has seen me here sleeping with her Woman:—If so, how low an Hypocrite to her must that Sight have prov'd me!—The Thought has made me despicable ev'n to my self—How mean a Vice is Lying? and how often have these empty Pleasures lull'd my Honour and my Conscience to a Lethargy,—while I grossly have abus'd her, poorly skulking behind a thousand Falshoods? Now I reflect, this has not been the first of her Discoveries—How contemptible a Figure must I have made to her!—A crowd of recollected Circumstances confirm me now, she has been long acquainted with my Follies, and yet with what amazing Prudence has she born the secret Pangs of injur'd Love, and wore an everlasting Smile to me!—This asks a little Thinking—something should be done—I'll see her instantly, and be resolv'd from her Behaviour.

[*Exit.*

SCENE VI.

The SCENE *changes to another Room.*

Enter Lady Easy *and* Edging.

Lady Ea. Where have you been, *Edging?*

Edg. Been, Madam! I–I–I–I came as soon as I heard you Ring, Madam.

Lady Ea. How Guilt confounds her! but she's below my Thought–[*Aside.*] Fetch my last new Scarf hither–I have a mind to alter it a little–make haste.

Edg. Yes, Madam–I see she does not suspect any thing. [*Exit.*

Lady Ea. Heigh ho! [*Sitting down.*] I had forgot–but I'm unfit for writing now–'Twas an hard Conflict–yet it's a Joy to think it over: A secret Pride, to tell my Heart my Conduct has been just–How low are vicious Minds that offer Injuries! how much superior Innocence that bears 'em!–Still there's a Pleasure ev'n in the Melancholy of a quiet Conscience–Away my Fears, it is not yet impossible–for while his human Nature is not quite shook off, I ought not to despair.

Re-enter Edging *with a Scarf.*

Edg. Here's the Scarf, Madam.

Lady Ea. So, sit down there–and, let me see–here–Rip off all that Silver.

Edg. Indeed, I always thought it would become your Ladyship better without it–But now suppose, Madam, you carry'd another Row of Gold round the Scollops, and then you take and lay this Silver Plain all along the Gathers, and your Ladyship will perfectly see it will give the Thing ten thousand times another Air.

Lady Ea. Prithee don't be impertinent, do as I bid you.

Edg. Nay, Madam, with all my Heart, your Ladyship may do as you please.

Lady Ea. This Creature grows so confident, and I dare not part with her, lest he should think it Jealousy. [*Aside.*

Enter Sir Charles.

Sir Cha. So, my Dear! What, at Work! How are you employ'd, pray?

Lady Ea. I was thinking to alter this Scarf here.

Sir Cha. What's amiss? methinks it's very pretty.

Edg. Yes, Sir, it's pretty enough for that matter, but my Lady has a mind it should be proper too.

Sir Cha. Indeed!

Lady Ea. I fancy plain Gold and Black would become me better.

Sir Cha. That's a grave Thought, my Dear.

Edg. O dear Sir, not at all, my Lady's much in the Right; I am sure as it is it's fit for nothing but a Girl.

Sir Cha. Leave the Room.

Edg. Lard, Sir! I can't stir—I must stay to—

Sir Cha. Go— [*Angrily.*

Edg. [*Throwing down the Work hastily, and crying aside.*] If ever I speak to him again, I'll be burn'd. [*Exit* Edging.

Sir Cha. Sit still, my Dear—I came to talk with you—and, which you well may wonder at, what I have to say is of Importance too, but 'tis in order to my hereafter always talking kindly to you.

Lady Ea. Your Words were never disobliging, nor can I charge you with a Look that ever had the Appearance of unkind.

Sir Cha. The perpetual Spring of your good Humour lets me draw no Merit from what I have appear'd to be, which makes me curious now to know your Thoughts of what I really am: And never having ask'd you this before, it puzzles me; nor can I (my strange Negligence consider'd) reconcile to Reason your first Thoughts of venturing upon Marriage with me.

Lady Ea. I never thought it such an Hazard.

Sir Cha. How could a Woman of your Restraint in Principles, Sedateness, Sense, and tender Disposition, propose to see an happy Life with one (now I reflect) that hardly took an Hour's Pains ev'n before Marriage, to appear but what I am? A loose unheeding Wretch, absent in all I do, Civil, and as often Rude without Design, unseasonably thoughtful, easy to a Fault, and in my best of Praise but carelessly good-natur'd; How shall I reconcile your Temper with having made so strange a Choice?

Lady Ea. Your own Words may answer you—Your having never seem'd to be but what you really were; and through that Carelessness of Temper there still shone forth to me an undesigning Honesty, I always doubted of in smoother Faces: Thus while I saw you took least Pains to win me, you pleas'd and woo'd me most: Nay,

I have often thought, that such a Temper could never be deliberately unkind: Or at the worst, I knew that Errors from want of Thinking might be born; at least, when probably one Moment's serious Thought would end 'em: These were my worst of Fears, and these, when weigh'd by growing Love against solid Hopes, were nothing.

Sir Cha. My Dear, your Understanding startles me, and justly calls my own in question: I blush to think I've worn so bright a Jewel in my Bosom, and till this Hour have scarce been curious once to look upon its Lustre.

Lady Ea. You set too high a Value on the common Qualities of an easy Wife.

Sir Cha. Virtues, like Benefits, are double when conceal'd: And, I confess, I yet suspect you of a higher Value far, than I have spoke you.

Lady Ea. I understand you not.

Sir Cha. I'll speak more plainly to you—be free and tell me—Where did you leave this Handkerchief?

Lady Ea. Hah!

Sir Cha. What is't you start at? You hear the Question.

Lady Ea. What shall I say? my Fears confound me.

Sir Cha. Be not concern'd, my Dear, be easy in the Truth, and tell me.

Lady Ea. I cannot speak—and I cou'd wish you'd not oblige me to it—'tis the only Thing I ever yet refus'd you—and tho' I want a Reason for my Will, let me not answer you.

Sir Cha. Your Will then be a Reason, and since I see you are so generously tender of reproaching me, 'tis fit I should be easy in my Gratitude, and make what ought to be my Shame, my Joy; let me be therefore pleas'd to tell you now, your wondrous Conduct has wak'd me to a Sense of your Disquiet past, and Resolution never to disturb it more—And (not that I offer it as a Merit, but yet in blind Compliance to my Will) let me beg you would immediately discharge your Woman.

Lady Ea. Alas! I think not of her—O, my Dear, distract me not with this Excess of Goodness. [*Weeping.*

Sir Cha. Nay, praise me not, lest I reflect how little I have deserv'd it—I see you are in Pain to give me this Confusion—Come, I will not shock your Softness by my untimely Blush for what is past, but rather sooth you to a Pleasure at my Sense of Joy, for my recover'd Happiness to come: Give then to my new-born Love what Name you please, it cannot, shall not be too kind: O! it cannot be too soft for what my Soul swells up with Emulation to deserve—Receive me then intire at last, and take what yet no Woman ever truly had, my conquer'd Heart.

Lady Ea. O the soft Treasure! O the dear Reward of long-desiring Love!—Now I am blest indeed, to see you kind without th' Expence of Pain in being so, to make you mine with Easiness: Thus! thus to have you mine is something more than Happiness, 'tis double Life, and Madness of abounding Joy. But 'twas a Pain intolerable to give you a Confusion.

Sir Cha. O thou engaging Virtue! But I'm too slow in doing Justice to thy Love: I know thy Softness will refuse me: but remember I insist upon it—let thy Woman be discharg'd this Minute.

Lady Ea. No, my Dear, think me not so low in Faith, to fear that, after what you have said, 'twill ever be in her Power to do me future Injury: When I can conveniently provide for her, I'll think on't: But to discharge her now, might let her guess at the Occasion; and methinks I wou'd have all our Differences, like our Endearments, be equally a Secret to our Servants.

Sir Cha. Still my Superior every way—be it as you have better thought—Well, my Dear, now I'll confess a thing that was not in your Power to accuse me of; to be short, I own this Creature is not the only one I have been to blame with.

Lady Ea. I know she is not, and was always less concern'd to find it so; for Constancy in Errors might have been fatal to me.

Sir Cha. What is't you know, my Dear? [*Surpriz'd.*

Lady Ea. Come, I am not afraid to accuse you now—my Lady *Graveairs*—Your Carelessness, my Dear, let all the World know it, and it would have been hard indeed, had it been only to me a Secret.

Sir Cha. My Dear, I'll ask no more Questions, for fear of being more ridiculous: I do confess, I thought my Discretion there had been a Masterpiece—How contemptible must I have look'd all this while?

Lady Ea. You shan't say so.

Sir Cha. Well, to let you see I had some Shame, as well as Nature in me, I had writ this to my Lady *Graveairs,* upon my first discovering that you knew I had wrong'd you: Read it.

Lady Ea. [*Reads.*] "Something has happen'd, that prevents
"the Visit I intended you; and I could gladly wish, you
"never wou'd reproach me, if I tell you, 'tis utterly in-
"convenient that I shou'd ever see you more.

This indeed was more than I had merited.

Enter a Servant.

Sir Cha. Who's there? Here–step with this to my Lady *Graveairs.* [*Seals the Letter, and gives it the Servant.*

Serv. Yes, Sir–Madam, my Lady *Betty*'s come.

Lady Ea. I'll wait on her.

Sir Cha. My Dear, I'm thinking there may be other things my Negligence may have wrong'd you in; but be assur'd, as I discover 'em, all shall be corrected: Is there any Part or Circumstance in your Fortune that I can change, or yet make easier to you?

Lady Ea. None, my Dear, your good Nature never stinted me in that; and now, methinks, I have less Occasion there than ever.

Re-enter Servant.

Serv. Sir, my Lord *Morelove*'s come.

Sir Cha. I am coming–I think I told you of the Design we had laid against Lady *Betty*.

Lady Ea. You did, and I shou'd be pleas'd to be my self concern'd in it.

Sir Cha. I believe we may employ you: I know he waits me with Impatience. But, my Dear, won't you think me tasteless to the Joy you've given me, to suffer at this time any Concern but you t'employ my Thoughts?

Lady Ea. Seasons must be obey'd; and since I know your Friend's Happiness depending, I cou'd not taste my own, shou'd you neglect it.

Sir Cha. Thou easy Sweetness–O! what a Waste on thy neglected Love has my unthinking Brain committed! But Time, and future Thrift of Tenderness, shall yet repair it all: The Hours will come, when this soft gliding Stream that swells my Heart, uninterrupted shall renew its Course–

And like the Ocean after Ebb, shall move
With constant Force of due returning Love. [*Exit.*

SCENE VII.

The SCENE *changes to another Room.*

And then Re-enter Lady Easy *and Lady* Betty.

Lady Bet. You have been in Tears, my Dear, and yet you look pleas'd too.

Lady Ea. You'll pardon me, if I can't let you into Circumstances: But be satisfied, Sir *Charles* has made me happy ev'n to a Pain of Joy.

Lady Bet. Indeed I am truly glad of it: tho' I am sorry to find that any one who has Generosity enough to do you Justice, should, unprovok'd, be so great an Enemy to me.

Lady Ea. Sir *Charles* your Enemy!

Lady Bet. My Dear, you'll pardon me, if I always thought him so, but now I am convinc'd of it.

Lady Ea. In what, pray? I can't think you'll find him so.

Lady Bet. O! Madam, it has been his whole Business of late to make an utter Breach between my Lord *Morelove* and me.

Lady Ea. That may be owing to your Usage of my Lord; perhaps he thought it would not disoblige you! I am confident you are mistaken in him.

Lady Bet. O! I don't use to be out in things of this Nature; I can see well enough: But I shall be able to tell you more when I have talk'd with my Lord.

Lady Ea. Here he comes; and because you shall talk with him—No Excuses—for positively I'll leave you together.

Lady Bet. Indeed, my Dear, I desire you would stay then; for, I know you think now, that I have a Mind to—to—

Lady Ea. To—to—ha! ha! ha! [*Going.*

Lady Bet. Well! remember this.

Enter Lord Morelove.

Lord Mo. I hope I don't fright you away, Madam.

Lady Ea. Not at all, my Lord; but I must beg your Pardon for a Moment, I'll wait upon you immediately. [*Exit.*

Lady Bet. My Lady *Easy* gone?

Lord Mo. Perhaps, Madam, in Friendship to you; she thinks I may have deserv'd the Coldness you of late have shewn me, and was willing to give you this Opportunity to convince me, you have not done it without just Grounds and Reason.

Lady Bet. How handsomly does he reproach me! But I can't bear that he should think I know it—[*Aside.*] My Lord, whatever has pass'd between you and me, I dare swear that could not be her Thoughts at this time: For when two People have appear'd professed Enemies, she can't but think one will as little care to give, as t'other to receive a Justification of their Actions.

Lord Mo. Passion indeed often does repented Injuries on both sides; but I don't remember in my Heat of Error, I ever yet profess'd my self your Enemy.

Lady Bet. My Lord, I shall be very free with you—I confess I do think now I have not a greater Enemy in the World.

Lord Mo. If having long loved you, to my own Disquiet, be injurious, I am contented then to stand the foremost of your Enemies.

Lady Bet. O, my Lord, there's no great fear of your being my Enemy that way, I dare say—

Lord Mo. There's no other way my Heart can bear to offend you now, and I foresee in that it will persist to my undoing.

Lady Bet. Fie, fie, my Lord, we know where your Heart is well enough.

Lord Mo. My Conduct has indeed deserv'd this Scorn, and therefore 'tis but just I should submit to your Resentment, and beg (tho' I am assur'd in vain) for Pardon. [*Kneels.*

Enter Sir Charles.

Sir Cha. How, my Lord! [*Lord* Morelove *rises.*

Lady Bet. Ha! he here? This was unlucky. [*Aside.*

Lord Mo. O pity my Confusion! [*To Lady* Betty.

Sir Cha. I am sorry to see you can so soon forget your self; methinks the Insults you have born from that Lady, by this Time, shou'd have warn'd you into a Disgust of her regardless Principles.

Lord Mo. Hold, Sir *Charles!* While you and I are Friends, I desire you would speak with Honour of this Lady—'Tis sufficient I have no Complaint against her, and—

Lady Bet. My Lord, I beg you would resent this thing no farther: An Injury like this is better punish'd with our Contempt; apparent Malice only should be laugh'd at.

Sir Cha. Ha! ha! the old Recourse. Offers of any Hopes to delude him from his Resentment; and then, as the Grand Monarch did with *Cavalier,* you are sure to keep your Word with him.

Lady Bet. Sir *Charles,* to let you know how far I am above your little Spleen, my Lord, your Hand from this Hour.—

Sir Cha. Pshah! Pshah! All Design! all Pique! meer Artifice, and disappointed Woman.

Lady Bet. Look you, Sir, not that I doubt my Lord's Opinion of me; yet—

Sir Cha. Look you, Madam, in short your Word has been too often taken to let you make up Quarrels, as you used to do, with a soft Look, and a fair Promise you never intended to keep.

Lady Bet. Was ever such an Insolence? he won't give me leave to speak.

Lord Mo. Sir *Charles!*

Lady Bet. No pray, my Lord, have Patience; and since his Malice seems to grow particular, I dare his worst, and urge him to the Proof on't: Pray, Sir, wherein can you charge me with Breach of Promise to my Lord?

Sir Cha. Death! you won't deny it? How often, to piece up a Quarrel, have you appointed him to visit you alone; and tho' you have promis'd to see no other Company the whole Day, when he has come, he has found you among the Laugh of noisy Fops, Coquets, and Coxcombs, dissolutely Gay, while your full Eyes ran o'er with Transport of their Flattery, and your own vain Power of Pleasing? How often, I say, have you been known to throw away, at least, four Hours of your Good Humour upon such Wretches; and the Minute they were gone, grew only dull to him, sunk into a distastful Spleen, complain'd you had talk'd your self into the Head-ach, and then indulg'd upon the dear Delight of seeing him in Pain? And by that time you had stretcht, and gap'd him heartily out of Patience, of a sudden most importunately remember you had out-sate your Appointment with my Lady *Fiddle-faddle;* and immediately order your Coach to the Park.

Lady Bet. Yet, Sir, have you done?

Sir Cha. No—tho' this might serve to shew the Nature of your Principles: But the noble Conquest you have gain'd at last, over defeated Sense of Reputation too, has made your Fame Immortal.

Lord Mo. How Sir?

Lady Bet. My Reputation?

Sir Cha. Ay, Madam, your Reputation—my Lord, if I advance a Falshood, then resent it—I say, your Reputation—'t has been your Life's whole Pride of late, to be the common Toast of every publick Table, vain ev'n in the infamous Addresses of a marry'd Man, my Lord *Foppington;* let that be reconcil'd with Reputation, I'll now shake Hands with Shame, and bow me to the low Contempt which you deserve from him; not but I suppose you'll yet endeavou to recover him: Now you find ill Usage in Danger of losing your Conquest, 'tis possible you'll stop at nothing to preserve it.

Lady Bet. Sir *Charles*— [*Walks disorder'd, and he after her.*

Sir Cha. I know your Vanity is so voracious, 'twill ev'n wound it self to feed it self; offer him a Blank, perhaps, to fill up with Hopes of what Nature he pleases, and part with ev'n your Pride to keep him.

Lady Bet. Sir *Charles,* I have not deserv'd this of you. [*Bursting into Tears.*

Sir Cha. Ah! True Woman, drop him a soft dissembling Tear, and then his just Resentment must be husht of Course.

Lord Mo. O *Charles!* I can bear no more, those Tears are too reproaching.

Sir Cha. Hist for your Life! [*Aside, and then aloud.*] My Lord, if you believe her, you're undone; the very next sight of my Lord *Foppington* would make her yet forswear all that she can promise.

Lady Bet. My Lord *Foppington!* is that the mighty Crime that must condemn me then? You know I us'd him but as a Tool of my Resentment, which you your self, by a pretended Friendship to us both, most artfully provok'd me to—

Lord Mo. Hold, I conjure you, Madam, I want not this Conviction.

Lady Bet. Send for him this Minute, and you and he shall both be Witnesses of the Contempt and Detestation I have for any forward Hopes his Vanity may have given him, or your Malice would insinuate.

Sir Cha. Death! you would as soon eat Fire, as soon part with your luxurious Taste of Folly, as dare to own the half of this before his Face, or any one, that wou'd make you blush to deny it to—Here comes my Wife, now you shall see—Ha! and my Lord *Foppington* with her—Now! now, we shall see this mighty Proof of your Sincerity—Now, my Lord, you'll have a Warning sure, and henceforth know me for your Friend indeed—

Enter Lady Easy *and Lord* Foppington.

Lady Ea. In Tears, my Dear! what's the matter?

Lady Bet. O, my Dear, all I told you's true: Sir *Charles* has shewn himself so inveterably my Enemy, that if I believ'd I deserv'd but half his Hate, 'twould make me hate my self.

Lord Fop. Hark you, *Charles,* prithee what is this Business?

Sir Cha. Why yours, my Lord, for ought I know—I have made such a Breach betwixt 'em—I can't promise much for the Courage of a Woman; but if hers holds, I am sure it's wide enough, you may enter ten a-breast, my Lord.

Lord Fop. Say'st thou so, *Charles?* Then I hold Six to Four I am the first Man in the Town.

Lady Ea. Sure there must be some Mistake in this; I hope he has not made my Lord your Enemy.

Lady Bet. I know not what he has done.

Lord Mo. Far be that Thought! Alas! I am too much in Fear my self, that what I have this Day committed, advis'd by his mistaken Friendship, may have done my Love irreparable Prejudice.

Lady Bet. No, my Lord, since I perceive his little Arts have not prevail'd upon your Good Nature to my Prejudice, I am bound in Gratitude, in Duty to my self, and to the Confession you have made, my Lord, to acknowledge now, I have been to blame too.

Lord Mo. Ha! Is't possible, can you own so much? O my transported Heart!

Lady Bet. He says, I have taken Pleasure in seeing you uneasy—I own it—but 'twas when that Uneasiness I thought proceeded from your Love; and if you did love—'twill not be much to pardon it.

Lord Mo. O let my Soul, thus bending to your Power, adore this soft descending Goodness.

Lady Bet. And since the giddy Woman's Slights I have shewn you too often, have been made publick, 'tis fit at last the Amends and Reparation should be so: Therefore what I offer'd to Sir *Charles,* I now repeat before this Company, my utter Detestation of any past, or future Gallantry, that has, or shall be offer'd me to your Uneasiness.

Lord Mo. O! be less Generous, or teach me to deserve it—Now blush, Sir *Charles,* at your injurious Accusation.

Lord Fop. Hah! *Pardi voila quelque Chose d'Extraordinaire.* [*Aside.*

Lady Bet. As for my Lord *Foppington,* I owe him Thanks for having been so friendly an Instrument of our Reconciliation; for tho' in the little outward Gallantry I receiv'd from him, I did not immediately trust him with my Design in it; yet I have a better Opinion of his Understanding, than to suppose he could mistake it.

Lord Fop. I am struck dumb with the Deliberation of her Assurance; and do not positively remember, that the *Non-Chalence* of my Temper ever had so bright an Occasion to shew it self before.

Lady Bet. My Lord, I hope you'll pardon the Freedom I have taken with you.

Lord Fop. O, Madam, don't be under the Confusion of an Apology upon my Account; for in cases of this Nature, I am never disappointed, but when I find a Lady of the same Mind two Hours together—Madam, I have lost a thousand fine Women in my time; but never had the ill Manners to be out of Humour with any one for refusing me, since I was born.

Lady Bet. My Lord, that's a very prudent Temper.

Lord Fop. Madam, to convince you that I am in an universal Peace with Mankind, since you own I have so far contributed to your Happiness, give me leave to have the Honour of compleating it, by joining your Hand where you have already offer'd up your Inclination.

Lady Bet. My Lord, that's a Favour I can't refuse you.

Lord Mo. Generous indeed, my Lord.

[*Lord* Foppington *joins their Hands.*

Lord Fop. And stap my Breath if ever I was better pleas'd since my first Entrance into Human Nature.

Sir Cha. How now, my Lord! What, throw up the Cards before you have lost the Game?

Lord Fop. Look you, *Charles,* 'tis true, I did design to have play'd with her alone: But he that will keep well with the Ladies, must sometimes be content to make one at a Poole with 'em: And since I know I must engage her in my Turn, I don't see any great Odds in letting him take the first Game with her.

Sir Cha. Wisely consider'd, my Lord.

Lady Bet. And now, Sir *Charles*—

Sir Cha. And now, Madam, I'll save you the Trouble of a long Speech; and, in one Word, confess that every thing I have done in regard to you this Day was purely Artificial—I saw there was no way to secure you to my Lord *Morelove,* but by allarming your Pride with the Danger of losing him: And since the Success must have by this time convinc'd you, that in Love nothing is more ridiculous than an over-acted Aversion; I am sure you won't take it ill, if we at last congratulate your good Nature, by heartily laughing at the Fright we had put you in. Ha! ha! ha!

Lady Ea. Ha! ha! ha!

Lady Bet. Why—well, I declare it now, I hate you worse than ever.

Sir Cha. Ha! ha! ha! And was it afraid they would take its Love from it—Poor Lady *Betty!* ha! ha!

Lady Ea. My Dear, I beg your Pardon; but 'tis impossible not to laugh when one's so heartily pleas'd.

Lord Fop. Really, Madam, I am afraid the good Humour of the Company will draw me into your Displeasure too; but if I were to expire this Moment, my last Breath would positively go out in a Laugh. Ha! ha! ha!

Lady Bet. Nay, I have deserv'd it all, that's the Truth on't—but I hope, my Lord, you were not in this Design against me.

Lord Mo. As a Proof, Madam, I am inclin'd never to deceive you more—I do confess I had my share in't.

Lady Bet. You do, my Lord!—then I declare 'twas a Design, one or other—the best carry'd on, that ever I knew in my Life; and (to my Shame I own it) for ought I know, the only thing that cou'd have prevail'd upon my Temper: 'Twas a foolish Pride, that has cost me many a bitten Lip to support it—I wish we don't both repent, my Lord.

Lord Mo. Don't You repent without Me, and we never shall.

Sir Cha. Well, Madam, now the worst that the World can say of your past Conduct is, that my Lord had Constancy, and you have try'd it.

Enter a Servant to Lord Morelove.

Serv. My Lord, Mr. *Le Fevre*'s below, and desires to know what time your Lordship will please to have the Musick begin.

Lord Mo. Sir *Charles,* what say you? Will you give me leave to bring 'em hither?

Sir Cha. As the Ladies think fit, my Lord.

Lady Bet. O! by all means; 'twill be better here, unless we could have the Terrace to our selves.

Lord Mo. Then pray desire 'em to come all hither immediately.

Serv. Yes, my Lord. [*Exit Servant.*

Enter Lady Graveairs.

Sir Cha. Lady *Graveairs!*

Lady Gra. Yes, you may well start! but don't suppose I am now come like a poor tame Fool to upbraid your Guilt; but, if I could, to blast you with a Look.

Sir Cha. Come, come, you have Sense—Don't expose your self—you are unhappy, and I own my self the Cause—The only Satisfaction I can offer you is to protest, no new Engagement takes me from you: But a sincere Reflection of the long Neglect and Injuries I've done the best of Wives; for whose amends and only sake I must part with You, and all the inconvenient Pleasures of my Life

Lady Gra. Have you then fallen into the low Contempt of exposing me, and to your Wife too?

Sir Cha. 'Twas impossible, without it, I could ever be sincere in my Conversion.

Lady Gra. Despicable!

Sir Cha. Do not think so—for my sake I know she'll not reproach you—nor, by her Carriage, ever let the World perceive you've wrong her.—My Dear—

Lady Ea. Lady *Graveairs,* I hope you'll Sup with us?

Lady Gra. I can't refuse so much good Company, Madam.

Sir Cha. You see the worst of her Resentment—In the mean time, don't endeavour to be her Friend, and she'll never be your Enemy.

Lady Gra. I am unfortunate—'tis what my Folly has deserv'd, and I submit to it.

Lord Mo. So! here's the Musick.

Lady Ea. Come, Ladies, shall we sit?

After the Musick a SONG.

Sabina *with an Angel's Face,*
By Love ordain'd for Joy,
Seems of the Syren's *Cruel Race,*
To Charm, and then Destroy:

With all the Arts of Look and Dress,
She fans the fatal Fire;
Through Pride, mistaken oft for Grace,
She bids the Swain expire.

The God of Love, enrag'd to see
The Nymph defy his Flame,
Pronounc'd this Merciless Decree
Against the Haughty Dame;

Let Age with double Speed o'ertake her,
Let Love the Room of Pride supply;
And when the Lovers all forsake her,
A Spotless Virgin let her Die.

Sir Charles *comes forward with Lady* Easy.

Sir Cha. Now, my Dear, I find my Happiness grow fast upon me; in all my past Experience of the Sex, I found ev'n among the better sort so much of Folly, Pride, Malice, Passion, and irresolute Desire, that I concluded thee but of the foremost Rank, and therefore scarce worthy my Concern; but thou hast stirr'd me with so severe a Proof of thy exalted Virtue, it gives me Wonder equal to my Love —If then the unkindly Thought of what I have been, hereafter should intrude upon thy growing Quiet, let this Reflection teach thee to be easy:

Thy Wrongs, when greatest, most thy Virtue prov'd,
And from that Virtue found, I blush'd, and truly lov'd. [*Exeunt.*

THE
EPILOGUE.

Conquest and Freedom are at length our own,
False Fears of Slavery no more are shown;
Nor Dread of paying Tribute to a Foreign Throne.
All Stations now the Fruits of Conquest share,
Except (if small with great things may compare)
Th' Opprest Condition of the Lab'ring Player.
We're still in Fears (as you of late from France*)*
Of the Despotic Power of Song, and Dance:
For while Subscription like a Tyrant Reigns,
Nature's Neglected, and the Stage in Chains,
And English *Actors Slaves to swell the* Frenchman's *Gains.*
Like Aesop's *Crow, the poor outwitted Stage,*
That liv'd on wholesom Plays i' th' latter Age,
Deluded once to Sing, ev'n justly serv'd,
Let fall her Cheese to th' Fox's Mouth, and starv'd.
O that your Judgment, as your Courage has
Your Fame extended, would assert our Cause,
That nothing English *might submit to Foreign Laws.*
If we but live to see that joyful Day
Then of the English *Stage reviv'd we may,*
As of your Honour now, with proper Application say.

So when the Gallick *Fox, by Fraud of Peace,*
Had lull'd the British *Lion into Ease,*
And saw that Sleep compos'd his Couchant Head,
He bids him Wake, and sees himself betray'd
In Toils of Treacherous Politicks around him laid:
Shews him, how one close Hour of Gallick *Thought*
Retook those Towns for which he Years had Fought.
At this th' Indignant Savage rowls his fiery Eyes,
Dauntless, tho' blushing at the base Surprize;

Pauses a while—but finds Delays are vain;
Compell'd to Fight, he shakes his shaggy Main;
He grinds his dreadful Fangs, and stalks to Blenheim*'s Plain.*
There with erected Crest, and horrid Roar,
He Furious, plunges on through Streams of Gore.
And dyes with False Bavarian *Blood the Purple* Danube*'s Shore;*
In one pusht Battel frees the Destin'd Slaves,
Revives old English *Honour, and an Empire saves.*

FINIS.

THE

LADY's Last STAKE,

OR, THE

WIFE's RESENTMENT.

A

COMEDY.

As it is Acted at the

QUEEN's THEATRE

IN THE

HAY-MARKET,

By Her MAJESTY's Servants.

To the Most NOBLE
The MARQUIS of *KENT*,
Lord Chamberlain of Her Majesty's Houshold, *&c.*

The utmost Success I ever propos'd from this Play, was, that it might reach the Taste of a few good Judges, and from thence plead a sort of Title to your Lordship's Protection: And, if the most just, and candid Criticks are not the greatest Flatterers, I have not fail'd in my Proposal. As for those Gentlemen, that thrust themselves forward upon the Stage, before a crowded Audience, as if they resolv'd to play themselves, and save the Actor the Trouble of presenting them; they indeed, as they are above Instruction, so they scorn to be diverted by it, and will as soon allow me a good Voice, as a Genius. I did not intend it shou'd entertain any, that never come with a Design to sit out a Play; and therefore, without being much mortified, am content such Persons shou'd dislike it. If I would have been less instructive, I might easily have had a louder, tho' not a more valuable Applause. But I shall always prefer a fixt, and general Attention before the noisy Roars of the Gallery. A Play, without a just Moral, is a poor and trivial Undertaking; and 'tis from the Success of such Pieces, that Mr. *Collier* was furnish'd with an Advantageous Pretence of laying his unmerciful Axe to the Root of the Stage. Gaming is a Vice, that has undone more innocent Principles, than any one Folly that's in Fashion; therefore I chose to expose it to the Fair Sex in its most hideous Form, by reducing a Woman of Honour to stand the presumptuous Addresses of a Man, whom neither her Virtue or Inclination wou'd let her have the least Taste to: Now 'tis not impossible but some Man of Fortune, who has a handsome Lady, and a great deal of Money to throw away, may from this startling hint think it worth his while to find his Wife some less hazardous Diversion. If that should ever happen, my End of writing this Play is answer'd; and if it may boast of any Favours from the Town, I now must own they are entirely owing to your Lordship's Protection of the Theatre. For, without a Union of the best Actors, it must have been impossible for it to have receiv'd a tolerable Justice in the Performance.

The Stage has for many Years, till late, groan'd under the greatest Discouragements; which have been very much, if not wholly owing to the Mismanagement or Avarice of those that have aukwardly govern'd it. Great Sums have been ventur'd upon empty Projects, and Hopes of immoderate Gains; and when those Hopes have fail'd, the Loss has been tyrannically deducted out of the Actors Sallery. And if your Lordship had not redeem'd 'em, they were very near being wholly laid aside, or at least, the Use of their Labour was to be swallow'd up, in the pretended Merit of Singing and Dancing. I don't offer this as a Reflexion upon Musick, (for I allow and feel its Charms) but it has been the Misfortune of That, as well as Poetry to have been too long in the Hands of those, whose Taste and Fancy are utterly insensible of their Use and Power. And tho' your Lordship foresaw, and Experience tells us, that both Diversions would be better encourag'd under their separate Endeavours, yet this was a Scheme, that cou'd never be beat into the impenetrable Heads of those that might have honestly paid the Labourers their Hire, and put the Profits of both into their own Pockets. Nay, even the Opera tho' the Town has neither grudg'd it Pay nor Equipage, from either the Wilfulness or Ignorance of the same General, we see, was not able to take the Field till *December*.

My Lord, there is nothing Difficult to a Body of *English* People, when they are unanimous, and well commanded: And tho' your Lordship's Tenderness of oppressing is so very just, that you have rather stay'd to convince a Man of your good Intentions to him, than to do him ev'n a Service against his Will: Yet since your Lordship has so happily begun the Establishment of the separate Diversions, we live in Hope, that the same Justice and Resolution will still persuade you to go as successfully through with it.

But while any Man is suffer'd to confound the Industry and Use of 'em, by acting publickly, in Opposition to your Lordship's equal Intentions, under a false and intricate Pretence of not being able to comply with 'em; the Town is likely to be more entertain'd with the private Dissentions, than the publick Performance of either, and the Actors in a perpetual Fear and Necessity of petitioning your Lordship every Season for new Relief.

To succour the Distress'd is the first Mark of Greatness, and your Lordship is eminently distinguish'd for a Virtue that certainly claims the next place to it. The disinterested Choice and Manner of your Lordship's disposing Places in your Gift, are Proofs that you always have the Claims of Merit under your first and tenderest Consideration. And from the Assurance of this Thought, my Lord, the Stage, the Poets, and the Players, lay their Cause, their Hopes, and utmost Expectations at Your Lordship's Feet for Support and Protection. I am,

My LORD,
Your Lordship's most Humble,
and most Obedient Servant,
Colley Cibber.

PROLOGUE.

Since Plays are but the Mirrours of our Lives,
And soon, or late Mankind are chain'd to Wives;
Since those dissolveless Fetters too, must be
Our greatest Happiness, or Misery;
What Subject ought, in Reason, more to please ye,
Than an Attempt to make those Chains sit easy?
Tho' in the Noose so many Souls seem curst,
Pray who's in Fault?—For when you've said your worst,
You all Did feel its Happiness—at first.
Therefore our Author drew you once the Life
Of Careless Husband, *and Enduring Wife,*
Who by her Patience (tho' much out of Fashion)
Retriev'd, at last, her Wanderer's Inclination.
Yet some there are, who still arraign the Play,
At her tame Temper shock'd, as who should say—
The Price, for a dull Husband, was too much to pay.
Had he been strangled sleeping, Who shou'd hurt ye?
When so provok'd—Revenge had been a Virtue.
—Well then—to do his former Moral Right,
Or set such Measures in a fairer Light,
He gives you now a Wife, he's sure's in Fashion,
Whose Wrongs use modern Means for Reparation.
No Fool, that will her Life in Sufferings waste,
But furious, proud, and insolently chaste;
Who more in Honour jealous, than in Love,
Resolves Resentment shall her Wrongs remove:
Not to be cheated with his civil Face,
But scorns his Falshood, and to prove him base,
Mobb'd up in Hack triumphant doggs him to the Place.
These modish Measures, we presume, you'll own,

Are oft what Wives of Gallantry have done;
But if their Consequence shou'd meet the Curse
Of making a provok'd Aversion worse,
Then you his former Moral must allow,
Or own the Satyr just he shews you now.
Some other Follies too, our Scenes present
Some warn the Fair from Gaming, when extravagant.
But when undone you see the dreadful Stake,
That hard-press'd Virtue is reduced to make;
Think not the Terrors, you behold her in,
Are rudely drawn t'expose what has been seen;
But, as the friendly Muses tender'st way,
To let such Dangers warn you from the Depth of Play.

Dramatis Personæ.

MEN.

Lord *Wronglove,*	Mr. *Wilks.*
Lord *George Brilliant,*	Mr. *Cibber.*
Sir *Friendly Moral,*	Mr. *Keene.*

WOMEN.

Lady *Wronglove,*	Mrs. *Barry.*
Lady *Gentle,*	Mrs. *Rogers.*
Mrs. *Conquest,*	Mrs. *Oldfield.*
Miss *Notable,*	Mrs. *Cross.*

THE
LADY's Last STAKE,
OR, THE
WIFE's RESENTMENT.

ACT I. SCENE I.

SCENE, *Lord* Wronglove*'s Apartment.*

Lord Wronglove *alone, musing.*

Lord Wrong. My Wife—as abundance of other Men of Quality's Wives are—is a miserable Woman: Ask her the Reason, she'll tell you—Husband, ask me: I say, Wife—all's entirely owing to her own Temper.

Enter Mrs. Hartshorn.

Mrs. Harts. My Lady desires to know if your Lordship pleases to spare her the Chariot this Morning?

Lord Wrong. Hah! That's as much as to say, I have a mind to guess when, and how you go out this Morning. [*Aside.*] Well, the Chariot is at her Service. [*Exit* Hartshorn.] This continual Jealousie is insupportable—What's to be done with her? What's her Complaint? Who's the Aggressor? I'll e'en refer the matter fairly to my own Conscience, and if she casts me there, I'll do her Justice; if not, tho' the Cost were ten times hers, I'll make my self easy, for the rest of my Life.—Let me see,—as to the Fact I'm charg'd with, *viz.* That I have feloniously embezzled my Inclinations among the rough and smooth Conversation of several undaunted Gentlewomen, and so forth.—That, I think, since it must be prov'd against me, I had best plead guilty to.—Be it so.—Very well!—A terrible Charge indeed: And now—

Enter Brush.

Brush. My Lady desires to know if your Lordship pleases to dine at home to Day?

Lord Wrong. Right! Another gentle Enquiry. [*Aside.*] Why tell her 'tis impossible to guess, but her Ladyship may do as she pleases. [*Exit* Brush.] But to go on,–Now let's hear the Defendant, and then proceed to Judgment and Damages. Well! the Defendant says, That 'tis true he was in love with Madam up to her proud Heart's Wishes, but hop'd that Marriage was his End of Servitude, that then her wise Reserve, her Pride, and other fine Lady's Airs wou'd be all laid aside.–No,–her Ladyship was still the same unconquer'd Heroine: If being endur'd cou'd give me Happiness, 'twas mine; if not, she knew her self, and shou'd not bend below her Sexes Value –I bore this long, then urg'd her Duty; that this Reserve of Humour was inconsistent with her being a Friend, a Wife, or a Companion.– She said 'twas Nature's Fault, and I but talk'd in vain.–Upon this I found my Patience began to have enough on't; so I e'en made her invincibleship a low Bow, and told her, I wou'd dispose of my time in Pleasures, which were a little more comeatable; which Pleasures I have found, and she–has found out, but truly she won't bear it: And tho' she scorn'd to love, she'll condescend to hate; she'll have Redress, Revenge, and Reparation; so that if I have a mind to be Easie at home, I need but tremble at her Anger, down on my Knees, confess, beg Pardon, promise Amendment, keep my Word, and the Bus'ness is done.–Now venerable, human Conscience, speak, must I do this only to purchase what the Greatness of her Soul has taught me to be indifferent to? Am I bound to fast, because her Ladyship has no Appetite? Shall Threats and Browbeatings fright me into Justice, where my own Will's a Law?–No, no, no, positively no:–I'm Lord of my own Heart sure, and whoever thinks to enter at my Humour shall speak me very fair.–Most generous Conscience, I give you Thanks for this Deliverance! And since I'm positive, I've little Nature on my side too, Madam may now go on with her noble Resentment as she pleases.

Enter Brush.

Brush. Lord *George Brilliant* gives his Service, and if your Lordship's at Leisure he'll wait upon you.

Lord Wrong. Give my Service, say I shall be glad to see him. [*Exit* Brush.

D'ye hear! *Brush!* [Brush *returns.*

Brush. My Lord!

Lord Wrong. Is the Footman come back yet?

Brush. Yes, my Lord, he call'd at *White*'s, but there's no Letter for your Lordship.

Lord Wrong. Very well. [*Exit* Brush.

I can't imagine the meaning of it,—Sure I havn't play'd with this Baby-fac'd Girl 'till I'm in love with her; and yet her disappointing me Yesterday does not slip so easily through my Memory, as things of this gentle Nature us'd to do.—A very Phlegmatick Symptome—And yet, if she had come, 'tis ten to one, the greatest Relief she cou'd have given me, wou'd have been a fair Excuse to get rid of her.—Hum! ay, ay, all's safe.—She has only stirr'd my Pride I find, my Heart's as sound as my Constitution,—and yet her not coming, nor excusing it; puzzles me.

Enter Brush.

Brush. A Letter for your Lordship.

Lord Wrong. Who brought it.

Brush. *Snug* the Chair-man.

Lord Wrong. O! 'tis right, now we shall be let into the Secret. [Reads.]

I Wo'n't beg your Pardon for not coming Yesterday, because it was not my Fault, but indeed I'm sorry I could not.

Kind however, tho' 'tis possible she may lye too.

To be short, old Teizer *smoaks the Business, poss—*

By her Stile, the Child seems to have a great Genius for Iniquity: But who the Duce is old *Teizer?* O! that must be her Unkle Sir *Friendly Moral! Smoaks the Business, poss!* Very well.

For he watch'd me all Day, as if he had been in love with me himself: But you may depend upon me this Afternoon, about five at the same Place, till when, dear Dismal, *adieu.*

[Tears the Letter.

Well said! I gad, this Girl will debauch me! what Pity 'tis, her Person does not spread like her Understanding—But she is one of Eve's own Sisters, born a Woman: Bid the Fellow stay for an Answer. [*Exit* Brush.

Enter Mrs. Hartshorn.

Mrs. Harts. My Lady desires to know, if your Lordship pleases to drink any Tea?

Lord Wrong. [*Aside.*] What a Mess of Impertinence have I had this Morning: But I'll make my Advantage of this. Pray thank your Lady, and tell her I desire she'll be pleas'd to come and drink some with me. [*Exit* Hartshorn.] When a Man has a little private Folly upon his Hands, 'tis Prudent to keep his Wife in good Humour, at least, till the Frailty's thoroughly committed. [*Exit.*

Enter Lady Wronglove *and* Brush.

Lady Wrong. Where's my Lord?

Brush. I believe he's writing in his Closet Madam; if your Ladyship pleases I'll go see.

Lady Wrong. No, stay—I'll—I'll—wait without.

Brush. Jealous by *Jupiter,* I must look sharp, I see. [*Retires.*

Lady Wrong. Writing! then I am confirm'd! Not a Day passes without some fresh Discovery of his Perfidiousness—This usage is beyond Patience—Sure Men think, that Wives are Stocks or Stones, without all Sense of Injuries, or only born, and bound to bear 'em! But since his Villanies want the Excuse of my deserving them, I'll let him see I dare resent 'em, as I ought. I'll prove 'em first, and then Revenge 'em with my Scorn—Hum! what's here, a torn Letter! ha! this Hand is new! O! my Patience! some fresh, some undiscover'd Slut! Here! *Hartshorn!*

Enter Hartshorn.

Go to the Door this Minute, and tell the impudent Fellow there, that my Lord says the Letter requires no Answer; and if he offers to bring any more, he'll have his Limbs broke.

Brush. [*Behind.*] Ha! this was a lucky Discovery; between my Lord, or my Lady, it's hard if I don't mend my Place by it.

Lady Wrong. It is not yet so torn, but I may read it—'Twill cost his Wit some Trouble to evade this Proof, I'm sure—I'll have it piec'd, and send it him—I'll let him see I know him still—A base, a mean—Auh!—now he's nauseous to me. [*Exit Lady* Wronglove.

Re-enter Lord Wronglove *with a Letter.*

Lord Wrong. Here, give this to the Porter.

Brush. My Lord, the Porter's gone. [*Smiling.*

Lord Wrong. Gone! how so! What does the Fellow snear at?

Brush. My Lord, I beg your Lordship's Pardon for my Boldness, but perhaps it may be more useful to you than my Silence; I saw something that happen'd just now—

Lord Wrong. What's the Matter?

Brush. While your Lordship was Writing within, my Lady, I fancy'd by her Looks, suspected something by *Snug*'s being at the Door (for she enquires every Mortal's Bussness that comes to speak with your Lordship) but here she came, and bid me go out of the Room: Upon which I made bold to watch her at the Door, where I saw her pick up the Pieces of that Letter your Lordship tore just now; and then she flew into a violent Passion, and order'd the Porter to be sent away without his Answer.

Lord Wrong. No Matter, you know where to find him?

Brush. Yes, my Lord, he plies at *White*'s.

Lord Wrong. Run after him quick, tell him it was a Mistake, and that's his Answer. [*Gives a Letter.*] [*Exit* Brush.] Let me see—I shall certainly hear of this Letter from my Wife; and 'tis probable her Pride will have as much Pleasure in Reproaching me, as her good Nature wou'd in finding me Innocent—I must take care not to let her grow upon me—To bear the open Insolence of a Wife is a Punishment, that exceeds both the Crime and the Pleasure of any Favours the Sex can give us—But why am I so apprehensive of a poor Woman's being out of Humour? My Gravity for the Matter wou'd be as Ridiculous as her Passion—The worst on't is, that in our Matrimonial Squabbles, one side's generally forc'd to make a Confidence with their Servants, I am reduc'd not to trust this Fellow—But I can make it his Interest to be Secret—

Enter Mrs. Hartshorn *with Tea.*

Mrs. Harts. Here's your Lordship's Tea.

Lord Wrong. O! thank you Mrs. *Hartshorn*—Where's your Lady?

Mrs. Harts. My Lord, she is not very well, and desir'd me to give your Lordship this. [*Gives a Letter.*

Lord Wrong. Soh! Now it comes—let's see—Ha! The Child's Letter Faith, carefully piec'd together again, how—here's some of her own hand too.

[Reads.]

Something has happen'd that makes me unfit for Tea, I wou'd tell you what, but that I find 'tis the Fashion for married People to have separate Secrets.

Humph! This is speaking pretty plain—Now if I take no Notice of it, I shall have her walk by me in the House with a Dumb, Gloomy Insolence for a Fortnight together—Suppose I let her—No—better talk with her—The most violent Jealousie is often subject to the grossest Credulity—I'll make one Push for't however, 'tis certainly more Prudent to come off if I can,—Mrs. *Hartshorn,* pray tell your Lady I must needs see her, I have something to say to her that will make her Laugh, though she was dying of the Vapours.

Mrs. Harts. My Lord, I'll tell her. [*Exit Mrs.* Hartshorn.

Lord Wrong. Or suppose her Jealousie is too wise for my Wit, say she won't be impos'd upon: At worst, I'll carry it on with such an Excess of Assurance, that I'll give her the Mortification of thinking, that I believe I have deciev'd her: She shan't have the Pleasure of knowing she insults me, I'll crush the very Hope of her Resentment; and by seeming always easie my self, make her Jealousie a private Plague to her Insolence! She shall never catch me owning any thing. Her Pride wou'd have its End indeed, if she cou'd once bring me to the humble Shame of Confession—O she's here!

Enter Lady Wronglove, *very Grave.*

Lady Wrong. D'ye want me for any thing?

Lord Wrong. Ay Child, sit down, *Hartshorn* told me you were not well, so I had a mind to divert you a little. Such a ridiculous Adventure sure—Ha! ha! ha!

Lady Wrong. I am as well as I expect to be, tho' perhaps not so easie to be diverted.

Lord Wrong. Ha! ha! ha! no matter for that, if I don't divert you—Here take your Dish Child—Ha! ha! ha!

Lady Wrong. I shan't drink any.

Lord Wrong. Hah! ha! ha! Do you know now, that I know what makes you so out of Humour? Ha! ha!

Lady Wrong. By my Soul, you've a good Assurance. [*Turning away*.

Lord Wrong. Ha! ha! ha! Do you know too, that I am now insulting you with the most ridiculous Malice, and yet with all the comical Justice in the World; Ha! ha! ha!

Lady Wrong. My Lord, all this is mightily thrown away upon me, I never had any great Genius to Humour; besides that little I have, you know I have now Reason to be out of: And to spare you the vain Trouble of endeavouring to impose upon me, I must tell you, that this Usage is fit only for the common Wretches you converse with.

Lord Wrong. By my Soul I don't believe the like ever happen'd in all the Accidents of Humane Life! Such an Incredible, such a Romantick Complication of Blunders, that, let me perish, if I think *Molier's Cocu Imaginare* has half so many Turns in it, as you shall hear Child—In the first Place, the Porter makes a Blunder by mistaking the Place for the Person, and enquires for me, instead of one at my House; my Blockhead *Brush* here carries it on, and with his own blundering Hand, gives his Mistress's Letter to me: No sooner was that Mistake set to rights, but the Pieces of the Letter fall into your Hands, and (as if Fortune resolv'd the Jest should not be lost) you really fancy'd it came from a Mistress of mine, and so by way of Comical Resentment, fall out of Humour with your Tea, and send it to me again. Ha, ha, ha.

Lady Wrong. This Evasion, my Lord, is the worst Stuff, that ever any sure was made of.

Lord Wrong. [*Aside*.] 'twon't do, I find, but it's no matter, I'll go on. Ha! ha! and so upon this, what does me I, but instead of making you easie, let's you go on in the Fancy, till I was thoroughly convinc'd your Suspicion was real, and then comes me about with the most unexpected Catastrophe, and tells you the whole Truth of the matter, Ha, ha, ha.

Lady Wrong. A very pretty Farce indeed, my Lord, but by the Thinness of the Plot, I see you have not given your self much trouble in the Contrivance.

Lord Wrong. No, upon my Soul, 'twas all so directly in Nature, that the least Fiction in the World had knockt it all to Pieces.

Lady Wrong. It's very well, my Lord, I am as much diverted with the Entertainment, I suppose, as you expect I should be.

Lord Wrong. Ha, ha, why did I not tell you I shou'd divert you?

Lady Wrong. You have indeed, my Lord, to astonishment. Tho' there's one Part of the Design you left out in the Relation, and that was the Answer, that you wrote, (by mistake, I suppose) to your Man's Mistress.

Lord Wrong. O that!—why that was—that was—the—the—the—the Answer? Ay, ay, the Answer was sent after the Porter, because, you know, if he had gone away without it, 'twas Fifty to One the poor Fellow's Mistress wou'd not have been reconcil'd to him again this Fortnight—But did you observe, Child, what a coarse familiar Style the Puss writes?

Lady Wrong. Coarseness of Style is no Proof that the Puss might not be Mistress to a Man of Quality: And I must tell you, my Lord, when Men of Quality can find their Account in engaging with Women, whose highest Modesty is Impudence, methinks they shou'd not wonder if Men of their own Principles, whose Impudence is so often mistaken for Wit, should talk their Wives into the same Failing.

Lord Wrong. Let me die, Child, if you han't a great deal of good Sense. [*Sipping his Tea.*

Lady Wrong. 'Tis not the first time that an affronted Wife has convinc'd the World of her Personal Merit, to the severe Repentance of her Husband.

Lord Wrong. Abundance of good Sense.

Enter Brush.

Brush. Lord *George,* my Lord.

Lord Wrong. Desire him to walk in—Nay you need not go, Child.

Lady Wrong. I am not in an Humour now for Company—There's a Couple of you. [*Exit Lady* Wronglove.

Lord Wrong. What Pains this silly Woman takes to weary me, always widening the Breach between us, as if 'twere her Interest to have no Hopes of Accommodation; as if she felt no pain in making her own Life wretched, so she cou'd but imbitter mine—Let her go on—Here's one that always sweetens it.

Enter Lord George.

Ah, my *Georgy!* Kiss.

Lord Geo. And kiss, and kiss again, my Dear—By *Ganymede* there's Nectar on thy Lips. O the pleasure of a Friend to tell the Joy!—O *Wronglove!* Such Hopes!

Lord Wrong. Hey-day! What's the matter?

Lord Geo. Such soft Ideas!—Such thrilling Thoughts of aching Pleasure!—In short, I have too much on't.

Lord Wrong. Thou strange Piece of wild Nature!

Lord Geo. Death! I tell thee Man, I'm above half Seas over.

Lord Wrong. One wou'd rather think half the Seas were over you; for, in my Mind, you don't talk like a Man above Water.

Lord Geo. Prithee forgive me: How is it possible I shou'd, when all my Faculties are drown'd in Joy?

Lord Wrong. Then prithee, my Dear, float about, shut down the Sluice of your Rapture, before the Nothingness of your Words gets over the Banks of your Understanding. In plain common Sense lets know the Business.

Lord Geo. Why the Business, in one Word—its impossible to tell you.

Lord Wrong. Impossible!—Will you drink any Tea?

Lord Geo. Tea! Thou soft, thou sober, sage, and venerable Liquid, thou innocent Pretence for bringing the Wicked of both Sexes together in a Morning; thou Female Tongue-running, Smile-smoothing, Heart-opening, Wink-tipping Cordial, to whose glorious Insipidity I owe the happiest Moment of my Life, let me fall prostrate thus, and s-p, s-p, s-p, thus adore thee. [*Kneels and sips the Tea.*

Lord Wrong. Come, come, you silly affected Rogue get up, and talk at least like a Fool to be understood.

Lord Geo. Don't you think there's Pleasure in Affectation, when one's heartily in good Humour. [*Very affectedly.*

Lord Wrong. Impertinent Puppy—Drink your Tea.

Lord Geo. O *Wronglove!* I have been drinking Tea. [*Transported.*

Lord Wrong. With some laughing Ladies, I presume, whose incessant Concussion of Words wou'd not let you put in a Syllable, and so you are come to ease yourself upon me.

Lord Geo. Then prithee be a Friend, and let me speak.

Lord Wrong. Not only Blank-Verse, but Rhime, if you please, in the Name of Nonsense go on.

Lord Geo. Swear then.

Lord Wrong. Swear!

Lord Geo. Ay, swear.

Lord Wrong. –Blood!

Lord Geo. Pshah! Prithee.

Lord Wrong. Nay, pray, Sir, give me leave to play the Fool in my Turn, the moment you speak to be understood, I'll secure you a reasonable Answer.

Lord Geo. Swear then never (to any Mortal) to trust from you, to hint, or speak of what I shall discover.

Lord Wrong. Upon Honour.

Lord Geo. Honour! the common Hackney-Oath of Fops, Rakes, and Sharpers; swear me by something dearer, than thy Eyes, than Life or Liberty.

Lord Wrong. Indeed!

Lord Geo. Swear me by all the tendrest Hopes in Love; by thy soft Sighs of Pain: proceeding from thy Pleasure; swear–

Lord Wrong. I do by something dearer to me yet–By my short Stay after possession; my my Chaise after hard Riding; by my Easie-Chair after Dinner, and by t'other Bottle after the Bill's paid, I will be secret.

Lord Geo. Ay, now be perjur'd if thou darest–Know then–at last, that Generous Lovely Creature has said behind my Back, that I am the most Sober, Good-humour'd, and Agreeably Inoffensive Young Fellow, that ever came into a Civil Family; to be short, she has made me a General Invitation to her House, upon which I have taken Lodgings, that look full into her Back-Closet-Window, and drank Tea with her alone this Morning.

Lord Wrong. Some humble Sinner, whose only Charm is being another Man's Mistress, I'll lay my Life on't. [*Aside.*] –Well, and what did you give her?

Lord Geo. A Bleeding-Heart, all studded o'er with Wounds of her Eyes own making.

Lord Wrong. That is, you pull'd out your Watch as you were going away, and she took a Fancy to one of the Seals: Tho' by the

Device, I presume, it was only a modern Bauble, so 'tis probable you might not have come off much cheaper at Mother *Davis's*.

Lord Geo. Profanation!—To be serious then at once, I have solid Hopes of my Lady *Gentle.*

Lord Wrong. Hoh! hoh! O thou vain, thou senseless Fop! Is all this mighty Rapture then only from a fine Woman's being commonly Civil to thee? The mere innocent Effect of her Good-Humour and Breeding.

Lord Geo. Pshah, tell not me of whence it is born, let it suffice, I've form'd it into Hope, let your Tame, Civil, Secret-Sighers, such as never think the Fair one sure, till they hear the Tag of her Lace click, think it no Cause for Joy; but I've a Soul, that wakes, that starts me up at the least dawning Cranny of a Hope, and sets my every Faculty on Fire—she must—she must—she shall be won—For since I have resolv'd to hope, my Fancy double paints her Beauties—O! she's all one Fragrant Field of Charms, to pamper up the Blood of wild Desire.

Lord Wrong. Ah, *George!* What luscious Morsels then must her Husband take of her?

Lord Geo. Why didst thou mention him? Death! I can't bear that Thought—Can she love him?—O the Verdant Vales, the Downy Lawns of Fruitful Bliss! The ever flowing Springs of Cool Refreshing Beauty, that happy Dog must Revel, Range, and Sport in!

Lord Wrong. Nay, the Woman's a Fine Creature, that's certain, it's a thousand Pities one can't laugh her out of that unfashionable Folly of liking her Husband, when here's a Man of undisputed Honour too, that knows the World, that understands Love and Ruin to a Tittle; that would at the least Tip of a Wink rid her of all her Incumbrances, set her at the very Top of the Mode, and qualifie her for a separate Maintenance, in the twinkling of an Hackney-Coach-Window.

Lord Geo. Can you be a moment serious?

Lord Wrong. Faith, Sir, if I am not, 'tis only to make you so.

Lord Geo. You seem to think this Business impracticable.

Lord Wrong. Why truly for any great Progress I see you have made, I don't think but it is: And if you'll take my Opinion of the Woman, I do think, provided you'll allow there's any such Thing in Nature, she's one of impregnable Virtue: That you can no more make a Breach in her Honour, than find a Flaw in her Features: Bate but a little of her Over-fondness for Play, she's the Perfection of a good Wife.

Lord Geo. O your Servant, Sir, you own she has a Passion for Play then.

Lord Wrong. That I can't deny, and what's worse, I doubt she likes it a great deal better than she understands it. I hear she has lost considerably to the Count of late.

Lord Geo. You must know then, that the Count is my Ingineer; he and I have a right understanding; whenever she plays we are sure of her Money: Now he has already stript her of all her Running Cash, besides eight hundred Pound upon Honour: For payment of which, I made him send her a downright pressing Letter, by me this Morning: I observ'd her a little startled when she read it, and took that opportunity to scrue my self into the Secret, and offer'd my Assistance; to be short, I address'd my self with so tender a Regard to her Confusion, that before we parted, I engag'd this Afternoon to lend her a Thousand Pound of her own Money to pay him.

Lord Wrong. I confess your Battery's rais'd against the only weak Side of her Virtue. But how are you sure you can work her to push her ill Fortune; she may give over Play: What will all your Advantages signifie, if she does not lose to you more than she can pay?

Lord Geo. O, I have an Expedient for that too—look you, in short, I won't spoil my Plot by discovering it; a few Hours will make it ripe for Execution, and then—but

There is no fear that I shou'd tell,
The Joys that are unspeakable.

Lord Wrong. Ha, ha, and so you are really in Love to the last Extremity of Passion.

Lord Geo. Prithee don't laugh at me. [*Affectedly.*

Lord Wrong. Don't you think I have heard you with a great deal of Patience?

Lord Geo. Nay, I know we Puppies in Love are tiresome.

Lord Wrong. And so you think that all this Extravagance of your Style and Gesture must have convinc'd me, that you really care Sixpence for this Woman?

Lord Geo. Wou'd you have me swear?

Lord Wrong. Ay come do a little.

Lord Geo. Why then, by all the Sacred Ties of Honour, Friendship, and Resistless Love, had I but Five thousand Pound in the whole World, and nothing else could purchase her—

Lord Wrong. I dare swear you'd give it every Shilling, that you really cou'd love her, tho' it were only to get rid of your Passion for Mrs. *Conquest.*

Lord Geo. Why then, look you—

Lord Wrong. You may swear till you are black in the Face; but you love her, her only, indeed you do: Your Passion for Lady *Gentle* is affected: Not but I grant you'll pursue it, for when nothing's in view, you're Indefatigable: You are a little uneasie at the smallness of Mrs. *Conquests* Fortune, and would fain persuade your self you are in love in another Place—but hark'e, you'll marry her.—And so if your Chariot's at the Door you shall carry me to *White*'s.

Lord Geo. Why then (except my self) thou art positively the most impudent Fellow upon the Face of the Earth. [*Exeunt.*

The End of the First Act.

ACT II. SCENE I.

SCENE *Continues.*

Lady Wronglove *alone.*

Lady Wrong. Why am I thus uneasie? Sure I am unreasonable in my Temper, I over-rate my self.—For if the Husband's Violation of his Marriage-Vow is in it self so foul an Injury, whence is it that the Law's so sparing in its Provision of Redress? And yet 'tis sure an Injury, because just Nature makes the Pain of bearing it outragious. O hard Condition! For if even that Pain provokes the Wife to move for Reparation, the World's gross Custom makes her perhaps a Jest to those that shou'd assist her.—If she offends, the Crime's unpardonable, yet if injur'd has no right to Compensation, it may be usual this, but sure 'tis un-natural.

Enter Mrs. Hartshorn.

Mrs. Harts. Madam, the Porter's come back.

Lady Wrong. Bring him in.

Enter Porter.

Well, Friend, how far have you followed 'em?

Port. Why, and it please your Honour, first they both went in Lord *George*'s Chariot to *White's.*

Lady Wrong. How long did they stay?

Port. Why and it please your Honour, they stay'd as near as I can guess, about a very little time.

Lady Wrong. Whither did they go then?

Port. Why then they stopt a little at the Coach-Maker's at *Charin Cross,* and look'd upon a small thing there, they call a Booby-Hutch and did not stay; and so then stop'd again at the Fruit-Shop in *Covent-Garden,* and then just went up to *Tom*'s Coffee-House, and then went away to the Toy-Shop at the *Temple-Gate,* and there the stay'd I can't tell how long, and please you.

Lady Wrong. Did they buy any thing?

Port. Yes, a number of things, truly.

Lady Wrong. Were they mostly for Men's Use, or how?

Port. Nay, I don't know; such sort of *Trangams* as the Gentry use:—I remember one was such a kind of a small Scizzar-Case as that by your Honour's side, my Lord *Wronglove* bought it.

Lady Wrong. So! that was not for me I am sure. [*Aside.*] Do you know what he paid for't?

Port. Troth, I cant say I do,—They came away, an't like your Honour, but I did not see them pay for any thing.—And so after that,—

Enter Mrs. Hartshorn.

Mrs. Harts. Young Mrs. *Notable* is come to wait upon your Ladyship.

Lady Wrong. Here, come into the next Room, Friend, I must employ you farther.—Desire her to walk in, I'll wait upon her presently. [*Exit Lady* Wronglove *and Porter.*

Re-enter Mrs. Hartshorn *with Miss* Notable.

Mrs. Harts. If your Ladyship pleases to walk in, my Lady knows you are here, Madam.—Dear Madam! how extreamly your Ladyship's grown within this half Year?

Miss Not. O fie, Mrs. *Hartshorn,* you don't think me taller, do you?

Mrs. Harts. O dear Madam! to an Infinity! Nay, and so plump too, so fresh-look'd. so round-hipp'd, and full-chested,—That—I'm sure, Madam, he! he! If I were a young Gentleman of Quality, Madam, he! he! Your Ladyship will pardon my Freedom.—I protest—he! he!— [*Curtsying and simpering.*

Miss Not. I vow, Mrs. *Hartshorn,* you have a great deal of good Humour; is not your Lady very fond of you?

Mrs. Harts. Truly, Madam, I have no Reason to complain of my Lady; but you must know, Madam, of late there have been some Concerns in the Family between my Lord and she, that I vow, my poor Lady is seldom in Humour with any Body.

Miss Not. I'm mighty sorry for that—What does my Lord give her any Occasion for Jealousie, think you?

Mrs. Harts. Occasion quoth'a! O Lard! Madam—But 'tis not fit for me to speak.

Miss Not. [*Aside.*] I'm glad to hear this—'Tis possible her Ladyship may be convinc'd that fifteen is as fit an Age for Love, as six and twenty.—And if her Jealousy's kindled already, I'll blow it into a Blaze before I part with her.

Mrs. Harts. Madam, I hear my Lady's coming—I humbly take my leave of your Ladyship: Your Ladyship's most obedient Servant. [*Impertinently cringing.*

Miss Not. Your Servant, good Mrs. *Hartshorn,* if you'll call to see me, I have a very pretty new Cross, that would become your Neck extremely—you'll pardon me.

Mrs. Harts. Dear Madam! your Ladyship's so obliging—I shall take an Opportunity to thank your Ladyship. [*Exit Mrs.* Hartshorn.

Enter Lady Wronglove.

Miss Not. My dear, dear Lady *Wronglove!* You'll forgive me; I always come unseasonably, but now 'tis pure Friendship, and my Concern for you, that brought me.

Lady Wrong. My dear you know I am always glad to see you,—but you'll excuse me if I am not the Company I wou'd be; I am mightily out of Order of late. I hope Sir *Friendly*'s well.

Miss Not. After the old Rate, past the Pleasures of Life himself, and always snarling at us that are just come into 'em.—I do make such Work with him—He reads me every Morning a Lecture against lightness, and gadding abroad, as he calls it; then do I teize him to Death, and threaten him, if he won't let me do what I please, I'll choose a new Guardian that will.

Lady Wrong. Come, don't disoblige him, my dear; for if you'll let me speak as a Friend, you have a good natural Town Wit, I own and a great many pretty Qualities; but, take my Word, your Interest and Reputation will find a better Account in trusting 'em under your Unkle's Conduct than your own.

Miss Not. I don't know that; for all his tedious self-denying Course of Philosophy is only to make me a good old Woman: Just the Condition of the Miser's Horse, when he had taught him to live upon one Oat a Day, the poor Creature dyed. So I am to spend all my Youth in learning to avoid Pleasures, that Nature won't let me be able to taste when I'm old.—Which is just as much as to say, Don't drink while you are thirsty, because if you will but stay till you are choak'd, you wont care whether you drink or no.

Lady Wrong. [*Aside.*] What an improving Age is this? But, my Dear, pray let me talk to you a little seriously, and I hope it won't be lost upon you; for you have an Understanding that's uncommon at your Age. I have observ'd among all the Unfortunate of our Sex, more Women have been undone by their Wit, than their Simplicity: Wit makes us vain, and when we are Warm in our Opinion of it, it sometimes hurries us through the very bounds of Prudence, Interest, and Reputation; have a care of being singled by the Men. Women, like Deer, are safest in the Herd; she that breaks away from her Acquaintance may be follow'd indeed, but the End of the Chace is very often Fatal.

Miss Not. But pray, Madam! Now with Submission, I think your Argument won't hold; for a Deer's Business is to escape, but a Woman's is to be caught, or else the World's strangely alter'd.

Lady Wrong. Honourably, I grant you.

Miss Not. Honourably! That is to stand still like a poor Dumb Thing, and be tamely shot out of the Herd—Now I think a young Creature that fairly trusts to her Heels, and leads you twenty, or thirty couple of brisk young Fellows after her Helter Skelter, over Hills, Hedges, Boggs, and Ditches, has ten times a fairer Chance for her Life; and if she is taken at last, I hold Twenty to one among any People of Taste, they'll say she's better Meat by half.

Lady Wrong. Well said Child! upon my Word you have a good Heart: Th' address of a Lover uses to be more Terrible at your Age—You seem to have resolv'd upon not dying a Maid already.

Miss Not. Between you and I, Lady *Wronglove,* I have been positive in that this Twelvemonth.

Lady Wrong. Why then, since we are upon Secrets, my Dear, I must tell you the Road you are in is quite out of the Way to be marry'd: Husbands and Lovers are not caught with the same Bait.

Miss Not. With all my Heart, let me but catch Lovers plenty I'm satisfied: For if having ones Will is the Pleasure of Life, I'm sure catching a Husband is catching a Tartar. No, give me dear precious Liberty—Content and a Cottage.

Lady Wrong. And wou'd not a good Husband content you?

Miss Not. And why must I expect a better than any of my Neighbours? Do but look into the private Comforts of the Dear,

Fond, Honourable Couples about this Town; and you'll find there's generally two Beds, two Purses, two Tables, two Coaches—Two ways—And so in most of their Pleasures, an unmolested Separation is the only Chain that keeps 'em together—Now pray, Madam, will you give me leave to be free, and ask you one Question?

Lady Wrong. Freely, my Dear.

Miss Not. Then did you yourself, never, upon no Occasion, repent your being marry'd?

Lady Wrong. That Question's very particular, my Dear.

Miss Not. Perhaps you'll Pardon me, when I give you my Reason for asking; but if you never did repent it, I am resolv'd I won't be the first that shews you Occasion to do it.

Lady Wrong. I don't know, my Dear, that ever I gave any body Reason to think me uneasie at Home; but you speak, Child, as if you knew something that ought to make me so.

Miss Not. Then depend upon't, unless I were sure you were uneasie already, I'd as soon be lock'd up as tell you any thing.

Lady Wrong. Well! suppose I am uneasie.

Miss Not. Pardon me—I can't suppose it—But suppose you are not, then I shou'd play a Fool's part, I'm sure to make you so.

Lady Wrong. I am sure you know something of my Lord, pray tell me.

Miss Not. Since I see you are uneasie, and I know you love him but too well; upon Condition you'll think I only do it to help your Cure, I will tell you; for when a Woman is once sure she has a substantial Reason to hate her Husband, I shou'd think the Business must be half over.

Lady Wrong. You make me impatient.

Miss Not. Let me think a little to soften it, as well as I can—What great Fools these wise over-grown Prudes are—to tell the greatest Secret of her Life to a Girl! To own her Husband false, and all her sober Charms neglected—But if she knew that young *Pill Garlick* were the occasion of it too—Lurd! how her Blood wou'd rise! What a disfigurable Condition wou'd my poor Headclothes be in? [*Aside* Well, Madam, to begin then with the end of my Story. In one word my Lord is grossly false to you, and to my Knowledge has an Appointment from a Mistress this very Afternoon, to meet her in an Hackney Coach in the Road to *Chelsea.*

Lady Wrong. All this, my Dear, except their Place of Meeting, I knew before, but how you come to know it I confess amazes me.

Miss Not. Look you, Madam, all I know is this—While my Lord *Wronglove,* and Lord *George* stay'd at our House, to speak with my Lady *Gentle* this Morning, I happen'd to sit in the next Room to 'em, reading the last new Play: Where among the rest of their precious Discourse, I over-heard my Lord *Wronglove* tell Lord *George,* the very Appointment, word for word, as I have now told it to you.

Lady Wrong. You did not hear her Name?

Miss Not. No, nor what she was; only that she's pretty Young: For I remember Lord *George* ridicul'd his Fancy, and call'd her *Green Fruit*—Little if you please, says t'other, but Ripe I'll warrant her: And I had rather gather my Fruit my self, than have it (like you) through the several Hands that bring it to *Covent-Garden*—

Lady Wrong. The brutal Thought!

Miss Not. When my Lady came down she made 'em stay Dinner; which was no sooner done, but I immediately slip'd away to tell you of it: For methought I was as much touch'd with the Wrong done to your Ladyship, as if it had been to my self.

Lady Wrong. My Dear, I am extremely oblig'd to you.

Miss Not. I'm sure I meant it well—For to know the worst, is not half so bad as to mistrust it.

Lady Wrong. Infinitely oblig'd to you.

Miss Not. Oh! she's deliciously uneasie. [*Aside and pleas'd.*] I'll tell you what I wou'd advise your Ladyship to do: Call for your Hood and Scarf, and an Hackney Coach to the Door this Minute—In the mean time I'll step Home again (for I am sure they are not gone yet; the Tea was but just call'd for when I came away) and the Moment my Lord *Wronglove* takes his leave, I'll send you word: Then may you clap on your Mask, drive after him, and in five Minutes I'll lay my Life you catch 'em together.

Lady Wrong. Why then if you'll do me the Favour to send me that word, my Dear, I shall have leisure in the mean time, perhaps to improve upon your Advice.

Miss Not. If you'll let one of your People send my Servant for a Chair, I'll go this Minute.

Lady Wrong. Here—who's there—[*Mrs.* Hartshorn *at the Door.*

Miss Not. Now I think I shall be ev'n with his Honour, I'll teach him to tell of Favours before he has 'em at least: If I had not discover'd him, in my Conscience he had let Madam discover me. [*Aside.*

Lady Wrong. I wou'd not but have known this for the World.

Miss Not. I am over-joy'd I can serve your Ladyship: You'll excuse my running away.

Enter Mrs. Hartshorn.

Mrs. Harts. Here's a Chair, Madam.

Miss Not. Well, I'll take no leave, for I'll call again by and by to know your Success.

Lady Wrong. My Dear I shall be extremely glad to see you; your Servant.

Miss Not. Your Servant, Servant. [*Runs off.*

Lady Wrong. Get me a Hood and Scarf, and a Mask, and bid one of the Footmen call an Hackney Coach to the Door immediately. [*Exit Mrs.* Hartshorn.] What will become of me? Shou'd not I strive to hate him?—I think I almost do—Is he not contemptible? Fogh!—What odious thing must this be, that he converses with! A Woman without Modesty has something sure of Horror in her Nature! What is it then in Men, that overlooks so foul a coarsness in the Heart, and makes 'em infamously fond of Shame and Outside?—I blush to think on't—How Tame must he suppose me, if I bear this Usage? I'll let him see I have a Spirit daring as his own, and as Resentful too: Since he dares be Base, I cannot bear but he should see I know him so. To sigh in Secret o're my Wrongs, and pay his Falshood the Regards I only owe his Truth, is more than Nature can submit to.

When once the Nuptial Bond's by him destroy'd,
The Obligations of the Wife are void. [Exit.

SCENE II.

SCENE *changes to the Lady* Gentle*'s House.*

Lady Gentle, *Lord* Wronglove, *Mrs.* Conquest, *and Lord* George *at a Tea-Table.*

Lady Gent. [*To Lord* Wronglove.] Come! come, my Lord, you must stay another Dish indeed.

Lord Wrong. Upon my Faith, Madam, my Business is of the last Concern; your Ladyship knows I don't use to start from good Company. [*Aside.*

Lady Gent. Well! I e'en give you over, you grow perfectly good for nothing.

Lord Wrong. The Truth on't is, Madam, we fond Husbands are fit for nothing—but our Wives.

Lady Gent. Come! none of your Raillery upon one that's too good for you.

Lord Wrong. Why, she has some high Qualities indeed, Madam, that I confess are far above my Merit, but I'm endeavouring every Day to deserve 'em, as fast as I can.

Lady Gent. Go, go! you deserve nothing at all, now you disoblige me.

Lord Wrong. I shall take a better Opportunity to make my self amends for going so soon, I am your Ladyship's most humble Servant—Mrs. *Conquest,* pray take care of Lord *George.*

Mrs. Con. O! he shall want for nothing, my Lord, pray do you take the same Care of the Lady you are going to.

Lord Wrong. Ha! ha! ha! [*Exit Lord* Wronglove.

Lord Geo. My Lord *Wronglove* is a very pretty Gentleman, and yet how unaccountable 'tis to hear good Sense jest upon Marriage.

Lady Gent. My Lord has so much good Sense, that he does not mean what he says, I dare swear for him.

Lord Geo. Indeed, Madam, I can't think he does, I never saw any thing amiss in his Actions, either at Home, or Abroad.

Lady Gent. Nor I indeed: And I think your Lordship very much to be commended; you love to put the fairest Construction upon things; it's a certain sign of good Sense, and good Principles.

Lord Geo. Your Ladyship has so much of both, that I can't help being Proud of any thing that recommends me to your Esteem.

Lady Gent. Upon my Word, my Lord, you have a great share on't, and I think very deservedly: 'Tis not a common thing in this Town, to find a Gentleman of your Figure, that has Courage enough to keep Marriage in Countenance, especially when it's so much the Mode to be severe upon't.

Lord Geo. Now that to me is an intolerable Vanity, to see a Man asham'd of being honourably Happy, because 'tis the Fashion to be viciously wretched—I don't know how it may be with other People, but if I were married, I shou'd as much Tremble to speak lightly of my Wife, as my Religion.

Mrs. Con. O! the hypocritical Monster—When he knows I know, [*Aside.*] if he were to be hang'd, he'd scarce think it a Reprive to be married—There's Roguery at the bottom of all this I'm sure—The Devil does not use to turn Saint for nothing.

Lady Gent. I am in hopes your Lordship's good Opinion of Marriage will persuade you not to be long out of it: We that feel the Happiness of a Condition our selves, naturally wish our Friends in it.

Mrs. Con. What do you think of me, my Lord, you know I have been about you a great while.

Lord Geo. Fy! fy! you marry! A meer Rake!

Mrs. Con. O but I fancy now, a Man of your Sobriety, and stay'd Temper wou'd soon reform me.

Lord Geo. [*Aside.*] This subtle Devil smoaks me!—'Ware Morals Faith—It shews her a little Jealous however.

Mrs. Con. I'll be whip'd if ever you marry more to your Mind; what signifies two or three thousand Pound in ones Fortune, where you are sure it wou'd be made up in good Humour and Obedience?

Lord Geo. And considering how intimate a Foot you and I have always convers'd upon: What a venerable Figure shou'd I make in the solemn Authority of an Husband pretending to command you?

Lady Gent. O! if you were married there wou'd be but one Will between you.

Lord Geo. There's the Danger, Madam, being but one, we shou'd certainly Squabble, who shou'd have it. I shou'd like Mrs. *Conquest* perhaps for my Wive's Companion: One as a light Allay to the softness of the others Temper: But if I were once fix'd in Love, and shou'd unfortunately bolt upon the least Glimpse of Jealousie, I am such a Slave to Tenderness, I know 'twould break my Heart.

Mrs. Con. Now cou'd I wash his Face with my Tea. [*Aside.*

Lady Gent. Well, I'm confident my Lord wou'd make an extreme good Husband.

Lord Geo. I don't know but I really might, Madam, if I cou'd persuade any Woman beside your Ladyship to think so.

Mrs. Con. [*Aside.*] How artfully the Monster scrues himself into her good Opinion; I must take him down a little—Pray, my Lord, how many Women have you had of late, by way of *Balm,* to heal the slight wound I gave you?

Lord Geo. Upon my Faith, Madam, I had my Wound and Cure from the same Person: My Passion for you went forward like *Penelope's* Web; whatever your Eyes did in the Day, a very short Reflexion upon your Temper unravell'd at Night; so that if you will needs know the Truth, I have not been reduc'd of late to apply my self for Relief to any body but your Ladyship. Ha! ha! ha! ha! [*Affects an insulting Laugh.*

Mrs. Con. Well, he has a glorious Assurance!

Lord Geo. I fancy Mrs. *Conquest,* you measure my Principles by your own; for by your Question you seem to think me a very wild Creature.

Mrs. Con. O fy, my Lord! so far from it, that I never saw any thing so astonishingly Modest.

Lord Geo. Not so modest neither, Madam, but if my Lady *Gentle* will give me leave, I dare use you most intolerably for this.

Lady Gent. Ev'n as you please, my Lord, for I confess her Assurance is enough to dash any out of Countenance.

Lord Geo. Does your Ladyship hear that, Madam? Remember now, that I am allow'd the modester Person; but to let you see, that in a just Cause I scorn to take the Advantage of my Character; I'll lay it aside for once, and with an honest Freedom tell you, your Attempts upon me are vain; you are Homely, downright Homely; and if she were not a Kin to me, I wou'd as soon marry my Grandmother.

Mrs. Con. Ah! poor Soul! every Body knows as well as my self, I am more than tolerably handsome: And (which you are ready to tear your Flesh at) the whole Town knows you think so.

Lord Geo. Madam—did your Ladyship ever hear so transcendant an Assurance.

Lady Gent. Nay, I'm on your side, my Lord—I think you can't be too free with her.

Lord Geo. I'll tell your Ladyship what this Creature did once: Such an Instance of her Intrepid Self-sufficiency—

Lady Gent. Pray let's hear it. Ha, ha.

Mrs. Con. With all my Heart, I'll be heard too.

Lord Geo. I'll tell you, Madam—About two Years ago I happen'd to make a Country-Visit to my Lady *Conquest,* her Mother, and one Day, at the Table, I remember, I was particularly pleas'd with the Entertainment, and upon Enquiry found that the Bill of Fare was under the Direction of *Mademoiselle* here: Now it happen'd at that Time, I was my self in want of a House-keeper; upon which Account I thought it wou'd not be amiss, if I now and then paid her a little particular Civility: To be short, I fairly told her, I had a great mind to have a plain good House-wife about me, and dropt some broad Hints, that the Place might be hers for asking—Wou'd you believe it, Madam, if I'm alive, the Creature grew so vain upon't, so deplorably mistook my Meaning, that she told me, her Fortune depended upon her Mother's Will, and therefore she could receive no Proposals of Marriage without her Consent: Ha, ha. Now after that unfortunate Blunder of hers, whether I ever gave my Lady the least trouble about the Business, I leave to the small Remainder of her own Conscience.

Mrs. Con. Madam, as I hope to be married, the poor Wretch fell downright in Love with me; for tho' he design'd only to make two Days stay with us, it was above three Months before I was able to get rid of him: When he came first indeed, he was a pretty sort of a tolerable impudent young Fellow, but before he left us, (O the power of Beauty!) I most barbarously reduc'd him to a sighing, humble, downright Dullness and Modesty.

Lady Gent. Ha, ha, Pray which of you Two am I to believe all this while?

Lord Geo. Madam, if there's any Faith in my Senses, her only Charms then were, and are still not in Raising of Passion, but Paste.

I own I did voraciously admire her prodigious Knack of making Cheescakes, Tarts, Custards, and Syllabubs, Ha, ha, ha.

Lady Gent. Ha, ha, ha.

Mrs. Con. You see, Madam, what 'tis to let him be never so little out of one's Hands: Now his very Modesty is Impudence: For to deny his being in Love with me to another, is ten times more Insolent, than his first owning it to me.

Lady Gent. Pshah, Words signifie nothing—Did he ever own it under his Hand?

Mrs. Con. His Hand! Ha, ha, ha, Madam—as I am a living Creature, if I have One, I have Five hundred *Billet-doux* of his, where he has confess'd such Things of my Wit, and Parts, and my Eyes, and my Air, and my Shape, and my Charms, that—Nay, he tells me in One, I have more natural Beauties the moment I rise out of my Bed in the Morning, than the whole Drawing-Room upon a Birth-Day by Candle-light. There's for you.

Lord Geo. And she beliẹv'd it, Madam—Ha, ha, ha, that's well enough.

Mrs. Con. Why I believe still you think so—Then every Line of 'em is so cramm'd with Sincerity, Sighs, Hopes, Fears, Flames, Darts, Pains, Pangs, and Passion, that in my Conscience, if a Body were to set 'em on fire, the Flame would never go out.

Lady Gent. Well, if you are in Love, ho, this is certainly the newest Way of Woing that ever was.

Lord Geo. Whether I'm in Love or no, I leave to your Ladyship.

Mrs. Con. And if your Ladyship should give it against him, whether or no, I have Reason to be vain upon't let the World judge.

Lady Gent. The World, I believe, will think better of you both, when you're married.

Lord Geo. In the mean time, I believe, our surest Comfort will be to think well of our selves, and let it alone. [*All rise.*

Mrs. Con. I am glad to find you have Modesty enough to suppose Marriage wou'd make us think worse of one another.

Lord Geo. O fie! Mrs. *Conquest,* the more you are known, the more you must be lik'd.

Mrs. Con. Is it then possible that you cou'd like me?

[*Both affectedly.*]

Lady Gent. Ha, ha. [*Going to the Tea-Table.*

Lord Geo. If it were possible I cou'd like any Thing out of Matrimony, it wou'd be you.

Mrs. Con. Well, but tell me, do you like me as I am, how do you know but you may persuade me into it.

Lord Geo. Like you—Umh! I can't tell—let's see—[*Looking on her.*]—give me your Hand.

Mrs. Con. There—[*Strikes it into his.*

Lord Geo. Now I must press it gently, to know if touching you keeps any Correspondence with my Heart—Humh!—A well flesht Hand indeed—[*Ogling her.*

Mrs. Con. O Lud! not so hard tho'.

Lord Geo. Now try your other Forces—look upon me.

Mrs. Con. There—[*Staring wildly on him.*

Lord Geo. [*Aside.*] She dares not tho' in Raillery look kindly on me—I like her for't—This over-acted Boldness to save her Modesty at this time, looks like secret Inclination.

Mrs. Con. Well, how do you find yourself? Have I Power—Do you burn much?

Lord Geo. Umh! No, I'm a little too low for a Fever—There's a small Pulse indeed—Different Sexes, like Steel and Flint can't well meet without a sort of striking Light between 'em; not but it goes out as fast as it comes in—One farther Tryal of your Power, and I'll tell you more.

Mrs. Con. Come, come, what is't? I'll do't.

Lord Geo. Turn away your Face, hold your Fan before it. Now draw your Hand slowly from me, and if you wou'd not have me think this Lightness of your Humour a direct Indifference, let me perceive a gentle Hold at parting, as though you left a tender Heart upon the Pressure. [*She does as directed, and runs from him.*

Mrs. Con. Has your Ladyship any Tea left?

Lord Geo. Death! that softning Touch has shot me to the Soul.

Mrs. Con. [*Aside.*] Let me observe him well, for Faith! I try'd my utmost Force, and even pleas'd my self in hopes to touch him.

Lord Geo. [*Aside.*] How vain a Coxcomb am I? This Girl has fool'd me to believe she likes me—That there should be such Pleasure in the Flattery of another's good Opinion!—There's something in the open Freedom of her Humour, so much beyond the

Close Reserves of Formal Prudery, that—Death, if she were of any Price but Marriage—But I'm a Fool to think of her— [*Walks apart.*

Mrs. Con. Humh! The Symptoms are right—Hah.—*Courage ma Fille,* the Gentleman has a Hole in his Heart yet.

Enter a Servant, who gives Lord George *a Letter.*

Lord Geo. Oh! There, come in good Time—Now to drive out one Poison with another—[*Goes to Lady* Gentle.] Madam, if your Ladyship's at leisure—I have the Bills ready.

Lady Gent. I am asham'd to give your Lordship this trouble.

Lord Geo. A Trifle, Madam, 1, 2, 3, 4, 5, 6, 7, 8, if your Ladyship pleases to look upon 'em, I think they are all hundred Pounds. The rest I have about me in Gold.

Lady Gent. If your Lordship pleases, we'll reckon in the next Room—Mrs. *Conquest.*

Mrs. Con. I'll wait upon your Ladyship.

[*Exit Lady* Gentle, *and Lord* George.

—Eight Hundred Pound, and the rest in Gold, upon her bare Word of Honour! He'd hardly make that Complement only to give me Jealousie—The Mortal's in earnest, that's certain—And what wicked way he proposes to find his Account with her; I am afraid to think—Let me see, I know there will be deep Play here to Night—I have a Thought in my Head, that perhaps may lay a Block in his way to her—Not but if there is such a thing as impregnable Vertue, I dare swear my Lady *Gentle* is Mistress of it; but then, on th' other side he has a consummate Assurance, that's full as unsurmountable. And when the impudent Hopes of a Lover are like his, cover'd with Modesty, it alters the Case strangely.—No Woman can then be positive what will become of her.—Her not suspecting his Design, puts him but in a fairer way of carrying it on.—Ah lud! I don't like it.—He'll certainly—Well! let him do what he will, he can't marry her, that's one Comfort, however. [*Exit.*

The End of the Second Act.

ACT III. SCENE I.

SCENE, *Lord* Wronglove*'s House.*

Enter Miss Notable *alone.*

Miss Not. So! this has been a Day of Business—I think now I am pretty even with his Lordship; and if I cou'd but draw in Lord *George* to be his Rival now, I should touch the very tip of Happiness—For then to have the Noise of these two Lovers draw two or three score more after me, which it certainly wou'd: For when once a Woman's the Fashion, every Body follows her; she fills like a Musick-Subscription, tho' there's nothing in't, no body will be out on't—And then to have the full Pleasure of mortifying Mrs. *Conquest* too, that's always holding her Nose over me, as if I was not fit to be out of my Bib and Apron. If I don't make as good a Rout in the Town as she 'tis very hard—Sure!—I'll forbid 'em all to toast her, that's positive!

Enter Lord George.

Lord Geo. [*Aside.*] Here she is, faith, and alone; now, if I can but flatter her into my Party, my Business is half over—So! my little *Venus!*

Miss Not. Bless me—This is lucky—I vow, my Lord, you frightned me.

Lord Geo. Well, and what makes your pretty Ladyship here, now none of the Family's at home?

Miss Not. O! my Lady will be at home presently! but pray how came your Lordship here then?

Lord Geo. Why, my Life, I chanc'd to be driving by, and perhaps saw you go in. [*Takes her by the Hand.*

Miss Not. Well, and what then?

Lord Geo. Why then, upon Inquiry, I found you were here alone and that made me come in—My dear Miss! how charming you look to Day!

Miss Not. P'shaw!

Lord Geo. What's the Matter, my Soul?

Miss Not. To tell me I look charming, and then call one Miss.

Lord Geo. O! I ask a thousand Pardons.

Miss Not. No dear Lord *Georgy,* never call me Miss again, you don't call Mrs. *Conquest* so; and tho' she's bigger, and more out of Shape, you know, than I, I'm sure I'm as much a Woman in my Heart, as she; nay, and in my Passions too: For I could kill any Woman that would rob me of a Lover, and dye for the dear Man that wou'd not be won from me.

Lord Geo. O the pretty Tenderness! But, my Dear, take heed how you look upon me, for I am fam'd for Assurance; and if once encourag'd, i'gad my Hope sets no Bounds to its Impudence, but falls downright to resolving, and cocks its Hat to the Fair ones Face, tho' in the very Fury of her Vertue.

Miss Not. I fancy now you're as gentle as the rest of your Brother Beaux, whose greatest Assurance is only in bragging of more than you have.

Lord Geo. Nay, if you doubt my Vertues, Child, I'll give you a Taste of 'em, my Dear. [*Kisses her.*

Miss Not. Hold! hold! O lud! The Duce take you for me.

Lord Geo. Death! what a pouting Lip the Rogue has! I gad. I think my Friend *Wronglove*'s in the right on't sure.

Miss Not. Besides do you think this bullying is any Proof of your Courage? [*Affectedly grave.*

Lord Geo. Why then, my Dear, to prevent all Mistakes for the future, I now give you fair Warning—If you have a Mind I shou'd not like you, don't flatter me any more; for I tell you, I'm a downright believing Puppy, and upon the least hint of a Hope, can no more forbear proceeding—

Miss Not. Look you, my Lord, all this is but Stuff, for, upon my Word, you'll find it no easie Matter to flatter me: I know well enough how you're disposed of.

Lord Geo. Why then, by all the Pains, Pangs, and Torments—In short, I'm a Fool; I won't speak a Word more to you.

Miss Not. Fie! fie! you had better give yourself these Airs to Mrs. *Conquest.*

Lord Geo. I don't know but I had, Madam, for I suppose you'll tell my Lord *Wronglove* of it.

Miss Not. Ah! poor Soul! if Mrs. *Conquest* lik'd you no better than I do my Lord *Wronglove,* you'd think yourself a miserable Creature.

Lord Geo. If Mrs. *Conquest* lik'd me but half so well, as I like you, I'm sure she'd be a miserable Creature.

Miss Not. Umh! How can you design upon me so?

Lord Geo. How can you think to impose upon me so?

Miss Not. My Lord, I shall take it very ill, if you tell me of my Lord *Wronglove.*

Lord Geo. Then perhaps, Madam, I shall'nt take it well to be told of Mrs. *Conquest.*

Miss Not. My Lord *Wronglove!*

Lord Geo. Mrs. *Conquest!*

Miss Not. I'd have you know, my Lord, of all Mankind, he's the farthest from my Thoughts.

Lord Geo. And I'd have you know, Madam, of all Womankind Mrs. *Conquest*'s as far out of mine.

Miss Not. Lard! the Assurance of some Men!

Lord Geo. Look you, Madam, in short, I can prove what I say; and I hold ten Pound of Tea to a Pinch of Snuff, you won't let me prove it: Come, and I'll take the same Bett of you, that you don't prove what you said to me of my Lord *Wronglove.*

Miss Not. Come, it's done!

Lord Geo. Done!

Miss Not. Done, for both!

Lord Geo. Done!

Miss Not. Why then, to prove that I am innocent of the least Inclination for him, I own he has teiz'd me these two Months, and because I was resolv'd to give him his Answer and his Punishment at the same time, I this very Afternoon made him an Appointment, then went immediately and told my Lady *Wronglove* he was to meet a Mistress at such an Hour, to my Knowledge, and so sent her in a Fury after him to catch 'em together.

Lord Geo. But how cou'd you escape yourself, all this while?

Miss Not. O! I did not tell her it was I: For as soon as I had blown up her Jealousie, I whip'd into a Hackney-Coach, and got to my Lord before her, where I just popp'd out my Head to him, and told him, in a pretended Fright, my Lady had dogg'd him, and

I durst not stay, then drove away as fast as I cou'd, and e'en left her to make up Accounts with him.

Lord Geo. Why then, my Life, I do pronounce, that the stoutest Wife of 'em all, with the Spirit of Revenge in her, could not have better bustled through this Business than you have.

Miss Not. And to let you see, Sir, that I never do design him any Favour, I give you leave to tell him, that I sent my Lady after him: —Which, if he does, I'm sure my Lord *Wronglove* must suspect an Intimacy between us. [*Aside.*] Nay, and if you'll but stay a Moment, you'll have an Opportunity, for I know he'll be at home presently.

Lord Geo. Then you are but just come from him?

Miss Not. The Minute you saw me come in.—And now, Sir, if you can but give me half as good a Proof, that your Heart is Innocent of Mrs. *Conquest.*—Why 'tis possible (when you have been about seven Years in the same Mine) I may then begin to think whether I shall consider of it or no.

Lord Geo. A notable Encouragement truly! But to let you see, Madam, I can't bear the Scandal of a Passion I'm not guilty of, as the last Proof of my Innocence, if either she doubts of my Indifference, or you of my Inclination, I am content to own both before both your Faces.

Miss Not. And so afterwards deny both, behind both our Backs. Indeed you must think again, that won't do.—An old Bite.

Lord Geo. Come, I'll do more—I'll pretend to trust you with my Passion for a third Person, and give you leave in the tenderest Touches Art or Woman's Wit can paint it, to tell it that third Person, while Mrs. *Conquest* is by.

Miss Not. Umh! This has a Face.

Lord Geo. Nay, with a Mask upon't too; for while I am convincing you, I dont care a Button for her, I impose upon a third Person purely to make a Secret of my Passion for you.

Miss Not. Better still—But, when I have a mind to pull off the Mask, you shan't refuse to show your Face; for I don't care a Man shou'd be asham'd of his Passion neither.

Lord Geo. As you please, for that.

Miss Not. I begin to like this strangely—This will teize Mrs. *Conquest* to Death—But now the Difficulty is to find out this third

Person—It must be one I'm acquainted with—What think you of my Lady *Wronglove?*

Lord Geo. Umh! No, I don't care to affront the Wife of my Friend.

Miss Not. Ah! Do you think any of the sober Souls about Town are ever angry in their Hearts to hear a Man likes 'em.

Lord Geo. That's true, 'tis possible her Resentment might let a Man die in his Bed after it—But 'tis not worth ones while to quarrel with him, about a Woman I don't like.

Miss Not. Nay, I wou'd not run you into any Hazard—unless 'twere upon my own Account—And now I think on't, I'll reserve that Quarrel for my self. [*Aside.*

Lord Geo. Come! I have found one—the properest Person in the World is my Lady *Gentle*—you know you are all in a House together her Husband, Sir *William's* in the Country, I have no Acquaintance with him; and if I lose hers by it, I don't care Sixpence.

Miss Not. I like your Choice very well—but I doubt it will require some Art to manage her; for to say the Truth, the Woman is most fantastically Simple: The very word Love out of any Mouth but her Husbands will make her Start, as if a Gun went off.

Lord Geo. Therefore, my Dear, it must be done as if you did not do it: You must go to her in all the disorder in the World, as if I had had the Impudence to endeavour to bribe you into my Assistance.

Miss Not. Right! or I'll go first and quarrel with my Uncle till he makes me Cry, and then come in with my Eyes swell'd, and sobbing as if I was almost choak'd with the Affront you had offer'd me, and then call you a thousand Villains for daring to propose such an impudent thing to me.

Lord Geo. Admirable! I gad, the Child's a Bars length in Experience above the stoutest of her Sex—Hark! I here a Coach stop!

Miss Not. Pshah! Duce take him, its certainly my Lord! how shall we do?

Lord Geo. Why, if you'll give me leave, my Life I'll call at your House in an Hour, and there we'll settle every Point to a Tittle.

Miss Not. With all my Heart, I won't stay for my Lady! I'll go Home now: But here comes my Lord, you shall see first how I'll use him.

Lord Geo. Don't trouble your self my Life, it will only give him a Jealousie, and do us no Service.

Miss Not. Indeed! methinks if I am not afraid of his Jealousie, you need not.

Lord Geo. My Soul! I ask ten thousand Pardons for my Stupidity.

Enter Lord Wronglove *and stops Miss* Notable, *who seems to talk gravely with him.*

Lord Geo. I gad, I can hardly believe my Senses; if this Girl's Character were in a Play, People that had not seen it wou'd swear the notableness of her Head were above Nature.

Lord Wrong. [*To Miss* Notable.] Did my Lord *George* tell you I told him you were to meet me?

Miss Not. That's no matter, it's sufficient I know you told him: But I thought at least you had seen enough of the World to know, that a Confident was the safest Disguise for a Rival.

Lord Wrong. I am sorry your Ladyship has such an Opinion of me.

Miss Not. Indeed, Sir, I shall not reproach you, I have satisfied my self in serving you, as you deserve for it—There's one can tell you how too, and so your Servant—My Lord, you'll remember. [*To Lord* George. [*Exit Miss* Notable.

Lord Wrong. Ha! ha! ha! Why, how now Friend! What are you my Rival?

Lord Geo. Ha! ha! ha! Why, Faith I am very near being one of 'em; for I believe the Child will think she has hard luck, if the whole Town is not so in a Fortnight.

Lord Wrong. But prithee how came she to know I ever made you a Confidence of my Affair with her? I am afraid you have been thoughtless.

Lord Geo. No, by all that's Honest—But she has told me more than you cou'd tell me.

Lord Wrong. What?

Lord Geo. That she her self told my Lady *Wronglove* of your Appointment with her this Afternoon, and (as I suppose you have since found) sent her in a Hackney Coach after you.

Lord Wrong. The Devil!

Lord Geo. Nay, 'twas a home push Faith!

Lord Wrong. Home! quotha! i'gad it's time for me to knock off, I shall never come up with her: But what cou'd she propose by telling you of it?

Lord Geo. Why, a fresh Lover I suppose—She found me a little Tardy here in addressing her, and imagining my small Virtue might proceed from a Regard to you: To convince me of her Indifference to you, she very fairly told me how she had serv'd you, to open an easier Passage in my Conscience for my Passion to her.

Lord Wrong. Sir, I give you Joy.

Lord Geo. And Faith, Sir, I expect it, though not as you do from the green Youth of her Person, but the plump Maturity of her Understanding—in helping me to another.

Lord Wrong. Riddles!

Lord Geo. To be short; I think I have bit the Babe; for in return, to convince her of my Indifference to Mrs. *Conquest,* I have impos'd upon her to discover my real Passion to Lady *Gentle,* before Mrs. *Conquest's* Face: And this, Sir, with your leave, is upon Honour all the Use I design to make of her.

Lord Wrong. Faith! 'tis a glorious one—All *Matchiavel* was Boys play to it—Look you, Sir, if you have a Fancy to the small remainder of her Composition—Pray be free—

Lord Geo. Dear Sir! not so much as the squeeze of her little Finger: But I thought I might make bold with her Virtue, and not rob your *Goust* of a Morsel.

Lord Wrong. Not a step farther Faith—I shall ev'n turn about my Nag and go Home, a little humble Hare hunting, by way of taking the Air, I can make a Shift to come up to; but to scamper Neck, or nothing, after a mad galloping Jade of a Hind, that will run you strait an end out of a Country, requires a little more Mettle than I am Master of.

Lord Geo. Come, come! you are Sportsman enough to know, that as Pride first humbles a Coquet into the loosest Encouragements to gain a Man, so the same Pride very often piques her into the granting the last Favour, rather than lose him.

Lord Wrong. I am sorry I have made this rout about it. I expect to have my Wife shock me too.

Lord Geo. O! pray, how did you come off? Did my Lady see you in the Coach?

Lord Wrong. I am not sure, Faith, but whether she did or not, she shan't convince me she did?

Lord Geo. Where did you leave her.

Lord Wrong. Why as soon as the Child told me from her Coach, that my Wife was in another behind me, I advis'd her to go off, then whipt up my wooden Glasses, and stood cross the Road, to prevent the Nymph's being follow'd, when she was out of sight, I order'd the Fellow to drive to Town as fast as *Black* and *Bay* cou'd lay Legs to the Ground; and having the Fortune of better Horses, I just got time enough to stop, and give a Fellow a Guinea to cut the Braces of the Coach that came after me, which while I drove gently on, I saw him do, so e'en came away, and left her Ladyship fairly overset in the middle of a swinging Shower, at *Hyde-Park-Corner.*

Lord Geo. How will she get Home?

Lord Wrong. Umh! She will have Wit enough in her Passion, I presume to send for another Coach, or, if not it will be a very pretty cool Walk over the Park for her.

Lord Geo. What an unfortunate Creature is a Jealous Wife?

Brush *Whispers Lord* Wronglove, *and Exit.*

Lord Wrong. My Wife's come Home: Now if you have a Curiosity, you shall see how I'll manage her.

Lord Geo. Pray, Sir, don't let me be Witness of your Conjugal Douceurs; but, if you please, I'll step into the next Room a little, for I have two or three Words to write: I must appoint the Count to meet me at my Lady *Gentle*'s after the Play.

Lord Wrong. Do so then—Take this Key, you'll find Paper in the Burreau.

Lord Geo. Quick, quick, I hear her—*Bon Voyage.*

[*Exit Lord* George.

Enter Lady Wronglove, *as from the Street, in a Hood and Scarf, and her Petticoat pinn'd up.*

Lady Wrong. So Sir, you are come home I see.

Lord Wrong. Yes, Madam, and you have been abroad I see, will you never give over making your self ridiculous to the very Servants? Was this a Dress to go out in, or a Condition for a Woman of your Quality to walk home in? Death! What must People take you for?—For shame!

Lady Wrong. My Lord, when a Husband grows monstrous, a Wife may well become ridiculous.

Lord Wrong. Look you, Madam, while your Jealousie keeps within Bounds I shall take little notice of it: But when its idle Extravagances break in upon my Reputation, I shall resent it as I ought: You may think me an ill Husband, if you please, but I won't have the World think so, till I give 'em occasion.

Lady Wrong. Insolent!

Lord Wrong. I thought I had told you in the Morning of a foolish Letter, that was brought by Mistake to me instead of my Servant: Your not taking my Word, methinks was not over Civil, Madam; and your since Dogging my Servant, instead of me, to the very Place of Appointment, was extremely obliging; the Fellow has confess'd to me, since he came home, that in his Fear to be seen, he got your Coach overthrown in the middle of the Highway, while you ridiculously pursued him: A mighty reputable Figure you must make, while you were getting out of it no doubt!

Lady Wrong. Come, come, my Lord, I have not lost my Senses yet—I follow'd you, and saw you in the Coach, when the confident Creature reach'd out to you from another, to tell you, I suppose, that I was just behind you. You may wrong me, but you can never blind me. [*In a scornful Smile*

Lord Wrong. Look you, Madam, that manner in speaking shews too much Transport, and—Colour does not become your Face—

Lady Wrong. [*Taking him up short.*] Some People think it does now: All Men are not of your Opinion, my Lord, my Complexion may not please you perhaps; but I have known many a Lover find an Appetite only from a Husband's losing it.

Lord Wrong. I won't suppose, Madam, you'll suffer any Man to like you more than he ought to do.

Lady Wrong. O Sir! don't you depend more upon my Discretion, than your own—We Wives, as well as our Husbands, love to have some idle Body or other to flatter us into Humour, when the Time hangs upon our Hands.

Lord Wrong. You are pleasant, Madam.

Lady Wrong. Marriage wou'd be an unfortunate Frolick indeed, if a Woman's Happiness were to die with her Husband's Inclination.

Lord Wrong. Waggish, I protest.

Lady Wrong. O there's nothing like a modish Husband to refine the unbred Vertue of a Wife into all the pretty Liberties in Fashion.

Lord Wrong. Good Company, or let me die.

Lady Wrong. I knew the Day when my Lady *Honey-Moon* wou'd have blusht almost into Tears at the Alarm of a bare civil thing from any Man but her Husband; but from the well-bred Example of his Conscience, she has now most undauntedly got the better of her own, and stands buff at the Head of the Mode, without the least Tincture of Vertue to put her out of Countenance.

Lord Wrong. Why now, my Dear—this is something, if you'd but always treat me with this good Humour, you and I shou'd never dispute as long as we live.

Lady Wrong. Monster!

Lord Wrong. For you know I have often told you, that if ever I shou'd be weak enough to wrong you, a gentle Complaint, and good Words wou'd work me to any thing; when the Pride of an insolent Reproach wou'd be but adding Fuel to my Folly, and make it flame the higher: But now I see that you are convinc'd that your Suspicions were groundless, and that you are sensible, if they had not that, Defiance is utterly the wrong Way to reform me: You shall find that all this Tenderness and Temper that you now treat me with, shall n't be thrown away upon me.

Lady Wrong. Insolent! Provoking Devil!

Lord Wrong. I am glad we are Friends with all my Heart, I am, upon my Soul, my Dear.

Lady Wrong. Villain!

Lord Wrong. O my Dear! I had like to have forgot one thing, and since we are now come to a Right Understanding, I'll tell you. If ever you and I should happen to disagree, I beg of you, for your own sake, never give me any hard Language; because there is no being certain, but in one of my brutal Fits, I may let you cry your self half blind for it, before I forgive you.

Lady Wrong. Forgive me! I have a Soul as much above the fear of you, as are your Injuries below my scorn—I laugh at both.

Lord Wrong. Ay but, my Life, I wou'd not have you trust me, for if ever you shou'd accuse me wrongfully, I know my foolish Temper so well, that, in my Conscience, in pure Spite, I believe—I believe—I believe I shou'd keep a Whore.

Lady Wrong. My Lord, this Affectation won't redress my Injuries, and however you deceive you self, in your unquestion'd Power of doing wrong, you'll find there is a Force of Justice yet above your Strength, a Curb of Law to check abandon'd Principles; nor am I yet so poor in Interest or Friends, jealous of my Wrongs, as of their own, but I may find a Time and place to make your proud Heart humble for this Usage.

Lord Wrong. Death! and Hell! dare to insult me with such another Thought, these Walls shall mark your Bounds of liberty: This dismal House becomes your Prison, debarr'd of Light, of Converse, or Relief, you live immured for Life: And, let me see that Big-mouth'd Friend, or Interest then, that can unlock a Husband's Power to keep you—When my Wife talks warmly to me, she shall ask my leave first.

Lady Wrong. Never—Such leave as you took to give me Cause for't, I take to tell you of it.

Lord Wrong. We are not upon an equal Foot: I won't have you so familiar in your Accusations: Be warn'd, and stir me not to use my Power: You may sooner make me an ill Husband than a tame one.

Lady Wrong. So may you me a Wife, my Lord: And what is't binds me more to bear an Injury, than you? I have seen you laugh at Passive Obedience between a Prince and People, and in the Sense of Nature, I can't see why 'tis not as ridiculous from a Wife to an injurious Husband?

Lord Wrong. Their Hazard is at least unequal: A People may be freed by struggling; but when a fetter'd Wife presumes, th' insulted Husband's sure to make her Chain the shorter.

Lady Wrong. Her Mind, at least, is more at liberty; the Ease of giving Shame for Pain, stands yet in some degree of pleasure: The

Wretch that's basely kill'd, falls better satisfied to see his Murtherer bleed.

Lord Wrong. Nay, now I crave your Mercy, Madam, I find I have mistook your Grievance all this while—it seems then, to be refus'd the pleasure of reproaching, is what you can't bear—and when you are wrong'd, to lock up your Tongue is the greatest Cruelty your Tyrant can impose upon you—if that be the Hardship, pray be easie, when you please in the Name of Thunder go on, spare no Invectives, but open the Spout of your Eloquence, and see with what a calm connubial Resignation, I will both hear and bow me to the Chastisement.

Lady Wrong. Poor helpless Affectation! This Shew of Temper is as much dissembled as your Innocence—I know, in spite of all your hardned Thoughts, to hear your Guilt confronted thus, must gall your Soul: Patients don't use to smile while their fresh Wounds are prob'd, nor Criminals to laugh under the smart of Justice.

Lord Wrong. My Life, you begin extremely well, and with abundance of Fire, only give me leave to observe one thing to you, that as you draw towards an End, don't forget the principal thing you were going to say.

Lady Wrong. How poor! How low! How wretched is a guilty Mind, that stands without a Blush the Shock of Accusation—

Lord Wrong. Hold, Madam, don't mistake me neither; for I allow you to accuse me of nothing, but of what we fine Gentlemen think is next to nothing—a little Whoredom.

Lady Wrong. Audacious! Horrid Wretch! and dare you own the Fact.

Lord Wrong. Own it: No, no, if I were guilty I wou'd not do that, but I give you leave to suppose me so, because, by what you say, I fancy it wou'd ease your Heart to reproach me, tho' methinks—it's very hard, that Demonstration won't convince you of my Innocence.

Lady Wrong. Demonstration!

Lord Wrong. Demonstration! Ay, Demonstration; For if I were guilty, pray who cou'd better know it than my self, and have not I told you with my own Mouth 'tis no such thing: Pray what Demonstration can be plainer?

Lady Wrong. I find you are resolv'd to stand it to the last; but since I know your Guilt, I owe my self the Justice to resent it. When the weak Wife transgresses, the Husband's Blood has leave to boil; his Fury's justified by Honour; the Wrong admits no measure of amends; his Reputation bleeds, and only Blood can stanch it. And I must tell you, Sir, that in the Scales of Conscience, the Husband's Falshood is an equal Injury, and equal too, you'll find the Wife's Resentment: Henceforth be sure you're private in your Shame; for if I trace you to another Proof, expect as little Mercy for the Wretch you doat on, as you your self wou'd shew to the felonious Lover.

My Wrongs through her shall shoot you to the Soul,
You shall not find I am an injur'd Fool. [Exit.

Lord Wrong. Well said I gad, if she cou'd but love with half the Fire she can hate, I wou'd not desire to pass my time in better Company—Not but between me, and my self, our Dear Consorts, have something a hard time on't: We are a little apt to take more Liberty than we give—But People in Power don't care to part with it, whether it be lawful or no; to bear her Insolence is positively intolerable—What shall I do with her—I know no way of making an honourable Peace, better than Sword in Hand—Ev'n let her Pride swell till it bursts, and then 'tis possible she may come to Reason.

Enter a Servant.

Serv. Here's Sir *Friendly Moral,* my Lord.

Lord Wrong. Desire him to walk in—I hold fifty Pound the old Gentleman comes to school me about his young Kinswoman; if he does, I know he'll do it handsomely: For give him his due, with all his severity of Principles, he is as good humour'd, and as well bred, as if he had no Principles at all.

Enter a Servant with Sir Friendly.

Sir Fr. My Lord, I am your most humble Servant.

Lord Wrong. Sir *Friendly!* this is kind indeed! Chairs there—Well! how goes the Gout Sir?

Sir Fr. In troth very untowardly; for I can hardly walk with it—Will your Lordship give me leave?

Lord Wrong. To stand upon any thing but Ceremony.

Enter Lord George *from the Inner Room.*

Lord Geo. Nuncle, I am glad to see you.

Sir Fr. Hah! Monsieur *Brilliant,* and in a sober Visit after Sun-set!

Lord Geo. O dear Sir, I'm grown a Fellow of the most retir'd Conversation in the World.

Sir Fr. Your Reformation is not of a very long Date, I'm afraid; for if I don't mistake, I saw you but Yesterday at the Thatch'd-house with a Napkin upon your Head, at the Window in very hopeless Company.

Lord Geo. How! how Nuncle! two Men of Title, and a foreign Count, hopeless Company!

Sir Fr. Most deplorable! Your Count's a Counter, and only passes for what he is in his own Country; your Men of Title indeed are no Counterfeits, every Body sees into their Worth, Sir *Bubble Squander,* and my Lord *Lawless:* But the Sparks I observ'd you with, were *Donefirst* the Jockey, and *Touchum* the Gamester; as infamous a Fellow as ever broke the Head of a Box-keeper.

Lord Geo. Pshah! People that Play keep all Company: But to let you see I had my Account in it, I had a mind to bite Sir *Bubble* in a Horse Match, and so took these two Fellows with me, to let him into the Secret.

Sir Fr. A fine Instance of our Modish Morals indeed! To make ones Conscience a Bawd, to the dishonour of biting a Wretch of perhaps a hundred Pound! What a Shame it is the World shou'd not call it by its true name Cheating, that Men of Honour might not be guilty of it.

Lord Geo. O, Sir, the name I grant you wou'd strangely alter the Case; but People of Rank, and Power, Nuncle, are wiser, and Nick-name one another's Infirmities.—Therefore 'tis your little Cheat you see, that's sent to *Newgate;* your great one's only turn'd out of his Place.

Sir Fr. Nay, 'tis a comfortable World indeed, for Knaves, Fools, Fops, Cowards, and Sharpers.

Lord Geo. Right! their Quality and Quantity keeps 'em in Countenance.

Sir Fr. So that a Man may be any one, or all of 'em, and yet appear no Monster in most of the publick Places about Town.

Lord Wrong. But with submission, Sir *Friendly,* if I meet with a Man of Figure, that talks agreeably over a Glass; what in the Name of good Nature have I to do with his Morals?

Sir Fr. 'Tis in my Opinion, as dishonest in a Man of Quality to converse with a well-bred Rogue, as 'twere unsafe for a Woman of Reputation to make a Companion of an agreeable Strumpet. People's Taste and Principles are very justly measur'd by their Choice of Acquaintance: Besides, a Man of Honour owes the discountenance of a Villain, as a Debt to his own Dignity. How poor a Spirit must it shew in our People of Fortune, to let Fellows, who deserve hanging every other Day of their lives, die at last of sitting up in the best Company? But my Lord *Wronglove,* I am afraid I have a Pardon to ask; the last time we three were together, did not the old Fellow a little over-shoot himself? I thought, when I parted, I had been freer in my Advice than became me?

Lord Wrong. So far from it, that your very Manner of speaking makes your most severe Reproofs an Obligation.

Sir Fr. Nay, I was only concern'd for what I had said to your Lordship: As for this Spark, I no more mind his Caprice, than I believe he does any thing I can say to him: And yet the Knave has something of good Humour in him, that makes me I can't help sometimes throwing away my words upon him. But give me your Hand; in troth, when I was at your Years, I had my Follies too.

Lord Geo. Ay! now you come to us Nuncle, and I hope you'll have good Nature enough, not to expect your Friends to be wiser than you were.

Sir Fr. Perhaps I don't expect it, but in troth, if they shou'd be wiser—for my Soul I can't see any Harm 'twould do 'em: And tho' I love with all my Heart, to see Spirit in a young Fellow, yet a little Prudence won't poison him. And if a Man that sets out into Life, shou'd carry a little general Esteem with him, as part of his Equipage he'd make never the worse Figure at the end of his Journey.

Lord Geo. We young Fellows that ride Post, never mind what Figures we make.

Sir Fr. Come! come! lets not contend for Victory, but Truth—I love you both—and wou'd have all that know you do so too—Don't think because you pass for Men of Wit, and modish Honour, that that's all you owe to your Condition: Fortune has given you

Titles to set your Actions in a fairer Light, and Nature Understanding to make 'em not only Just, but generous. Troth! It grieves me to think you can abuse such Happiness, and have no more Ambition, or regard to real Honour, than the wretched fine Genlemen in most of our Modern Comedies!—Will you forgive me—Upon my Faith, I don't speak thus of you to other People, nor wou'd I now speak so to you, but to prevent other Peoples speaking thus of you to me.

Lord Geo. Nuncle, depend upon't I'm always pleas'd to hear you.

Lord Wrong. I take it kindly.

Sir Fr. Then first to you, Lord *George,*—What can you think the honest part of the World will say of you, when you have seduc'd the innocent Inclinations of one of the best Wives, from perhaps one of the best Husbands in the World.—To be plain, I mean my Lady *Gentle;*—You see, my Lord, with all your Discretion, your Design's no Secret.

Lord Geo. Upon my Life, Nuncle, if I were half the Fellow you think me, I shou'd be asham'd to look People in the Face.

Sir Fr. Fie, fie! how useless is the Force of Understanding, when only Age can give us Vertue?

Lord Wrong. Come, Sir, you see he's incorrigible, you'll have better Success with me, I hope; for, to tell you the Truth, I have few Pleasures, that you can call it Vertue in me to part with.

Sir Fr. I am glad to hear it, my Lord,—I shall be as favourable as I can; but, since we are in search of Truth, must freely tell you, The Man that violates himself the sacred Honours of his Wife's chast Bed (I must be plain, my Lord) ought at least to fear, as she's the frailer Sex, the same from her; the Injury to her strikes deeper than the Head, often to the Heart. And then her Provocation is in Nature greater; and injur'd Minds think nothing is unjust that's natural. This ought to make a wise Man tremble: For, in the Point of real Honour, there's very little Difference between being a Cuckold, and deserving to be one: And to come a little closer to your Lordship's Case, to see so fine a Woman as my Lady *Wronglove,* even in her Flower of Beauty, slighted for the unblown Pleasures of a Green-sick Girl, besides th' imprudent part, argues at best a thin and sickly Appetite.

Lord Wrong. Sir *Friendly,* I am almost asham'd to answer you, —Your Reproach indeed has touch'd me; I mean for my Attempts upon your young Kinswoman; but, because 'tis not fit you shou'd take my Word, after my owning so unfair an Action, here's one can bear me Witness, that not half an Hour before you came in, I had resolv'd never to persue her more.

Sir Fr. My Lord, I came not to reproach you with a Wrong to me, but to yourself; had the Girl had no Relation to me, I still had said the same; not but I now am doubly bound to thank you.

Lord Geo. And now, Nuncle, I'll give you a piece of Advice: Dispose of the Child as soon as you can, rather under-match her, than not at all: For, if you'll allow me to know any thing of the Mathematicks, that before she's five Weeks older she will be totally unqualified for an Ape-leader, you may as positively depend upon, as that she is of the Feminine Gender.

Sir Fr. I am pretty well acquainted with the Ripeness of her Inclinations, and have provided for 'em; unless some such Spark as you (now my Lord has laid 'em down) whips up the Cudgels in the mean time.

Lord Geo. Not I, upon Honour, depend upon't; her Person's quite out of my Goust, nor have I any more Concern about it than I have to know who will be the next King of *Poland,* or who is the true Original of Strops for Razors.

Lord Wrong. Sir *Friendly,* I own I have been no Stranger in other Places to the Follies you have charg'd me with; yet I am so far inclin'd to part with them, that were it possible I could be, my own way, and properly, reconcil'd to my Wife, I wou'd not wish a Thought of Happiness beyond it.

Sir Fr. My Lord, I know her Temper, and her Spirit.

Lord Wrong. O! human Patience can't bear it.

Sir Fr. I warrant you! A wise Man will bear a greater Weakness from a Woman: And, since I find your good Nature is not wholly disoblig'd, I could wish, for both your Sakes, I had your Lordship's secret leave to talk with her.

Lord Wrong. Um! Cou'd not it as well be done without my Leave, Sir *Friendly?* I shou'd not Care to have her think I made Advances—

Sir Fr. O!—I am a Friend to both, and will betray neither of you.

Enter a Servant.

Serv. Sir, there's a Gentleman come out of the City, and stays at your House to speak with you.

Sir Fr. I'll wait on him.—My Lord, will you excuse me?

Lord Wrong. I cou'd rather wish your Business wou'd, Sir *Friendly.*

Sir Fr. Upon my Word, my Lord, 'tis urgent; this Man brings me Money: I am discharging my self of my Guardianship to Mrs. *Conquest,* and my Business is now to pay her in the last Sum of her Fortune.

Lord Geo. What's the Sum total, Nuncle, if a Man shou'd happen to set a Price upon his Liberty?

Sir Fr. Come, come, the Liberties you value, my Lord, are not worth keeping: An honest Smile from the good Humour of that Girl is worth all the sodden Favours of your whole *Seraglio*—Will four thousand Pound do any good, my Lord.

Lord Geo. Look you, Sir *Friendly,* Marriage is very honourable and wise, and—and—it—it—it's—it's an extreme fine thing, no doubt; but I am one of those frank-hearted Fellows that had rather see my Friends happy that way than my self.—My Lord, your Servant,—If you are going home, Nuncle, I'll carry you, for I have Business at your House too.

Lord Wrong. Who's there? Light out!—Lord *George,* is your new Chariot at the Door?

Lord Geo. Yes; and positively the prettiest that ever roll'd in the Rear of six Horses.

Lord Wrong. I have a Mind to look at it. [*Exeunt.*

The End of the Third Act.

ACT IV. SCENE I.

SCENE, *Lord* Wronglove*'s House.*

Enter Lady Wronglove *and Mrs.* Hartshorn.

Lady Wrong. Was Sir *Friendly* within.

Mrs. Harts. Yes, Madam, he gives his humble Service, and says he will certainly be at home at eight a Clock, and expect your Ladyship's Commands.

Lady Wrong. Did the Fellow give my Service to my Lady *Gentle* too, and to Mrs. *Conquest?*

Mrs. Harts. He did not say any thing of it to me, Madam.

Lady Wrong. What Blockhead is it you always find out to neglect my Business? Whom did you send?

Mrs. Harts. James, Madam.

Lady Wrong. Call him in, I find I must always give my Orders my self.

Mrs. Harts. He's gone to the Play to keep your Ladyship's Places

Lady Wrong. The Play! sure the People are all out of their Senses! Why I shall'nt go to Day.

Mrs. Harts. He say'd, Madam, your Ladyship order'd him, right or wrong, to keep Places every *Saturday.*

Lady Wrong. Pshah!

Mrs. Harts. I hope your Ladyship is not angry at me, Madam.

Lady Wrong. No! Prithee! I don't know what I say.

Mrs. Harts. Ah, poor Lady! [*Aside.*

Lady Wrong. What is the Play to Day?

Mrs. Harts. The—the—*Husband,* something—the *Careful Husband* I think, Madam.

Lady Wrong. The *Careful;* the *Careless Husband,* you mean sure tho' I never saw it.

Mrs. Harts. Yes, yes, Madam—it's that Play, that my Lady *Wear-breeches* hates so, that I saw once, Madam—where there's a Lady that comes in, and catches her Husband fast asleep with her own

Woman, and then takes her Handkercher off her Neck, and then goes softly to him—

Lady Wrong. And strangles him in his Sleep?

Mrs. Harts. No, Madam.

Lady Wrong. Oh, strangles the Woman.

Mrs. Harts. No, Madam, she only lays it gently over his Head, for fear he shou'd catch Cold, and so steals out of the Room, without so much as offering to wake him.

Lady Wrong. Horrid! And what becomes of the poor spirited Creature?

Mrs. Harts. O! Madam, when the Gentleman wakes, and finds that his Lady has been there without taking any notice of it to him, he grows so sham'd of his Wickedness, and so sensible of her Vertues, that he afterwards proves the civilest Gentleman, and the best Husband in the World to her.

Lady Wrong. Foh! were I an Husband, a Wife with such a tame enduring Spirit wou'd make me scorn her, or, at best, but sleep at her groveling Vertue—Is my Lord within?

Mrs. Harts. Yes, Madam, he's reading in his Closet.

Lady Wrong. Any thing, the dullest Solitude more pleases him than my Company—Hoh! [*Sighing.*

Mrs. Harts. [*Aside.*] Ah poor Lady! it makes me weep to see her grieve at Heart so.

Lady Wrong. Go to my Lord, and say I desire to speak with him. [*Exit Mrs.* Hartshorn.] O! for a Draught of cold Indifference to chill this lukewarm Love, that wou'd rebel against my Peace, that I may leave without a Pang this hardned Wretch, and to the rude Riots of his gross Desire give him up for ever—He comes, keep down my swelling Heart, and let tame Patience speak my Wrongs for once, for Wrongs like mine need not the Force, or Fire of Passion to present 'em.

Enter Lord Wronglove.

Lord Wrong. I am told, Madam, you desire to speak with me!

Lady Wrong. Yes, my Lord, and which perhaps you'll not dislike, to talk with you in Temper too, if you're in Temper to receive it.

Lord Wrong. While you're in Temper, Madam, I shall always think I owe you the respect of keeping mine, and when you are not, I shall keep it in respect to my self.

Lady Wrong. My Lord I never had occasion to question your knowing what you ought to do: But you are not bound, you'll say, to make your Inclination a Slave to your Understanding: And therefore 'tis possible you won't want Arguments to convince me, that a Wife's obliged to bear all Faults in her Husband, that are not in her Power to punish.

Lord Wrong. Proceed.

Lady Wrong. Now I must tell you, my Lord, when any one injures me, because 'tis in their Power, I shall certainly hate 'em for't because that's in my Power.

Lord Wrong. I am sorry you think it worth your while to make use of so unprofitable a Power.

Lady Wrong. I am sorry I have Occasion for it.

Lord Wrong. Um—That's half a Question—but go on.

Lady Wrong. And therefore since I find the more I endeavour to detect you, the more you persist in your Resolution to use me ill. Since my honest Resentment, and your Actions have made us a mutual Grievance to one another, I see no way in Nature to make us mutually Just, but by cancelling our Obligations. If we agree to part, th'uneasie Bond of Wife or Husband no longer lies in force against us—And since I am contented to remit the Breaches you have made of the Conditions on your Part, I suppose you won't think it inconsistent with your Reputation, to allow me part of the Fortune I brought you, as a separate Maintenance.

Lord Wrong. When you and I part, Madam, you shall leave none of your Fortune behind you: But shou'd I now yield to your Proposal, the World might think I own'd the Breaches you accuse me of, and then 'twere only parting to indulge your Pride: But if the sincere Sorrow of your humble Heart can find a way to make it as consistent with my Reputation, as my private Peace, I'll sign to your Relief this moment.

Lady Wrong. Your Reputation! No, my Lord, that's your Business to secure. I've taken care to let my Actions justifie my own; if you have been remiss, the Fault's not mine to answer—I'm glad at least to see you own where 'tis your Weakness lies.

Lord Wrong. To bear such Insults from a Wife, is not, perhaps, my least Weakness—Nay, I've another too (which I might own with equal Blushing). A tame forgiving Pity of your unfortunate Temper, that pauses yet to take th' Advantage of your Distraction to undo you.

Lady Wrong. Horrid! Insolent Assertion, to do me Injury; and call my innocent Endeavours at Redress, Distraction.

Lord Wrong. Innocent! Away! You take the Rudest, Fiercest, Falsest Means for Reparation, if you had a Wrong.

Lady Wrong. If I had! Insupportable! To be out-fac'd that my own Eyes deceive me!

Lord Wrong. Death, and Confusion! Suppose your Wrongs were true—think what they are—speak 'em with a modest Tongue, and blush at all this Redness of Resentment.

Lady Wrong. Nay now, my Lord, we are past all Argument.

Lord Wrong. 'Tis fit we shou'd be so—the Subject ought to be below your Thoughts—don't misuse your Pride, till I am taught to think you've none. Death! I've known the Spirit of a Strumpet in the Misfortunes of her slighted Love shew more than you; who tho' her Heart was bleeding with the inward Pain, yet to her Lover's Face took Pride and Ease to seem concernless at his Falshood.

Lady Wrong. My Lord, your having a better Opinion of such Creatures than your Wife, is no new Thing to me, but I must tell you, I have not deserv'd your vile Comparison. Nor shall I ever buy an Husband's Inclination, by being like the horrid Things you doat on.

Lord Wrong. Come, since you are Incorrigible, I'll give your Pride the vain Relief you ask for—Your Temper is at last intolerable, and now 'tis mutual Ease to part with you: Yet to let you see 'tis not in the Power of all your Follies to provoke me to an Injustice; I will not trust your Wishes with your own Discretion; but if you have a Friend, that's not an Enemy to me, whose Honesty and Sense you dare depend on, let him be Umpire of the Conditions, of what's proper both of us should yield to when we part, and here's my Hand, my Word, my Honour, I'll sign them on demand.

Lady Wrong. Keep but your Word in this, my Lord, and I have henceforth no Injuries to reproach you with.

Lord Wrong. If in the least Article I shrink from it, conclude me then the mean, the servile Wretch you'd make me.

Lady Wrong. I'd make you Just, my Lord, if that's my fault, I never shall repent it.

Lord Wrong. We are now no longer our own Judges: Madam, name the Person you appeal to.

Lady Wrong. O! my Lord, you can't be more in haste than I am. Sir *Friendly Moral,* and I think you can have no Objection to his Integrity—I appeal to him.

Lord Wrong. The Man o'th' World I wou'd have chose my self; and if you please, Madam, I'll wait upon you to him immediately.

Lady Wrong. No, my Lord, I think it won't be unreasonable, if I speak with him alone first.

Lord Wrong. With all my Heart; in half an Hour then I'll follow you.

Lady Wrong. My Lord, you need not affect this Indifference, I have Provocations enough without it—I'll go, depend upon't.

Lord Wrong. I thought you had been gone, Madam. How now. [*Passing hastily by him*

Enter a Servant, who whispers Lord Wronglove.

Serv. Sir *Friendly Moral* desires to speak with your Lordship, he stays in the next Room, and begs my Lady may not know he's her

Lady Wrong. [*Turning.*] What can that Whisper mean? But I have done with Jealousie.

Lord Wrong. When your Lady's gone out, desire him to walk in. [*Exit Servant.*] In half an Hour, as I told you, I'll positively be with you.

Lady Wrong. O! my Lord, I shall n't stay to interrupt your Privacies. [*Exit Lady* Wronglove

Lord Wrong. How unfortunate must this Woman's Temper be when e'en this Affectation of Indifference is the greatest Proof I ever receiv'd of her Inclination—What can this come to?—By Sir *Friendly*'s being here, I fansy she has been disclosing her Grievanc already; and when she has made the very worst of it, I am mistake if his Temper and Understanding won't convince her, that 'tis bel the Pride and Prudence of a Wife, to take so violent a Notice of it— But here he comes—[*Enter Sir* Friendly Moral.] Sir *Friendly,* you most humble Servant—Come, we are alone, I guess the Business—my Wife has been talking with you.

Sir Fr. No, my Lord, and unless you give me your Word to be secret, I dare not tell you my Business.

Lord Wrong. Upon my Honour.

Sir Fr. Then, there, my Lord, I just now receiv'd that Letter from her.

Lord Wrong. [Reads.]

At last I find there's no way of being easie in my Life, but parting for ever with my Lord: And I wou'd willingly do it in such a manner, as might least blame me to the World: Your Friendship to both our Families will, I'm sure, engage you to advise me in the safest Method: Therefore I beg you'll be at home some time this Evening, that I may speak with you: For Life, as it is, is insupportable.

I am, Sir, *&c.*

Well, Sir *Friendly,* then I can tell you, half your Trouble's over; for we have agreed to part already, and both have chosen you the Umpire of the Conditions.

Sir Fr. How, my Lord! cou'd Passion be so far your Master too?

Lord Wrong. Why Faith, Sir *Friendly,* Patience cou'd endure it no longer—'Twas her own Proposal, and she found the way at last to provoke me, to take her at her word.

Sir Fr. Her word, fy! fy! because she'd lame her Reputation to cripple yours, shall you revenge her Folly on yourself? Come, come, your understanding ought to have more Compassion for the Misfortune of a weak Woman's Temper.

Lord Wrong. Oh! she's implacable!

Sir Fr. That quality punishes it self, my Lord; and since the Provocation's yours, it might sometimes be pardon'd. Do but imagine how it must gall the Heart of a Woman of Spirit, to see the loose *Coquets* of her Acquaintance smile at her modish Husband's sleeping in a separate Bed from her.

Lord Wrong. Humph! there's something in what you say—I own—Not but you'll laugh at me, shou'd I tell you the true and honest occasion of it.

Sir Fr. Not if it be true, and honest, my Lord.

Lord Wrong. Upon my Faith, it was not the least distaste of her Person, but her being downright an intolerable Bedfellow.

Sir Fr. How do you mean?

Lord Wrong. I cou'd never Sleep with her—For though she loves late Hours, yet when she has seen me gape for Bed like a Waiter at the Groom Porters in a Morning, she wou'd still reserve to her self the tedious Decorum of being first sollicited for her Company; so that she usually contriv'd to let me be three quarters Asleep, before she wou'd do me the Honour to disturb me. Then besides this, I was seldom less than two Nights in Four, but in the very middle of my first comfortable Nap, I was awaken'd with th' Alarum of Tingle, Tingle, Tingle, for a quarter of an Hour together, that you'd swear she wanted a Doctor, or a Midwife: And by and by down comes Madamoiselle with a single Under-petticoat in one Hand, and rubbing her Eyes with the t'other; and then after about half an Hours weighty Arguments on both sides, poor Madamoiselle is guilty of not having pull'd the Sheet smooth at her Feet; by which unpardonable neglect her Ladyship's little Toe had lain at least two Hours upon the Rack of a Wrinkle, that had almost put her into a Fever—This, when I civilly complain'd of, she said she must either be easie in the Bed, or go out of it—I told her that was exactly my Case, so I very fairly step'd into the next Room, where I have ever since slept most profoundly sound, without so much as once dreaming of her?

Sir Fr. An unfortunate Circumstance truly, but I see a little matter, my Lord, will part People that don't care for Company.

Lord Wrong. But, Sir *Friendly,* (not to trouble you with a long Particular of the Provocations I had from her Temper, to run a roguing at first) suppose I have play'd the Fool, is the Fault unpardonable? Is a Wife's Reputation like a Husband's, mean, or infamous, because she overlooks the Folly?

Sir Fr. No—but did you, my Lord, ever give her any signs of a Repentance?

Lord Wrong. As far as I thought the nature of the Crime requir'd—I've often receiv'd her moderate Reproaches with a Smile, and Raillery—given her leave to guess, in hopes her Understanding wou'd have smil'd again, and pardon'd it.

Sir Fr. And what Effect had that?

Lord Wrong. O! none in Nature! For, Sir, her Pride has possess' her with so horrid an Idea of the Crime, that my making slight on't but more incenses her: And when once her Passion takes the Liberty of her Tongue to me, I neither spare Authority, nor ill Nature to provoke, or silence her—This generally is our course of Conversation; and for ought I see, if we shou'd not agree upon parting, we are in as fair a way of heartily plaguing one another for Life, as er'e a comfortable Couple in *Europe*.

Sir Fr. My Lord, the thought's too Melancholy to jest upon.

Lord Wrong. Why Faith, I have so far a Concern for her, that cou'd any means of an Accommodation be found, that were not unfit for an Husband to submit to, I shou'd not yet refuse to come into it.

Sir Fr. Spoken like a Man, my Lord: How far the Fault's in you, I partly see; and when I have made the same Enquiry into my Ladies Grief, I doubt not then I shall be better able to advise.

Lord Wrong. You've now an Opportunity; for she's gone this very Minute to my Lady *Gentle*'s, to speak with you.

Sir Fr. 'Twere best to lose no time then, my Lord, I'll take my leave—nay, no Ceremony.

Lord Wrong. No, I'm going part of your way—upon my word. [*Exeunt.*

Enter Lady Gentle *reading a Letter, and Mrs.* Conquest.

Mrs. Con. I hope Sir *William*'s well, Madam.

Lady Gent. Yes, very well, my Dear, and desires his *Bais mains* to your Ladyship.

Mrs. Con. Does he say any thing of coming to Town?

Lady Gent. No, nothing yet.

Mrs. Con. No! Pray, Madam don't you think his good Worship begins to be a little fonder of Fox Hunting than you cou'd wish he were?

Lady Gent. I am always pleas'd while he's diverted; if you saw his Letters to me, you wou'd not think I had any reason to complain.

Mrs. Con. Nay, the World owns your Ladyship has the perfect Secret of making a good Husband.

Lady Gent. Believe me Child, the matter's not so difficult as People wou'd have it. If you but knew what Trifles, in the complyance of a Woman's Temper sooth a Man to Fondness, you'd admire to what childish Obstinacy so many Women owe their uneasiness.

Enter Miss crying.

Miss Not. Oh! Oh!

Lady Gent. How now! what's the Matter, my Dear?

Miss Not. Oh! Oh! Madam! Madam!

Mrs. Con. Bless me! what ails the Child?

Miss Not. I have been so abus'd! so affronted!

Lady Gent. Abus'd! by whom, my Dear?

Miss Not. That Monster of Men, my Lord *George Brilliant.*

Mrs. Con. My Lord *George.*

Miss Not. Oh! I can't speak for Passion!

Lady Gent. I'm amaz'd! what has he done, Child?

Miss Not. The most provoking, impudent thing that ever was offer'd to a young Creature sure: Oh! Oh!

Mrs. Con. [*Aside.*] This must be some strange thing indeed: For if I don't mistake, her young Ladyship thinks her self old enough for most sorts of Impudence, that a Man can offer to her.

Lady Gent. Has he offer'd any Love, or Rudeness to you?

Miss Not. O worse! worse! a thousand times.

Mrs. Con. Worse! what can that be Child?—unless it be, that he has not made love to her? [*Aside.*

Miss Not. O! Madam! 'tis not my self alone, but your Ladyship and Mrs. *Conquest* too, that are affronted.

Mrs. Con. Am I in? But it's no Novelty to me—I have so far the better of both of you, I am us'd to his Impudence, and know how to bear it.

Lady Gent. I am amaz'd! Pray let's hear, Child.

Miss Not. O! I cou'd tear his Flesh for having such a Thought of me.

Lady Gent. What Thought, my Dear?

Miss Not. O! Madam! cou'd any thing, but the greatest Villain upon Earth, think to make me a Procuress.

Lady Gent. Child! you startle me!

Miss Not. Or any Mortal, but from a most profligate Principle of the most provoking Vanity, nourish but the least living hope against your Ladyship's Vertue.

Lady Gent. How Child!

Miss Not. Or any Monster, but the most ungrateful, most audacious of Mankind propose too, that I shou'd discover his odious Inclinations to your Ladyship, before the very Face of one who innocently loves him: O! I am past Patience!—I think I do it bravely. [*Aside.*] [*Walks in disorder.*

Lady Gent. I am all Confusion!

Mrs. Con. [*Aside.*] If this Girl's Passion is not all an Air, and his own Contrivance, then will I be bound to endure the Success of it.

Lady Gent. His Inclination! and to me! and yet propos'd, that you shou'd discover it before Mrs. *Conquest* too: To Glory in such Insolence! This seems a Contradiction.

Miss Not. Or else said he, 'twould never be believ'd; for having the idle Reputation of liking one, I am oblig'd that both should know it, that she I really love may see I'm wholly free from any former Passion.

Mrs. Con. This Lye must be his own, by the Extremity of its Impudence. [*Aside.*

Lady Gent. But when he us'd my Name, Child, why were you not shock'd at first? why did not you leave him to tell his idle Story to the Wind?

Miss Not. O Madam! that was it betray'd me into hearing him: For when he first began he nam'd no Names; that he reserv'd till last, till he had told me all to clinch the Secret with.

Lady Gent. But, pray Child, how did he begin it? What was his manner of first attempting you?

Mrs. Con. Her Ladyship grows a little inquisitive, methinks. [*Aside.*

Miss Not. O! with all the subtle Softness that ever humble Love inspir'd:—Then of a sudden, rousing from his Fear, he gave himself such an animated Air of Confidence, threw back his Wig, and cry'd aloud: *But why should she asham'd, or angry be,*
To be belov'd by me?

Mrs. Con. What do you think of his Modesty now, Madam.

Lady Gent. I am amaz'd, indeed.

Miss Not. Then he turn'd to me, press'd me by the Hand, and, kneeling, begg'd my Friendship, and threw into my Lap such untold Heaps of Gold, forc'd upon my Finger too a sparking Diamond, I thought must beggar him to purchase—But when I heard him close his impudent Story with offering me a Letter to give your Ladyship while Mrs. *Conquest* was by.—I started up, and told him, Yes, my Lord, I'll do your Errand, but without your Letter, in another manner than your infamous Principles have propos'd it; my Lady shall know your Passion, but know it, as I do, to avoid, to loath, and scorn you for such a villainous Thought. While I was saying this, I threw his filthy Gold upon the Floor, his Letter into the Fire, his Diamond out of the Window, and left him to gather 'em up, as he pleas'd, without expecting an Answer.

Lady Gent. Sure! 'tis impossible a Man shou'd wear a Face, that cou'd so stedfastly belye his Heart.

Miss Not. So I was resolv'd to tell your Ladyship—Besides, I thought it proper Mrs. *Conquest* should know his Brutality to her too.

Mrs. Con. O! I am mightily oblig'd to you, my Dear, but I knew him before.

Miss Not. [*Aside.*] Hah! how affectedly indifferent the vain thing is?

Lady Gent. My Dear, I'm at a Loss how far to doubt, or to believe this Folly of him.—Pray advise me. [*To Mrs.* Conquest.

Mrs. Con. If your Ladyship wou'd take my Opinion, I'd be entirely easie, I'd neither doubt or believe any thing of the Matter, till I had it confirm'd from his own Behaviour.

Miss Not. [*Aside.*] I can't bear this,—She shalln't be so easie,—I'll tell her the whole Truth of his addressing to me, but I'll humble her.

Lady Gent. Now, you know, he was to be here with other Company at Cards to Night, but if you'll do me the Favour to sit with me, I'll keep my Chamber, say I'm indispos'd, and see no Company at all.—What think you?

Mrs. Con. I think it won't be worth that Trouble, Madam.

Enter a Servant.

Serv. Madam, the Company's come.

Lady Gent. Is my Lord *George* there?

Serv. Yes, Madam.

Lady Gent. What shall we do now?

Mrs. Con. By all means go and receive him among the rest, as you us'd to do, and take no notice of any thing,—I'll wait upon your Ladyship in two Minutes.

Lady Gent. If you don't I shall certainly betray my self, I'll come and fetch you. [*Exit Lady* Gentle.

Mrs. Con. As you please, Madam.—I have observ'd a thoughtful Smile upon this Girl's Face, that makes me fancy her Secret is but half out yet.—If I guess right, I'll e'en pique her little Pride till she tells me, for I know the Chit does not care for me. [*Aside.*

Miss Not. Oh! Mrs. *Vanity*'s a little upon the hum-drum at last, I see, I'll make her sob before I have done with her.—Mrs. *Conquest* you seem a little concern'd about this Matter; now, if I were you, I'd take no manner of notice of it, he shou'd not have the Pride to think 'twas in his Power to give me a Moment's Uneasiness.

Mrs. Con. My dear, you advise me very well, but, upon my Word, I am not uneasie.

Miss Not. Pooh! That's such a Jest! as if you did not love my Lord *George.*

Mrs. Con. Did he ever tell you I did?

Miss Not. Tell me!—No:—But—One sees that well enough.

Mrs. Con. Why then if I do love him, Child, you may depend upon't, it's only from the Assurances I have of his loving me only.

Miss Not. But since you see (as the World will too, in a little time) how false those Assurances are, had not you better seem to leave him, than lie under the Scandal of his leaving you.

Mrs. Con. No, Child; I'll still keep up my Pretensions, if it be only to hinder other vain Creatures from coming into Hopes of him: For I know, were I once to own my self disengag'd, then ev'ry impertinent Coquet in Town would be giving Airs to him.

Miss Not. Was ever any thing so stupidly vain? [*Aside.*] Lard! Madam, you have a mighty Opinion of your Perfections sure, to think it impossible a Man can be false to you: Some Women wou'd ha' been a top of the House, by this time, if they had only heard of their Lover's common Civility to another.—You are strangely happy sure, when his owning a Passion to your Friend, before your Face, can't make you uneasie, Heh! heh!

Mrs. Con. Methinks, Child, my want of jealousie from what you've said, gives you a little uneasiness—I shou'd be loath to think his idle way of Raillery had taught you to think of Love so soon.

Miss Not. So soon! I suppose, Madam, if I had the Forwardness of your Ladyship's Inclination, I might produce as good Proofs of his Passion for me, as you can of his Constancy to you.

Mrs. Con. So! she's stirr'd—I must have the rest on't. [*Aside.*] His Passion to thee, Love, that were impossible—Have a Passion for any thing so uncapable to conceive it—Why Love's a thing you won't be fit to think of these two Years.

Miss Not. Not think of it! I'd have you to know, Madam, there are Men in the World that think me as fit for a Lover as your Ladyship.

Mrs. Con. So! now it's coming. [*Aside.*

Miss Not. And however unfit you think me, Madam, I'd advise you next time any Man's idle Raillery flatters you into a Passion for him, don't let me know it; I say, don't let me know it, for fear my Unfitness should undeceive your Vanity, by taking him from you—Not think of it!—I shall live to see you burst with Envy, Madam—Do you observe me? Burst! burst!—Not think of it!

Mrs. Con. Nay, now I am convinc'd—This Passion, I dare swear, is real—He has certainly said some civil thing to thee, before he was aware.—But for what you said of him, just now, to my Lady *Gentle,* my pretty One—

Miss Not. Pretty One!—Pray Madam!—Tho' I'm sorry I can't say the same of your Ladyship.

Mrs. Con. I say, all your late sobbing, and pretending to throw Gold about the Room, and Diamonds out of the Window, and all that Stuff, my Honey, I am now confirm'd was all, from first to last, the pretty Fiction of thy own little Pride and Jealousie, only to have the Ease of giving me Pain from his suppos'd forsaking me.

Miss Not. Hah! ha! ha! I am glad to see your Vanity so swell'd, Madam, but since I find 'tis your Disease, I'll be your Friend for once, and work your Cure by bursting it: Know then you've guess'd a Truth that has undone you: The part I've acted of his pretended Passion to another, was, as you said indeed, a Fiction all, and only play'd to give my Pride the Diversion of his owning to your Face, how little he regards you. But know the fatal Face to which you owe your Ruine, was not my Lady *Gentle*'s (that was my own Invention) but Mine; not Her, nor You, but Me, and Me alone he loves—These poor unfit Features have seduc'd him from you—And now let all the World (that sees how barbarously your Vanity, or mine, has mistaken idle Raillery for Love) judge who's most fit to think of it. [*Exit.*

Mrs. Con. Now the Mystery's unfolded—O! this subtle Devil! how artfully has he fool'd this forward Girl to his Assistance—Well! there's something in the barefac'd excess of his Assurance that makes me Smile: I'm loath to say he's impudent, but he has an undaunted Modesty, that's certain, and for that very one Quality 'twill be worth my while not to trust him even with my Lady *Gentle*—O Sir—

Enter Sir Friendly Moral.

Sir Fr. So Child, how stand Affairs now? Any fresh Discovery?

Mrs. Con. Only a trifling confirmation or two, Sir, of what we suspected before—Therefore what we do must be done quickly—Have you consider'd what I propos'd, Sir?

Sir Fr. In troth 'tis a wild Thought, but you have a wild Spark to deal with, and for ought I know, his own Snares may be likeliest to hold him. Only take this general Caution with you, that the warmth of your Undertaking don't carry you into any Action, that the discretion of your Sex can't answer.

Mrs. Con. Fear not, Sir, I know my Man, and know my self.

Sir Fr. Then here's your Letter writ, and seal'd, as you directed.

Mrs. Con. And here comes my Lady, 'twill be now a fit occasion to make use of it.

Sir Fr. I'll leave you then.

Mrs. Con. When I have done with her, Sir, I wou'd consult you farther.

Sir Fr. I'll expect you in my Chamber. [*Exit Sir* Friendly.

Enter Lady Gentle.

Lady Gent. O Child I'm glad I have found you.

Mrs. Con. What's the Matter, Madam?

Lady Gent. I think I was never more provok'd in my Life.

Mrs. Con. Any thing from my Lord *George?*

Lady Gent. Yes—something that makes me shudder at the Thought.

Mrs. Con. Bless me!

Lady Gent. Something so grossly insolent in the over respectfulness of his Behaviour, such an affected Awe when he but speaks to me, something that shews within his Heart so vain, so arrogant a Hope; it more provokes me than all the awkward Follies of a bare-fac'd Impudence: And since I find he secretly presumes upon my knowing his odious Secret, 'twill be therefore but equal Justice to my self and you, to crush his idle Hopes at once: For not to check is to encourage 'em: And when once a Woman's known to be follow'd, let her Virtue be never so fam'd, or fortified, the good natur'd Town always conclude the Lover successful.

Mrs. Con. You did not seem to understand his Behaviour?

Lady Gent. I can't tell whether he understood me, or no; but I cou'd not help saying in a very grave manner, that whatever strait I put my self to, his 1000 *l.* shou'd certainly be paid him next Week.

Mrs. Con. And how did he take it?

Lady Gent. O! he is not to be put out of Countenance, that I see, for he press'd me with a world of easie Civility, not to give my self the least Concern; for if I pleas'd, he wou'd immediately give me a very fair chance to pay him without ever drawing a Line for it.

Mrs. Con. A fair chance! What was it?

Lady Gent. Why, he offer'd me indeed at Picquet such odds, as I am sure he is not able to give me; for Count *Tailly,* who stood by, thought it so considerable an Advantage, that he beg'd he might go my halfs, or what part of the Money I pleas'd.

Mrs. Con. Well said Count—This may come to something—She must play with him—for positively there's no other way of seeing a quick end of his Hopes, or my own.

Lady Gent. The extravagance of his offer I confess surpriz'd me, so I only told him I'd consider on't, and came to you for Advice.

Mrs. Con. Then certainly, Madam, take him at his word; and since you know his dishonest end, in offering such an Advantage, ev'n make use on't, and let his very baseness punish it self.

Lady Gent. As how?

Mrs. Con. Look you, the best way to disappoint his Hopes, is first to raise 'em—Go to him this Minute—call for Cards—and put on all the coquet Airs imaginable: Smile at his Respect, and glance him out of his affected Modesty. By this means you will certainly encourage his Vanity, not only to the Gallantry of letting you win your Money again, but more than probably of losing his own to you.

Lady Gent. I vow you tempt me strangely—I boggle at nothing, but those Airs you speak of, I shall do it so aukwardly—

Mrs. Con. Pooh! I warrant you, trust to Nature; it's nothing, one cannot set one's Hair in a Glass without 'em—If it were not a sure Card, you can't think I'd advise you to play it, for my own Sake.

Lady Gent. That, indeed, leaves me nothing to say.—Well, upon your Encouragement, I will venture, and the very Moment I get home the Sum I am out to him, I'll throw up my Cards, and fairly tell him, I know when its time to give over.

Mrs. Con. Admirable.

Lady Gent. Nay, and because I don't think I owe him the Regard of declaring it my self, I'll go down into *Sussex* to Morrow Morning, and leave you, if you think fit, to tell him the Occasion.

Mrs. Con. No, Madam, to let your Ladyship see I think every thing as entirely safe under your Discretion, as my own, I am resolv'd to go out of Town this Moment.

Lady Gent. What do you mean?

Mrs. Con. I have receiv'd a Letter here from my Brother Sir *John,* my Twin-Brother, Madam, whom I have not seen these nine Years; he arriv'd but last Night from *Italy,* to take Possession of his Estate, he's now at his House in *Essex,* and a little indispos'd after his Voyage, he has sent his Coach, and begs if possible, I would be with him to Night.

Lady Gent. To Night! Impossible! Go as early in the Morning, Child, as you please.

Mrs. Con. No, dear Madam, pardon me, the Moon shines, and I had rather defer my Sleep, than break it.

Lady Gent. Well, my Dear, since you won't be persuaded, I wish you a good Journey—I shall see you before you go.

Mrs. Con. I have just a Moment's Business with Sir *Friendly,* and then I'll wait upon your Ladyship. [*Exit Lady* Gentle.] Well, there she goes–How she will come off I can't tell. The good Woman I dare swear, is truly Innocent in her Intentions, but good looking after, I fancy, can do her no Injury: For Virtue, tho' she's of a Noble Spirit, and a Great Conqueror, 'tis true; yet, as she's Stout, alas! we know she's Merciful, and when sly Humility and Nature kneel hopeless to her unquestion'd Power, they look so pitiful, speak in such a gentle Tone, and sigh their Griefs with such Submission, that cruel Virtue loses all its Anger for Compassion–Compassion kindles Hope, Hope arms Assurance, and then–Tho' Virtue may have Courage enough to give a stout Knock with her Heel, for some body to come in–still, I say, if some body shou'd come in–'twou'd be ungrateful in any Woman alive not to allow, that good Attendance sometimes may do her Virtue considerable Service.–

[*Exit.*

The End of the Fourth Act.

ACT V. SCENE I.

The SCENE *continues.*

Enter Lord George, *and Miss* Notable.

Miss Not. So when I found that wou'd not take down her Vanity, I e'en told her the whole Truth of the Matter, that it was not my Lady *Gentle,* but her humble Servant was her Rival.

Lord Geo. Well said: What did Mrs. *Conquest* say upon that?

Miss Not. She did not say much, but the poor Soul's gone out of Town upon't.

Lord Geo. Out of Town at this time of Night! What d'ye mean?

Miss Not. Just as I say, Sir—Her Brother, it seems, is come from Travel, so the Fullness of her Stomach laid hold on that Occasion, and she pretends she's gone to meet him—Now what I expect from you is this; since I see nothing but Demonstration will heartily humble her Ladyship, you shall confess all I told her of your Addressing to me, under your own Hand, in a Billet to me, which I'll inclose in a stinging Letter from my self to her, and send it immediately.

Lord Geo. So, so, I am like to be drawn into a fine Business here: The Jest must not go so far neither: The Child has a strange Vivacity in her good Nature— [*Aside.*

Miss Not. You pause upon't—

Lord Geo. Well, Madam, to let you see I scorn to profess more than I'll stand to, do you draw up the Letter to your Mind, I'll copy it, and—and—and—and—put the Change upon you. [*Aside.*

Miss Not. Ay, now you say something, I'll about it immediately.

Lord Geo. Do so, I'll stay here till you have done it. [*Exit Miss* Notable.] Who says I am not a provident Lover? For now by that Time my Harvest of Lady *Gentle* is over, the early Inclination I have sown in this Girl will be just ripe and ready for the Sicle—A true Woman's Man should breed his Mistresses, as an old What-d'ye-call—'um does young Girls in a Play-House, one under another, that he may have always something fit for the Desire of several

Persons of Quality--But here comes my Lady *Gentle*--Assurance, stand fast, and don't let the insolent Awe of a fine Woman's Virtue look thee out of Countenance.

Enter Lady Gentle.

Lady Gent. Come, come, my Lord, where do you run? the Cards stay for you.

Lord Geo. I did not know your Ladyship had resolv'd to do me the Honour of accepting the Match I propos'd you.

Lady Gent. O your Servant grave Sir--you have a Mind to be off on't, I suppose--but as meer a Country-Gentlewoman as you think me, you'll find I am enough in the Mode not to refuse a good Offer, whether I deserve it or no.

Lord Geo. Coquet by all that's lovely. [*Aside.*]--I must confess, Madam, I shou'd be glad to see your Ladyship a little better reconcil'd to the Diversions in Fashion.

Lady Gent. And if I have any Skill in Faces, whatever solemn Airs you give your self, no body is more a private Friend to 'em than your Lordship.

Lord Geo. I can't disown a secret Tenderness for every Thing that ought to move the Heart, but Reputation shou'd be always sacred: And he that does not take some care of his own, can never hope to be much trusted with other People's: For were a Woman of Condition generously to make that Trust, what Consequence upon Earth cou'd be more terrible to her, than the Folly, or Baseness of her Lover's exposing the Secret.

Lady Gent. Very modish Morals, upon my Word, so that a prudent regard to her Reputation is all the Virtue you think a Woman has occasion for--Fie, fie, I'll swear my Lord, I took you for quite another Man.

Lord Geo. I never was deceiv'd in your Ladyship, for I always took you for a Woman of the first and quickest Understanding.

Lady Gent. Are not you a wicked Creature? How can you have the Assurance to think any Woman that knows you, will be commonly civil to you?

Lord Geo. I do think the most impudent thing a Man can offer a Woman, is to ask the least Favour of her before he has done something to deserve it, and so, if you please, Madam, we'll e'en sit down to Picquet, and make an end of our Argument afterwards.

Lady Gent. [*Aside.*] How blind is Vanity? that this Wretch can't see I fool him all this while?—Well, my Lord, for once I won't baulk your Gallantry. [*Enter Sir* Friendly.] Come, Sir *Friendly,* my Lord and I are going to Picquet, have you a mind to look on a little?

Sir Fr. Troth, Madam, I have often lookt on, and have as often wondred, to see two very good Friends sit fairly down, and in cool Blood, agree to wish one another heartily inconvenienc'd in their Fortune.

Lord Geo. O Fie! Nuncle, that's driving the Consequence too far.

Sir Fr. Not a Jot—And 'tis amazing, that so many good Families shou'd daily encourage a Diversion, whose utmost Pleasure is founded upon Avarice and ill Nature: For those are always the secret Principles of deep Play.

Re-enter Miss, and winks to Lord George.

Lord Geo. I'll wait upon your Ladyship in a moment. [*Exit.*

Lady Gent. I don't know, Play is a Diversion that always keeps the Spirits awake, methinks, whether one wins or loses.

Sir Fr. I have very little to say against a moderate use of it—but we grow serious—Pray, Madam, is my Lady *Wronglove* in the next Room.

Lady Gent. I left her there, she was enquiring for you—Here she is.

Enter Lady Wronglove.

Lady Gent. Well, Madam! What are they doing within?

Lady Wrong. There's like to be no Bank, I find, they are all broke into Ombre and Picquet.

Lady Gent. Your Ladyship is not for Play then?

Lady Wrong. Not yet, Madam; I have a word or two with Sir *Friendly,* and I'll endeavour to wait on your Ladyship.

Enter a Servant.

Serv. Madam, here's Sir *John Conquest* just come to Town, he enquires for your Ladyship, or Sir *Friendly Moral.*

Lady Gent. Sir *John!* What a Mistake has poor Mrs. *Conquest* made now? She went but an Hour ago to meet him?

Sir Fr. Will your Ladyship give me leave to wait on him?

Lady Gent. If you please to give yourself that trouble, Sir *Friendly*. Pray desire him to walk in. [*Exit Sir* Friendly.] Is my Lord *Wronglove* come, Madam?

Lady Wrong. He said he would be here; but you must not expect him the more for that.

Lady Gent. He does not much stand upon Forms, indeed; but he's extremely good humour'd, when one has him.

Lady Wrong. How can People taste good Humour, where there's no Principle?

Lady Gent. And what dull Company wou'd the strictest Principle be without good Humour?

Lady Wrong. And yet the best Temper's but a Cheat without 'em

Lady Gent. He must be a Man indeed that lives without a Fault; but there are some, that 'tis always a Woman's Interest to overlook in a Husband: Our Frowns may govern Lovers, but Husbands must be smil'd on.

Lady Wrong. I shou'd despise the Man that must be flatter'd to be just.

Lady Gent. Alas! The Price is very little, and let me tell you, Madam; the Man that's just is not to be despis'd.

Lady Wrong. He that lives in a profess'd Contempt of Obligation can never be belov'd—'tis better to release 'em: You'll shortly see me easie.

Lady Gent. I shall ever wish you so.

Enter Sir Friendly *with Mrs.* Conquest, *in Man's Habit.*

Sir Fr. This, Sir, is my Lady *Gentle.* [*They salute.*

Lady Gent. You are welcome into *England,* Sir.

Enter Lord George *who seeing Mrs.* Conquest, *whispers Sir* Friendly.

Mrs. Con. I hope your Ladyship will excuse my unseasonable Visit, but I rather chose to be troublesome than slow in the Acknowledgments I owe your Ladyship for your many Favours to my Sister.

Lady Gent. Mrs. *Conquest* and her Friends are always welcome to me—My Lady *Wronglove,* pray, know Sir *John!*

Sir Fr. My Lord *George,* and Sir *John,* Will you give me leave to recommend a Friendship between you.

Lord Geo. Sir, I shall be proud to embrace it.

Mrs. Con. 'Twill be a Charity in a Man of your Lordship's Figure to give a raw young Fellow a little Countenance at his first Arrival.

Lord Geo. Your Appearance, Sir, I am confident, will never want a Friendship among the Men of Taste, or the Ladies.

Sir Fr. This young Lady, Sir *John,* is a near Relation of mine; and if you have not left your heart abroad, will endanger it here as far as e're a Southern Beauty of 'em all.

Mrs. Con. If the Lady's Good-nature were equal to her Beauty, 'twould be dispos'd this minute.

Lord Geo. Faith, he's a pretty Fellow.

Miss Not. A sweet Creature! [*Aside.*

Lady Wrong. He's extremely like his Sister.

Lady Gent. The very Image of her.

Mrs. Con. We were both made at the same time, Ladies, I only wish she had been born to Breeches too: For I fansy that wild Humour of hers is dismally put to't under the Confinement of Petticoats. [*Lady* Wronglove *goes to Sir* Friendly.

Lady Gent. I find, Sir *John,* you are Twins in your good humour, as well as your Persons.

Mrs. Con. We always took a Liberty with one another, Madam, tho' I believe the Girl may be honest at the bottom.

Lord Geo. Methinks you lose time with the young Lady, Sir *John* [*Aside.*

Mrs. Con. To tell you the Truth, my Lord, I find my self a little too sharp set for a formal Gallantry, I have had a tedious Voyage, and wou'd be as glad of a small Recommendation to any humble extempore Favour.

Lord Geo. Faith I am a little out of—Gentlewomen, my self at present: But if your Occasions are not very pressing, I'll put you out of a despairing Condition—I'll carry you behind the Scenes, and there are Ladies of all sorts, Coquets, Prudes, and Virgins (they say) serious and Comical, Vocal,—and Instrumental.

Mrs. Con. We shall find a time, my Lord.

Miss Not. I must have a Friendship with him, that's Poss. Let me see—ay, that will do it.—What a dear Pleasure 'tis, be in what Company one will, to have all the young Fellows particular. [*Aside.*

Mrs. Con. [*To Lady* Gentle.] I am afraid, Madam, we interrupt the Diversion of the good Company, I heard Cards call'd for as we came in.

Lady Gent. If you please then, Sir *John,* we'll step into the next Room—my Lady *Wronglove,* we'll expect you.

[*Exeunt all but Lady* Wronglove *and Sir* Friendly.

Lady Wrong. I'll wait upon your Ladyship.

Sir Fr. I am sorry, Madam, to find the Misunderstanding carried to such Extremities.

Lady Wrong. After such Usage 'tis impossible to live with him.

Sir Fr. And have you in your calmer Thoughts e'er weigh'd the miserable Consequence of parting?

Lady Wrong. 'Twill shew the World, at least, I am not like the World; but scorn on any Terms t'endure the Man that wrongs me. Since too he still persists in his Defiance of my Resentment, what Remedy on Earth have I but parting?

Sir Fr. Is there no Cure for Wounds but bleeding dead?—You'll say he has wrong'd you—Grant it—that Wrong has been severely punish'd in your severe Resentment.

Lady Wrong. But still it has not cur'd the Wrong.

Sir Fr. Then, certainly, 'twas wrong to use it.

Lady Wrong. I've been reduc'd to use it: Nor cou'd I bear the loose, malicious Fleerings of the World without a just Resentment upon him.

Sir Fr. Nor wou'd I have you bear it—no;—but disappoint their empty fashionable Malice, close up this unprofitable Breach, 'tis still within your Power, and fix him yet more firmly yours.

Lady Wrong. Alas, 'tis now too late! We have agreed on other Terms: He too, at last, is willing we shou'd part.

Sir Fr. Bury that Thought: Come, come, there's yet a gentler Cure, cou'd you suppress your Temper to go through it: This rash and fruitless struggling with a broken Limb gives you but more outragious Pain, inflames the Wound, and brings your very Life of Peace in Danger: Think what a glorious Conquest it wou'd be, ev'n in the Face of the censorious and insulting World, to tame this

Wanderer, whose frail Inconstancy has sought a vain and false Relief abroad: To lure him home with soft Affection, to lull him into Blushes, Peace, and envied Happiness. One Word, one tender Look secures your Triumph: Is there no Virtue, think you, in Remission? Nothing persuasive in the Reproach of patient Love?

Lady Wrong. I see to what your Friendship wou'd persuade me, but were it possible my flatter'd Hopes cou'd lose the Memory of my Wrongs for ever—Say I cou'd this Moment hush my Woman's Pride to all the Tenderness of soft Affection, cou'd sigh, cou'd weep, and earn for Reconcilement! Where cou'd a Wretch, unheeded in her Wrongs like me, find shelter? Where is the Friendly Bosome wou'd receive me? How can I hope for Comfort from that Breast, that now I fear is hardned to my undoing?

Sir Fr. Cherish that softning Thought, and all may yet be well: O! there's a meritable Goodness in those Fears that cannot fail to Conquer. Do not suppose, I can be partial to his Errors, and not a Friend to your Complaints. Resentment can but at best revenge, but never redress 'em. Repose 'em with a Friend for once, and be assur'd, as of my Honesty, I'll make you no dishonourable Peace.

Lady Wrong. I don't doubt of your sincere Endeavours. But who can answer for another's Morals? Think how much more miserable you make me, shou'd he insult upon my Patience.

Sir Fr. By that Sincerity you trust in, I know him of a softer Nature, friendly, generous, and tender; only to Opposition, obstinately cool; to Gentleness, submissive as a Lover.

Lady Wrong. Do what you will with me. [*Sits down weeping.*

Sir Fr. He comes! be comforted! Depend upon my Friendship.

Enter Lord Wronglove.

My Lord, I grieve to see you here on this occasion.

Lord Wrong. I'm not my self transported at it, Sir *Friendly*—I come—t'obey my Summons.

Sir Fr. How easily we pay Obedience to our Wishes! Was it well done, my Lord, to work the Weakness of a Woman to ask for what you knew was her undoing? A Mind, which your Unkindness had distemper'd, deserv'd a tenderer care, than reaching it a Corrosive for a Cordial. Your Judgment cou'd not but foresee the Resolution of a Love-sick Wife must stagger in the Shock of Separation.

Lord Wrong. Ha! [*Lady* Wronglove *weeping.*

Sir Fr. Look there; and while those softning Tears reproach you, think on the long watched, restless Hours, she already has endur'd from your Misdoing: Nor cou'd you blame her, if in the torturing Pain she thought her only Help was cutting off th'infected Limb: But you! You to hold the horrid Knife prepar'd, while your hard Heart was conscious of a gentler Cure, was Cruelty beyond a humane Nature.

Lord Wrong. Mistake me not: I need not these Reproaches, to be just. I never sought this Separation, never wish'd it; and when it can be prov'd unkind in me to accept it, my Ruine shou'd as soon be welcome. And tho' perhaps my negligence of Temper may have stood the Frowns of Love unmov'd, yet I can find no Guard within, that can support me 'gainst its Tears. [*Goes to Lady* Wronglove.

Sir Fr. Now, my Lord, you are indeed a Man.

Lord Wrong. Welcome or not, I must not see you thus, Madam, without an offer'd Hand to raise you. What is't disturbs you?

Lady Wrong. Nothing.

Lord Wrong. If I can never more deserve the soft Reception of a Lover, give me at least the honest Freedom of a Friend's Concern, to wish you well; to search your inmost Griefs, and share 'em.

Lady Wrong. I cannot speak to you.

Sir Fr. My Lord, that tender Silence tells you all.

Lord Wrong. Too much indeed for Sense of Shame to bear.—Now, I shou'd blush ever to have deserv'd these just reproachful Tears; but when I think they spring from the dissolving Rock of secret Love, I triumph in the thought; and in this wild irruption of its Joy, my parching Heart cou'd drink the Cordial Dew.

Lady Wrong. What means this soft Effusion in my Breast! an aching Tenderness ne'er felt before?

Lord Wrong. I cannot bear that melting Eloquence of Eyes.—Yet nearer, closer to my Heart, and live for ever there.—Thus blending our dissolving Souls in dumb inutterable Softness.

Sir Fr. Age has not yet so drain'd me, but when I see a Tenderness in Virtue's Eye, my Heart will soften, and its Springs will flow.

Lady Wrong. Pity this new Confusion of my Woman's Heart, that wou'd (but knows not how to) make returns for this Endearment; that fears, yet wishes, that burns and blushes, with my Sex's

Shame in yielding.—Can you forgive, my Lord, the late uncurb'd Expressions of a disorder'd Mind?—but think they were my Passion's fault, and pardon 'em.

Lord Wrong. O never! never let us think we ever disagreed! since our sick Love is heal'd, for ever be its cause forgotten, and remov'd.

Lady Wrong. But let the kind Physician that restor'd us, be for ever in our Thanks remember'd. Had not his tender Care observ'd the Crisis of my distemper'd Mind, how rashly had I languish'd out a wretched Being?

Lord Wrong. This was indeed beyond a Friend,—a Father's Care.

Sir Fr. My Lord, what I have done, your mutual Peace has overpaid: I knew you both had Virtues, and was too far concern'd indeed to see 'em lost in Passion.

Lord Wrong. If Heaven wou'd mark our Bounds of Happiness below, or Humane Wisdom were allow'd to chuse from Virtue's largest Store; in Joys, like ours, the needless Search wou'd end.

Sir Fr. In such soft Wives.

Lady Wrong. —So kind a Husband.

Lord Wrong. —Such a Friend.

Enter Mrs. Conquest, *and Miss* Notable.

Mrs. Con. I'm all Amazement, all Rapture, Madam! Is't possible so fair, and young a Creature, can have so just, so exquisite a sense of Love?

Miss Not. Why not? If I have any Sense, 'tis natural to have our first Views of Happiness from Love.

Mrs. Con. My little Soul you charm me! You have a mind to Pique Lord *George,* you say.

Miss Not. To a Rapidity!—Yet, methinks, not so much upon my own Account, as Yours: for his dishonourable Usage, as I told you, of your Sister. And to convince you of my Friendship,—there's his own Hand to accuse him of it:—Read it.—Hold! hold!—here's my Unkle,—put it up.

Mrs. Con. Can't I steal into your Room by and by?

Miss Not. With all my Heart.—Then I'll tell you more.

[*Exit Miss* Notable.

Enter Sir Friendly.

Sir Fr. So, Child! you are making way, I see! What have you got in your Hand there?

Mrs. Con. Why young Madam tells me, 'tis something under my Lord *George*'s Hand, that will convince me of his abusing my Sister —me.

Sir Fr. Pray read it.

Mrs. Con. [Reads.] To Mrs. *Conquest.*

If you design to make any stay in the Country, 'twill be obliging to return the Lampoon you stole from me, it being the only Copy from the Face of this Globe to the Sky, that is to be had for Malice, or Money. I am, dear Madam, with all due Extremity, most invincibly yours, BRILLIANT.

A very tender Epistle truly.

Sir Fr. 'Tis like all the rest of him.

Mrs. Con. I'm glad to find, however, he has good Humour enough not to let the little Malice of that Chit fool him, to affront me; which I find she has been heartily driving at.

Sir Fr. In troth, it shews some sense of Honour in him.

Mrs. Con. Depend upon it, Sir, he does not want it upon an honourable occasion.

Sir Fr. And 'twou'd be hard indeed, not to make some allowances for Youth.

Mrs. Con. But if I am not ev'n with her young Ladyship—

Sir Fr. I'm glad you have so innocent a Revenge in your Hands; persue your Addresses to her: To make her Coquettry a little ridiculous will do her no harm. Well! how go Affairs within? How is my Lady *Gentle* like to come off with his Lordship at play?

Mrs. Con. Just as I expected: I left her in the last Game of losing about double the Sum she owes him. That Fellow, the Count, is certainly his Confederate; his going her halfs, is only a pretence to look on, and so, by private Signs, to tell my Lord every Card in her Hand.

Sir Fr. Not unlikely: What's to be done next?

Mrs. Con. Only, Sir, do you engage the Company still in the next Room, while I take my Post. Hark! they have done Play.— I heard the Table move: Away.

Sir Fr. Success to you— [*Exeunt severally.*

SCENE II.

The SCENE *opening discovers Lord* George *and Lady* Gentle *rising from Play.*

Lord Geo. Have we done, Madam?

Lady Gent. I have, my Lord, and I think for ever;–'please to tell that. Intolerable Fortune. [*Throws down Money.*

Lord Geo. The Count gone!

Lady Gent. O yes, my Lord; he had not Patience, you see.–He run away when the Game was scarce up.

Lord Geo. This Bill is his then.

Lady Gent. It was; but it's yours now, I suppose.

Lord Geo. Here's Forty Pound, Madam.

Lady Gent. There's a Hundred, and Sixty. [*Gives a Bill.*] What do I owe you now, my Lord?

Lord Geo. Forty!–a Hundred, and Sixty!–um–just 1000 *l.* Madam.

Lady Gent. Very well!–and 1000 *l.* more borrow'd this Morning! and all fool'd away!–fool'd!–fool'd away! [*Fretting.*

Lord Geo. Oh! does it bite. [*Aside.*

Lady Gent. O Wretch! Wretch! miserable forsaken Wretch!–Ay! do! think! think! and sigh upon the Consequence of what thou'st done! the Ruin! Ruin! the sure Ruin that's before thee!

Lord Geo. Suppose, Madam, you try your Fortune at some other Game.

Lady Gent. Talk not of Play,–for I have done with it for ever.

Lord Geo. I can't see you, under this Confusion, at your ill Fortune, Madam, without offering all, within my power, to make you easie.

Lady Gent. My Lord, I can't be easie under an Obligation, which I have no prospect of returning.

Lord Geo. Come, come, you're not so poor, as your hard Fears wou'd make you. There are a thousand trifles in your power to grant, that you wou'd never miss, yet a Heart less sensible of your Concern than mine, wou'd prize beyond a tenfold value of your Losses.

Lady Gent. I'm poor in every thing but Folly, and a just Will to answer for its Miscarriages. On this, my Lord, you may depend: I'll strain my utmost to be just to you.

Lord Geo. Alas! you do not know the plenty Nature has endow'd you with. There's not a tender Sigh that heaves that lovely Bosom, but might, if giv'n in soft Compassion to a Lover's Pain, release you of the *Indies,* had you lost 'em. Can you suppose, that sordid Avarice alone, has push'd my Fortune to this Height? Was the poor lucre of a little Pelf worth all this wild Extravagance of Hazard I have run?—Give it at least a View more generous, tho' less successful; and think, that all I've done was in your greatest need to prove my self your firmest Friend.

Lady Gent. My Lord, 'twou'd now be Affectation not to understand you. But I'm concern'd, that you shou'd think, that Fortune ever cou'd reduce me to stand the hearing of a dishonourable Thought from any Man; or, if I cou'd be won to Folly, at least I wou'd make a Gift, and not a Bargain of my Heart: Therefore, if the worst must be, I'll own the Sum, and Sir *William* shall pay it on demand.

Lord Geo. [*Aside.*] Shall he? I know what will become of your Ladyship—You may Flounce, and run away with my Line if you please, but you will find at the end of it a lovely bearded Hook, that will strangely persuade you to come back again—A Debt of two thousand Pounds is not so easily slipt out of.

Lady Gent. Now, my Lord, if after all I've said, you have Honour enough to do a handsome thing, and not let him know of it.

Lord Geo. O do you feel it, Madam? [*Aside.*

Lady Gent. 'Tis but being a better House-wife in Pins; and if an hundred Pound, a Quarter of that will satisfie you till the whole's paid, you may depend upon't: A little more Prudence, and a Winter or two in the Country will soon recover it.

Lord Geo. Press me not with so unkind a Thought. To drive you from the Town, e're you have scarce run through half the Diversions of it, wou'd be barbarous indeed?

Lady Gent. Wou'd I had never seen it.

Lord Geo. Since I see, Madam, how much you dread an Obligation to me, say I cou'd find the Means to free you of this Debt, without my obliging you, nay, without a possibility of your losing more: I wou'd ev'n unthank'd relieve you.

Lady Gent. That's a Proposal I can't comprehend, my Lord.

Lord Geo. I'll make it more engaging yet: For give but a Promise you'll weigh the Offer in one Moment's Thought before you answer to it; and in return, by all my Hearts last bleeding Hopes, I swear, that ev'n your refusal then shall silence my offensive Love, and seal its Lips for ever.

Lady Gent. I think, my Lord, on that Condition, I may safely hear you.

Lord Geo. Thus then I offer–I'll tailly to you on one single Card, which if your Fortune wins, the Sums you owe me then shall all be quit, and my offensive hopes of Love be Dumb for ever: If I win, those Sums shall still be paid you back with this Reserve, That I have then your silent leave to Hope.

Lady Gent. My Lord–

Lord Geo. I beg you do not answer yet–Consider first, This Offer shuts out my very humblest Hope from Merit, is certain to recover all you've lost, with equal Chance, to rid you of (I fear) a hateful Lover, and but at worst, makes it your avoidless Fortune to endure him.

Lady Gent. A bold and artful Bait indeed. [*Aside.*

Lord Geo. Iv'e done, and leave you to the moment's Pause you promis'd.

Lady Gent. [*Aside.*] A certainty to quit the Sums I owe! A Chance with it, to rid me of his assaulting Love! A blest deliverance indeed! But then the Lot is equal too, of being oblig'd to give him Hope, my secret, conscious, leave to love–That thought imbitters all again; 'tis horrid loathsome, and my Disease less formidable than such a Cure–Why do I hold it in a moment's thought? Be bold and tell him so; for while I Pause he hopes in spite of me–Hold–

Lord Geo. Ay! think a little better on't. [*Aside.*

Lady Gent. [*Aside.*] To do it rashly, may incense him to my Ruine: He has it in his Power. He may demand my losings of my Husband's Honour; who tho' 'twill make his Fortune bleed to do't, I'm sure will pay 'em. Two thousand Pounds, with what Iv'e lately lost, might shock the Measures of a larger Income. What Face must I appear with then? whose shameful Conduct is the Cause on't–The consequence of that must, like an inward Canker, feed upon our future Quiet! His former friendly Confidence must wear a face of Strangeness to me: His ease of Thought, his chearful Smiles, with all the Thousand hoarded Pleasures of his indulgent Love, are lost: Then lost for ever! Insupportable Dilemma! What will become of me!

Lord Geo. [*Aside.*] Ah! poor Lady! it's a hard Tug indeed; but by the Grace of Necessity, Virtue may get over it.

Lady Gent. [*Aside.*] If some Women had this offer now, they'd make a Trifle of the Hazard! Nay, even of their losing it.

Lord Geo. [*Aside.*] Well said! take Courage!—There's nothing in't—it's a good round Sum—half ready Money too—think of that. Suppose I shou'd touch the Cards a little.

Lady Gent. [*Aside.*] Hope! he hopes already from his Offer: But then he offers me the means to kill it too! Say he shou'd win, he takes that Hope but from his Fortune, not my Virtue! Beside—am I so sure to lose? Is't in his Fate, that he must ever win? Why shall'nt I rather think, that Providence has brought me to this Stress, only to set my Follies dreadful in my view, and reaches now, at last, its Hand to save and warn me on the Precipice?—It must—it is—my flattering Hope will have it so—Impossible so critical a Chance can lose—My Fancy strengthens on the Thought, my Heart grows bold, and bids me venture.

Lord Geo. Shall I deal, Madam?—or—

Lady Gent. Quick, quickly then, and take me while my Courage can support it. [*He shuffles the Cards.*] Forgive me Virtue, if I this once depend on Fortune to relieve thee.

Lord Geo. Then Fortune for the Bold—I've dealt—'Tis fix'd for one of us.

Lady Gent. There [*She sets upon the King.*

Lord Geo. The King—'tis mine.

[*Lord* George *Taillys, and Lady* Gentle *loses.*

Lady Gent. Distraction!—Madness—Madness only can relieve me now.

Lord Geo. Soh! my venture is arriv'd at last—Now to unlade it. These Bills, Madam, now are yours again. [*Lays 'em down.*] But wh this hard, unkind Concern? Be just at least, and don't, in these reluctant Tears, drown all the humble Hopes that Fortune has bequeath'd me: Or if they press too rude and sudden for their Welcome, chide 'em but gently, they're soft as Infant wishes, one tende word will hush them into Whispers.

Lady Gent. Thus then with low Submission, on my Knees, I beg for Pity of my Fortune! O save me! save me from your cruel Power: Pity the hard distresses of a trembling Wretch, whom Folly has betray'd to Ruin. O! think not I can ever stain my Virtue, and preserve my Senses! For while I think, my shrinking Heart will shudder at the Horror: This trembling Hand will wither in your Touch, or end me in distraction. If you've a humane Soul, O yet be greatly good, and save me from eternal Ruine.

Lord Geo. These bugbear Terrors (Pray be rais'd—

Lady Gent. O never!)

Lord Geo. Which inexperience forms, wou'd vanish in a moments just or generous Thought: And since the right of Fortune has decreed me Hope, your Word, your Faith, your Honour stands engag'd to pay it—

Enter a Stranger bluntly with a Letter.

Strang. Lady?

Lady Gent. Ah!

Lord Geo. How now! what's the meaning of this?

Strang. I have sworn to deliver this into your own Hands, tho' I shou'd find you at your Prayers.

Lady Gent. Who are you, Sir?

Strang. No body.

Lady Gent. Whence come you?

Strang. From no body—Good b'y. [*Exit.*

Lord Geo. Fire and Furies! what a ridiculous Interruption is this?

Lady Gent. I'm amaz'd.

Lord Geo. What can it mean?

Lady Gent. Ha! what's here! Bank Bills of two thousand Pounds! The very Sums I have lost!—No advice! Not a Line with 'em! No matter whence they came! From no Enemy I'm sure; better owe 'em any where, than here.

Lord Geo. I fansy, Madam, the next Room were—were—

Lady Gent. No, my Lord—our Accounts now need no Privacy—there's your two thousand Pound.

Lord Geo. What mean you, Madam.

Lady Gent. To be as you wou'd have me, Just, and pay my Debts of Honour: For those that you demand against my Honour, by the known Laws of Play, are void: Where Honour cannot win, Honour can never lose. And now, my Lord, 'tis time to leave my Folly, and its Danger—Fare you well.

Lord Geo. Hold, Madam, our short Account is not made ev'n yet: Your Tears indeed might fool me into Pity, but this unfair Defiance never can: Since you wou'd poorly falsifie your Word, you've nothing but your Sex to guard you now, and all the Favour that you can Hope is, that I'll give your Virtue ev'n its last Excuse, and force you to be just.

Lady Gent. Ah!

Enter Mrs. Conquest *with her Sword drawn.*

Mrs. Con. Hold, Sir! unhand the Lady.

Lord Geo. Death again! [*Draws.*

Mrs. Con. My Lord, this is no place to use our Swords in; this Lady's Presence may Sheath 'em here without dishonour. Your Pardon, Madam, for this rude intrusion, which your Protection, and my own injur'd Honour have compell'd me to.

Lord Geo. Let me advise you, Sir, to have more regard to this Lady's Honour, than to suppose my being innocently here at Cards, was upon the least ill thought against it.

Mrs. Con. My Lord, that's answer'd, in owning I have overheard every word you have said this half Hour.

Lord Geo. The Devil! He loves her sure! You are to be found, Sir—

Mrs. Con. O! my Lord, I shall not part with you; but I have first a Message to you from my Sister, which you must answer instantly: Not but I know her Pride contemns the baseness you have us'd her with; for which she'd think perhaps, your disappointment here an over-pay'd Revenge: But there's a jealous Honour in our Family, whose injuries are above the feeble Spirit of a Girl to punish, that lies on me to vindicate, and calls for warmer Reparation—Follow me.

Lady Gent. Good, Sir!—my Lord, I beg for pity's sake, compose this Breach some milder way—If Blood shou'd follow on your going hence, what must the World report of me? my Fame's undone for ever—Let me intreat you, Sir, be pacify'd, my Lord will think of honourable Means to right your Sister—My Lord, for Mercy's sake—

Lord Geo. Your Pardon, Madam, Honour must be free before it can repair: Compulsion stains it into Cowardice—Away, Sir—I follow you. [*Exeunt Lord* George *and Mrs.* Conquest.

Lady Gent. O miserable Wretch! to what a sure distruction has thy Folly brought thee!

Enter Sir Friendly Moral.

Sir Fr. Dear, Madam, what's the matter, I heard high words within, no harm I hope?

Lady Gent. Murther, I fear, if not prevented; my Lord *George,* and Sir *John Conquest* have quarrell'd, and are gone out this Moment in their Heat to end it.

Sir Fr. How?

Lady Gent. I beg you, Sir, go after 'em, shou'd there be Mischief, the World will certainly report from false Appearances, that I'm the Cause.

Sir Fr. Don't think so, Madam, I'll use my best endeavour to prevent it! in the mean time take heed your Disorder don't Alarm the Company within—Which way went they?

Lady Gent. That Door, Sir. [*Exit Sir* Friendly.] Who's there. [*Enter a Servant.*] Run quick, and see if the Garden Door into the Park be lock'd—[*Exit Servant.*] How strict a Guard should Virtue keep upon its Innocence? How dangerous, how faithless are its lawful Pleasures, when habitual! This Vice of Play, that has, I fear undone me, appear'd at first an harmless, safe, Amusement; but stealing into Habit, its greatest Hazards grew so familiar, that ev'n the Face of Ruine lost its Terror to me. O! Reflection how I shudder at thee! the shameful Memory, of what I have done this Night will live with me for ever.

Re-enter Servant.

Serv. Madam, the Garden Door was wide open.

Lady Gent. Did you hear no Noise, or Bustle in the Park.

Serv. No Madam. [*Exit Servant.*

Lady Gent. They're certainly gone out that way, and Sir *Friendly* must miss of 'em—O Wretch! Wretch! that stoodst the foremost in the Rank of Prudent, Happy Wives, art now become the branded Mark of Infamy and Shame. [*Exit.*

SCENE III.

SCENE *changes to the Park.*

Enter Lord George.

Lord Geo. So, I think we've lost the Fellows that observ'd us, and if my Gentleman's Stomach holds, now I'm at leisure to entertain him. Death! was ever glorious Hope so inveterably disappointed! To bring her to her last Stake, to have her fast upon my Hook, nay in my Hand, and after all, to have her whip through my Fingers like an Eel, was the very Impudence of Fortune—What not come yet? He has not thought better on't, I hope—It's a lovely clear Moon—I wish it does not shine through some body presently.

Enter Four Fellows at a distance.

1. *Fel.* Stand close, softly and we have him—By your leave, Sir. [*They seize him.*

Lord Geo. So! Here's like to be no sport to Night then—I'm taken care of, I see—Nay, pray Gentlemen, you need not be so boisterous—I am sensible we are prevented.

2. *Fel.* Damn your Sense, Sir. [*Trips up his Heels.*

1. *Fel.* Blood, Sir, make the least Noise, I'll stick you to the Ground.

Lord Geo. I beg your Pardon, Gentlemen, I find I am mistaken, I thought you had only come to preserve my Person, but I find 'tis my Purse you have a Passion for—You're in the wrong Pocket, upon my Faith Sir.

1. *Fel.* Pull off his Breeches, make sure work, over his Heels with 'em that's the shortest way.

Lord Geo. With submission, Sir, there's a shorter—and if you pull off my Skin, you won't find another Sixpence in the inside on't.

2. *Fel.* What's this?

Lord Geo. Only a Table-Book, you don't deal in Paper, I presume?

1. *Fel.* Rot your Paper, Sir, we'll trust no Man, Money down's our Business.

Enter Mrs. Conquest.

Mrs. Con. How now, Gentlemen, what are you doing here?

Lord Geo. Only borrowing a little Money, Sir, the Gentlemen will be gone presently.

1. *Fel.* Hark you, you Bastardly Beau, get about your Business—or—lay hold on him *Jack*—

Mrs. Con. Me! Raskal—look you Dogs—release that Gentleman quick—give him his Sword again this Minute—or—[*Presents a Pistol.*

Lord Geo. And my Money, I beseech you, Sir.

1. *Fel.* Blood! Stand him *Jack.* Five to One he don't kill. The Dog has a good Coat on, and may have Money in his Pocket.

2. *Fel.* Drop your Pistol, Sir, or spill my Blood, I'll stick you.

Mrs. Con. Do you brave me Villains—Have at you.

[*She Presents, and misses Fire.*

1. *Fel.* O ho! Mr. Bully, have we met with you—come on Sir—there, Sir, that will do, I believe. [*Two of 'em secure Lord* George.

3. *Fel.* What is he down? Strip him. [*They push, she falls.*

2. *Fel.* No, rot him he's not worth it—Let's brush off. [*Exeunt.*

Lord Geo. Barbarous Dogs! How is it Sir?

Mrs. Con. I'm kill'd—I fear the Wound's quite through me.

Lord Geo. Mercy forbid! Where is't?

Mrs. Con. O! don't touch me—I beg you call for help, or any one to witness that my last Words confess you guiltless of this Accident.

Lord Geo. This generous Reproach has more than vanquish'd me—I think I see a Chair in the *Mall*—Chair, Chair,—they come—Believe me, Sir, I have so just a Sense of your Misfortune, and your Honour, that my full Heart now bleeds with shame to think how grossly I have wrong'd you in your Sister's Goodness: But if you live, the future study of my Life shall be with utmost Reparation to deserve your Friendship.

Mrs. Con. I shall never think that dearly bought, my Lord.

Enter Chairmen.

Chair. Here: Who calls Chair?

Lord Geo. Here, Friend, help up this Gentleman, he's wounded by some Foot-Pads, that just now set upon us—Softly—Carry him to Sir *William Gentle*'s, in—in—

Chair. I know it very well, Sir.

[*Exit Chairmen with Mrs.* Conquest.

Lord Geo. Make haste, while I run for a Surgeon. Death! how this Misfortune shocks and alters me.

SCENE IV.

The SCENE *changes to Lady* Gentle's.

Enter Miss Notable, [*Alone.*]

Miss Not. So, my Plot takes, I find: the Family's in a terrible Confusion: Sir *John* has certainly call'd him to an Account for the Letter I gave him—If the Town does not allow me the Reputation of this Quarrel—I have very hard Fortune—Lord! What a mortified Creature will poor Mrs. *Conquest* be, when she hears in the lonesome Country, that her own Brother has fought with her only Lover, for his Offers of Love to me? Dear Soul! What must it think, when such a raw unfit thing as I, gives such a great Creature as she so unexpected a Confusion? She can't take it ill sure, if one shou'd smile when one sees her next.

Enter to her Mrs. Hartshorn *crying.*

Mrs. Harts. O Dear Madam! Sad News.

Miss Not. What's the matter?

Mrs. Harts. My Lord *George* has kill'd Sir *John Conquest.*

Miss Not. O Heav'ns! Upon my Account! Art sure he's kill'd? Didst see him dead?

Mrs. Harts. No Madam, he's alive yet: They've just brought him in a Hackney-Chair; but they say the Wound's quite through his Body: O! 'tis a ghastly Sight—

Miss Not. Malicious Fortune! Had it been t'others Fate, I cou'd have born it. To take from me the only Life I ever really lov'd, is insupportable.

Mrs. Harts. Won't your Ladyship go in and see him, Madam?

Miss Not. Prithee leave me to my Griefs alone.

Mrs. Harts. Ah! poor Gentleman— [*Exit.*

Miss Not. Pretty Creature! I must see him—but it shall be in an

Undress—it will be proper at least, to give my Concern the Advantage of as much Disorder as I can. [*Exit.*

SCENE V.

The SCENE *drawing, discovers Mrs.* Conquest *in an arm'd Chair, with Lady* Gentle, *Lady* Wronglove, *Lord* Wronglove, *and Servants about her.*

Mrs. Con. No Surgeon yet?

Lord Wrong. Here's my Lord *George,* and I believe the Surgeon with him.

Enter Lord George, *Sir* Friendly, *and Surgeon.*

Lord Geo. Come, Sir, pray be quick, there's your Patient. How is it, Sir?

Mrs. Con. Oh!

Sir Fr. 'Twas not in my Fortune, Madam, to prevent this Accident. [*To Lady* Gentle.

Sur. By your leave Sir—Your Coat must come off, Sir.

Mrs. Con. Hold—Hark you Sir. [*Whispers the Surgeon.*

Sur. I am surpriz'd indeed—A Woman, but don't be uneasie, Madam, I shall have all due regard to your Sex.

Omnes. A Woman!

Lord Geo. Ha!

Mrs. Con. To raise your Wonder, Ladies, equal to your Pity, know then, I am not what I seem, the injur'd Brother of Mrs. *Conquest;* but she, her self, the feeble Champion of my own Despair.

Lord Geo. Distraction!

Lady Gent. O my fatal Folly! What Ruin art thou now the Cause of?

Lady Wrong. Poor unhappy Creature!

Lord Wrong. What have you done, my Lord?

Lord Geo. O blind besotted Sense! Not by a thousand pointing Circumstances to fore-know this Secret, and prevent its Consequence. How shall I look on her?

Sur. No hopes, indeed, Sir.

Sir Fr. Take heed.—Art sure, 'tis mortal?

Sur. Sir, 'tis impossible she can live three hours:—The best way will be to convey the Lady to Bed, and let her take a large Dose of Opium: All the help I can give her, is the hopes of going off in her Sleep.

Lady Gent. [*Weeping.*] O piteous Creature!

Lord Wrong. A Heart so generous indeed, deserv'd a kinder Fate.

Lord Geo. [*Throwing himself at Mrs.* Conquest*'s Feet.*] O pardon injur'd Goodness! Pardon the ungrateful Follies of a thoughtless Wretch, that burns to be forgiven: Cou'd I have e'er suppos'd your generous Soul had set at half this fatal Price my tendrest Vows, how gladly lavish had I paid 'em to deserve such Virtue?

Mrs. Con. My Death, my Lord, is not half so terrible, as the wide Wound this rash Attempt must give my bleeding Reputation.

Lord Geo. —To cure that Virgin Fear, this Moment, I conjure you, then, before your latest Breath forsakes you, let the pronouncing Priest, in sacred Union of our hands, unite our Honour too, and in this full Reduction of my vanquish'd Heart silence all envious Questions on your Fame for ever.

Mrs. Con. 'Twou'd be, I own, an Ease in Death, to give me the Excuse of dying honourably yours.

Lord Geo. My Lord, your Chaplain's near, I beg he may be sent for.

Lord Wrong. This Minute—

Lady Wrong. An honourable, tho' unfortunate Amends.

Mrs. Con. We have seen happier Hours, my Lord; but little thought our many cheerful Evenings wou'd have so dark a Night to end 'em.

Lady Gent. Mournful indeed!

Lord Geo. How gladly wou'd I pay down future Life to purchase back one past, one fatal Hour!

Mrs. Con. Is't possible!

Lord Geo. What?

Mrs. Con. The World shou'd judge, my Lord, so widely of your Heart, that only what was grossly sensual cou'd affect it:—Now, Sir, [*To Sir* Friendly.] what think you? With all this Headlong Wildness of a youthful Heat, one Moment's Thought, you see, produces Love, Compassion, Tenderness and Honour: And now, my

Lord, to let you see it was not Interest but innocent Revenge, that made me thus turn Champion to my Sexes Honour; since by this just exposing the Weakness of your Inconstancy, I have reduc'd you fairly to confess the forceful power of honourable Love: I thus release you of the Chain: For, know, I am as well in Health as ever. [*Walks from her Chair.*

Lord Geo. Ha! [*Joyfully surpriz'd.*

Mrs. Con. And if the darling Pleasures of abandon'd Liberty have yet a more prevailing Charm, you now again are free; return and revel in the Transport.

Lord Geo. Is there a Transport under Heav'n like this?

Lady Gent. O blest Deliverance!

Lord Wrong. Surprizing Change!

Lady Wrong. No Wound, nor danger then at last?

Mrs. Con. All! all! in every Circumstance I've done this Night, my Wound, the Robbery, the Surgeon, (here's one can witness) all was equally dissembled as my Person.

Lord Geo. Is't possible?

Lord Wrong. The most consummate Bite, my Lord, that ever happen'd in all the Circumstances of Humane Nature.

Lord Geo. O! for a Strain of Thought t'out-do this spiteful Virtue.

Lord Wrong. Why Faith, my Lord, 'twas smartly handsome, not to cheat you into Marriage, when 'twas so provokingly in her Power.

Mrs. Con. If you think it worth your Revenge, my Lord—Come! for once I'll give your Vanity leave to humble my Pride, and laugh in your Turn at the notable stir I have made about you.

Lord Geo. Since you provoke me then, prepare to start, and tremble at my Revenge—I will not only marry thee this Instant, but the next spiteful Moment insolently Bed thee too, and make such ravenous Havock of thy Beauties, that thou shalt call in vain for Mercy of my Power. Ho! within there! call the Chaplain.

Mrs. Con. Hold, my Lord!

Lord Geo. Nay, no resistance—by the transporting Fury thou hast rais'd I'll do't.

Mrs. Con. This is down-right Violence—my Lord *Wronglove*— [*Strugling.*

Lord Wrong. Don't be concern'd, Madam, he never does any harm in these Fits.

Mrs. Con. Have you no Shame!

Lord Geo. By Earth, Seas, Air, and by the glorious impudence of substantial Darkness, I am fix'd.

Mrs. Con. Will no one help me—Sir *Friendly.*

Sir Fr. Not I in troth, Madam, I think his Revenge is a very honest one.

Lord Geo. Confess me Victor, or expect no Mercy: Not all the Adamantine Rocks of Virgin Coyness, not all your Trembling, Sighs, Prayers, Threats, Promisses, or Tears shall save you. O transport of devouring Joy! [*Closely embracing her.*

Mrs. Con. Oh!—Quarter! Quarter! O spare my Perriwig.

Lord Wrong. Victoria! Victoria! The Town's our own.

Sir Fr. Fairly won indeed, my Lord!

Lord Geo. Sword in Hand, by *Jupiter*—And now, Madam, I put my self into Garrison for Life.

Mrs. Con. Oh! that won't be long I'm sure; for you've almost kill'd me.

Lord Geo. I warrant you moderate Exercise will bring you to your Wind again.

Mrs. Con. [*Aside.*] Well! People may say what they will; but upon some Occasions, an agreeable Impudence saves one a world of impertinent Confusion.

Lord Geo. And now, Madam, to let you see you have as much subdu'd my Follies, as my Heart.—First, let me humbly ask a Pardon for Offences—Here—[*To Lady* Gentle.] These Sums, Madam, I now must own to serve my shameful Ends, were all unfairly won of you; which since I never meant to keep, I thus restore, and with 'em give a friendly Warning of your too mix'd a Company in Play.

Lady Gent. My Lord, I thank you—and shall henceforth study to deserve the Providence that sav'd me—If I mistake not too, I have some Bills that call for restitution, Here. [*To Mrs.* Conquest.] No one cou'd, I'm sure, be more concern'd to send 'em. Friendship's conceal'd are double Obligations.

Mrs. Con. I sent 'em to relieve you, Madam, but since your dange has no farther need of 'em— [*Takes the Bills.*

Sir Fr. Now, Child, I claim your Promise, here comes another of your small Accounts that is not made up yet.

Mrs. Con. Fear not, Sir, I'll pay it to a Scruple.

Enter Miss Notable *weeping, in a Night dress.*

Miss Not. O where's this mournful sight: Your Pardon Ladies, if my intruding Tears confess the weakness of a harmless Passion, that now 'twould be ungrateful to conceal: Had I not lov'd too well, this fatal Accident had never been.

Mrs. Con. Well don't be concern'd, dear Madam, for the worst part of the Accident is, that I am found at last, it seems, to be no more fit for a Wife, than as I told you, you were for a Husband.

Miss Not. Ha! [*In Confusion.*

Mrs. Con. Not but I had some thoughts of marrying you too; but then I fansy'd you'd soon be uneasy under the cold Comfort of Petticoats—so—I don't know—the good Company has ev'n persuaded me to pull off my Breeches, and marry Lord *George.*

Miss Not. Marry'd! base Man! is this the proof of your Indifference to Mrs. *Conquest!* [*Aside to Lord* George.

Lord Geo. 'Tis not a Proof yet indeed—But I believe I shall marry her to Night; and then you know, my Life, I am in a fair way to it.

Miss Not. Jeer'd by him too! I'll lock my self up in some dark Room, and never see the World again. [*Exit.*

Lady Wrong. [*To Lord* Wronglove.] Was she? that Creature then the little wicked cause of my Disquiet?—How ridiculous have you made my Jealousie? Farewel the Folly and the Pain.

Lord Wrong. Farewel the Cause of it for ever.

Lady Gent. [*To Sir* Friendly.] The Count say you, his Accomplice! How I tremble. But I have done with it for Life; such ruinous Hazards, need no second Warning.

Lord Geo. I fancy, Nuncle, I begin to make a very ridiculous Figure here, and have given my self the Air of more Looseness than I have been able to come up to.

Mrs. Con. I'm afraid that's giving your self the Air of more Virtue than you'll be able to come up to—But however, since I can't help it, I had as good trust you.

Lord Geo. And when I wrong that Trust, may you deceive me.

Sir Fr. And now a lasting Happiness to all.
[*Coming forward to the Audience.*

Let those that here, as in a Mirror see
These Follies, and the Dangers they have run
Be cheaply warn'd, and think these Scapes their own.

THE END.

EPILOGUE.

Spoken by Mr. CIBBER.

I'm thinking, when poor Plays are quite cry'd down,
(As nothing's strange in this revolving Town,
Tho' what the latter Age had thought amazing,)
What we poor Slaves shall do, when turn'd a Grazing.
Perhaps great Caesar, *who the World commanded,*
May snuff the Opera Candles when disbanded;
And proud Roxana, *from her high Disdain,*
Most vilely stoop to spread Tofftissa's *Train.*
Not but our Women may see better Lives,
And make some honest Citts—(troth!)—comfortable Wives.
Let no fair Damsel think this said t'affront her,
(For howsoe'er the Stages Hopes may mount her)
Beauty may drive as good a Trade behind a Counter.
As here some Chapmen, *there some Heads with Sorrow.* [*The Pit and Gallery.
May give, and feel, sore Proofs before this time to Morrow:
But I, whose Beauty only is Grimace,
Have no such Prospects from this hatchet Face.
All I can do must be—
With humble Ale, and Toast, round Sea-Coal Fire,
At Nights my pensive Spouse, and Brats t'inspire,
With Taggs of Crambo Rhimes, and tack 'em to th' Italian *Lyre.*
Nay, e'en when Hunger prompts 'em for Relief,
I'll make 'em ask for Food in Recitative:
As thus, [Sings in Recitative.] *"Mamma!—Well! what, what is't you mutter?*
"Pray cut me a great Piece of Bread and Butter.
[Then this to the Air of *Yes, yes, 'tis all I want,* &c.
There's all you're like to have,
Nor can you ask for Supper;
'Tis cut quite round the Loaf,
'Tis under side, and Upper.

Who knows in time, but this in Bills inserted,
May croud a House, when Shakespear *is deserted.*
Or say that I my self–
Since painted Nature no Recruits will bring in,
Shou'd e'en, in Spite of Nature, stick to Singing,
My Voice, t'is true, the Gipsy's but unkind to,
Tho' that's a Fault you ev'ry Day are blind to.
But if I change my Name, that half will win ye,
O! the soft Sound of Seignior Cibberini.
Imagine then, that thus with am'rous Air
I give you Raptures, while I squall Despair. [Sings *Italian.*]
If this won't do, I'll try another Touch,
Half French, *some* English, *and a spice of* Dutch. [Sings in broken [*English.*
Now, Sirs, you've seen the utmost I can do,
As Poet, Player, and as Songster too;
But if you can't allow my Voice inviting,
E'en let me live by Acting, and by Writing.

APPENDICES

Appendix I

A Scene from the Early Quartos of *Love's Last Shift*

The following scene opens *Love's Last Shift,* Act IV, in the quartos of 1695/6 and 1702, but does not appear in the *Plays* of 1721, nor in any subsequent London edition. It is included in the 1725 Dublin edition, and in the T. Johnson Hague editions of 1711 and [1720]. The text printed here is that of the first quarto.

ACT IV.

The SCENE continues.

Enter two Bullies, and Sir William Wisewou'd *observing them.*

1*st. Bully*. Damme! *Jack,* let's after him, and fight him; 'tis not to be put up.

2*d. Bull.* No! Dam him! no body saw the affront, and what need we take notice of it?

1*st. Bul.* Why that's true!—But Damme! I have much ado to forbear cutting his Throat.

Sir Will. Pray Gentlemen, what's the matter? Why are you in such a Passion?

1*st. B.* What's that to you, Sir? What wou'd you have?

Sir Will. I hope, Sir, a Man may ask a Civil Question.

1*st. B.* Damme! Sir, we are Men of Honour, we dare answer any Man.

Sir Will. But why are you angry, Gentlemen? Have you received any wrong?

2*d. B.* We have been called Rascals, Sir, have had the Lye given us, and had like to have been kickt!

Sir Will. But I hope, you were not kickt, Gentlemen.

2*d. B.* How, Sir! we kickt!

Sir Will. Nor do I presume, that you are Rascals!

1*st. B.* Bloud! and Thunder! Sir, let any Man say it that wears an head! we Rascals!

Sir Will. Very good! since then you are not Rascals, he rather was one, who maliciously call'd you so:—'Pray take my Advice, Gentlemen; never disturb your selves, for any ill your enemy says of you; for from an Enemy the World will not believe it: Now you must know, Gentlemen, that a Flea-bite is to me more offensive, than the severest Affront any Man can offer me!

1*st. B.* What, and so you wou'd have us put it up! Damme! Sir, don't preach Cowardice to us, we are Men of Valour: you won't find us Cowards, Sir.

2*d. B.* No, Sir! we are no Cowards, tho' you are.

1*st. B.* Hang him, let him alone, I see a Coward in his face.

Sir Will. If my face make any Reflection, Sir, 'tis against my will.

2*d. B.* Prithee *Tom,* let's Affront him, and raise his Spleen a little.

Sir Will. Raise my Spleen! that's more than any Man cou'd ever boast of.

1*st. B.* You Lye.

Sir Will. I am not angry yet, therefore I do not Lye, Sir: Now one of us must lye, I do not lye. *Ergo*—

1*st. B.* Damme! Sir, have a care! Don't give me the Lye, I shan't take it, Sir.

Sir Will. I need not, Sir! you give it your self.

1*st. B.* Well, Sir, what then? if I make bold with my self, every old Puppy shall not pretend to do it.

Sir Will. Ha! ha! ha! ha! ha!

1*st. B.* Damme, Sir, what do you laugh at!

Sir Will. To let you see, that I am no Puppy, Sir, for Puppies are Brutes, now Brutes have not Risibility: But I laugh, therefore I am no Puppy, ha! ha!

1*st. B.* Bloud and Thunder, Sir! dare you fight?

Sir Will. Not in cool blood, Sir, and I confess 'tis impossible to make me angry.

2d. B. I'le try that! Heark ye, don't you know you are a sniveling old Cuckold?

Sir Will. No, really, Sir.

2d. B. Why then I know you to be one.

Sir Will. Look you, Sir, my Reason weighs this Injury, which is so light, it will not raise my Anger in the other Scale.

1st. B. Oon's! what a tame old Prig's this? I'll give you better weight then. I know who got all your Children.

Sir Will. Not so well as my Wife I presume—Now she tells me, 'twas my self, and I believe her too.

1st. B. She tells you so, because the poor Rogue that got 'em is not able to keep 'em.

Sir Will. Then my keeping them is Charity.

1st. B. Bloud and Thunder, Sir, this is an Affront to us, not to be Angry after all these Provocations—Damme! *Jack,* let's souse him in the Canal. (*as they lay hold on him*)

Enter El. Worthy, *Young* Worthy, Nar., *and* Hill.

Y. Wor. S'Death, what's here? Sir *William* in the Rogues hands that affronted the Ladies—Oh, forbear, forbear—

(*Strikes them.*)

E. Wor. So, Gentlemen, I thought you had fair warning before, now you shall pay for't. (*Enter three or four Sentinels.*) Heark you, honest Soldiers, pray do me the favour to wash these Rascals in the Canal, and there's a Guinea for your trouble.

Bullies. Damme, Sir! we shall expect satisfaction.

[*Exeunt dragging the Bullies.*

Sir Will. Oh dear Gentlemen, I am obliged to you, for I was just going to the Canal my self, if you had not come as you did.

E. Wor. Pray, Sir, what had you done to 'em?

Sir Will. Why, hearing the Musick from my Parlour Window, and being invited by the sweetness of the Evening, I ev'n took a Walk to see if I could meet with you, when the first Objects that presented themselves were these Bullies, threatning to cut some bodies Throat: Now, I endeavouring to allay their Fury, occasioned their giving me scurrilous Language: and finding they cou'd not make me as angry as themselves, they off'red to fling me into the Water.

E. Wor. I am glad we stept to your deliverance.

Sir Will. Oh, I thank you, Gentlemen.—I'll e'en go home, and recover my fright. Good Night, Good Night to you all. [*Exit.*

E. W. Harry, see Sir *William* safe to his Lodging. [*To his Servant.*

Appendix II
The Music

The music for the song and the masque in *Love's Last Shift* was sufficiently popular to have been included in collections of new songs printed in 1696. The song in Act IV.iii appeared in *Deliciae Musicae: A Collection of the newest and best Songs* . . . (The First Book of the Second Volume [London: J. Heptinstall, 1696], 17). It was set by Henry Purcell's younger brother Daniel (c. 1660-1717), who, between 1696 and 1707, had devoted himself to writing music for plays, among them another of Cibber's plays, *Love Makes a Man* (*Grove's Dictionary of Music and Musicians,* 5th ed. [New York: Macmillan, 1954], VI, 1019).

The song in the masque appeared in *Thesaurus Musicus: Being a Collection of the Newest Songs Performed At His Majesties Theatres* (The Fifth Book [London: J. Heptinstall, 1696], 8-10). It was set by Johann Wolfgang Franck, one-time director of music at the Hamburg cathedral, who had come to London around 1690. He composed songs in English and gave concerts there for two or three years. The song for *Love's Last Shift* is considered the last of his English songs (*Grove's Dictionary,* III, 476-77).

B.M. Add. MS. 38,189, fol. 31^{v} reversed, contains further music for *Love's Last Shift,* with the following notation: "Play this [ ] times over, & the last play the Repeit, in the Love's Last Shift." There is no indication in the manuscript at what point in the play it was to be played. The MS., its front cover labeled "Dancing Booke Violins," contains other tunes for plays and may have belonged to a theater musician.

The song "Sabina with an Angel's Face" survives in printed form in only one copy that I have been able to trace. It is a single sheet folded, bearing the title "A SONG *in the* Careless Husband *Sung by* Mr Leveridge/Set by Mr Daniell Purcell," and is included in a collection of a number of similar items in the Music Library of the Birmingham Public Libraries. Of the other items in the collection, those which can be identified were published in London between 1705 and 1710. Richard Leveridge was a bass singer and composer who frequently sang songs in the plays at Drury Lane as well as in concert (*Grove's Dictionary,* V, 152-53). He was also engaged as music master at Drury Lane (Nicoll, II, 277). *The London Stage* (pt. 2, p. 83) records that he and Miss Cross, who also sang in *Love's Last Shift,* provided singing entertainment for performances of *The Careless Husband,* starting on December 16, 1704.

The air "Yes, yes, 'tis all I want," which Cibber used in the Epilogue to *The Lady's Last Stake,* is from Niccolo Haym's *Camilla,* an opera popular on the London stage at the time, and the focus of Cibber's quarrel with Italian opera. *Camilla* is an adaptation of *Il Trionfo di Camilla* by Silvio Stampiglia, with music by Antonio Maria Buononcini (see the Epistle Dedicatory to *The Lady's Last Stake,* ll. 52-55n.). The manuscript music for this air is B.M. Add. MS. 31,993, fols. 37-38^{v}.

There is in *The Dancing Master: Vol. the Second . . .* (3rd ed. [London: W. Pearson, 1718], 147), a dance tune labeled "The Ladies last Stake/ Longways for as many as will," followed by instructions for the dancers. There is no indication of a dance in any edition of Cibber's play, nor any record of dancing at any of the performances of the play up to 1718.

The manuscript music for the air "Yes, yes, 'tis all I want" has been reproduced with the permission of the Trustees of the British Museum. Photographic copies of the music for *Love's Last Shift* have been supplied by the Music Department of the Library of Congress, and those of the song in *The Careless Husband,* by the Birmingham Public Libraries, England.

[17]
A Song, Sett by Mr. Daniel Purcell, Sung in Love's Last Shift.
WHat un-grate-full De-vil moves you! Come, come my Friend; the Truth de-
-clare; You Love Sylvia, Sylvia Loves you; why, why then will you Wed the Fair?
Marriage-joyning does dis-co-ver, but Love-free-ing joyns for Life: Wou'd you,
wou'd you, wou'd you Love the Nymph for ever? Never, never, never, never, never,
never let her be your Wife.

A Song in the *Mask* for the *Lover's Last-Shift*, Sung by Mrs. *Cross* and the Boy, upon a Marriage Life. Sett by Mr. *Francks*.

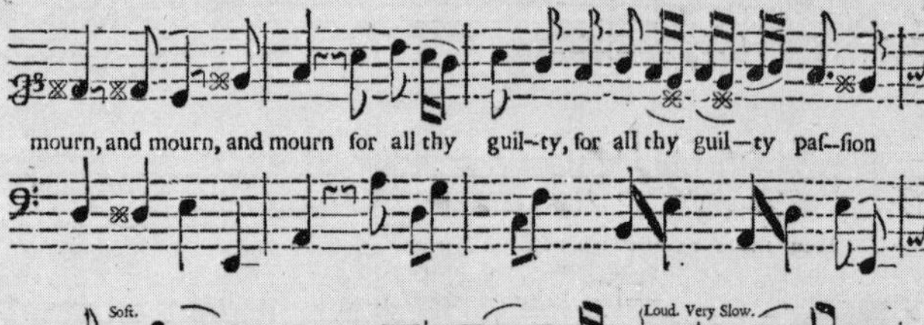

pas——sion past: Then thou shall find those Joy
pas——sion past: Then thou shall find those Joy
——s, those Joys re-turn, those Joy
——s, those Joys re—turn, those Joy
Loud.
——s, those Joys re—turn, those Joy——s, those, those Joys re--turn:
——s, those Joys re—turn, those Joys, those Joy—s, those, those Joys re—turn:
Which shall for ever, for ever, for ever, for ever, for ever
Which shall for ever, for ever, for

laſt; which ſhall for ever, for ever, for ever, for ever
ever, for ever, laſt; which ſhall for ever, for ever
laſt, for ever, for ever, for ever, for ever, for e—ver laſt, for
laſt, for ever, for ever, for ever, for ever, for e—ver laſt, for
ever, for ever, for ever, for ever, for e—ver laſt, for ever, for
ever, for ever, for ever, for ever, for e—ver laſt, for ever, for
ever, ever, e——ver laſt.
ever, ever, e——ver laſt.

A SONG in the Careless Husband Sung by Mr Leveridge
Set by Mr Daniell Purcell
Sabina with an Angels Face, by Love or_daind for Joy,
seems of the Syrens Cruell Race, to Cha________rm and then de_
_stroy, to Cha________rm and then destroy.
With all the Arts of Look and Dress, She Fa________ns y Fatal
Fire, thro Pride mistaken oft for Grace, She bids the Swain expire, thro Pride
mistaken oft for Grace, She bids the Swain, She bids the Swain expire.
The God of Love enrag'd, the God of Love enrag'd to see y
Nymph defy his Flame, Pronounc'd this mercyless Decree, a gainst the
haughty Dame, Pronounc'd this mercyless Decree, a gainst the haughty Dame,

Let Age with double Speed or'e take her, let Love the roome of
Pride supply, and when her Lovers all for_sake her, let her then, then,
then let her, then un_pi_tied Dye, and when her Lovers all for_
sake her, let her then, then, then let her, then, then, then let her, then un
_pi_tied Dye. Let her then un_pi_tied Dye.
for the flute

Camilla
37
Sym:
yes, yes, 'tis all I want
Volti

woud I better thrive (yes, yes tis all I want, nor woud I better
Thrive a heart for a heart is all a lover can gaine a
heart for heart, is all a Lover can gaine all, all, a
Lover can gaine all, all a lover can gaine,

38
a happyness I feele to
mortall can reveall, if all you have you give I nere must com-
Sym
=plain
if all you have you
give I nere must complain, I nere must complain if

all you have you give I nère must com=plain
Da Capo

Appendix III
The Text

The copy-text is that of the large quarto *Plays Written by Mr. Cibber. In Two Volumes,* published by subscription in London in 1721. This edition is based on the copy in the Sterling Memorial Library of Yale University, and is transcribed with the permission of the library. It follows the copy-text at all points, except in modernizing long "s," in correcting obvious printer's errors, such as turned and wrong-font letters, and in rendering consistent certain accidentals—such as the use of roman and italic type and square brackets in stage directions, and the abbreviation of names in speech-prefixes—all of which have been done silently. Names abbreviated in the text or in stage directions have been silently expanded. This edition does not reproduce small capitals, factotums, ornamental or large capital initials, nor does it capitalize initial words or parts of words following ornamental initials.

The spelling and punctuation—including the presence or absence of the apostrophe in genitives, in contractions, and occasionally in plurals—are those of the copy-text, which appears to follow the accepted practice of Cibber's time. Variants in spelling have been recorded only where they suggest the possibility of a different word. Ambiguous spelling has been emended only where clarity seemed to require it. Thus "Spear" has been changed to "spare" (*The Lady's Last Stake,* I.i.6), following the reading in all other editions of the play. Emendations of spelling not indisputably erroneous are noted in the textual notes. The spelling of Latin and French words, no more consistent than contemporary English spelling, has been reproduced as it is in the copy-text.

The original punctuation has been preserved, except where an emendation was necessary to the sense. For example, the copy-text reads, "this was a lucky Discovery between my Lord, or my Lady, it's hard if I don't mend my Place by it" (*The Lady's Last Stake,* I.i.114-15); this has been clarified by the insertion of a semi-colon after "Discovery," a correction made in the editions of 1732 and 1736. Such an emendation is recorded in the textual notes. In the few instances where a speech ends without final punctuation, it has been supplied silently. Scene numbers have been added where necessary, and line numbers have been supplied throughout.

Substantive emendations have been made in only a very few instances, where it seemed necessary to correct a clearly erroneous reading or to supply a carelessly omitted word. In most cases the correction has been made by referring to the reading in the early quartos. All such emendations have been recorded in the textual notes.

All recorded variants appear in the textual notes, where the lemma reproduces the reading in this edition, and the sigla, all variant readings in chronological order. In the case of emendations, the lemma reproduces the emended reading in this text, and the sigla, the variant readings in chronological order. Where variants differ one from another in font, case, spelling, or punctuation, I have recorded only the form of the earliest variant. Variant forms of words like "beside" and "besides"—though they appear to have been interchangeable in the copy-text—and substantive variants in the stage directions have been recorded. Variant contractions of two words into one—"I am" to "I'm"—have been recorded as substantive. Variants in the use of parentheses in the text of speeches have not been recorded, nor have variants in the bracketing of asides. The general practice seems to have been to bracket only the term "Aside" in the earlier editions of the plays, while the later duodecimos usually bracket all of the speech to be spoken aside.

Characters omitted from the stage directions at the head of scenes in which they have a part have been duly added where there is no indication that they entered later in the scene. The Epilogue of *Love's Last Shift,* which followed the Prologue in the 1721 edition, has been moved to the end of the play to conform to the practice followed in *The Careless Husband* and *The Lady's Last Stake.*

TEXTUAL NOTES

Textual Notes

LOVE'S LAST SHIFT

Love's Last Shift was first published in small quarto in 1695/6. Its dedication is dated "Febr. 7," and the first notice of publication appears in *The London Gazette* for February 10-13, 1695/6. Another edition appeared in 1702, a carelessly printed small quarto with no clearly authorial revisions. The play was included, with authorial revisions, in Volume I of *Plays Written by Mr. Cibber. In Two Volumes,* published by subscription in large quarto in 1721. It was reprinted without further authoritative textual changes in duodecimo editions of 1730, 1733, 1735, 1747, and 1752. The 1735 edition appears also in Volume III of *The Dramatick Works of Colley Cibber, Esq; In Five Volumes,* published in 1735; the 1752 edition, in Volume I of *The Dramatick Works of Colley Cibber, Esq; In Four Volumes,* published in 1754. The play is included in two collections published after Cibber's death—in Volume I of the four-volume 1760 *Dramatic Works,* and in Volume I of the five-volume 1777 *Dramatic Works.*

An octavo edition printed in Dublin in 1725 follows the editions of 1695/6 and 1702. A 1711 octavo, bearing a London imprint, but printed in The Hague for T. Johnson (in Volume IX of *A Collection of the Best English Plays,* a twelve-volume collection dated 1711, but actually published between 1710 and 1718, with Volume IX dated 1712), follows the 1702 quarto, reproducing two errors found only in that edition: "Fornification" (Q2, p. 4; 1711, p. 16) and "Hallaria" (Q2, p. 6; 1711, p. 19). Another Johnson edition, "Printed for the Company of Booksellers" [*ca.* 1720], and part of Johnson's sixteen-volume second *Collection of the Best English Plays* (1720-1722), follows the early quartos by including the "Bullies" scene in Act IV, and reproduces "Hallaria" (Q2, p. 6; [1720], p. 17). An edition of 1740, "Printed for the Booksellers in Town and Country" by R. Walker—who had been a printer for Jacob Tonson and who later sold some of Tonson's plays under his own imprint, without Tonson's consent—incorporates the revisions of the 1721 edition and may have been prepared from the 1735 edition, since it prints "*Vision*" for "*Vision's*" in the masque, a change first made in 1735. An edition in Volume VI of the sixteen-volume *A Select Collection of the Best Modern English Plays,* "Printed for the Company of Booksellers" (The Hague, 1750) by H. Scheurleer, jun.,

Johnson's successor, follows the early quartos. The Dublin and Hague editions have no textual authority, however, and I have omitted them from the textual apparatus.

The 1721 large quarto of *Love's Last Shift* was apparently printed from a copy of the 1702 second quarto. Though the second quarto is substantially the same as the first, it offers certain distinctive readings which do not appear in the first quarto, but which are reprinted in the 1721 edition. The following is a list of some significant readings that first occur in the 1702 edition (the act-scene-line numbers refer to the present edition):

I.i.228	What Beau's Box now (Q1 omits "now")
III.i.107-08	she immediately rejects (Q1–he immediately rejects)
IV.i.85	Whether (Q1–whither)
V.iv.s.d.	The heading for the masque follows Q2 rather than Q1
V.iv.8	*such idle Joys* (Q1–*such fleeting Toys;* Q2–*such Joys*)

The last two changes in particular suggest that the printer had before him a copy of the second quarto.

The editions of 1730 and 1733 follow the large quarto of 1721 closely, with few substantive variants. A number of changes appear in the edition of 1735–none of them clearly authorial–in the bracketing of asides, in the correction of "beside" to "besides" where warranted, in contractions, and in punctuation. Furthermore, the 1735 and 1747 editions make some substantive changes which seem to indicate a slight deterioration of the text: for example, in 1735 Amanda's "dreaded" task becomes "dreadful" (V.ii.10), and in 1747 "luxurious" love becomes "luxuriant" (V.ii.224). Each of these deteriorations in the text is repeated in subsequent editions to 1752.

In a few instances the duodecimos restore readings from the early quartos, but it is by no means clear that these restorations required that the printer consult the quartos, except perhaps in the case of "Thou sweetest, softest Creature Heav'n e'er form'd" (IV.iii.175), where "form'd" is restored in place of the erroneous "found" in the 1721 edition.

Extensive revisions were made in the 1721 edition of *Love's Last Shift,* the most striking of these being the attempt to streamline Act IV by excising the original opening scene. In this short scene, two bullies, infuriated by their inability to make Sir William Wisewoud fight, attack him in the park. The scene is horseplay, and as such it serves only to distract the spectator by anticipating the ear-boxing Sir Novelty receives from his jealous mistress in the episode that follows it.

In further significant revisions, Cibber deleted some, though certainly not all vulgar passages from the speeches of "genteel" characters, especially in conversations which anticipate the pleasures of the wedding night (I.i.501-02 and IV.i.129-30; see Dougald MacMillan, "The Text of *Love's Last Shift," Modern Language Notes,* 46 [1931], 518-19). Specific physical terms are replaced by more general ones: "Maidenhead" becomes "Maid" (IV.i.37); "hot Raging Lus becomes "all the dotage of undone Desire" (IV.i.108); the lover is "new-blest in receiving what he ne'er enjoyed" rather than "new Ravished" (IV.iii.210). References to bad breath and belching are cut (IV.i.25, 38 and IV.iii.247). In addition to these, Cibber substituted "a very good Periwig" for "a very good Walk" (II.i.165) as Sir Novelty's criterion for a gentleman. This last change is not only more suitable to Sir Novelty's standards, but also suggests Sir Novelty's own stage periwig, which by 1721 had become famous with the audience (see *Love's Last Shift*, II.i.123-24n.).

Textual abbreviations, with locations of copies used:

Q1 First quarto. London: Samuel Briscoe, 1696. Yale.
Q2 Second quarto. London: H. Rhodes, R. Parker, R. Wellington, 1702. Yale.
P In *Plays Written by Mr. Cibber. In Two Volumes.* Vol. I. London: Jacob Tonson, Bernard Lintot, William Mears, William Chetwood, 1721. Yale; University of Pennsylvania (two copies).
D3 First duodecimo. London: B. Lintot, T. Saunders, et al., 1730. Yale.
D4 Second duodecimo. London: B. Lintot, W. Feales, et al., 1733. Harvard.
D5 Third duodecimo. London: B. Lintot, J. Clarke, et al., 1735. Harvard.
D6 Fourth duodecimo. London: H. Lintot, R. Wellington, et al., 1747. Duke.
D7 Fifth duodecimo. London: H. Lintot, R. Wellington, et al., 1752. Harvard.

Title page
jure] *jura* Q1, D6-7

Dedication
9 your Candour] *the smoothness of your Temper* Q1-2
17-18 Pleasures] Pleasure Q2
19 can] cou'd Q1-2
44 them . . . a] *my self for a Defensive* Q1-2
61 *Colley*] C. D5-7. Q1 adds date: "Febr. 7. 169$\frac{5}{6}$." Though the year "$\frac{5}{6}$" is not entirely legible, both Nicoll (I, 397) and *The London Stage* (pt. 1, p. 457) accept 1695/6. Cibber himself says it was performed in "*January* 1695" (*Apology*, I, 213), and the first notice of publication appears in *The London Gazette* for February 10-13, 1695/6.

Prologue
VERBRUGGEN] VERBRUGHEN P

14 *the expected*] *th'expected* D5-7
24 *t'expect*] *to expect* Q1-2
26 *Features find*] *find Features* Q1-2

Dramatis Personae
12 Gentleman] Gent. Q1
18 *Mills*] *Wills* P. D3-7 give a later cast which shows the following changes: Loveless, Mr. Wilks; Young Worthy, Mr. Mills; Snap, Mr. Cibber, jun.; Sly, Mr. Miller; Lawyer, Mr. Rosco; Amanda, Mrs. Porter; Narcissa, Mrs. Thurmond; Hillaria, Mrs. Heron; Flareit, Mrs. Mills.
25 Mistress] Mrs. Q1-2
28 Servants, *&c.*] Servants, Centinels, Porter, Bullies, and Musick. Q1-2

I.i

HT Love's Last Shift: OR, *The FOOL in FASHION.*] Love's Last Shift, &c. Q1; Love's Last Shift. Q2
1 Counsel,] Counsel's Q1-2
9 'em] them Q1-2
39 S'bud] odsbud Q1-2
55 this!] this? [*Aside.*] D5-7
67 has] hath D4-7
67-68 are forc'd] are forc't Q1-2; forc'd P, D3-7
71 *William*] *Will.* Q1-2
74 Beside] Besides D4-7
102 I'm] I am Q1-2
114 has] hath D4-7
118 I'm] I am Q1-2
123 other's] others Q1-2, D5-7
127 it] *om.* Q1-2
129 o' the] a Q1-2
134 wilt thou] will you Q1-2
135 Money is] Money's Q1-2, D3-7
140 beside] besides D4-7
163 Inclinations] Inclination D7
189 you] thee D7
196 *] *om.* Q1-2; P, D3-7 add note "*Guineas went then at 30 *s.*" at foot of page.
210 the] *om.* Q1-2
216 is it] it is D4-7
228 Beau's] Beaux Q1-2; Beaux's P
228 now] *om.* Q1
230 Novel] a Novel D5-7
231 Come, come] Come Q1
235 and the] the Q1-2
243 on] upon Q1-2
252 any] every Q1-2
252 Master] the Master Q1-2
261 me, he] me, is that he Q1
262 not] *om.* Q1-2
288 the] to the D4-7
289 in't] in it D4-7
308 an] a D4-7
309 for it] for't Q1-2
311 Virtue's self] Virtue itself D4-7
336 Warning] Counsel Q1-2
343-44 ends only] only ends D3-7
396 an] not an Q1-2
431 a] *om.* Q1-2
436 he's] he is D3
444 in] in a Q1
445 Design] designs Q1-2
451 take] have taken Q1-2
465 had] have had Q1-2
468 it.] it. *Aside.*] D5-6; it. [*Aside.*] D7
476 can,] can P, D3
478 Lye!] Lye? [*Aside.* D5-7
492 Beauties] Beauty's Q1-2
493 Then,] Then, Madam, Q1
499 small] *om.* D5-7
501 Insolence! D'ye] Insolence! if it once comes to that I don't question but you have been familiar with me in your Imagination. Marry you! What lye in a naked bed with you! Trembling by your side, like a tame Lamb for Sacrifice! De'e Q1-2
502 kiss, and] kiss him, Q1-2
512 happy] Rushing Q1-2

II.i

6-7 If . . . Eyes.] [If . . . Eyes. *Aside.*] D5-7
19 there is] there's D5-7
21 Why] Why, D5-7
24 a stale] an Stale Q1
25 in a Morning] at a Rehearsal Q1-2
40 him.] him. *Aside.*] Q1-2, D5
46 you] *om.* Q1-2
61 Fashion] Fashions D6-7
85 *Merveil*] *Mervielle* Q1; *Merville* Q2

86 Cousin.] Cousin. *Aside.*] D5-7
90 'twou'd] it would D4-7
104 it.] it. *Aside.*] D5-7
121 I'm] I am Q1-2
133 Come,] Come, come, Q1
135 Hand] Hands Q1-2
157-58 *What . . . lose.*] Q1 prints as prose.
160 Resentment] Fury Q1-2
165 Periwig] Walk Q1-2
206 you'll] you will Q1-2
206 half] but half Q1-2
210 I'll] I will D5-7
246 for't.] for't. *Aside.*] D5-7
248 greater] greatest D4-7
250 a] *om.* Q1-2
251 upon?] upon? *Aside.*] D5-7
267 the Bardash] Bardash P, D3-7
272 end?] end? [*Aside.* D5-7
286 their] *om.* P
297 Glass.] Glass. [*Aside.* D5-7
301 I have] have I Q1-2
313 cold] *om.* Q2
313 Compliment.] Compliment. *Aside.*] D5-7
318 bow-Court'sy] Bow'd Curtesie Q1-2
331 following you] following Q1-2
333 Woman is] Woman's D4-7
337 I'm] I am Q1-2
344 Hand] hands Q1-2
353 farther] further Q2
353 an] a D4-7
380 you] your D3-7
394 bitter] better Q1

III.i

2 fain wou'd be] wou'd be fain Q1-2
7 Counsel] Council Q1-2
7 a] *om.* Q1-2
12-15 Why . . . of.] Why should Women affect Ignorance among themselves, when we converse with Men indeed? Modesty and Good Breeding Oblige us not to understand, what sometimes we can't help thinking of. Q1-2
27 Undertaking] Understanding Q1-2
32 I'm] I am Q1-2
58 Beside] Besides D6-7
60 farther] further Q1-2
60 Mr.] Young Q1-2
107 he] she Q2, P, D3-7. The sense clearly requires "he." The introduction of "she" in Q2 may have been one of the many careless errors in that edition.
168 be] me Q1-2
185 with,] *om.* Q1-2
207 that] *om.* Q1-2, D3-7
208s.d. *Servant*] *Footman* D5-7
210 Hand] hands Q1-2
220 will; tho'] will too D6-7
231 not it] it not D5-7
234 I shou'd] shou'd Q1
237 Ha! ha! ha! ha!] ha! ha! ha! he! Q1

III.ii

30 Souls] Soul Q1
47 take] do take Q1-2
58 *Sonata.*] *Sonata,* [*The Musick prepare to Play.*] Q1-2
60 a] *om.* Q1-2
72 surveying] a surveying Q1-2
76 a Separation] an Absence Q1-2
80 then] when Q1-2
84 it's] 'tis D3-7
85 an] a D4-7
98-99 Stuff as are here] Stuffs as here is Q1-2
119 Footmen] Footman Q1-2
119 that] and D5-7

126 The] That Q1-2
127 it] *om.* Q1-2
131 she] *om.* Q1-2
136 an] a D3-7
157 goes] go Q1-2
170 no] *om.* D4-7
181 have] ha' Q1-2
186 it's] 'tis D6-7
191 Rogue makes] Rogues make Q1-2
197 What] What the Devil Q1-2
209 long a] a long Q1-2

IV.i

s.d. *Enter* . . . Narcissa.] *Enter two Bullies, and Sir* William Wisewou'd *observing them.* Q1-2. In these two editions, Act IV opens with a park scene in which two bullies thrash Sir William. Elder Worthy, Young Worthy, Hillaria, and Narcissa enter at the end of the encounter as the bullies are about to throw him into the canal. The deleted scene is preserved in Appendix I above.
1 'tis] it's Q1-2
1 walking.] walking too. Q1-2. The omitted scene closes with Elder Worthy's commands to see Sir William home, hence the suggestion that the others be "walking too."
4 Effects] effect Q1-2
11 Heav'ns] Heav'n D6-7
20 Flame.] Flame. [*Throwing back her Hoods.* Q1-2
25 ago.] ago for her stinking breath! Q1-2
37 Maid] Maidenhead Q1-2
38 Foh!] Foh! my breath stinks does it! Q1-2
84 her.] her. *Aside.*] D5-7
101 Blood!] Blood! [*Raving.* Q1
108 all . . . Desire] hot Raging Lust Q1-2
111 *his, his*] *his* D3-7
112 *I'd*] *I'll* D7
112 [Exit.] [*Exit in a fury.* Q1-2
116 troublesome and so] very troublesome and Q1-2
128 Ladies,] Ladies, considering how little rest you'll have to morrow night, Q1-2
129 longer. See] longer.
Y. Wor. Nay as for that mat ter, the night before a Weddin is as unfit to sleep in, as the Night following: Imagination' a very troublesome Bedfellow —Your Pardon, Ladies, I only speak for my self.
El. Wor. See Q1-2
130 *Servants*] *Servant* Q1-2

IV.ii

8 order'd?] order'd it? Q1-2

IV.iii

s.d. *Periwig*] *Peruque* D4-7
11s.d. *Man,*] *Man and* D5-7
48 her.] you. D3-4; her. *Aside.* D5-7
82 brought] brought me Q1-2
91 Hand] hands Q1-2
103 in] with Q1-2
109 hundred] a hundred D3-7
116 it.] it, Madam. Q1-2
119 purpose] propose Q1-2
132 to] and Q1-2
136 a] her Q1-2
146 as little] a little P
170 burning] Raging Q1-2
175 form'd] found P
197 all the] all Q1-2
198 have] *om.* D5-7
206 burns] burn Q1-2
210 new-blest] new Ravish'd Q1-2

227 it's] 'tis Q1-2
243 us] *om.* D3-7
247 stinks.] stinks. (*He belches.*) Q1-2

IV.iv

9 so, however] so, however; Q2; so however, P, D3-7
14 you are] you're D5-7
21 your] your own Q1-2

V.i

s.d. *a Writing*] *Writing* Q1-2
5 on] upon Q1-2
6 Pound] Pounds D6-7
7 it not] not it Q1-2
15 Pound] Pounds D5-7
34 I] *om.* Q1-2
37 Pounds] pound Q1-2
38 Pounds] pound Q1-2
46 Pounds] pound Q1-2
54 Pounds] pound Q1-2
55 Parties] Party's Q1
55 do't] do it D5-7
71 your] his Q1-2
78 Pounds] Pound Q1-2
98 I wou'd] I'd D5-7
99 [*Aside.*]] *om.* D5-7
102 it.] it. *Aside.*] D5-7
102 at present] *om.* D3-7
111 Pound] Pounds D5-7
115 Bond to] Bond, P, D3-7. The bond is actually Wisewoud's to Worthy, and is handed by the lawyer to Wisewoud for signing, so that the reading "Bond to Mr. *Worthy*," as it appears in Q1-2, seems the correct one.
137 Witnesses of] Witnesses to D5-7
138 of] *om.* Q1-2

V.ii

10 dreaded] dreadful D5-7
29 ask] ask of D4-7
50 World] World free Q1-2
56 Pounds] Pound Q1-2
60 of] *om.* Q1-2
95 bright] brighter D5-7
98 her.] her. *Aside.*] D5-7
114 upon] on Q1-2
126 an] *om.* Q1-2
142 awaken'd] awak'd Q1-2
153 It will not] I wonot Q1-2
217 on] upon Q1-2
222 travel] travail Q1-2
224 luxurious] luxuriant D6-7

V.iii

7 here] in Here Q1-2
10 better.] better. [3*d* Serv. P; better. 3 *Serv.* Q1-2. What appears in P to be an unnecessary stage direction, occurs in Q1 at the right-hand margin, three lines from the bottom of the page. It seems to have been intended as a catchword which was not deleted when the two lines of text were added. It is reproduced in Q2 in the upper half of the page, and later reprinted in P.
34 her] his Q1-2
37 Adviser] promoter Q1-2
56-57 Passion, for me,] Passion; for me Q1-2; Passion for me, D4-7
74 have] am Q1-2
89 you'll] you will Q1-2
98 Beaux'] Beaux Q1-2; Beau's P, D3-7
100 Pounds] pound Q1-2
106 the Women] but the Women Q1-2
128 off] off of Q1-2
131 Pounds] Pound Q1-2
165 Pounds] Pound Q1-2
167 Pounds] Pound Q1-2

167 on] upon Q1-2
173 Pounds] Pound Q1-2
190 Pounds] Pound Q1-2
201 I'll] I Q1-2
223 you] you have Q1-2
236 Blessing] Blessings D5-7

V.iv

s.d. The . . . CHORUS.] *A* SONG, *Sett by* Mr. Frank./ Love is Seated on a Throne, attended with/ a CHORUS. Q1. "A Song in the *Mask* for the *Lover's* [*sic*] *Last-Shift.* Sung by Mrs. *Cross* and the Boy, upon a Marriage Life. Sett by Mr. Francks." appeared in *Thesaurus Musicus: Being, A Collection of the Newest Songs . . .* The Fifth Book (London, 1696), pp. 8-10; it is included in Appendix II above.

8 *such idle Joys*] *such fleeting Toys* Q1; *such Joys* Q2
17 *What*] Q1-2, D5-7 add speech-prefix "Honor."
32 *Vision's*] *Vision* D5-7
38 *find it in*] *find in it* P; *find it, in* D3, 5-7
52 *Love.*] Q1-2, D3-4 add *"FINIS."*

Epilogue

EPILOGUE] Q1-2, P, D3-4 print the Epilogue immediately following the Prologue.
4 *a*] *one* Q1-2
5 *if you*] *if you'l* Q1-2
11 *he's*] *ha's* Q1-2
19 *were*] *was* Q1-2
25 *subdue.*] D5-7 add "FINIS." since Epilogue follows text of play.

THE CARELESS HUSBAND

The Careless Husband was first published in a small quarto dated 1705, with a dedication dated "Decem. 15. 1704." *The Daily Courant* for December 19, 1704, advertises: "This day is publish'd, The Careless Husband"; *The London Gazette* for December 18-21 also advertises the publication. The second edition, also a small quarto, appeared later in the same year, with no significant revisions. The third edition, "Revis'd by the Author," appeared in duodecimo in 1713; in it Cibber made his major changes in the text of the play. This edition appears to have been printed from the first quarto: in III.i.77, the first quarto reads "you would things"; the second quarto attempts to clarify this ambiguous phrase with "you'd dispose things"; and the third edition, instead of reprinting this perfectly clear reading, prints "you'd think of things." While this may, of course, be one of Cibber's revisions, it does suggest that the third edition was printed from the first quarto rather than the second. The fourth edition was published in 1714, the fifth, in 1718—both in duodecimo—with no further specifically authorial revisions.

In 1721 *The Careless Husband* was included in Volume I of the large quarto *Plays Written by Mr. Cibber. In Two Volumes.* This edition of the play, which appears to have been printed either from a copy of the fourth edition of 1714, or from a copy of the fifth edition of 1718 with certain of its inferior readings corrected, reprints the following readings that appear for the first time in 1714:

Ded. 1. 53	farther (Q1-2, D3–further)
I.i.42	torn (Q1-2, D3–tore)
I.i.239	–I (Q1-2, D3–nay I)
II.ii.26	on (Q1-2, D3–of)
II.ii.112	Add (Q1-2, D3–And)
II.ii.249	but she did (Q1-2–that she did not; D3–that she did)
IV.i.6	ingenuously (Q1-2, D3–ingeniously)

The edition of 1718 reprints these changes; it also introduces the following inferior readings which are not reprinted in the 1721 large quarto:

II.ii.266	turn'd upon her Heel, and gave a crack (Q1-2, D3-4, P–turn'd upon her Heel, gave a crack)
V.vi.60	unheeded (Q1-2, D3-4, P–unheeding)
V.vi.70	I have thought (Q1-2, D3-4, P–I have often thought)

and the following readings which are included in 1721:

Dramatis Personae	[headings] Men [and] Women (Q1-2, D3-4 use no headings)
III.i.469	Rally (Q1-2–Railery, D3-4–Railly)
V.iii.70-71	shall not we make (Q1-2, D3-4–shall not we go make)

Six duodecimo editions of *The Careless Husband* followed the large quarto of 1721: the sixth edition in 1725, the seventh edition in 1731, the eighth edition in 1734, followed by editions in 1735, 1750, and 1756. Some copies of the duodecimo dated 1735 are really only reissues of the seventh edition of 1731, with a cancel title of the 1735 edition, and therefore of no real bibliographical interest to this edition. The edition of 1735 is also included in Volume II of the *Dramatick Works* of 1736, and the 1750 edition, in Volume I of the *Dramatick Works* of 1754. The play is included in the collections of 1760 and 1777.

A "Sixth Edition" of the play was published in Dublin in 1723; a duodecimo in sixes, it appears to follow the London fifth edition of 1718, printing "unheeded" for "unheeding" (V.vi.60), a change that appeared for the first time in the fifth edition. An "Eighth Edition" was published in Dublin in 1733, and appears to have been printed from one of the earlier London editions, probably the seventh edition of 1731. An edition printed in Dublin in 1752 incorporates some, but not all, of the slight changes introduced for the first time in the London edition of 1750.

The Careless Husband, like *Love's Last Shift,* is included in Volume IX (1712) of T. Johnson's *A Collection of the Best English Plays* (1711). This octavo edition of the play is dated 1710 and follows the second quarto, repeating "dispose" (III.i.77), a reading found only in the second quarto. A second T. Johnson edition, an octavo published in 1721, also follows the second quarto, reprinting "dispose." Since these editions have no textual authority, I have not included them in the textual apparatus.

The London sixth edition appears to have been printed from the earlier duodecimos, probably the fifth edition, rather than from the edition of 1721, since it fails to include many of the fine points corrected in the large quarto. Each subsequent duodecimo edition appears to be printed from the immediately preceding edition, and there is a noticeable deterioration of the text in the course of these later editions, of which the following are but a sampling. The sixth edition prints "silly" for "sillily" (I.i.284), "really" for "readily" (III.i.333), "unheeded" for "unheeding" (V.vi.60); the seventh edition prints "repeated" for "repented" (V.vii.41); in the eighth edition "being her Jest" (I.i.298) was obviously misread, and "her being in Jest" was supplied instead. The edition of 1750 prints "wrongfully" for "wrongly" (II.i.12), and "cold" for "cool" (II.ii.32). In only one instance is an earlier, better reading restored: the seventh and eighth editions print the erroneous "you see" for "you, I see" (IV.i.253), and the reading is corrected in the edition of 1735 and all editions thereafter.

In *The Careless Husband,* the significant authorial revisions, made in the third edition, constitute for the most part refinements of phrasing. For example, Lady Easy's warning to Lady Betty to beware of "being too eagerly Fond of Power" is changed to "trusting too far to Power alone" (II.i.148-49), and Sir Charles's admonition to Lord Foppington, "Nay, nay, we must have it—come, come, your Real Business here?" is changed to "Nay, nay, this is too much among Friends, my Lord; come, come—we must have it, your Real Business here?" (II.ii.65-66). In some cases Cibber simply shortened a speech. Sometimes an unsuitable figure is deleted, as in the case of Lord Foppington's comparison of a "Fine Woman" to a "Fine Oyster" (III.i.355t.n.). Elsewhere Cibber adds fanciful embellishment: in the quartos Sir Charles says, "a fine Woman's an Excuse for any thing," while in the revised editions he adds, "and the Scandal of being her Jest, is a Jest it self; we are all forc'd to be their Fools, before we can be their Favourites" (I.i.297-99).

The revisions in the 1721 edition make further refinements. For example, "Remains" becomes "small Remains" (III.i.229); "importantly" becomes "importunately" (V.vii.101); and Lady Betty's maltreatment of Lord Morelove, originally "public," is more precisely referred to as "made public" (V.vii.178). The changes in the 1721 edition are few, but since all the editions printed after 1721 seem to derive from the earlier duodecimos, the 1721 edition does, in fact, stand as the latest authoritative version of the text.

Textual abbreviations, with locations of copies used:

Q1 First quarto. London: William Davis, 1705. Yale.
Q2 Second quarto. The Second Edition. London: W. Davis, 1705. Yale.
D3 Duodecimo. The Third Edition. London: Jacob Tonson, 1713. Folger.
D4 Duodecimo. The Fourth Edition. London: Jacob Tonson, 1714. B.M.
D5 Duodecimo. The Fifth Edition. London: J. Tonson, 1718. B.M.

P In *Plays Written by Mr. Cibber. In Two Volumes.* Vol. I. London: Jacob Tonson, Bernard Lintot, William Mears, William Chetwood, 1721. Yale; B.M.; University of Pennsylvania.
D6 Duodecimo. The Sixth Edition. London: J. Tonson, 1725. B.M.
D7 Duodecimo. The Seventh Edition. London: J. Tonson, 1731. Yale.
D8 Duodecimo. The Eighth Edition. London: J. Tonson, 1734. Folger.
D9 Ninth duodecimo. London: Jacob Tonson, 1734. Yale.
D10 Tenth duodecimo. London: J. and R. Tonson, S. Draper, 1750. Harvard.
D11 Eleventh duodecimo. London: J. and R. Tonson, 1756. Folger.

Title page
Prol. to Sir FOP.] *om.* Q1

Dedication
DUKE of ARGYLE.] *Duke and Earl of* Argile, *Marquis of* Lorne, *Lord* Kintyre, Campbel *and* Lorne, *Heretable Master of the Houshold, Colonel and Captain of her Majesty's Troop of Horse-Guards in* Scotland, *and Knight of the most Ancient and Noble Order of St.* Andrew. Q1 *Duke of* Argyle, *Her Majesty's Lord High Commissioner for the Kingdom of* Scotland, *Marquis of* Kintyre *and* Lorne, *Earl of* Campbel, *&c. Heretable Justice General for the Shire of* Argyle, *Isles, and others; Heretable* Sheriff *of the said Shire; Heritable Great Master of the Houshold in* Scotland, *one of the extraordinary Lords of the Sessions; Brigadier General and Captain of Her Majesty's Life Guard of Horse; Brigadier General and Colonel of a Regiment of Fusiliers, in the Service of their High and Mightinesses the States General, one of Her Majesty's most Honourable Privy Council, and Knight of the most Ancient and most Noble Order of the* Thistle. Q2
17 World] Word D6
28 proper] a proper Q1-2, D3-11
30 stopt] stop D10
35 for me] me for Q1-2, D3
53 farther] further Q1-2, D3
58 CIBBER.] Q1-2, D3-11 add date: "Decem. 15. 1704."

Prologue Upon the last Campaign
31 *make*] *made* D6-11
55 *cease.*] Q1-2 print Epilogue following Prologue Upon the last Campaign.

Dramatis Personae
Dramatis Personae] The Persons Q1-2
MEN.] *om.* Q1-2, D3-4
WOMEN.] *om.* Q1-2, D3-4
SCENE] The *SCENE* Q1-2

I.i
7 Th'] The D6-11
42 torn] tore Q1-2, D3
49 of] or Q1-2, D3-11
58 he's] he is D5-11
71 I] *om.* Q1-2, D3-11
80 you not] not you Q1-2, D3-11
84 say to] do with Q1-2
148 [*Exit.*] *om.* Q1-2
149 Soldiers–] Soldiers–[*Ex.* Edg. Q1-2

186 Upon . . . don't.] I don't really Q1-2
197 I–I–] –I– D7-11
206 you] *om.* D6-11
239 –I] –nay I Q1-2, D3
247 my] *om.* D6-11
266 so.] so. [*Re-enter the Servant.* Q1-2
284 sillily] silly D6-11
297-99 thing . . . Favourites.] thing. Q1-2
298 being her] her being in D8-11
300 are willing] take a great deal of Pains Q1-2
302 I'm] I am Q1-2, D3-5
310 late] *om.* Q1-2
320 Commoner] Gentleman Q1-2
341 I'm] I am Q1-2, D3-11
343 think . . . that] think that Q1-2
351 a Clock] o'clock D10-11
357 an] a Q1-2
357 and] *om.* Q1-2
375 he is] he's Q1-2, D3-11

II.i

5 What] What, Q1, D3, 5-10
12 wrongly] wrongfully D10-11
14 I'm] I am Q1
33 had] wou'd Q1-2, D3-11
54 'em] them D9-11
59 not] not to Q1
63 in it] in't Q1-2, D3-11
109 generally] always Q1-2
109 that that] that D9-11
120 there] with her D8-11
120 seen,] seen her Q1-2
131 is] are D7-11
131 makes] make D6-11
146 in] *om.* D5
147 'em] them D7-11
148-49 trusting . . . alone] being too eagerly Fond of Power Q1-2
166 *Arm in Arm*] *om.* Q1-2

II.ii

8 there] here D9-10
10 There–[*Paying the Money.*] *om.* Q1-2
12 on?] forward?–here– Q1-2
13 agreeably] agreeable Q2, D3
20 convince] satisfie Q1-2
21 &c.] *om.* Q1-2
25 Well-jointured] Well-jointed Q1-2
26 on] of Q1-2, D3
31 you] ye D10-11
32 cool] cold D10-11
35 *Foppington!*] *Foppington*'s come. Q1-2
38 you–] you–My Dear Q1; you–My Dear. Q2
39 My dear] *om.* Q1-2
44 a] *om.* Q1-2
46 so,] so, my Lord, Q1-2, D3-1
51 Come, come] Come, come, my Lord, Q1-2
52 there] here Q1-2
63 Pox! prithee] prithee Pax! Q1-2
65-66 this . . . it] we must have it–come, come, Q1-2
70 Thousand] Thousand Pound Q1-2
71 or so;] *om.* Q1-2
74 manage] menage Q1
75 of] of some Q1-2
77 O!] Pshah! Q1-2
79 For] For, all this while, Q1-2
80 Bet] Bet, that Q1-2
82 happen] Happens Q1-2
86 Pound] Pounds D8-11
96 Month] Fortnight Q1-2
107 Husband's Inclinations] Husband Q1-2
112 Add] And Q1-2, D3
113 extremely] very Q1-2
141 But . . . Lord,] my Lord, but since you are thus indifferent, Q1-2

148 so] *om.* Q1-2
150 had been] were Q1-2
151 me in] her into Q1-2
151 Thousand] Thousand Pound, Q1-2
171 chief] *om.* Q1-2
176 of] of Having Q1-2
185 Lord,] Lord, since the World sees you make so little of the Difficulty, Q1-2
186 so] too Q1-2
189 stop] stap Q1-2, D3
192 let 'em] let them Q1-2, D7-11
196 them] 'em Q1-2
202 it] it on Q1-2
206-07 Candle-light.] Candle-light, ha! ha! Q1-2
210 Woman.] Woman, ha! ha! Q1-2
225 severe] formal Q1-2
228 o'the] on the Q1-2
228 Duce] Devil Q1-2
241 very] *om.* Q1-2
245 a] the Q1-2
248 you] you, that Q1-2
249 but she did] that she did not Q1-2; that she did D3
261 before] before; ha! ha! Q1-2
265 O,] *om.* Q1-2
266 burst] Busted Q1-2
266 Heel,] Heel, and D5-11
268s.d. [*A* . . . Charles.] Q1-2 print s.d. following line 269.
276 within] within, that Q1-2
278 guess who] know whom Q1-2
281 making] *om.* Q1-2

III.i

SCENE I.] *om.* Q1-2
29 her] her late Q1-2
37 you] you a Q1-2
51 are] were Q1-2
62 satisfy'd,] satisfy'd, that Q1-2
63 all] all that Q1-2
63 not] *om.* Q1-2
74 oblige the] oblige Q1-2, D3-11
77 you . . . of] you would Q1; you'd dispose Q2; you'd think of D3-11
77s.d. [*Going . . . her.*] *om.* Q1-2
79 I . . . Ladyship;] I have got it in my Head too, Q1-2; I'm as ready as your Ladyship; D6-11
81 ye] you Q1-2, D3
83 ye] the Q1-2
87 your] this Q1-2
88 you would] you'd Q1-2, D3-11
88 Soul] Eyes Q1-2
106 keep] kept Q2
110 [*Aside.*]] *om.* Q1-2
115 [*Aside.*] *om.* Q1-2
116 keeping a Letter] keeping-Letter Q2. In some copies of Q1, e.g. University of Chicago and Bodleian [Malone 122(3)], the "a," which occurs at the end of a line, does not appear; in another Bodleian copy [Douce P. subt. 74(5)] neither the "a" nor the "g" of "Keeping" appears. This probably resulted in the erroneous reading in Q2. The 1710 T. Johnson piracy attempts to correct the error by altering to "keeping Letters."
119 my] my Hood and Q1-2
122 [*Aside.*] *om.* Q1-2
125 *Exit smiling.*] *Exit.* [*After some Pause Lady* Graveairs *speaks.* Q1-2
128 is't] is it Q1-2, D3-11
131 this] it Q1-2
132s.d. *with a Scarf.*] *om.* Q1-2
137 before] at first Q1-2

140	Then] Why then Q1-2
145	Pleasure] Diversion Q1-2
145	rises] arises D7-11
145	of] of an Q1-2
162	Humh] Hah Q1-2
162	he is] he's Q1-2, D3-11
171	'em] them D7
178	No;] O! Q1-2
178	You] No, you Q1-2
185	Madam–I] Madam, I have told you that Reproaches will never do your Business with me: I Q1-2
191	*an*] *a* D10-11
204	I have] I've Q1
208	some] some Remedy for Q1-2
211	ha! ha!] *om.* Q1-2
212	she] she has Q1-2
213	Nature] Humour Q1-2
215	at the last she] she at last Q1-2
216	ha!] *om.* Q1-2
218	between . . . her] before my Lord Q1-2
229	small] *om.* Q1-2, D3-11
231	Handkerchief] Handkercher Q1
233	[*In . . . Tone.*] *om.* Q1-2
234	me?] me? [*Smiling.* Q1-2
250	stap] stop D9-11
255	her] *om.* Q1-2
270	That's] [*aside.*] That's Q1-2
270	Bite] a Bite D7-11
270	I'm] I am D6-11
270	sure–he'd] sure, I know he'd Q1-2
271	[*Aside.*] *om.* Q1-2
274	Nothing] O! Nothing Q1-2
278	him] him. [*Goes to L.* Fop. Q1-2
284s.d.	*Struggles*] *Struggling* D6-11
285	ha! ha!] *om.* Q1-2
285s.d.	*Struggling*] *Struggles* D6-11
286	Well–if] Well seriously, if Q1-2
304	immediately] when there's Occasion Q1-2
304	*Exit.*] *Exit Sir* Cha. Q1; *Exit Sir* Charles Q2
310s.d.	*earnestly on*] *very earnestly upon* Q1-2
319	therefore] and therefore Q1-2
333	readily] really D6-11
336	sometimes] *om.* Q1-2
345	once a Lady] a Lady once Q1-2
346	good Nature] Honour Q1-2
351	Goust] Gust D7-11
353	So!] So! [*Aside.* Q1-2
355	Zested.] Zested; a Fine Woman, like a Fine Oyster, needs no Sawce but her own Q1-2
368	Company.] Company, ha! h Q1-2
370s.d.	*her.*] *her Manner.* Q1-2
375	I see] *om.* Q1-2
375	her;] her, I find; Q1-2
379	you] it Q1-2
384	heh! heh! heh!] heh! heh! ha! Q1-2
392	I once] once I Q1-2, D8-11
407	Ay] Ah Q1-2, D3-11
411	Ladyship's] Ladyship is D1
421	ha! ha! ha!] *om.* Q1-2
422	[*Aside.*]] [*disdainfully, and aside.*] Q1-2
426	'em] them D8-11
428	imagine] Imagine, that Q1-
441s.d.	[*Lady . . .* Foppington.] *om* Q1-2
442	O!] *om.* Q1-2
451	I have] I've Q1-2, D3-11
469	Rally] Railery Q1-2; Railly D3-4
471	I am] I'm Q1-2, D3-11
476	[*Aside.*] *om.* Q1-2
502	in] at Q1-2
507	with all] withal Q1-2

511-12 Well . . . how] But how, Madam, Q1-2
521 fail,] fail Q1-2, D7-8
522 Ha! ha! ha!] Ha! ha! Q1-2
542 No, no;] No, Q1-2
550 [*Exit.*] [*Exit L.* Betty. Q1-2
561 Tittle] Title Q2
564 all] *om.* Q1-2
565 [*Exit.*] Q1 adds "*The End of the Third ACT.*"

IV.i

SCENE I.] *om.* Q1-2
s.d. SCENE . . . Easy.] *The* Scene *the* Terrace./ *Enter Lady* Easy *and Lady* Betty. Q1-2
6 ingenuously] ingeniously Q1-2, D3
14 addressings] addressing Q1-2, D3-11
15 I] Humh [*Smiling.*] I Q1-2
31 Were] Was Q1-2
33 Hah] Hay Q1
39 for] *om.* Q1-2
42 comfortably] comfortable Q2
52 give] proceed to Q1-2
60 No,] *om.* Q1-2
81 Ha!] *om.* Q1-2
86 Hugh] Auh Q1-2; Huh D3
88 Address] Address to Q1-2, D3-10
93 Friend] Friends Q1-2
112 as] and D7-11
113 chuse] chose Q1-2, D3
145 them] 'em Q1-2, D3-11
146 Moment] Minute Q1-2
156 or] or the Q1-2
164 owing] owning D4-5
175 least] least distant Q1-2
192 this] his D7-11
193 Danger] Dangers Q1-2
198 into] to Q1-2
199 dares] dare D6-11
202 [*Walking disorder'd.*] *om.* D10-11
203 *Lady Ea.*] La. *Bet.* P; La. *Ea.* [*Aside.*] Q1-2
206 [*Aside.*] *om.* Q1-2
208 Oh!] 'Pshah! Q1-2
216 this] the D6-11
220 it] indeed it Q1-2, D3-11
220 Indifference] Indifferent Q1-2
225s.d. *a*] *and a* Q1-2
229 O,] *om.* Q1-2
231 hear 'em,] have 'em, for Q1-2
244 And] Ha! ha! And Q1-2
253 you, I] you D7-8
255 so!] so! Ha! Ha! Q1-2
258 find] see Q1-2
264 that] this D7-11
270 it's] 'tis D8-11
275 the] that Q1-2
284 Preferments] Preferment Q1-2
288 all] always D10-11
292 Ha! ha!] *om.* Q1-2
296 great] such Q1-2
306 she's] she is Q1-2
332 Privilege] Privilege that Q1-2
373 Ha! ha! ha!] *om.* Q1-2
394 dem me] demme Q1-2, D3-11
414 Ladyship's.] Ladyship's. [*Goes from her.* Q1-2
424 with all] withal Q1-2
444 dares] dare Q1-2
455 *Singing.*] Q1 adds "*The End of the Fourth Act.*"

V.i

SCENE I.] *om.* Q1-2
8 as] *om.* D9-11
46 a Clock] o'clock D11
51 [*Exit.*] [*Exit. L.* Gra. Q1-2
69 not] *om.* Q1-2
82-83 ha! ha! ha!] ha! ha! ha! ha! Q1-2

87 *Betty.*] Q1-2 add another line, "L. *Bett.* Pshah!" before [*Exeunt.*

V.ii.

7 where] when D6-11
11 besides] beside Q1-2
21 Fancy] great Fancy Q1-2
24 Besides] Beside Q1-2
29s.d. *Sits*] *He sits* Q1-2. Q1-2 print s.d. following *l.* 30.
39 Faces] Face D6-11
44 I'm] I am Q1-2, D3-11

V.iii

6 easily be] be easily D5-11
14 with all] withal Q1
36 'em] them D7-11
46 Ha! ha! ha!] Ha! ha! D7-11
48 too] *om.* D7-11
50 Lady] Ha! ha! Lady Q1-2
60 a] *om.* Q1. In Q1 the "a" would have occurred at the end of a line, under the "f" of "of" in the line above. It appears that in some copies the "a" slipped out of the line and the "f" dropped down into its place, producing the reading "f Lampoon."
64 we] one Q1-2, D3-11
71 we] we go Q1-2, D3-4
76 [*Exit* . . . Easy.]] Q1-2 print s.d. following *l.* 77.
78 Oh!] *om.* Q1-2
84 come] comes Q2

V.iv

6 on't] on it Q1-2, D3-11

V.v

s.d. *Then*] *And then* Q1-2
s.d. *trembles, some time*] *trembles some time,* Q1
15 Where] When D6-11
18 warm] warms Q2
22 th'] the Q1-2
23-27 But . . . it.] Q1-2 print as prose.
25 its] his Q1-2
27s.d. *Takes . . . Head.*] *Takes her Steinkirk from her Neck, an lays it gently over his Head.* Q1-2
29s.d. Edging *wakes,*] *at which the Maid waking starts,* Q1-2
33 [*Bell*] [*Runs to the Glass. Bell* Q1-2
34-35 [*Runs to the Glass.*] *om.* Q1-2
38 [*Puts . . . Wig.*] *om.* Q1-2
40 not] *om.* D7
51 confirm] confirms D7-11

V.vi

2 I–I–I–I] I–I–I Q1-2
5 [*Aside.*]] *om.* Q1-2, D3-11
8 Heigh . . . *down.*]] [*Sitting down.*] Heigh ho! Q1-2
13 Fears] Tears Q1-2
21 the] those Q1-2
43 *Work*] *Scarf* Q1-2
53 my] that Q1-2
56 an] a D6-11
60 unheeding] unheeded D5-1
70 often] *om.* D5-11
82 a] an Q1-2, D3-11
93 a] *om.* D10-11
98 be] *om.* Q1-2
106 you are] you're Q2, D3-11
116 th'] the D11
124 you have] you've Q1-2, D3-11
153s.d. *it*] *it to* Q1-2, D3, 5-11
167 waits] waits for D6-11
180 *Exit*] *Exeunt* Q1-2

V.vii

1 You have] You've Q1-2, D3-11

3 can't] can't yet Q1-2
6 Indeed I am] Indeed I'm D6-11
20 Lord.] Lord, ha! ha! ha! Q1-2
22 I'll] I will Q1-2, D3-11
29 [*Exit.*] *om.* Q1-2
38 Thoughts] Thought Q1-2
41 repented] repeated D7-11
57 I am] I'm Q1-2, D3-11
62 Insults] Insult D7-11
69 only should] shou'd only D6-11
92 has] was D10-11
100 had] *om.* Q1-2
101 importunately] importantly Q1-2, D3-11
145 you] we Q1-2, D3-11
151 inveterably] inveterately Q1-2 (see also *The Lady's Last Stake,* V.iii.3 t.n.). Though Arthur E. Case corrects to "inveterately" (*British Dramatists from Dryden to Sheridan,* p. 434), I have retained it as it reads in the copy-text. Since it occurs twice, both times in editions to which the author is supposed to have set his hand, it may be a Cibberism.
178 made] *om.* Q1-2, D3-11
181 offer'd] offer'd by D6-11
192 the] *om.* P
205 an] a Q1-2
214 the] your Q1-2
235 take] take away D7-11
237 'tis] it's D11
241 in] with D8-11
249 I own] own D8-11
251 bitten] Bitter Q1-2
267 Yes,] Ye! D7-10
270 you] you yet Q1-2
275 I] I now Q1-2, D3-11
281 think] think it Q1-2, D3-6
303 *this*] *his* D7-11
319s.d. *Exeunt.*] Q1-2 add "*FINIS.*"

Epilogue

EPILOGUE.] Q1-2 print Epilogue following Prologue Upon the last Campaign.
7 *from*] *in* D8-11
15 *Fox's*] *Fox* D9-11
16 *your Judgment*] *our Judgment* D8-11
FINIS.] *om.* Q1-2

THE LADY'S LAST STAKE

The Lady's Last Stake was first published in small quarto in 1707. This quarto is undated, and 1708 is accepted as the date of publication by Nicoll (II, 310) and *The London Stage* (pt. 2, p. 160). However, *The Daily Courant* for December 29, 1707, advertises: "To Morrow will be publish'd, The Last new Comedy entitul'd, The Lady's Last Stake, or, The Wife's Resentment." The *Courant* for December 31, 1707, notes that the play was "Just Publish'd," and *The London Gazette* for January 1-5, 1707/8, advertises: "This Day is publish'd, The Lady's last Stake; or, The Wife's Resentment."

The play was not published again until it was included, with authorial revisions, in Volume II of *Plays Written by Mr. Cibber. In Two Volumes,* in 1721. The third edition appeared, without further authoritative changes, in duodecimo in 1732; it was reprinted, still as the third edition, in 1736, and again in 1747, though not this time as the third edition. Some copies of the 1736 edition are really only reissues of the edition of 1732, differing from it only in the cancel title of 1736, and therefore are of no real bibliographical interest to this edition. The 1736 third edition appears also in Volume III of the *Dramatick Works* of 1736; the 1747 edition appears also in Volume I of the *Dramatick Works* of 1754. It is included in the collections of 1760 and 1777.

The 1721 edition of *The Lady's Last Stake* was apparently printed from a corrected copy of the first quarto. Cibber anglicized Lord George's name from Brillant to Brilliant throughout the 1721 edition, but in two instances—in both of which the name appears set off from the text by spacing or by upper-case type (in the Dramatis Personae and in the signature of a letter, V.i.326)—the spelling of the quarto is retained.

The duodecimo edition of 1732 reprints most of the revisions made in the 1721 edition, but in some instances restores the reading in the quarto. For example, "*her Dangers*" is restored in place of "*such Dangers*" (Prologue, l. 43); "sorry I have made this rout about it, Sir," in place of "sorry I have made this rout about it" (III.i.250); and "Belief," in place of "Relief" (V.i.208). The editions of 1736 and 1747 follow that of 1732 in this respect.

The edition of 1732 also introduces many variant readings which indicate slight deterioration of the text. It prints "I see you have not given your self much Contrivance" where the 1721 edition prints "I see you have not given your self much trouble in the Contrivance" (I.i.221-22). "Restless Love" replaces "Resistless Love" (I.i.412), and an entire line (V.iii.58) has been omitted. The edition of 1747 deteriorates still further, printing "W'are Mortals" for "'Ware Morals" (II.ii.57).

Cibber made few changes in *The Lady's Last Stake*, but in one instance, at least, he refined the dialogue. He cut an insulting comparison from Lord Wronglove's reprimand of his wife (III.i.286t.n.), and a long passage from Lord George's speculation on the success of his trap for Lady Gentle (V.ii.120t.n.). In addition he made many small changes to improve the sense. Typical of these is Lord George's protest, in response to Sir John's request for a "humble extempore favour," that he is "out of—Gentlewomen, my self at present" (V.i.164), where Q reads "out of order, Gentlewomen."

Textual abbreviations, with locations of copies used:

- Q1 First quarto. London: Bernard Lintott, [1707]. Yale.
- P In *Plays Written by Mr. Cibber. In Two Volumes.* Vol. II. London: B. Lintot, W. Mears, W. Chetwood, 1721. Yale; University of Pennsylvania (two copies).
- D3 Duodecimo. The Third Edition. London: B. Lintot, W. Feales, 1732. Folger.
- D4 Duodecimo. The Third Edition. London: W. Feales, 1736. Folger.
- D5 Third Duodecimo. London: Henry Lintot, 1747. Rochester.

Epistle Dedicatory

16 trivial] mercenary Q
22 presumptuous] presuming Q
49 Labourers] Labourer Q, P
56 of oppressing] to oppress Q

58 to] *om.* Q
67 the Actors] we Q

Prologue
7 *seem*] *seem'd* D3-5
21 *sure's*] *sure* D5
39 *That . . . make*] *That flatter'd Hope lets hard-press'd Virtue make* Q
43 *such*] *her* Q, D3-5

Dramatis Personae
2 Lord *George Brilliant*] Sir *George Brillant* Q; Lord *George Brillant* P

I,i
6 spare] spear P
24 to] *om.* D3-5
70 excusing it;] excusing, it Q; excusing it, D3-5
98 go] go and D3-5
113 Discovery;] Discovery Q, P; Discovery! D5
118 Auh] Huh D5
128 Bussness] Business Q, D3-5
136 it was] 'twas Q
214 me] *om.* Q
221 trouble in the] *om.* D3-5
253 an] a D4
266 I have] I've Q
321 Agreeably] Agreeable D4
363 an] a D4
412 Resistless] Restless D3-5

II.i
3 it self] its self D3-5
14 it] *om.* Q
35 them] 'em Q
83 I'll] to Q
107 be] be most Q, D3-5
130 a Husband] an Husband Q
138 'em] them D4
141 no] *om.* Q
153 me] *om.* D5
169 of] *om.* P
171 from] of D4
171 an] a D5
195 I'm] I am Q
239 Exit] Exeunt Q, P, D3-5

II.ii
s.d. *Mrs.* Conquest,] *om.* Q, P, D3-5
45 Reprive] Reprieve Q, D3-5
57 'Ware Morals] W'are Mortals D5
60 Pound] Pounds D3-5
68 shou'd like] shou'd, like Q, P
89 he has] h'as D4
98 any] any one Q
126 dropt] dropt her Q
160 the Morning] a Morning Q
170 I'm] I am D4
204 Flint] Flints Q
236 Pound] Pounds D3-5
244 th'] the D3-5
The End of the Second Act.] *om.* Q

III.i
32 *Georgy*] *George* D4-5
49 *Lord Geo.*] *om.* Q The speech thus reads as a continuation of Miss Notable's.
56 a] *om.* Q
173 here] hear Q, D3-5
176 Life] Life, Q, D3-5
181 self] self, D3-5
186s.d. *gravely*] *very gravely* D4
191 him] him that D3-5
193 seen] known D4
200 Friend] my Friend Q
202 Ha! ha! ha!] Ha! ha! Q
206 Confidence] Confidant D3, 5; Confidante D4
213 a] an Q
238 Virtue] Virtues Q
250 it.] it, Sir. Q, D3-5
281s.d. *Street*] *Stairs* Q

286 for?—] for?—In just such a Trim have I seen a trigg'd up *Drury-Lane* Gentlewoman come daggled along from Market with a comfortable Pound of Beef-stakes upon a Scuer— Q
387 from] for Q
396 have] *om.* D3-5
433 the Husband's] Husband's Q
480 *Touchum*] *Touch 'em* D4
484 these] those Q
494 one's] one D5
524 Hand] Hands Q
570 nothing is] nothing's Q
576 Girl . . . part,] Girl; besides, th' imprudent part Q, P
586 doubly bound to] bound to doubly Q

IV.i
30 Handkercher] Steinkirk Q; Handkerchief D3-5
72 her Husband] a Husband Q, D3-5
106 th'] the D3-5
137 them] 'em Q, D3-5
187 *I'm*] *I am* D3-5
223 awaken'd] wak'd Q
225 she] she either Q
242 a Husband's] an Husband's Q, D3-5
253 more] the more D3-5
346 it] what D3-5
353 of] upon Q
361 sparking] sparkling Q, D3-5
419 from] for Q
451 undeceive] deceive D3-5
467 you've] you have D3-5
528 fair] *om.* P
549 your] your own D4
559 its] 'tis Q, D3-5
565 as entirely] is entirely D3-5
569 *John*] *Charles* Q, P, D3-5. He is called "Sir John" in every other instance in the play, but "*Charles*" is the reading here in all editions.

V.i
25 provident] very provident Q
72 are] am P
97 just] just now Q
164 of—Gentlewomen] of order, Gentlewomen Q
168 Instrumental] Instrumental. [*Aside.* Q
174 Diversion] Diversions D4
186 my] his Q
208 Relief] Belief Q, D3-5
247 th'] the D3-5
256 Tears] Fears Q
333-34 an honourable] a sincere Q
350 move: Away] move away Q

V.ii
6 run] ran Q
30 yet] and not Q
38 that] that from the Aim of Q
39 has] I've Q
47-48 I wou'd] I'd Q
52 Ladyship—] Ladyship then— Q
61 Pound] Pounds D3-5
69 the] a Q
109 inward] envious Q
120 that.] that a little. I fancy few Women have been better brib'd this Winter; and yet—let me see—if I succeed—wha will this whole Affair stand me in?—Um—half a Crown—eighteen Pence—and—eighteen Pence—Ay, just five and six Pence, Chair hire—not one single Tester more, but her own Money again by all that's—Greatly brought abou

If she complies—what a transcendant happy Dog am I? Q

148 them] 'em Q

182 Pound] Pounds D3-5

V.iii

3 inveterably] inveterately Q, D3-5 (see *The Careless Husband,* V.vii.149t.n.)

18 Purse] Purse that D4

30 Gentlemen] Gentleman P

43 *'em*] *them* D3-5

44 *They push,*] *om.* Q

58 Mrs. . . . Lord.] *om.* D3-5

58s.d. *Chairmen*] *Chairman* P, D3-5

V.v

s.d. *Lord* Wronglove] *om.* D3-5

11 surpriz'd] persuaded D4

31 help] hopes Q; helps D3-5

48 Excuse] Excuse at least Q

66 it was] 'twas Q, D3-5

66 Interest] my Jealous Love Q; my Interest D3-5

68 just] *om.* D3-5

82 dissembled] deceitful Q

86 t'] to D3-5

132 give] too Q

149 last, it seems,] last; it seems Q, P

150 you,] *om.* P

THE END.] FINIS. D3-5

Epilogue

EPILOGUE.] Q prints Epilogue immediately following Prologue.

13 *a Counter*] *the Counter* D3-5

26 *you're*] *you are* D3-5

35 *t'is*] *'tis* Q, D3-5

38 *Sound*] *Name* Q

NOTES

Abbreviations

Apology	*An Apology for the Life of Mr. Colley Cibber, Written by Himself.* Ed. Robert W. Lowe. 2 vols. London: John C. Nimmo, 1889.
Barker	Barker, Richard Hindry. *Mr. Cibber of Drury Lane.* New York: Columbia University Press, 1939.
Bateson	Bateson, F. W. *English Comic Drama, 1700-1750.* Oxford: Clarendon Press, 1929.
Bernbaum	Bernbaum, Ernest. *The Drama of Sensibility.* Cambridge, Mass.: Harvard University Press, 1915.
Blackmore	Blackmore, Sir Richard. Preface to *Prince Arthur, An Heroick Poem,* in *Critical Essays of the Seventeenth Century.* Ed. J. E. Spingarn. 3 vols. Bloomington, Indiana: Indiana University Press, 1957. III, 227-41.
Collier	Collier, Jeremy. *A Short View of the Immorality, and Profaneness of the English Stage . . . .* London, 1698.
Companion	[Baker, David Erskine]. *The Companion to the Playhouse: Or, An Historical Account of all the Dramatic Writers (and their Works) . . . down to the Present Year 1764. Composed in the Form of a Dictionary.* 2 vols. London, 1764.
Comparison	*A Comparison Between the Two Stages, With an Examen of the Generous Conqueror; And Some Critical Remarks on the Funeral, or Grief Alamode, The False Friend, Tamerlane and others. In Dialogue.* London, 1702.
Congreve	*The Complete Plays of William Congreve.* Ed. Herbert Davis. Chicago: University of Chicago Press, 1967.
Croissant	Croissant, DeWitt C. *Studies in the Work of Colley Cibber.* Bulletin of the University of Kansas Humanistic Studies, I(1912), 1-69.
Cunningham	Cunningham, George H. *London, a Comprehensive Survey of the History, Traditions and Historical Associations of Buildings and Monuments.* London: J. M. Dent, 1931.

Davies	Davies, Thomas. *Dramatic Miscellanies: A New Edition.* 3 vols. London, 1785.
Dryden	*The Works of John Dryden.* Ed. Sir Walter Scott, rev. and corr. George Saintsbury. 18 vols. Edinburgh: W. Paterson, 1882-93.
ELH	*A Journal of English Literary History.*
Essays	*Essays of John Dryden.* Ed. W. P. Ker. 2 vols. Oxford: Clarendon Press, 1900.
Genest	Genest, John. *Some Account of the English Stage, From the Restoration in 1660 to 1830.* 10 vols. Bath, 1832.
Hill	Hill, Georgiana. *A History of English Dress.* 2 vols. New York: G. P. Putnam's Sons, 1883.
Laureat	*The Laureat: or the Right Side of Colley Cibber, Esq; . . . .* London, 1740.
The London Stage	*The London Stage, A Calendar of Plays, Entertainments . . . .* Ed. William Van Lennep, Emmett L. Avery, Arthur H. Scouten, George Winchester Stone, Jr., Charles Beecher Hogan. 5 pts. in 11 vols. Carbondale: Southern Illinois University Press, 1960-68.
Macaulay	Macaulay, Thomas Babington. *The History of England from the Accession of James II.* Ed. Douglas Jerrold. 4 vols. London: J. M. Dent, Everyman's Library, 1962.
Nicoll	Nicoll, Allardyce. *A History of English Drama, 1660-1900.* 6 vols. Cambridge: The University Press, 1965. Vol. I, 4th edition Vol. II, 3rd edition.
Pepys	*The Diary of Samuel Pepys.* Ed. Henry B. Wheatley. 8 vols. London: G. Bell, 1923.
PMLA	*Publications of the Modern Language Association of America.*
Pope	*The Poems of Alexander Pope: A One-Volume Edition of the Twickenham Text.* Ed. John Butt. New Haven: Yale University Press, 1963.
Rogers	Rogers, James E. Thorold. *The First Nine Years of the Bank of England.* Oxford: Clarendon Press, 1887.
Spectator	*The Spectator.* Ed. Donald F. Bond. 5 vols. Oxford: Clarendon Press, 1965.
Wycherley	*The Complete Works of William Wycherley.* Ed. Montague Summers. 4 vols. London: The Nonesuch Press, 1924.

HT	Head title
RT	Running title
s.d.	Stage direction
t.n.	Textual note

Notes to Preface

1 *The First Epistle of the Second Book of Horace Imitated,* l. 92, *Pope,* p. 639.
2 *Companion,* II, Article "Cibber."
3 Davies, III, 504.
4 Ernest Bernbaum in *The Drama of Sensibility* (1915); F. W. Bateson in *English Comic Drama, 1700-1750* (1929); Joseph Wood Krutch in *Comedy and Conscience After the Restoration* (New York: Columbia University Press, 1949); and Allardyce Nicoll in *A History of English Drama, 1660-1900,* I (1965).
5 This term is Cibber's designation for *The Rival Queans, with the Humours of Alexander the Great.*
6 For the canon and classifications I have relied chiefly on Allardyce Nicoll's handlists (I, 397; II, 306-13, 433-34). Croissant (pp. 2, 5, 9-10) ascribes *Bulls and Bears,* a farce, and *Cinna's Conspiracy,* a tragedy, to Cibber. Nicoll includes both among plays of unknown authors (II, 367-68), noting that the tragedy is "ascribed" to Cibber. John Nichols (*Literary Anecdotes of the Eighteenth Century,* VIII [London, 1814], 295) records that on March 16, 1712, Bernard Lintot paid Cibber £13 for *Cinna's Conspiracy,* but this may indicate only that he had a managerial and not an authorial interest in it. The play does not appear in editions of his collected plays printed during his lifetime. *Hob, or the Country Wake,* accepted as Cibber's by Nicoll, is regarded as an attribution by Leonard R. N. Ashley (*Colley Cibber* [New York: Twayne, 1965], p. 206) and by Richard Hindry Barker (p. 266).
7 *The Dunciad* (1743), I, 128-33, *Pope,* p. 726.
8 His *Love Makes a Man* (1700) combines Fletcher's *The Elder Brother* with *The Custom of the Country. She Wou'd and She Wou'd Not* (1702) is an adaptation of John Learned's *The Counterfeits. The Comical Lovers* (1706/7) draws on Dryden's *Secret Love, or The Maiden Queen* and *Marriage à la Mode. The Double Gallant* (1707) derives from two plays by William Burnaby, and from Mrs. Centlivre's *Love at a Venture. The Rival Fools* (1708/9) is based on Fletcher's *Wit at Several Weapons. The Non-Juror* (1717) and *The Refusal, or the Ladies Philosophy* (1720/1) derive from Molière's *Tartuffe* and *Les Femmes Savantes* respectively. *The Provok'd*

Husband (1727/8) is an adaptation and completion of Vanbrugh's unfinished *A Journey to London.* Of the tragedies, *The Tragical History of King Richard III* (1699/1700) and *Papal Tyranny in the Reign of King John* (1744/5) are adaptations of Shakespeare; *Ximena, or the Heroick Daughter* (1712) is based on Corneille's *Le Cid;* and *Caesar in Egypt* (1724) uses something of Fletcher's *The False One* and Corneille's *Pompée.* In addition to borrowing, Cibber recast material from his own earlier works. He took his farce, *The School Boy; or, The Comical Rival* (1702) from the comic subplot of his *Woman's Wit* (1696). His second ballad opera, *Damon and Phillida* (1720), had been a comic plot in his first, *Love in a Riddle,* performed unsuccessfully earlier in the same year (see Croissant, pp. 2-27).

9 *Apology,* I, 264.

10 *Bell's British Theatre,* 20 vols. (London, 1776-80) prints *The Careless Husband* (Vol. VIII), *Love's Last Shift* (Vol. XVII), and *The Lady's Last Stake* (Vol. XIX). *Bell's* also includes Cibber's *The Provok'd Husband, Love Makes a Man, She Wou'd and She Wou'd Not, The Refusal,* and *The Double Gallant. Jones's British Theatre,* 9 vols. (Dublin, 1795) includes *The Careless Husband,* as do *The British Drama; Comprehending the Best Plays in the English Language,* 5 vols. (London, 1804), edited by Sir Walter Scott, and *The British Theatre,* 25 vols. (London, 1808), edited by Mrs. Inchbald. The most enduring of Cibber's plays, *The Careless Husband* was included in the following later collections: *The British Drama: A Collection of the Most Esteemed Tragedies, Comedies, Operas, and Farces, in the English Language,* 2 vols. (London, 1829; Philadelphia, 1832); *The London Stage,* 4 vols. (London, [c. 1843]). These collections all present, not critical texts, but versions taken from acting texts.

Love's Last Shift has appeared in two twentieth-century anthologies, *Plays of the Restoration and Eighteenth Century,* ed. Dougald MacMillan and Howard Mumford Jones (New York, 1931) and *Representative English Drama from Dryden to Sheridan,* ed. Frederick Tupper and James W. Tupper (New York, 1934). Both editions use the first quarto as the copy-text. The MacMillan-Jones anthology prints the play with corrections from later editions, but without a full textual apparatus; the Tupper edition indicates that collations have been made, but no textual notes are given. There are five modern publications of *The Careless Husband.* D. M. E. Habbema's edition, in *An Appreciation of Colley Cibber, Actor and Dramatist* (Amsterdam, 1928), is based on the first quarto, collated with the 1710 T. Johnson Hague edition, the 1721 large quarto, the 1723 Dublin sixth edition, and the London editions of 1731 and 1733. F. Dorothy Senior's *The Life and Times of Colley Cibber* (London, 1928) includes a reprint of the play, but does not provide a critical edition. The play appears in *British Plays from the Restoration to 1820,* ed. Montrose J. Moses (Boston, 1929), in a text based on one of the early quartos, with no textual notes. William W. Appleton has edited the play for the Regents Restoration Drama Series (Lincoln,

Nebraska, 1966), using the first quarto as copy-text and collating only the second quarto and the large quarto of 1721. Arthur E. Case's edition in *British Dramatists from Dryden to Sheridan,* ed. George H. Nettleton and Arthur E. Case (Boston, 1939), is by far the best of these editions. It uses the 1721 large quarto as copy-text, collating it with the early quartos and with a representative selection of the later duodecimo editions. None of the modern editors has, however, collated all of the London editions printed during Cibber's lifetime, and none has had access to the crucial third edition, in which the major textual alterations occur. There is no modern edition of *The Lady's Last Stake.*

11 *Apology,* I, 264.

12 For a discussion of the nature of these revisions, see Appendix III.

Notes to Introduction

THE PLAYS

1 *Apology*, I, 213.
2 Davies, III, 439.
3 *Apology*, I, 214.
4 *Ibid.*, pp. 185-86.
5 *Ibid.*, pp. 205-09.
6 *Ibid.*, p. 212.
7 *Ibid.*, p. 135.
8 Anthony Aston, *A Brief Supplement to Colley Cibber, Esq; His Lives of the Late Famous Actors and Actresses*, in *Apology*, II, 311.
9 *The London Stage*, pt. 1, p. cv.
10 See Davies, III, 88-89.
11 *Apology*, I, 220.
12 See *The London Stage*, pt. 2, and George C. D. Odell, *Annals of the New York Stage* (New York: Columbia University Press, 1927), I, 63. For the suggestion of an earlier, private presentation in Virginia, see Carl R. Dolmetsch, "William Byrd II: Comic Dramatist?", *Early American Literature* 6 (1971), 18-19. (The chief contention of this article, that Byrd may have had a hand in the composition of *The Careless Husband*, is an interesting speculation, based on Byrd's incorporation of the song from the play into one of his notebooks. There is no real proof, however, that Byrd's copy antedates the first performance of the play.)
13 *A Selection of the Letters of Horace Walpole*, ed. W. S. Lewis (New York: Harper and Brothers, 1926), II, 396; *Companion*, I, Article "*The Careless Husband.*"
14 *Apology*, I, 308.
15 *Ibid.*, p. 309. See also William Egerton, *Faithful Memoirs of the Life, Amours and Performances, of That justly Celebrated, and most Eminent Actress of her Time, Mrs. Anne Oldfield* (London, 1731), p. 3.
16 Barker, pp. 65-66; see also Percy Fitzgerald, *A New History of the English Stage* (London: Tinsley, 1882), I, 236-65.
17 Barker, pp. 67-73.
18 *Apology*, II, 2.
19 *Ibid.*, I, 160.

20 *Ibid.*, p. 314.

21 Cibber boasted, in his dedication of the play: "the Fable is entirely my own." He was, of course, using traditional comic formulae. Amanda's lure is part of a tradition as old as Tamar's use of a harlot's disguise to conceive twin sons by Judah. Boccaccio's ninth novel of the third day—Giletta's conception of twins by Beltramo and the securing of his ring as proof—presents the story in the form Shakespeare used in *All's Well That Ends Well.* In James Shirley's *The Gamester,* Wilding orders his meek-seeming wife to bring her cousin Penelope to his bed and finds instead Mrs. Wilding in disguise.

Among contemporary plays, Thomas D'Urfey's *Madam Fickle, or The Witty False One* (1676) and *The Virtuous Wife, or Good Luck at Last* (1679) both deal with the situation of a wife resorting to trickery to win her husband back. Cibber's familiarity with D'Urfey's *Love for Money, or, The Boarding School* (1690) seems to be evident in the dialogue between Loveless and Young Worthy in Act I. There and in Act I of D'Urfey's play, two young gallants rail against hypocritical morality and discuss the arrangements they have made to secure their futures by duping old fools out of fortunes.

It seems probable that Cibber had James Carlile's *The Fortune Hunters; or, Two Fools Well Met* (1689) in mind when he worked out the subplot of *Love's Last Shift.* Though the similarities are only superficial, the subplot of *The Fortune Hunters* presents a pair of sons, the younger a disinherited rake; a switch of brides in a wedding in the dark; and a repentant old father. Carlile's two fops, Shamtown and Littlegad, anticipate the follies of Sir Novelty, the one being an affecter of intrigues, the other of clothing. Like Sir Novelty, Shamtown meets public disgrace in a plot which substitutes a disguised Littlegad where he expects to find his mistress.

22 Nicoll, I, 278. Bonamy Dobrée, too, accuses Cibber of "having in the first four acts given a loose rein to the most lubric fancy" (*English Literature in the Early Eighteenth Century, 1700-1740* [Oxford: Clarendon Press, 1964], p. 228).

THE CONTEXTS

23 Nicoll (II, 180) cites the "deliberate enunciation of a moral or social problem"; Bernbaum (p. 2) writes that "confidence in the goodness of average human nature is the mainspring of sentimentalism"; Bateson (p. 6) refers to "sensitiveness . . . to the claims of one's neighbors, and to an abstract ideal of order."

24 Krutch finds sentimentalism to be "merely facile and, usually, shallow, illogical emotion" (*Comedy and Conscience After the Restoration*, p. 192). Bernbaum (p. 10) considers that moving the emotions is the way good nature is revealed.

25 Smith, "Shadwell, the Ladies, and the Change in Comedy," in *Restoration Drama,* ed. John Loftis (New York: Oxford University Press, 1966), p. 238; Sherbo, *English Sentimental Drama* (East Lansing, Michigan: Michiga State University Press, 1957), pp. 32-71.

26 Sherbo, p. 100.

27 *The Plays of Richard Steele,* ed. Shirley Strum Kenny (Oxford: Clarendon Press, 1971), pp. 299-300.

28 "An Essay on the Theatre; Or, A Comparison Between Laughing and Senti mental Comedy," *Westminster Magazine,* I (January, 1773), 4-6.

29 See L. J. Potts, *Comedy* (London: Hutchinson, 1949), p. 50; also Norman N. Holland, *The First Modern Comedies* (Cambridge, Mass.: Harvard University Press, 1959), pp. 29-37.

30 Perhaps we are justified in rejecting Lamb's description of the comedy of manners ("On the Artificial Comedy of the Last Century," *The Works of Charles and Mary Lamb,* ed. E. V. Lucas [London: Methuen, 1903], II, 142) as "that happy breathing-place from the burthen of a perpetual moral questioning." But his vision of the "artificial" world of the comedy of ma ners has something to be said for it. It is, Lamb says (p. 143), "altogether a speculative scene of things," where "pleasure is duty, and the manners perfect freedom." Lamb's ideas have inspired the most consistent single body of criticism about the comedy of manners, excepting the equal torrent that flows from the moralists down to L. C. Knights. John Palmer (*The Comedy of Manners* [London: G. Bell, 1913], p. 289) accepts the "artificial" world of Lamb, but goes a step further, acknowledging the con nection between the work of art and its historical context. The picture of life is "conditioned by the period in which [the artist] lives, the moral law which his moods and characters unconsciously obey. He does not aim at enforcing or weakening the moral code; but in the result he necessarily does so." Bonamy Dobrée (*Restoration Comedy* [Oxford: Oxford Univers Press, 1924], p. 32) judges that the characters and dialogues of the comed of manners exist only for "crushing ridicule." He thinks that this kind of comedy tries as hard as Elizabethan comedy to "reveal mankind and consider the effect of passions." But he, too, is of the school of Lamb, agreein that the comedy of manners is intellectual, "entirely without the metaphysical element." Finally, Thomas H. Fujimura (*The Restoration Comedy of Wit* [Princeton: Princeton University Press, 1952], p. 59) describes the comedy of manners as the "aesthetic" view of life. The artist and his chara ters, by means of their wit, observe and arrange life in patterns to suit thei pleasure.

31 *Shakespeare and the Allegory of Evil* (New York: Columbia University Press, 1958), p. 151. See also Chapter V, "Emergence of the Vice," pp. 130-150.

32 I.i.200-02, *The Dramatic Works of Sir George Etherege,* ed. H. F. B. Brett-Smith, Percy Reprints, No. 6, 2 vols. (Boston: Houghton Mifflin, 1927), II, 195.

33 II.ii.
34 IV.i.51-53, *Etherege,* II, 246.
35 I.i, *Wycherley,* II, 14.
36 *The Way of the World,* IV.i.270, 207-09, *Congreve,* pp. 450-51.
37 See Fujimura, *Restoration Comedy of Wit,* for a thorough discussion of wit, both intellectual and verbal, as the central focus of the comedy of manners.
38 *Preface to Albion and Albanius, Essays,* I, 270.
39 V.i, *Wycherley,* II, 79.
40 II.i.409-23, *Congreve,* pp. 420-21.
41 IV.i.280, *ibid.,* p. 452.
42 II.i, *Wycherley,* II, 27.
43 IV.i, *ibid.,* p. 58.
44 I.i, *ibid.,* p. 106.
45 For an account of the contrast between engagement and detachment, between "dry" or unintentional wit and "sly" intentional wit, see Maynard Mack, "Engagement and Detachment in Shakespeare's Plays," *Essays on Shakespeare and Elizabethan Drama in Honor of Hardin Craig,* ed. Richard Hosley (Columbia, Missouri: University of Missouri Press, 1962), pp. 275-96.
46 See Nicoll, I, 284-342.
47 *Comparison,* p. 14.
48 While the playhouses were having financial difficulties, Bunyan's *Pilgrim's Progress* was selling twelve editions in the ten years between its first appearance in 1678 and Bunyan's death.
49 Macaulay, in fact, thought the wit of the comedy of manners was a deliberate rejection of Puritan thinking (Macaulay, I, 300-01).
50 See Richard C. Boys, *Sir Richard Blackmore and the Wits* (Ann Arbor, Michigan: University of Michigan Press, 1949), pp. 1-36.
51 Blackmore, p. 229.
52 *Ibid.*
53 *Ibid.*
54 Gilbert Burnet, Bishop of Salisbury, wrote (*History of His Own Time,* I [London, 1724], 186) that this "new set of men" was so influential in the early years of the Restoration that had they not appeared "the Church had quite lost her esteem over the Nation." See also R. S. Crane, "Suggestions Toward a Genealogy of the 'Man of Feeling'," *ELH,* 1 (December, 1934), 205-30.
55 *The Works of the Most Reverend Dr. John Tillotson* (London, 1712), II, 399, 394.
56 *The Works of the Learned Isaac Barrow, D.D.* (London, 1700), I, 165.
57 Tillotson, II, 54.
58 Ed. Rae Blanchard (Oxford: Oxford University Press, 1932), p. 77.
59 Anthony Ashley Cooper, third earl of Shaftesbury, *Characteristicks of Men, Manners, Opinions, Times* ([London], 1711), II, 175-76.

60 *His Majesties Letter to the Lord Bishop of London* (London, 1689), p. 4.
61 [Josiah Woodward], *An Account of the Societies for Reformation of Manners, In England and Ireland,* 3rd ed. (London, 1700). The Queen's letter is reprinted as a preface.
62 *Ibid.*, pp. 4-12.
63 *Comparison*, pp. 142-43.
64 *Laureat*, p. 53.
65 Collier, p. 1.
66 *Ibid.*, pp. 140-41.
67 *Ibid.*, p. 35.
68 *Ibid.*, pp. 8-16, 97-139.
69 *Ibid.*, p. 62.
70 *Ibid.*, pp. 82-83.
71 IV.i.67-72, *Congreve*, p. 77.
72 *Spectator* (No. 10, March 12, 1711), I, 44-46.
73 See John Loftis, *Comedy and Society from Congreve to Fielding* (Stanford: Stanford University Press, 1959), pp. 79-80.
74 *Pepys*, III, 2 (January 1, 1662/3); II, 400 (December 27, 1662).
75 *Ibid.*, VII, 104 (September 12, 1667). The play was *Tu Quoque; or, the Cit Gallant,* Davenant's adaptation of John Cooke's *Tu Quoque*, published in 1614 (see *The London Stage*, pt. 1, p. 117).
76 Ernest Berbaum cites the gratification of idealism and of "the yearning toward moral excellence" that the heroic spirit provided for later drama (Berrbaum, p. 53).
77 "Of Heroic Plays," *Essays*, I, 149.
78 *Ibid.*, p. 151.
79 M. C. Bradbrook, *English Dramatic Form, A History of Its Development* (London: Chatto and Windus, 1965), p. 115.
80 "Of Heroic Plays," *Essays*, I, 149.
81 *Ibid.*
82 Dedication to *The Conquest of Granada, Dryden*, IV, 11.
83 *Apology*, II, 27-28.
84 *The Herculean Hero in Marlowe, Chapman, Shakespeare and Dryden* (New York: Columbia University Press, 1962), p. 11.
85 *The Conquest of Granada*, Part I, IV.ii, *Dryden*, IV, 96.
86 *Aureng-Zebe*, III.i, *Dryden*, V, 255-56.
87 V.i, *ibid.*, p. 281.
88 "Of Heroic Plays," *Essays*, I, 148.
89 IV.ii, *Dryden*, IV, 94.
90 Part I, III.i, *ibid.*, p. 71.
91 For a detailed discussion of the rhetoric and imagery of heroic drama see Moody E. Prior, *The Language of Tragedy* (New York: Columbia University Press, 1947).
92 Kathleen Lynch, "Conventions of Platonic Drama in the Heroic Plays of Orrery and Dryden," *PMLA*, 44 (June, 1929), 461-63.

93 *Ibid.*, pp. 465-68.
94 Bernbaum, pp. 4-5. DeWitt Croissant calls sentimental drama "a continuation of the romanticism which was brought over from the Caroline drama" ("Early Sentimental Comedy," *Parrott Presentation Volume* [Princeton: Princeton University Press, 1935], p. 51).
95 *Anatomy of Criticism* (Princeton: Princeton University Press, 1957), p. 182.
96 The term is Frye's, *ibid.*
97 See Ian Watt, *The Rise of the Novel* (Berkeley: University of California Press, 1962), pp. 135-57.
98 Samuel Richardson, *Pamela: Or Virtue Rewarded* (London, 1741), I, 290.

Notes to the Plays

LOVE'S LAST SHIFT

Title Page

Fuit . . . maritis: Horace, *Ars Poetica,* 396, 398: "In days of yore, this was wisdom . . . to check vagrant union, to give rules for wedded life." Cibber does not include line 397, "publica privatis secernere, sacra profanis," "to draw a line between public and private rights, between things sacred and things common" (*Satires, Epistles and Ars Poetica,* trans. H. Rushton Fairclough, Loeb Classical Library [London: Heinemann, 1961], pp. 482-83).

Dedication

Richard Norton: Richard Norton (1666-1732) of Southwick, Hampshire, a man of "a family very ancient in this county, and of good note," who was "a great admirer of theatrical entertainments; and for his own and his neighbours' diversion, he used, during the summer's vacation, to have the best actors from the theatres in London, which he entertained at his house, with a good band of music; and had an apartment fitted up with scenes and other decorations, on a handsome stage, whereon he himself performed several parts, particularly that of the Spanish Friar, in which character he was great" (Richard Warner, *Collections for the History of Hampshire, and the Bishopric of Winchester* [London, (1795)], I, Part 2, 182-83). In April, 1696, a tragedy called *Pausanias, the Betrayer of His Country* had appeared at Drury Lane, promoted, like *Love's Last Shift,* by Thomas Southerne. Genest records that it was "said to have been written by Norton" (II, 76).

Norton's association with the theater appears to have been lifelong. In his will he bequeathed a "Pulling-clock" from his bedchamber to John Mills, his "long Acquaintance, living now in Drury-Lane" (*Gentleman's Magazine,* III [1733], 60). This may have been the John Mills who played the Lawyer and later Young Worthy in Cibber's play.

19 Country's Weal: Norton was a member of the House of Commons in 1696.

37 What . . . contrary: Accusations sprang not from evidence of plagiarism,

but rather from a general unwillingness to believe Cibber capable of writing the play. In the anonymous pamphlet *Visits from the Shades: Or, Dialogues Serious, Comical and Political* (London, 1704), the playwright "Nat. Lee" accuses Cibber of claiming a Vanbrugh play for his own: "The Style of the *Relapse,* the Constitution and carrying on the Plot, the resemblance of Characters, and pretty turns of Thought, have such a consonancy to the first part [*i.e., Love's Last Shift*]; that till you can prove a parity of Intellectuals between the ingenious Capt. *Van----k* and your self, you may as well lay a claim to the *Sequel,* as own the Precedent" (Dialogue III, p. 26). In 1742 similar accusations were still being made; another pamphlet, *Sawney and Colley,* speculated "That modest R---RS, (COLLEY, --Hey!)/ Who *wrote* the *Prologue,* wrote the *Play,*" the secret author supposedly a relation of Cibber's (*Sawney and Colley [1742] and Other Pope Pamphlets,* Augustan Reprint Society, No. 83 [Los Angeles, 1960], p. 8 and n.).

49 Galleries: The upper seats where, according to Swift, "Bombast and Buffoonry" come to rest in "a suitable Colony, who greedily intercept them in their Passage" (*A Tale of a Tub,* 2nd ed., ed. A. C. Guthkelch and D. Nicoll Smith [Oxford: Clarendon Press, 1958], p. 61).

54-55 Mr. *Southern's* . . . Success: According to Cibber, the playwright Thomas Southerne "happened to like it so well that he immediately recommended it to the Patentees, and it was accordingly acted in *January* 1695." Cibber also reports that as he was preparing to prompt the Prologue at the first performance Southerne said: "*Young Man! I pronounce thy Play a good one; I will answer for its Success, if thou dost not spoil it by thy own Action*" (*Apology,* I, 212-13).

Prologue

A FRIEND: There is no sound evidence for the friend's identity. The anonymous *Sawney and Colley* (1742) assumes that Cibber's relation, "modest R---RS," wrote the Prologue (see Dedication, 1. 37n.).

Mr. *VERBRUGGEN:* John Verbruggen, who acted the part of Loveless.

Dramatis Personae

23 Fortune: Heiress.

I.i

31 S'bud: I.e., either God's body (a shortened form of 'Od's bodikins) or God's blood (OED).

40-41 Actress . . . Maiden-head: Actresses were proverbially loose women (see *The Lady's Last Stake,* V.i.28-31, 165-68).

55 S'death: I.e., God's death.

91 Souse: Sou.

132 Flux: A cure, by fluxing or purging, for venereal disease.

145 Swinging: Large, "whopping."

182 Shift herself: Change her clothes.

188 Fiddles: Wedding-night serenade.

194 *Blue Posts:* A popular tavern in the Haymarket, mentioned by Otway in *The Souldiers Fortune,* I.i.294 (ed. J. C. Ghosh [Oxford: Clarendon Press, 1932], II, 104). Another by the same name, in Spring Gardens, Charing Cross, was the resort of Jacobites, and a plot to assassinate William III was uncovered there in 1696 (Cunningham, pp. 331, 662).

196 *Guineas: "*Guineas went then at 30 *s.*" [Cibber's note.] The guinea was first struck in 1663 with the nominal value of twenty shillings. During the first years of the Bank of England (founded in 1694), its value soared; during the period from May 24, 1695, to December 13, 1695, it was valued at twenty-nine shillings or more, and on June 14 of that year it was valued at exactly thirty shillings (Rogers, Table V).

231 *Basset:* A card game of French origin, popular in fashionable circles. The players bet on the order in which certain cards would appear when taken singly from the top of the pack.

257-58 Fool . . . Name: Herostratus, who set fire to the temple of Diana at Ephesus in 356 B.C. He was sentenced to death, and a law was passed that his name should never again be mentioned (see *Harper's Dictionary of Classical Literature and Antiquities,* ed. Harry Thurston Peck [New York, 1896]).

283 Meaking: Submissive, from "meaken," an obsolete (14th to 17th centuries) form of "meeken," which in the intransitive sense means to become meek or submissive. The participial adjective is properly "meakening" (OED).

321 Occasions: Requirements.

402-03 So . . . Country: Addison wrote describing Genoese whom he saw clad only in shirts: "and indeed without this natural Benefit of their Climates, the extream Misery and Poverty, that are in most of the *Italian* Governments would be insupportable" (*Remarks on Several Parts of Italy, &c. In the Years 1701, 1702, 1703* [London, 1705], p. 5). He also found Italian gentlemen unable to carry off the elegant French mode of dress (pp. 43-44).

490 Coffee-Criticks . . . *Arthur:* Sir Richard Blackmore's heroic poem, *Prince Arthur,* appeared in 1695 and was the beginning of his quarrel with the "wits," who, like Dryden, Congreve, and other frequenters of the famous Will's Coffee House, scorned him.

509 *Caelia:* Traditional name for one's mistress in seventeenth-century poetry.

II.i

44-45 Dresses . . . Militia: The militia was the "citizen army" (OED) made up, as Macaulay describes it, of "ploughmen officered by Justices of the Peace" (Macaulay, I, 219).

46 Pink: The "flower" or embodied perfection. Johnson defines it as "Any thing supremely excellent."

51 Late Mourning: Queen Mary died on December 28, 1694.

53 Second Mourning: Attire in which white, grey, lavender, or purple replace the black of full mourning.

83-84 *Bien Entendue:* As "*bien entendu*" this may be translated as "but of course," indicating details the *beau monde* need hardly mention. If the phrase is used adjectivally, it means "artfully arranged" or "tastefully done." Robert (*Dictionnaire alphabétique et analogique de la Langue Française* [Paris, 1966]) cites examples of such usage from Voltaire and Bossuet.

85 *A Merveil:* I.e., *À Merveille,* marvelously.

93-94 Rough . . . Corporal: While this comparison reflects the conventional English opinion of Dutch manners, it may refer more specifically to the contrast between the plain dress of the Dutch soldiers who followed William to England and the elegant red coats of the British soldiers.

123-24 Unpowder'd Periwig: Inelegantly dressed. The wig Cibber wore as Sir Novelty became a legend. He writes of the attraction it had for Henry Brett, who later became the controlling patentee of Drury Lane: "And though possibly the Charms of our Theatrical Nymphs might have their Share in drawing him thither, yet in my Observation the most visible Cause of his first coming was a more sincere Passion he had conceived for a fair full-bottom'd Perriwig which I then wore in my first Play of the *Fool in Fashion* in the Year 1695" (*Apology,* II, 35). Pope, in a note to *The Dunciad* (1743), tells us: "This remarkable Periwig usually made its entrance upon the stage in a sedan, brought in by two chairmen, with infinite approbation of the audience" (I, 167n., *Pope,* p. 728).

131 Demme: I.e., Damn or damn me.

157-58 *What . . . lose:* Quoted inaccurately from the Player-King in *Hamlet,* III.ii.184-85, where the second line of the couplet reads "The passion ending, doth the purpose lose" (*Variorum,* 13th ed. [Philadelphia, 1905], p. 252).

174 Legerdemain: Magician.

255 Name of *Beau:* The famous Beau Nash (Richard Nash, 1674-1761) had, by this time, distinguished himself as a student of the Inner Temple by his manners, by his dress, and "by leading so gay a life without visible means of support that his most intimate friends suspected him of being a highwayman." In 1695 he declined knighthood, supposedly because he felt he would not be able to support the title (DNB). Earlier, Beau Feilding (Robert Feilding, 1651?-1712) had been notorious at the court of Charles II for his amorous intrigues. He followed James to Ireland and in 1691-92 was trying to obtain a pardon. In 1696 he returned to England (DNB).

263-64 Raise . . . Goldsmiths: Before the establishment of the Bank of England in 1694, goldsmiths, who acted as bankers, made fortunes by clipping the edges of gold coins and melting the clippings into bullion, which was much more valuable than coin (Rogers, pp. 30-32).

266 Cravat-string: A ribbon passed around the two ends of a flowing cravat and tied in a bow under the chin.

267 Sword-knot: A ribbon or tassel used to ornament the hilt of a sword.

267 Centurine: A belt.

267 Bardash: A fringed sash or cravat. A loosely knotted sash was sometimes worn over the coat in the sixties and seventies; later, in the nineties, it was tied with short ends hanging level over the coat or vest (see Francis M. Kelly and Randolph Schwabe, *Historic Costume* [New York: Scribners, 1925], p. 169).

267 Steinkirk: A neck scarf having long, laced ends loosely folded, looped, or passed through a ring or buttonhole. It was adopted from the hastily donned neckerchief of French soldiers at the battle of Steenkirk, Belgium, in August, 1692. Ladies wore them, too, draped about their shoulders (see *The Careless Husband,* V.v).

268 Full Peruque: A long, flowing wig with luxuriant curls.

277 Conveniency . . . Play-houses: On March 25, 1695, the Drury Lane actor Thomas Betterton received a license to re-open the old theater in Lincoln's Inn Fields. Many actors, dissatisfied with Christopher Rich's management of Drury Lane, followed him, and during the 1695/96 season the rivalry between the two houses was intense.

334-35 Separate Maintenance: Support given by a husband to a wife when they are separated. Here, of course, it applies to a mistress (see also *The Careless Husband,* II.ii.131-32, and *The Lady's Last Stake,* IV.i.91).

367 News-Letters: Newspapers of a single sheet, either handwritten or printed in type resembling handwriting, offering news both political and social and often leaving blank spaces so that the purchaser could write in his own "news" before circulating it among his friends. John Dyer's *News-Letter* was being published at the time of *Love's Last Shift,* and Ichabod Dawkes' paper began in August, 1696 (see *Spectator,* I, 182n.; IV, 111-12n.; H. R. Fox Bourne, *English Newspapers* [London: Chatto and Windus, 1887], I, 57-58).

369 Musick-Meeting: A meeting of one of the fashionable music clubs where members practiced music and sometimes listened to concerts. Pepys reports two visits to "the Musique-meeting at the Post-office" (the Black Swan, Bishopsgate) in 1664 (*Pepys,* IV, 200, 243).

378-79 Bank . . . Goldsmiths: The Bank of England not only put an end to the goldsmiths' practice of clipping and melting (see II.i.263-64n.), but provided further attraction for investors by offering interest on bank bills.

390-91 Jesuit's Powder: Quinine, introduced into England from South America by the Jesuits.

III.i

57 Jointure: Joint property held in tail as a provision for the wife in the event of her widowhood.

58 Subsistence: An allowance for maintenance.

102-03 Mechanical: Common.

111-12 *In ordine ad:* Probably dog latin for "in order to." The editors of the

MacMillan-Jones anthology edition suggest "*In Ordinem adducere,*" "to reduce to order" (*Plays of the Restoration and Eighteenth Century,* ed. Dougald MacMillan and Howard Mumford Jones [New York: Holt, 1931], p. 325).

165-66 Another famous Comedy: *She Would If She Could* (1668), a comedy by Etherege, in which Lady Cockwood affects the coquette with neither the youth nor the beauty to be one.

214-15 Rosamond's Pond: A pond in St. James's Park (see III.ii.s.d.n.). It was famous as a meeting place for lovers and intriguers until it was filled up in 1770. Warburton writes to Hurd that it was "long consecrated to disastrous love, and *elegiac* poetry" (*Letters from a Late Eminent Prelate to One of His Friends,* 2nd ed. [London, 1809], p. 151).

222 The Musick: A serenade by a band of hired musicians.

237 *Diogenes:* The Greek philosopher (412-323 B.C.), known for his self-possession.

241 Demn: I.e., damn.

III.ii

s.d. St. James's-Park: Once a private park attached to St. James's Palace, it became a fashionable promenade during the Restoration. At the same time, because it was unlighted, it was the haunt of bullies.

10 Back: Constitution. Compare the aspirations of Sir Epicure Mammon (*The Alchemist,* II.ii.34-39):

For I doe meane
To haue a list of wiues, and concubines,
Equall with SALOMON; who had the *stone*
Alike, with me: and I will make me, a back
With the *elixir,* that shall be as tough
As HERCVLES, to encounter fiftie a night.

[*Ben Jonson,* ed. C. H. Herford and Percy Simpson (Oxford: Clarendon Press, 1937), V, 318-19.]

17 Debased: The practice of clipping coins diminished their value.

17-18 Maidenheads . . . Crowns: Clipped coins ceased to be current before the new milled coins appeared (Rogers, pp. 62-63).

18-19 *Dei . . .* Shilling: Coins debased by clipping might no longer carry the inscription *Dei Gratia* and the name of the sovereign around the edge. Young Worthy believes that the debasing of virtue has made it equally difficult to find the grace of God in young girls.

44 Hautboys: Oboe players.

55 The Musick: The band of musicians.

65s.d. *Masks:* Masked women, usually prostitutes, though ladies wore masks when they wished to disguise themselves. Presumably the "masks" are part of the crowd which gathers around Sir Novelty's "Musick," since they have not been introduced previously.

87 Since . . . accomplish'd: The accession of William and Mary, which estab-

lished constitutional monarchy and protestant succession, and set in motion a reform of manners.

108 Coach: The hackney coach was the customary conveyance for a mistress.

110-11, 113-14 Paul E. Parnell questions the attribution of these two speeches to Elder Worthy on the grounds that they are more suitable to Young Worthy, and that Narcissa's "too" (117) indicates that she has been talking to the younger brother all along ("An Incorrectly Attributed Speech-Prefix in 'Love's Last Shift'," *Notes and Queries,* 204 [June, 1959], 212-13). These speeches are, however, attributed to Elder Worthy in every edition and though they evince a worldly curiosity against which he protests, they are sufficiently priggish to belong to him.

135 Dishabillee: I.e., *Déshabille,* partial undress, or perhaps the undistinguished dress of a disguise.

135 High Head: The fashionable manner of hair-dressing in which the hair was drawn up over high frames or cushions, then pomaded, powdered, and trimmed with ribbons and lace.

163 The *Gridiron:* Presumably a tavern.

175-76 Point Head-Cloths: Women in high headdresses. Ned Ward writes in *The London Spy* (1698-1700) that his friend could tell "a kind of First Rate *Punks* by their Riging, of about a Guinea purchase" (Part II [London, 1698], 6).

183 Odsbud: I.e., God's body or God's blood (see I.i.31n.).

188 Odsheart: I.e., God's heart.

198 Oon's: I.e., God's wounds.

199 Shoot: Force.

IV.i

85 Whether: I.e., whither.

125 In Second: In second guard or parry; in fencing, a defensive position against a low outside blow.

IV.ii

8-9 Ply him home: Give him enough to put him in the desired condition.

IV.iii

44s.d. *A Song here: "A Song, Sett by Mr. Daniel Purcell, Sung in Love's Last Shift"* appeared in *Deliciae Musicae: Being a Collection of the Newest and Best Songs . . .* The First Book of the Second Volume (London, 1696), 17. See Appendix II above.

59 *Supernaculum:* To the very last drop—literally "over the nail"—referring to the custom of turning a glass over the left thumbnail to show that it was empty (OED).

243 A': I.e., he.

249 *Jacobite:* At that time, an adherent of James II.

V.i

35 Odso: I.e., God so.

68 Odd: I.e., God.

145 With a wet Finger: Easily (OED), perhaps from the practice of wetting the finger to pick up a piece of paper easily.

V.ii

19-20 Tavern-Bush: Sign of a tavern. Ivy, sacred to Bacchus, was the vintner's symbol.

49 Pip: Disappointment, melancholy.

V.iii

58 Smell Powder: Powder for wigs was perfumed with musk, civet, ambergris, bergamot, rose, violet, almond, or orange-flower to mask the odor of rancid pomatum, the grease used to make the powder adhere (Hill, II, 12-13).

81 Temple Beau: A dandy who lived in the Temple, of whom Fielding's Mr. Wilson said: "the beaus of the Temple are only the shadows of the others. They are the affectation of affectation" (*Joseph Andrews*, ed. Martin C. Battestin [Boston: Houghton Mifflin, 1961], p. 173). The famous Beau Nash lived in the Inner Temple (see II.i.255n.).

88 Chocolate-house: Probably White's Chocolate House, St. James's Street, Piccadilly (see *The Lady's Last Stake*, I.i.59n.).

97 Cloud of Powder: Wigs were often powdered with as much as two pounds of powder (Hill, II, 12).

107-08 Kept my Place: Servants were sent to the theaters to hold places for their masters.

109 Side-Box: An enclosed box at the side of the theater where "people of quality" sat.

134 Gentile: I.e., genteel.

203 The Groom-Porter's: The Groom Porter was an official of the Royal Household, appointed by the Lord Chamberlain to regulate gaming. He had his own gaming-house, usually in Whitehall, where the nobility played. Lesser members of the fashionable world also gambled there: Pepys records a visit to see "how people in ordinary clothes shall come hither, and play away 100, or 2 or 300 guinnys without any kind of difficulty" (*Pepys*, VII, 246).

204 Fourth . . . Play: In Cibber's time the playwright was allowed the receipts, less house charges, on the third night of a new play.

V.iv

See Appendix II for "A Song in the *Mask* for the *Lover's* [*sic*] *Last-Shift*, Sung by Mrs. *Cross* / and the Boy, upon a Marriage Life. Sett by Mr. *Francks.*"

Epilogue

Miss *Cross:* Miss Cross, who sang in the masque above and who later played Miss Notable in *The Lady's Last Stake,* was about twelve years old when *Love's Last Shift* was presented. Nicoll writes (I, 21, 266) that Restoration audiences delighted in hearing young girls recite bawdy or obscene verses in prologues and epilogues.

2 *City-Gentlemen:* The merchant class, which was, on the one hand, the class most active in the reformation of manners, and on the other, the group most frequently cuckolded on the Restoration stage.

THE CARELESS HUSBAND

Title Page

Yet . . . All: This couplet is taken, not from the Prologue, but from the "Epilogue by Mr. Dryden," written for Etherege's *The Man of Mode, or, Sir Fopling Flutter* (1676).

Qui . . . facit: If the cap fits, wear it (Latin proverb).

Dedication

JOHN, DUKE of ARGYLE: John Campbell (1678-1743), second Duke of Argyle, was a distinguished soldier who had acquitted himself well as colonel of the 14th Regiment of Horse Guards in the siege of Keyserswaert on April 16, 1702. He was at this time a great admirer of the Duke of Marlborough, whose triumph at Blenheim on August 13, 1704, only months before the publication of Cibber's dedication, would have been very much in the minds of his readers. This dedication, the *Prologue Upon the last Campaign,* and the *Epilogue* are concerned with Marlborough's successes in the war of the Spanish Succession.

If Argyle's military activities made him a timely object of Cibber's dedication, the receipt of a long poem on the war may have been further inspiration. It was generally thought that Argyle had written the *Prologue Upon the last Campaign:* in 1742 the anonymous *Sawney and Colley* claimed:

> Who call'st the *Careless Husband* thine,
> Tho' great A___LL wrote ev'ry Line;

thus imputing the play as well as the prologue to Argyle (*Sawney and Colley* [*1742*] *and Other Pope Pamphlets,* p. 8). Argyle's "pleasure in wit, poetry, and the belles-lettres"—as described by his great-niece Lady Louisa Stuart (*Some Account of John, Duke of Argyll, and His Family,* in *Lady Louisa Stuart, Selections From Her Manuscripts* [New York: Harper and Brothers, 1899], p. 16)—supports the possibility that he would celebrate Marlborough's triumph in verse. Though there is no evidence of his interest in the theater at this time in his career, two anecdotes from his later life, telling of his response to Gay's *Beggar's Opera,* suggest that he was a frequenter of the playhouse, and that he was acquainted with Cibber. One reports his enthusiasm for Gay's piece: he is said to have cried out before the end of the first act, "It will do,—it must do!—I see it in the eyes of them" (Joseph Spence, *Observations, Anecdotes, and Characters of Books and Men,* ed. James M. Osborne [New Haven: Yale University Press, 1966], I, 107). The other, from *Polly Peachum's Jests* ([London, 1728], Jest VIII, pp. 3-4), alludes to a meeting of Cibber and Argyle behind the scenes at *The Beggar's Opera* before the first edition was published. The Duke asked Cibber how he liked it and Cibber replied: "Why it makes one laugh, my Lord . . . upon the Stage, but how will it do in print." The Duke answered, "O very well, by G-d . . . *if you don't write the Preface.*"

8 It . . . own: The same charge, equally unsupported, that was levelled at *Love's Last Shift* (see note above, and *Love's Last Shift,* Dedication, l. 37n.).

23-25 Can't . . . Boxes: Can be understood by the lower classes, who occupied the galleries, as well as by the genteel audience in the boxes (see Dedication to *Love's Last Shift,* l. 49 and n.).

35 Third and Sixth Day: Days on which the poet was entitled to the profits, less house expenses (see *Love's Last Shift,* V.iii.204n.).

48 *Tragedy:* Cibber had, in fact, already written an unsuccessful tragedy, *Xerxes* (1698/9), and an adáptation of Shakespeare's *Richard III* (1699). His next attempt, also unsuccessful, was *Perolla and Izadora,* first presented at Drury Lane in December, 1705.

Prologue

6 *Citts:* Citizens. Johnson defined a "cit" as "A pert low tradesman."

7 *Cullies:* Dupes.

16 Newgate *or* Bedlam: Newgate Prison or Bethlehem (Bedlam) Hospital, the madhouse.

PROLOGUE . . . Quality: For a discussion of the possible ascription of this prologue to the Duke of Argyle, see the note to "John, Duke of Argyle" in the Dedication.

In B.M. Add. MS. 23,904, fol. 23, there is a manuscript poem titled "The Epilogue in the Play called the/ Careless Husband or the Carefull wife/ 1706." The manuscript appears to be part of a commonplace book, in an unidentified hand; it was purchased from Bernard Quaritch on July 19, 1860. It contains, in one long poem, most of the lines of the published *Prologue Upon the last Campaign,* as well as many of those in the Epilogue to the published play. It includes, in addition, many lines which do not appear in either.

If this is a copy of an early draft of the poem, before it was appended to the play, it casts doubt on Argyle's authorship, since the theatrical controversy (found in the lines which appear in the published Epilogue) was a favorite theme of Cibber's, one which he pursued in the Dedication and Epilogue to *The Lady's Last Stake* only three years later. The manuscript may, on the other hand, be a copy of a spoken epilogue which attempted to make use of lines from the *Prologue Upon the last Campaign* which we know from its subtitle was "design'd for the Sixth Day, but not spoken."

Prologue Upon the last Campaign

1 *Paying . . . Trade:* If Argyle did indeed write the prologue, his opening line expresses characteristic Tory sentiment: the Tories felt that the war was being financed at their expense (see G. M. Trevelyan, *England Under the Stuarts* [London: Methuen, 1949], p. 388).

2 *Lingring . . . made:* G. M. Trevelyan writes (*History of England,* 3rd ed. [London: Longmans, Green, 1945], pp. 495-96) that "warfare of the age of Louis XIV was largely an affair of fortresses" and led to "stagnation in military enterprise and mobility." Marlborough, "when he took over the command, found the French far in advance of their usual line of fortresses. He seized the opportunity to restore the war of movement."

32-55 Minerva . . . *cease:* If this prologue is Argyle's, his flattering opinion of Marlborough changed in the five years before 1710 when the General was ultimately dismissed by the new Tory ministry. When Marlborough returned to London in 1709, Argyle was apparently instrumental in organizing a cold reception. As Robert Campbell wrote in *The Life of the Most Illustrious Prince John, Duke of Argyle and Greenwich:* "His [Marlborough's] Friends in the House of Lords, by the Earl of *Scarborough,* had moved for the Thanks of that House, but were disappointed on account of some Objections *His Grace the Duke of Argyle* had started" ([London, 1745], p. 68).

Dramatis Personae

WINDSOR: Fashionable society resorted to Windsor when the court was in residence there.

I.i

100 Blue and Green Ribbons: The blue ribbon was worn by members of the Order of the Garter, the green by members of the Order of the Thistle.

101 Falbala: Flounced, ruffled.

155 Church: Probably Saint George's Chapel. Pepys visited Windsor and went to prayers at the chapel on February 26, 1666, recording this account: "It is a noble place indeed, and a good Quire of voices. Great bowing by all the people, and the poor Knights [an order, founded by Edward III in the fourteenth century and later called the Military Knights of Windsor, which resided in the Castle] particularly, to the Alter" (*Pepys,* V, 220).

321 Cane . . . Button: Canes, carried especially by fops, usually dangled by a ribbon from the wrist, but they may also have been hung from a button, as were muffs (see C. Willett and Phyllis Cunnington, *Handbook of*

English Costume in the Seventeenth Century [London: Faber and Faber, 1955], p. 168).

337 Chaise: A light open carriage for one or two persons.

340 *Hounslow:* A town about half-way between Windsor and London.

357 *Ecclarcisement:* I.e., *éclaircissement,* a mutual explanation of conduct, an understanding.

II.i

48 *Tendresse:* A gesture of affection.

65 Meer *Indian* Damask: An Indian damask would have come not from India, but from the East Indies, that is, China. Cibber was writing at the height of English propaganda against Chinese silks on behalf of English silk-weavers, hence the description "meer." (John Irwin, Keeper of the Indian Department, Victoria and Albert Museum.)

141-42 King . . . Word: In 1700, Louis XIV had recognized the will of Charles II of Spain, which left the whole Spanish inheritance to Philip of Anjou, thereby violating the Treaty of Partition of 1699 by which he had agreed that upon Charles II's death, Spain, the Spanish Netherlands, and Spanish America would be allotted to the Archduke Charles, son of the Emperor Leopold. In 1701, Louis violated the Treaty of Ryswick (1697) by recognizing the son of James II as James III on his father's death.

143 Confederates: The members of the Grand Alliance—England, the Netherlands, and Austria.

147 Bobs . . . Lips: Ornamental pendants, worn imbedded in the flesh by some natives of the West Indies.

II.ii

1 Tout: Complete victory.

40-41 *Que . . . veu:* Let me kiss you! By Jove! It's been a hundred years since I've seen you.

47 *Vermeile:* I.e., *vermeille,* a rosy glow.

48 *Brillant:* Sparkle, luster.

67-68 *Fille de Joye:* Woman of pleasure.

86 Five . . . deep: In debt to the extent of five hundred pounds.

130 Hackney: A hired coach (see *Love's Last Shift,* III.ii.108n.).

131-32 Separate Maintenance: The husband's support of a separated wife (see *Love's Last Shift,* II.i.334-35, and *The Lady's Last Stake,* IV.i.91).

161-62 *Toutjours Chapons Bouilles:* Always boiled capon, a bland diet.

166 *Banstead:* Banstead Downs, about fifteen miles from London, was famous for its sheep; it was "covered with a short grass intermixed with thyme, and other fragrant herbs, that render the mutton of this tract, though small, remarkable for its sweetness" (*London and Its Environs Described,* [London, 1761], I, 246).

169 Ortolan: A small European bird of delicate flavor.

199 *Partie Quarrie:* A party of two men and two women.

200 *Indian* House: A shop where goods from the East Indies were sold. Turberville reprints (*English Men and Manners in the Eighteenth Century* [Oxford: Clarendon Press, 1926], p. 443) an advertisement of a sale by lottery of Indian goods, taken from Houghton's *Collection* for January 5, 1693/4. Among the items of interest to the ladies are "*Several Sets of fine* China *Jarrs . . . Rich* Indian *Silks . . . fine* Indian *Fanns, Muslins and Callicoes.*" These were to be sold "at the Sign of the *Black Bell* in *Bedford-street Covent Garden.*"

285-86 "Women . . . Bold": The source of this couplet may be William Burnaby's *The Reform'd Wife* (1700), where it closes Act I.

III.i

51 Basset: See *Love's Last Shift,* I.i.231n.

52 Tally: Deal, or act the banker.

125 Pure: Slang for excellent, fine.

250 *Chagrin:* Disappointed.

263 *Pignus . . . Pertinaci:* Sir Novelty's misquotation is from Horace, *Odes,* I.ix.23-24. The lines read "pignusque dereptum lacertis/ aut digito male pertinaci," "and the forfeit snatched from her arm or finger that but feigns resistance" (*The Odes and Epodes,* trans. C. E. Bennett, Loeb Classical Library [London: Heinemann, 1964], pp. 28-29).

328 Mask: The customary disguise of women in an intrigue (see *Love's Last Shift,* III.ii.65s.d.n.).

351 Goust: I.e., *goût,* taste (see *The Lady's Last Stake,* III.i.239).

389 Lies: Holds, remains.

391-92 Unharbour'd: Driven from covert.

395 Rid down: Exhausted, of a horse.

405 *Tayo:* Tally-ho in the French manner (from *taïaut*).

406 'Ware Hanches: Beware of bites.

408 Stand: Standstill.

535 Rally: Ridicule.

553 Confederates: The member of the Grand Alliance (see II.i.143n.).

564 Rat: I.e., drat.

565 *Donc . . . faite:* Then the business is done.

IV.i

45 Gave the Musick: Gave a serenade (see *Love's Last Shift,* III.i.222n.).

150 Hautboys: Oboe players (see *Love's Last Shift,* III.ii.44).

275 *Canaille:* Mob.

350 Live buried in Woollen: Live with an old woman. In support of the British woolen industry, the law required that shrouds be made of wool.

351 Swan-skin: A thick, soft flannel. Young women would most likely have worn more fashionable petticoats of taffeta or silk.

362-63 Keep . . . Line: I'll try to play your backhand strokes (to free you for forecourt play). But you are so good, you could even let me play in the forecourt without endangering your game.

364 Rest: Rally, rapid and continuous exchange of strokes.

367 *Allons . . . lor:* Come! play in earnest, my lord.

373 *Bien joue:* Well played.

454 Is . . . go, *&c.:* Sir Charles goes off singing a song called "The Careless Swain," from the *Westminster Drollery* (*Or, A Choice Collection of the Newest Songs & Poems Both At Court and Theatres.* By A Person of Quality. With Additions [London, 1672], p. 81):

1. IS she gone? let her go; faith Boys, I care not,
I'l not sue after her, I dare not, I dare not.
Though she'as more Land than I by many an Acre,
I have plow'd in her ground, who may take her.

2. She is a witty one, and she is fair too;
She must have all the Land that she is Heir to:
But as for Free Land she has not any,
For hers is *Lammas* ground, common to many.

3. Were it in Several, 'twere a great favour,
It might be an inriching to him that shall have her:
But hers is common ground, and without bounding,
You may graze in her ground, and fear no pounding.

V.iii

65 Late . . . View: Jeremy Collier's *A Short View of the Immorality, and Profaneness of the English Stage* (1698) in which Collier denounced witty comedy that pretended to expose vice by satiric representation on the stage (see Introduction, The Contexts, pp. xxxviii-ix).

V.v

27s.d. Steinkirk: A scarf tied loosely about the neck (see *Love's Last Shift,* II.i.267n.). This famous scene was presumably drawn from an incident in the life of Colonel Henry Brett, the controlling patentee of the Drury Lane theater, who, in 1700, had married Ann Mason, divorced wife of the Earl of Macclesfield and mother of the poet Richard Savage. Boswell reports the incident in *The Life of Samuel Johnson:* "Miss Mason, after having forfeited the title of Lady Macclesfield by divorce, was married to Colonel Brett, and, it is said, was well known in all the polite circles. Colley Cibber, I am informed, had so high an opinion of her taste and judgment as to genteel life and manners, that he submitted every scene of his 'Careless Husband' to Mrs. Brett's revisal and correction. Colonel Brett was reported to be too free in his gallantry with his Lady's maid. Mrs. Brett came into a room one day in her own house, and found the

Colonel and her maid both fast asleep in two chairs. She tied a white handkerchief round her husband's neck, which was a sufficient proof that she had discovered his intrigue; but she never at any time took notice of it to him. This incident, I am told, gave occasion to the well-wrought scene of Sir Charles and Lady Easy and Edging" (ed. G. B. Hill, rev. L. F. Powell [Oxford: Clarendon Press, 1934], I, 174n.).

V.vi

176 Thrift: Prosperous growth.

V.vii

71-72 Grand . . . *Cavalier:* Jean Cavalier (1681-1740) was a leader of the Camisards, militant French protestant peasants of the region of Cevennes, from 1702 to 1705. This group offered organized military resistance to the government's revocation of the Edict of Nantes in 1685. On May 16, 1704, Cavalier submitted to Louis XIV, who then refused to grant liberty of conscience to Cavalier's soldiers. They deserted him as a traitor, Louis refused to see him, and so Cavalier rejoined the Camisards. In 1707 he fought under British command in Spain.

100 Gap'd: Yawned.

129 Hist . . . Life!: Keep still, to save your life.

185 *Pardi . . . Extraordinaire:* By Jove, there's something extraordinary.

193 *Non-Chalence:* I.e., nonchalance.

218 One at a Poole: One of the number of players required for a game in which there is a pool.

293 Sabina . . . *Face:* See Appendix II for "A SONG *in the* Careless Husband *Sung by* Mr Leveridge / Set by Mr Daniell Purcell." In this version of the song, the last line reads "let her then unpitied Dye."

Epilogue

EPILOGUE: Resuming the theme of the *Prologue Upon the last Campaign* the epilogue draws an analogy between the French military threat to England and the domination of the English stage by foreign entertainments. Edmund Curll wrote that about 1698 "the *English* Theatre was not only pestered with Tumblers, and Rope-Dancers from *France,* but likewise with Dancing-Masters, Dancing Dogs; shoals of *Italian* Squallers were daily imported; and the *Drury-Lane* Company almost broke" (*The Life of That Eminent Comedian Robert Wilks, Esq;* [London, 1733], p. 8). See also the Epilogue to *The Lady's Last Stake.*

9 *Subscription:* Opera especially supported itself by seasonal subscriptions which guaranteed a certain fixed income and thus gave it an advantage over drama. In the 1706-07 season, the Queen's Theatre, Haymarket, offered three plays by subscription, to give them some of the strength of opera, but subscription never became the custom for plays (see *The London Stage,* pt. 2, pp. lix-lx).

10 *Nature's Neglected:* In this case, comedy is neglected in favor of "un-

natural" spectacular performances such as rope dancers and Italian opera.

15 *Fox:* A symbol of France; Renart was the embodiment of *l'esprit gaulois.*

22-25 *So . . . betray'd:* A reference to Louis XIV's treachery (see II.i.141-42n.).

28 *Retook . . . Fought:* Trevelyan writes: "The war of the League of Augsburg (1688-97) included four distinct wars on land—those on the Flemish, the Rhenish, the Alpine, and the Pyrenean frontiers of France. The war of the Spanish Succession included the same four wars, but the seat of each had been removed by Louis far into the enemy's country. . . . Thus the Allies had again to undertake the same four wars, no longer as wars of defence but as wars of recovery" (*England Under the Stuarts,* p. 398).

36 *False* Bavarian *Blood:* Bavaria entered into an alliance with Louis XIV in 1703.

THE LADY'S LAST STAKE

Epistle Dedicatory

MARQUIS . . . Houshold: The Lord Chamberlain, in this case Henry Grey, Marquess of Kent, who held the office from 1704 to 1710, had in his charge the regulation of the activities of the theaters. It was to him that Cibber, and others concerned in the affairs of the Theatre Royal in Drury Lane, appealed when Christopher Rich, the most influential of the patentees of the theater, began to devote himself to the production of operas and other spectacular entertainments at the expense of comedy. Rich refused to obey the order that no singers should appear on the stage at Drury Lane, and in March, 1709, the Lord Chamberlain "silenced" his share of the patent (see Barker, pp. 73-78). Cibber's Epilogue considers further the effect of the stage controversy on the actors.

5-6 Gentlemen . . . Stage: Cibber writes (*Apology,* II, 246) of "those idle Gentlemen, who seem'd more delighted to be pretty Objects themselves, than capable of any Pleasure from the Play: Who took their daily Stands where they might best elbow the Actor, and come in for their Share of the Auditor's Attention." Genest recalls (III,57) that Drury Lane was closed for several days in February, 1720/1, as a result of a riot started when a drunken Earl "crossed over the stage among the performers" to join a companion on the other side.

17 Mr. *Collier:* Jeremy Collier, author of *A Short View of the Immorality, and Profaneness of the English Stage* (1698).

31 Union . . . Actors: On December 31, 1707, the Lord Chamberlain had ordered the union of the theaters, separating comedy at Drury Lane from opera at the Queen's Theatre, Haymarket. Cibber had written *The Lady's Last Stake* for production at the Haymarket after fleeing, with others of the Drury Lane company, the skulduggery of Christopher

Rich. The Haymarket was acoustically unsuitable, the makeshift company unsatisfactory, so that Cibber was undoubtedly happy to return to Drury Lane, especially since he could hope that the theater would be reserved for comedy and for a stable company of actors (see *Apology*, II, 49n.; Barker, pp. 73-78).

35-38 Mismanagement . . . Sallery: Rich's practice was to reduce the actors' salaries to meet the high cost of spectacular entertainment (see Barker, pp. 54-57).

50-53 Opera . . . *December:* Actually, the first opera of the 1707/08 season was presented at Drury Lane on November 15, 1707. It was, according to *The London Stage* (pt. 2, p. 158), Niccolo Haym's *Camilla.* Haym was best known, however, as a musical adapter, and his *Camilla* was an adaptation of *Il Trionfo di Camilla* by Silvio Stampiglia, with music by Antonio Maria Buononcini, performed in Naples a decade earlier (the *British Museum Catalogue of Manuscript Music* [II, 249] dates the opera 1693; the *Library of Congress Catalogue of Opera Librettos Printed Before 1800* [II, 252] dates the libretto 1696). Haym had apparently engaged a Mr. Northman to translate the Italian into English verse (see Nicoll, II, 274-75). The air—"Yes, yes, 'tis all I want"—in Cibber's Epilogue is taken from the English version (see Epilogue, l. 25s.d.n.).

68 Every . . . Relief: Though this is not precisely what happened, the union of the actors at Drury Lane did not prove a permanent solution. Rich continued his financial mismanagement, and the actors again appealed to the Lord Chamberlain. Queen Anne, in response, closed Drury Lane on June 6, 1709. The situation was not relieved until the installation of the actor-managers in 1710 (see *Apology*, II, 73n.).

I.i

12 Casts me: Finds me guilty.

59 *White*'s: White's Chocolate House, St. James's Street, Piccadilly, was notorious as a gambling place for the aristocracy. One of its rooms was the setting for Plate VI of Hogarth's "Rake's Progress" (Cunningham, p. 607; see *Love's Last Shift*, V.iii.88).

78 *Poss:* Positively.

166 The Vapours: Melancholy.

214-18 What . . . Truth: The sense of this complicated speech is as follows: "What do I set myself to but, instead of making you easy, letting you go on in the fancy till I was thoroughly convinced your suspicion was real, and then I turn about with the most unexpected reversal, and tell you the whole truth."

261 *Ganymede:* The bearer of nectar to the gods.

268 Above half Seas over: More than half way to the goal, or more than half intoxicated. In this case both are applicable.

283 Wink-tipping: Encouraging winking.

334 Mother *Davis*'s: Presumably a brothel.

348 Pamper up: Feed.

II.i

21 Booby-Hutch: A small cart intended for a single person.

23 *Tom's* Coffee-House: A coffee-house established in 1700 in the south corner of Covent Garden and later frequented by such literary figures as Fielding, Smollett, Garrick, Johnson, and Cibber (Cunningham, pp. 575-76).

24 Toy-Shop: A shop for trinkets and knick-knacks.

29 *Trangams:* Trinkets.

166 Young *Pill Garlick:* Little me. "Pilgarlic" is a mock-contemptuous reference to self.

168 Head-clothes: Headdress (see *Love's Last Shift,* III.ii.135n.).

187-88 Several . . . *Covent-Garden:* Both fruit-sellers and prostitutes transacted their business in Covent Garden.

II.ii

62 Foot: Footing.

III.i

7 Musick-Subscription: Probably a series of concerts for which an annual fee was paid. One of the most famous of these series, Britton's, was fashionable when Cibber wrote *The Lady's Last Stake.* Thomas Britton, a London coal-merchant and self-taught musician, had converted the loft above his coal-house into a music room where, among others, Handel and Pepusch played frequently. Though admission was at first free, Britton later imposed a subscription price of ten shillings a year. The series began in 1678 and ended with Britton's death in 1714 (see Percy A. Scholes, *The Oxford Companion to Music* [London: Oxford University Press, 1970], p. 228; see also "Musick-Meeting," *Love's Last Shift,* II.i.369n.).

133 This has a Face: This looks promising.

172 A Bars length: In contests of strength where a bar was thrown, the distance was measured in lengths of the bar.

239 *Goust:* I.e., *goût,* taste, liking (see *The Careless Husband,* III.i.351).

244 Strait an end: Immediately.

259 Wooden Glasses: A substitute for glass windows. Ned Ward wrote of riding in a hackney coach with tin ones: "For want of Glasses to our Coach, having drawn up our Tin Sashes, pink'd like the bottom of a Cullender, that the Air might pass thro' the holes . . . we were convey'd from the Fair" (*The London Spy,* Part III [London, 1699], 3).

266 Swinging: Heavy (see *Love's Last Shift,* I.i.145).

333 Stands buff: Endures without flinching.

471-72 The Thatch'd-house: A tavern in St. James's Street, Piccadilly. Sullen, Ramble, and Critick chose it as the scene of their discussion of the stage in *A Comparison Between the Two Stages* (p. 6). Later, Johnson's Club met there (Cunningham, p. 607).

476 Counter: Of no intrinsic value.

481 Box-keeper: Keeper of the dice-box or the money-box.

576 Green-sick: Anemic, especially of young girls.

591 Ape-leader: An old maid. To lead apes in hell was said to be the fate of those who died old maids.

595 Whips up the Cudgels: Takes up the game.

599 Next King of *Poland:* Augustus II had been elected to the throne of Poland in 1697, from among eighteen contenders. From 1704 to 1709, during the Northern War, Polish allegiance was divided between Augustus and Stanislaw Leszczynski, who was recognized and supported as king of Poland by Charles XII of Sweden.

600 Original . . . Razors: The following advertisement appeared in *The London Gazette* for December 28-January 1, 1704/5: "The Original Author of Strops for Setting Razors and Penknives upon, does hereby give Notice, That he hath now brought 'em to such a Perfection, that not only Razors and Penknives, but likewise Launcets, or any other fine Cutting Instrument may be set thereon; and are to be Sold only by Mr. Shipton at John's Coffee-house in Swithen's Alley by the Royal Exchange, ready fixed on Boards, with Directions affixed to the same. Price 1 s. each."

IV.i

91 Separate Maintenance: Support given by a husband to a wife when they are separated (see *Love's Last Shift,* II.i.334-35 and *The Careless Husband,* II.ii.131-32).

218 Groom Porters: The gaming house operated by the Groom Porter (see *Love's Last Shift,* V.iii.203n.).

273 *Bais mains:* Compliment (a kiss of the hands).

528 Drawing a Line: Writing an order to pay.

V.i

28-29 As . . . Play-House: As a manager prepares understudies. The proverbial reputation of actresses is further attested to in V.i.166-68 below, and in *Love's Last Shift,* I.i.40-41. Dryden, in *Mac Flecknoe* (1682), had associated the Nursery—a playhouse for the training of young actors and actresses, located at that time in the Barbican—with the brothels in that area:

> Near these a Nursery erects its head,
> Where Queens are form'd, and future Hero's bred;
> Where unfledg'd Actors learn to laugh and cry,
> Where infant Punks their tender Voices try.

[*The Poems of John Dryden,* ed. James Kinsley (Oxford: Clarendon Press, 1958), I, 267, ll. 74-77.]

166 Behind the Scenes: I.e., at the playhouse.

216 Earn: Yearn.

V.ii

60 Being . . . Pins: Economizing in small things.

80-81 Tailly . . . Card: Settle by matching a single card.

V.iii

26 Table-book: Pocket notebook.

38 Stand him: Stand up to him.

61 Foot-Pads: Robbers on foot.

Epilogue

1 *Poor . . . down:* Cibber's Epilogue expands the theme of the Epistle Dedicatory, the competition between comedy and opera. He wrote (*Apology*, II, 6) of "the Majority, who could more easily comprehend any thing they *saw* than the daintiest things that could be said to them."

5 Cæsar: The title role in Shakespeare's *Julius Caesar* had been played, in April, 1707, by Barton Booth, later one of the managers of Drury Lane, of whom Cibber wrote (*Apology*, II, 240): "*Booth* seem'd to think nothing valuable that was not tragically Great or Marvellous."

7 Roxana: The heroine in Nathaniel Lee's tragedy, *The Rival Queens.* On December 30, 1707, the part of Roxana had been played by Mrs. Elizabeth Barry, whom Cibber (*Apology*, I, 160) praised: "Mrs. *Barry*, in Characters of Greatness, had a Presence of elevated Dignity, her Mien and Motion superb and gracefully majestick; . . . In the Art of exciting Pity she had a Power beyond all the Actresses I have yet seen, or what your Imagination can conceive. Of the former of these two great Excellencies she gave the most delightful Proofs in almost all the Heroic Plays of *Dryden* and *Lee.*"

8 Tofftissa: Catherine Tofts, an English soprano and notorious prima donna, who starred in Italian opera, had sung the title role in Haym's *Camilla* (see Epistle Dedicatory, ll. 50-53n.) at Drury Lane on December 6, 1707. Her vanity was so well known that *The Spectator* (No. 443, IV, 55-56) published a letter from "Camilla" in which the lady deplored English insensitivity to her talents and told of her removal to Italy where she was properly acclaimed.

14 *Chapmen:* Merchants.

25s.d. *Yes . . . want:* The air is taken from Haym's *Camilla* (see Epistle Dedicatory, ll. 50-53n.). Though his name does not appear on the title page of the printed libretto, Mr. Northman is presumably responsible for the English words:

> Yes, yes, 'tis all I want,
> Nor wou'd I better thrive:
> A Heart for Heart is all
> A Lover can gain.
> A Happiness I feel,
> No Mortal can reveal.
> If all you have you give,
> I n'er must complain.

[*Camilla. An Opera.* (London, 1706), III.iv, pp. 29-30.] The music is included in Appendix II.

31 *May . . . House:* Actually, Cibber's Epilogue ran for two weeks after the

play itself had closed. *The Lady's Last Stake* played for the last time in December on the 19th, but the Epilogue was recited after John Crowne's *The Country Wit* on December 20 and 22, after John Banks' *The Unhappy Favourite* on December 26, and after *Mackbeth* on December 27 and 29 (see *The London Stage*, pt. 2, pp. 160-62).

35 *My . . . to:* It was not his fortune to have a good singing voice.